Brothers and Sisters

Brothers and Sisters

Diversity in College
Fraternities and Sororities

Edited by

Craig L. Torbenson
and Gregory S. Parks

Madison • Teaneck
Fairleigh Dickinson University Press

Associated University Presses
2010 Eastpark Boulevard
Cranbury, NJ 08512

The paper used in this publication meets the requirements of the American National Standard for Permanence of Paper for Printed Library Materials Z39.48-1984.

Library of Congress Cataloging-in-Publication Data

Brothers and sisters : diversity in college fraternities and sororities / edited by Craig L. Torbenson and Gregory S. Parks.
p. cm.
Includes bibliographical references and index.
ISBN 978-0-8386-4194-1 (alk. paper)
1. Greek letter societies—United States. 2. Minority college students—United States—Societies, etc. 3. Discrimination in higher education—United States. 4. Education, Higher—Social aspects—United States. I. Torbenson, Craig L. (Craig LaRon), 1956– II. Parks, Gregory, 1974–
LJ51.B767 2009
378.1′985—dc22

2008039476

PRINTED IN THE UNITED STATES OF AMERICA

Contents

Foreword

CRAIG L. TORBENSON AND GREGORY S. PARKS HAVE COLLABORATED to offer insight into a neglected area of scholarship involving Greek-letter student organizations. This effort, *Brothers and Sisters: Diversity in College Fraternities and Sororities*, widens the scope of study to include the breadth of diversity that exists among Greek-letter organizations. As college and university student populations become increasingly heterogeneous, student organizations, including Greek-letter organizations, have reflected the increasing diversity in students' interests and needs.

Torbenson and Parks's earlier works and prior collaborations have focused on the origins and development of black Greek-letter organizations. This book includes emerging scholarship on Greek groups involving Asian Americans, Latino/as, Native Americans, gays, multicultural and multiethnic students, and those who seek a religiously-affiliated Greek experience. Faculty and administrators need to understand the issues related to these groups if effective learning inside and outside the classroom is to occur. Also, as campus faculty and staff work with students to help them learn holistically, an understanding of the Greek experience can be revealing. The fraternity or sorority setting—be it white, black, Latino or other—can provide an important educational forum for critical discussion about a myriad of issues related to diversity, and the subsequent learning which occurs from that discussion.

A key question for the reader is how best to promote and support the diversity of the Greek experience—a question all of us in higher education must keep at the forefront. Torbenson and Parks's work also raises a number of questions regarding this experience related to race, ethnicity, gender and related issues which college administrators, and those who study student culture, should address. Although some progress has been made to open up the membership of Greek organizations, they remain predominantly white and heterosexual. This collection calls us to confront what Deborah E. Whaley in her chapter refers to as the "invisible norms" of white, heterosexual, and Christian. As colleges and universities struggle to diversify their campuses, educate students about the importance of celebrating and embracing multiculturalism, and deal with the myriad of related societal problems permeating campuses, this book highlights the challenges students from different backgrounds and cultures face in assimilating into historically white fraternities and sororities. In addition, the work underscores a student's desire to become part of a smaller group where he or she can find much needed support.

While sharing some similar aims of leadership, service, scholarship, brotherhood and sisterhood, and features like rituals, and letters, the Greek experience of today's college students is widely varied. The reader will come to understand that all groups struggle with identity even when individuals come together in a more narrowly defined purpose. Those of us working with groups from different cultures, backgrounds, and experiences must continually focus on how we are going to structure learning environments, such as fraternities and sororities, where students can be successful, both in and out of the classroom, regardless of race, ethnicity, sexual orientation, or religious belief.

—Edward G. Whipple
Vice President for Student Affairs
Bowling Green State University

Preface

IN 1955, ALFRED MCCLUNG LEE'S SEMINAL WORK, *FRATERNITIES WITHout Brotherhood: A Study of Prejudice on the American Campus*, was published by Beacon Press. In his book, Lee discussed the history of racial and religious exclusion largely on the part of white Anglo-Saxon Protestant (WASP) groups. *Fraternities Without Brotherhood* was the first and, unfortunately, the last book to take up the issue of diversity, broadly defined, within American college fraternities and sororities. Since Lee's publication, there has been some progress in way of reducing the amount of discrimination that takes place in WASP groups' selection of members and how their members treat others. However, incidents such as the one at Auburn University in 1999, where members of Pi Kappa Alpha fraternity wore Halloween costumes including Klansman outfits, members in blackface, and other members in blackface with nooses around their necks remind us of how far we have to go. More recently, on September 17, 2004, an initiate to Chi Psi Fraternity at the University of Colorado-Boulder died in relation to excessive alcohol consumption while at the fraternity's house. It was reported that while he lay passed out, vulgarities were written on his body including the word "nigger." Added to these incidents and others, the proliferation of groups catering to the unique needs of various minority and other student groups indicates there is a diverse fraternity and sorority culture that researchers, university administrators, and the general public fail to take into account. We take these issues into account in our book.

This book examines the variety of cultural-interest fraternities and sororities that can be found on college campuses. As a social institution, then, the college fraternity and sorority can be viewed today as a vibrant organization, capable of expanding its boundaries to include a variety of students' needs and interests, hence, its diversity. That has not always been the case. While arguments can be made for a brotherhood or sisterhood of like-minded individuals in forming a fraternity or sorority, others would argue that it is cultural diversity within each organization that makes it a social organization. It is the variety of fraternities and sororities within the social fraternity system that is a manifestation of the vitality and viability of this institution. The college fraternity system is able to absorb students who have diverse perspectives and outlooks on life and come from a variety of social, economic, ethnic, religious, or racial backgrounds. That is the beauty of the system, meeting the needs of a diverse student body. This book, then, examines the variety of cultural-interest fraternities and sororities based on ethnicity, race, sexual preference, and religion.

Craig L. Torbenson outlines the history of college fraternities and sororities, in general, and their first attempts to diversify across racial and religious lines. Deborah E. Whaley, Edith When-Chu Chen, Susana M. Muñoz and Juan R. Guardia, and Linda Kelley each look at the history and culture of fraternities and sororities developed for various racial groups (that is, African American, Asian American, Latino/a American, and Native American). Since there is such a paucity of information on Asian American groups, the author of that chapter explores what little research is available by primarily focusing on Asian American women in sororities. Amy E. Wells and Mark K. Dolan explore the history and culture of fraternities and sororities with a multicultural thrust. King-To Yeung takes a look at the history of fraternities and sororities founded for gay, bisexual, and lesbian individuals. However, the primary focus of this chapter is to take an in-depth case study of one particular gay fraternity. Craig L. Torbenson takes up the issue of religion within college fraternities and sororities while Matthew W. Hughey explores cross-racial membership within organizations that are predominantly black or white. An approach such as the one we take substantially builds upon *Fraternities Without Brotherhood.*

It is our hope that this book might find itself in the hands of a wide array of readers. College and university student affairs personnel might glean some insight into the breadth, depth, and complexities of their "Greek" communities. With that insight, they may be able to better serve their diverse student groups and better facilitate appreciation and collaboration across groups. Researchers are another group of readers who might find this book useful. The vast majority of research conducted on fraternities and sororities focuses on predominantly white groups. There does, also, seem to be a small yet growing body of literature on black Greek-letter organizations (BGLOs). Little work, however, focuses on groups catering to other racial minorities or nonheterosexuals. There is also limited research on multicultural organizations or fraternities and sororities with a religious emphasis. Hopefully, this book will provide some insight on and catalyst for research on these groups. With that in mind, and in an effort not to be redundant, a fairly exhaustive bibliography that may be used toward this end can be found in *African American Fraternities and Sororities: The Legacy and the Vision*—a book on which both of us worked. A final group that might find this book useful is the members of the respective diverse organizations. Very few of the diverse groups have their own history book, and there are few books exploring the history any of the collective groups (for example, Asian American, multicultural, religious). As such, this book is the first place many of them might see their history, which will hopefully provide them with a better understanding of their own organization and suggest to the world that they are here and here to stay!

Brothers and Sisters

From the Beginning: A History of College Fraternities and Sororities

Craig L. Torbenson

THE FIRST COLLEGE FRATERNITY BEGAN WHEN A GROUP OF FIVE young men attending William and Mary College in Virginia gathered December 5, 1776, to establish a student organization.[1] These young men, John Heath, Thomas Smith, Richard Booker, Armistead Smith, and John Jones, designed a square silver medal engraved with SP, the initials for Latin Societas Philosophiae. On the other side of the medal were the Greek initials Φ. . .β. . .κ.[2]

Phi Beta Kappa, then, became the first Greek-letter fraternity in the United States, the precursor to a variety of fraternal and sororal organizations. While there are numerous professional, recognition, and honor societies that use Greek letters, today there are more than three hundred and fifty national fraternity and sorority organizations classified as social fraternities. This is, however, only part of the story; at least another hundred national organizations have ceased to exist.

Although some may think all social fraternities and sororities are similar, there is, in fact, a great deal of diversity. Some are conservative in policies, but others are more open-minded. Some tend to establish chapters at certain types of colleges and universities; others are associated with particular religious, racial, or ethnic groups. Some are regional in distribution, while others are more national or even international. Despite these differences, the fraternity institution has had a notable role in the lives of countless students both before and after graduation. This chapter examines the origins of early social fraternities dominated by white, Protestant males and the later white, female sororities. With the expansion of colleges and the inclusion of other races, religions, and ethnic groups, the stage was set for the subsequent establishment of organizations specific to each group.

Student Life at Early U.S. Colleges

With the establishment of colleges during the colonial period, a subculture of student college life emerged that still exists today. This subculture embraces the educational and extracurricular experiences that students share while attending college. Within this subculture, numerous organizations—including college fraternities and sororities—developed to meet the intellectual and social needs of students.

The majority of early colleges in the United States patterned themselves after Harvard, which had modeled itself after Oxford and Cambridge Universities in England. In terms of structure (buildings, administration, and curriculum) and the collegiate way (dormitories, dining halls, and discipline), early American colleges tried to duplicate these two English prototypes as best they could. This section examines the early American attempts to replicate important physical and social features of English colleges and their subsequent modification, all of which provided the framework for student college life in U.S. colleges.[3]

Colonial schools quickly recognized the difficulties of duplicating the physical structure of their English examples. Because the population in the colonies was dispersed, colleges followed this same pattern, resulting in an educational system that was diffused and decentralized. Most colonial colleges lacked the resources to follow the architectural plans of their English models, which centered on enclosed quadrangles with only one exit. American colleges were often found to erect one structure at a time.[4]

Most colonial colleges followed the English model of using memorization and recitation as methods of classroom learning. Structured around the Greek and Latin languages and literature, the curriculum consisted of a group of courses taken by all; there was no flexibility, despite individual interest or professional plans. Information presented in class was not to be criticized or analyzed, but rather memorized or translated and then recited in Greek or Latin. This approach left little opportunity for students to expand their thinking and tended to be tiresome and dull.[5]

The idea of the collegiate way grew out of the concept of colleges as large family-like institutions. The faculty, acting as surrogate parents, assumed responsibility for discipline. Although the faculty members viewed college as a place to impart knowledge, they also saw it as a place to develop strong religious and moral character. Religion had a dominant role, and everyone observed a routine of "daily prayer, religious study, and Sunday church."[6]

In the colonies the faculty had the dual responsibility of teaching and meting out discipline, which frustrated attempts to foster any student-faculty relations. This differed from the English model, where deans and proctors were responsible for discipline and the faculty concentrated on teaching and developing close associations with their students. This paternalistic attitude of the colonial faculty resulted in highly structured everyday lives for students. Eating, sleeping, studying, and socializing were all supervised. A long list of "don'ts" left students with little freedom to diverge from a routine that some described as "pay, pray, study, and accept." For those guilty of infractions, the ultimate punishment was dismissal, though this was used sparingly, since the college relied financially on student tuition.[7]

The colonial college also tried to duplicate the dormitory, which was the heart of the English educational experience. In the English model, dormitories encouraged interaction, brought students and faculty together outside of the classroom, and enabled the faculty to keep a close eye on students. The colonial dormitory, however, was less successful. With limited funds, American colleges constructed one building at a time, and when a dormitory was built, it was often located some distance from the classroom buildings, making it difficult to enforce the rules and regulations.[8]

The colonial dormitories were crude and lacked many of the simple comforts of life. For the young men inhabiting the dormitories, the spartan conditions aggravated the situation. Tempers wore thin as frequent confrontations erupted. Several disputes resulted in death, such as when two students at South Carolina College grabbed the same plate of food and resolved their conflict with a duel in 1833. In such a difficult environment, students were easily incited to protest a variety of issues related to the educational process. They often led boycotts and rebellions that resulted in the destruction of school property. The faculty, and often the public, viewed these actions as inappropriate behavior, but the students saw these activities as a break from a boring curriculum of memorization and recitation.[9]

The colonial college copied the English system of dividing a student body into freshman, sophomore, junior, and senior classes. This class division is central to understanding certain aspects of college life in America. Since enrollments were small, students who entered college lived, studied, socialized, and graduated together. Class designation was therefore the first form of student association. Though never an official organization, each class had its own rituals, customs, insignia, and clothes and provided important social activities for members. In this hierarchy, the freshmen were on the bottom in a position of servitude to members of the upper classes. This strengthened the bonding of each incoming class and made interclass rivalry a significant part of college life. By 1725, social class standing also became important for students at Harvard, where members of each class were ranked according to their father's social position.[10]

Many aspects of student life found new meaning and purpose in college fraternities and sororities. Freshman servitude in the colonies, known as "fagging" in English colleges, evolved to become hazing by the early 1800s. Incidents of hazing were often humiliating and sometimes dangerous. Typical hazing incidents included consuming large amounts of drink or food, performing worthless and mundane tasks, or participating in various stunts. One aspect of hazing was rush. Initially an all-out fight or brawl between freshman and sophomore classes, rush later became an organized activity such as a wrestling match or football game.[11]

Although class standing was an important foundation for many student organizations, its role declined as some colleges ceased to provide housing for students. The college fraternity also had a role in this demise. Early in their history, fraternities selected members from one class only; thus, there were sophomore, junior, and senior fraternities. By the 1900s, however, college fraternities selected members from all four classes.[12]

Within this early collegiate world the student had little freedom. While the faculty saw college as a period of self-denial, the students saw college as a time to be enjoyed while preparing for the future. These differing viewpoints created tensions and frequent clashes between the faculty and students. Students attempted to take control of college life with the establishment of clubs, societies, and fraternities. The faculty had different ideas, however, and responded with stricter rules as they supervised many student organizations. Despite faculty control, or perhaps because of it, these organizations functioned well, giving students an outlet to interact with others in a social and intellectual atmosphere. In time, however, students wanted more freedom to pursue their own interests without faculty intervention. The result was a proliferation of student organizations to meet the various needs of the student body.[13]

Student Organizations

In 1703, the first-known student organization in British North America was established at Harvard. Its purpose was to allow students to pray together and mingle under faculty guidance within a religious context. Like the colonial college, early student organizations had religious orientations. By 1719, however, a number of more secular organizations had been established. Meeting in student rooms, members read poems and discussed topics while smoking and drinking.[14]

The formation of a student organization was often based on a specific interest or idea of a few individuals. Most of these organizations were short-lived and when their members graduated, they ceased to exist. Despite a proliferation of student organizations in the early eighteenth century, it was not until the late eighteenth century that student organizations recruited members and were thereby able to exist beyond the college careers of those who established them.[15]

Literary societies or debating clubs, which enjoyed their greatest popularity between 1760 and 1860, emerged as the most important organization for students. The proliferation of these societies and clubs can be attributed to the general atmosphere of political excitement in the colonies and to the changes brought about by the Enlightenment. Literary societies helped fill a void in the educational process by providing students with the opportunity to develop skills in speaking and writing. They also provided a spirit of intellectualism that was lacking in the college classroom because of the emphasis on rote learning and recitation.[16]

Usually, each campus had two or three literary societies that vied for members, student positions, and honors. Competition was often fierce. Each society was essentially a college within a college. It enrolled students, had classes, published magazines, and passed out diplomas. The literary society sometimes had a larger and better library than the college itself. To distinguish their members, many societies used secret initiation rites, mottos, and badges. As a result, membership and activities in literary societies often became more important than the curriculum of the college.[17]

College Fraternities and Sororities

Although other factors contributed to the decline of literary societies, their demise is closely associated with the rise of fraternities and sororities, which generated a higher degree of loyalty. The idea of fraternity or brotherhood was not peculiar to college students in the United States: many student organizations existed in Europe. Although attempts have been made to establish a link between European student organizations and the American college fraternity, the evidence suggests the social fraternity is unique to the United States.[18]

A particular fraternity or sorority was the creation of a few individuals who had similar values and ideals and who wanted to maintain close associations while in college. Their goals often included correcting the perceived wrongs of the college administration, providing social activities for students, and obtaining more rights for students. In reality, however, their purpose was to create a compatible brotherhood or sisterhood for friendship.[19]

Fraternities and sororities had many similar characteristics with the literary societies, including the use of pins, badges, secret initiation rites, and mottos. The fraternity system differed, however, with its use of Greek letters representing the organization's motto, and a reliance on initiation rituals from the Masonic Order. Rush and hazing, which were part of the early college tradition, took on new meaning within the social fraternity system. The initial documents of many fraternities and later, sororities, set out the goals for these organizations, which generally included maintaining high standards of scholarship, perpetuating brotherhood or sisterhood, striving for excellence as an individual, developing leadership qualities, and for some organizations, participating in service activities at school and in the community. Thus, whereas literary societies once filled the intellectual vacuum of college life, Greek-letter fraternities filled the social vacuum. In a fraternity, one could find brotherhood and escape from mundane class work and religious training. Drinking, smoking, card playing, singing, and womanizing—behavior not generally condoned—became institutionalized in the fraternity. While these activities had always been a way of escape for college students, the fraternity gave the behavior new opportunities.[20]

The First Fraternities

Phi Beta Kappa, the prototype of the college fraternity, was established at William and Mary College in Williamsburg, Virginia, in 1776. Similar to other student organizations of the time, Phi Beta Kappa functioned as a literary society, sponsoring essay writing, debates, and orations. It had its own rules for debate, and some of the discussion topics included "the advantages of an established Church," "the justice of African slavery," and "whether anything is more dangerous to civil liberty in a free state than a standing army in time of peace." Besides the scholarly activities of Phi Beta Kappa, this organization departed from the norm by also serving as a vehicle for social activities. The members devised a number of secret aspects, such as the handshake, motto, sign, and password, to identify those who belonged. An initiation ritual in Greek and Latin explained the organization's secrets. This aspect was not unique to Phi Beta Kappa, for other student organizations often used secrecy, but never with such a heavy emphasis.[21]

Two of the founders of Phi Beta Kappa and eight subsequent members were Masons; therefore, Masonic influence can be assumed. Certainly a model of symbology was provided from which adaptations could be made. One Masonic characteristic Phi Beta Kappa most likely adopted was the idea of establishing chapters at other locations in Virginia. However, the idea of expansion to other states was an innovation unique to Phi Beta Kappa. The expansion process worked as follows: the mother chapter at William and Mary granted a charter to an individual who wanted to establish a chapter. This individual took the charter, a piece of paper on which the fraternity's constitution was written, and tore it in half. The mother chapter kept half of the charter, and the new chapter retained the other half. This charter could be withdrawn if the new chapter proved unworthy of the fraternity's ideals.[22]

Phi Beta Kappa expanded initially into the South. By 1780, the fraternity had established chapters at some twenty colleges and within numerous communities. These early chapters are known as the "lost chapters," since there are no accurate records available. Expansion to the North occurred at Yale College and Harvard University in 1780 and 1781. Between 1787 and 1830, additional chapters at Dartmouth College (1787), Union College (1817) in New York, Bowdoin College (1825) in Maine, and Brown College (1830) in Rhode Island increased the geographic territory and influence of this organization. Since communication among these early chapters was infrequent, each developed and operated as an autonomous unit. Consequently, a variety of traditions and practices emerged at each school.[23]

During the latter part of the 1820s, an antisecrecy movement swept the country, prompted by the disappearance of William Morgan, who was about to publish a book exposing the secrets of Masonry. Throughout the United States, many people were increasingly of the opinion that Masons exerted undue political, social, and economic control or influence. A public outcry against such secret organizations culminated in the establishment of the Anti-Masonic Party in 1831; its main platform was the elimination of all secret societies. Phi Beta Kappa was often associated with the Masons, however, in 1831, Phi Beta Kappa published its secret rites and became an honorary society.[24]

The next recorded appearance of a Greek-letter organization occurred thirty-six years after the founding of Phi Beta Kappa. In 1812, four one-time initiates of Phi Beta Kappa at the University of North Carolina organized Kappa Alpha, which eventually expanded to include some twenty-one chapters throughout the South. It is very likely this fraternity was an offspring of one of the community chapters of Phi Beta Kappa, for its constitution, rituals, and secrets were very similar. Local fraternities were established at Union (1813), Yale (1821), and Princeton College (1824). Many local organizations were established because their petition for a Phi Beta Kappa charter was not promptly acted on or had been denied.[25]

Although Phi Beta Kappa is recognized as the first fraternity, it was not until the late 1820s and early 1830s that the fraternity movement became firmly established. With the establishment of a Phi Beta Kappa chapter at Union (1817) there was now competition with a local fraternity. Both organizations eventually came under faculty control, leading students to establish three new organizations that used Greek letters and implemented many of the characteristics of Phi Beta Kappa. Known as the Union Triad, Kappa Alpha Society (1825), Sigma Phi (1827), and Delta Phi (1827) launched the fraternity movement and set the pattern for the creation of new fraternities. Because three additional fraternities, Psi Upsilon (1833), Chi Psi (1841), and Theta Delta Chi (1847), were also established at Union, this school is referred to as the "Mother of Fraternities."[26]

The emergence of the fraternity, then, is the culmination of processes that involved early colonial colleges and the subsequent development of student college life. Certainly the struggle over whether the faculty or students should control student college life had a major role in the creation of the social fraternity. As the prototype fraternity, Phi Beta Kappa left its legacy to the college fraternity movement, with its heavy emphasis on secrecy and expansion to other colleges.

The First Sororities

The origins of women's fraternities, or sororities, are associated with the coeducational colleges of the Midwest and South, not the women's colleges of the East. Since they were a minority on coeducational campuses, women organized to unite their small numbers and give them a stronger position in campus activities. Clearly, the creation of women's organizations was an imitation of the already well-established men's fraternities.[27]

Before the 1830s, few women attended male-dominated colleges; rather, they went to female "academies" or "seminaries." As the number of women attending college increased, however, many predominantly male colleges opted to become coeducational. The question logically arose as to whether women should be allowed to join fraternities. There was no ban on women members, for this had never been an issue, and although a few fraternities allowed women to join, most excluded them. There are a few recorded examples of women joining chapters of national fraternities. One of the earliest is from a chapter of Sigma Alpha

Epsilon at the Kentucky Military Institute around 1860–61. Beta Theta Pi, Phi Delta Theta, and Pi Kappa Alpha were other organizations known to have female members. The women of Pi Kappa Alpha seem to have been members of the community and used their homes for entertainment, provided food for fraternity members, and decorated the chapter hall. Some national organizations debated for several years whether women should be admitted as members. Attempts were made to include women by giving them some sort of peripheral status, but many women objected and insisted on full membership. When this was not obtained, they created their own organizations to provide comparable activities.[28]

The earliest women's organizations were established at the first women's college—Wesleyan (Georgia) in 1851 and 1852. These secret literary societies used classical names that were later changed to the Greek Alpha Delta Pi and Phi Mu. They remained local organizations until the early 1900s. Pi Beta Phi (or I. C. Sorosis until 1888) has the distinction of being the first national women's fraternity. Organized in 1867 at Monmouth College (Illinois), it patterned itself after the male fraternity in organization and manner of expansion. With the establishment of its second chapter in 1869, it became a national organization.[29]

The first women's organization to use Greek letters was Kappa Alpha Theta, organized by Bettie Locke in 1870 at DePauw University (Indiana). Both her father and brother belonged to a fraternity. When her brother's fraternity offered her a pin so she could champion the organization, she asked to be a full member. The chapter members turned her down and her father suggested she begin her own organization. The first sorority was established in 1874 at Syracuse University. Gamma Phi Beta was a "society" prior to 1882, when a Latin professor suggested the use of the term *sorority*. This term became popular to distinguish between female and male fraternities.[30]

Geographic Patterns of Origin

Five geographic areas are important in terms of the origin of college fraternities and sororities. In chronological order, they are east-central New York, Virginia, west-central New York, the Midwest, and California. The "Cradle of Social Fraternities" formed in east-central New York, can be separated into a northern and southern core. The northern core was in place by 1835 and centered on Union College, where four fraternities had been established by 1834. Two other colleges formed this northern core—Hamilton and Williams—each of which had a fraternity. Of the five colleges in the region, three had fraternities. The southern core focused on Yale in Connecticut, where three fraternities had been established by 1848. The three other institutions in this southern core—Wesleyan, New York University, and Columbia—each had one fraternity. By 1848, Union had also added two new fraternities. Of the nine colleges located in the southern core, four were birthplaces for college fraternities. By 1848, the northern and southern cores had merged to form a fraternity culture hearth, or core area. This region extended from metropolitan New York up the Hudson and Mohawk Rivers to Schenectady and Clinton. The eastern boundary included the western half of Connecticut and western third of Massachusetts. Of the fifteen fraternities established from 1825 to 1848, fourteen were located in this region, and of the fifteen schools in the area, seven were places of origin.

The Virginia region became important as a place of origin following the Civil War. Seven schools in this area gave rise to fraternities and sororities between 1855 and 1901. Longwood and Washington and Lee Colleges each had four—Longwood with sororities and Washington and Lee with fraternities. The University of Virginia and the Virginia Military Institute each had three, followed by Roanoke with two. Falling just outside this Virginia region is Howard University in the District of Columbia and two other Virginian schools, Richmond and William and Mary. Howard was the place of origin for six black Greek-letter organizations—three fraternities and three sororities.

The next two regions of importance, west-central New York and the Midwest, gained significance during the early 1900s. In west-central New York, Cornell and Syracuse University formed the core, with seven and five new fraternities and sororities respectively. Other schools included Hobart College, SUNY–Buffalo, and the University of Rochester. Prior to 1910, only four college fraternities had originated at these schools, but by 1924, another seven had been established. In the Midwest (from the western border of Pennsylvania to Missouri), Miami University was the core, with five fraternities and three sororities. Other schools included Missouri with four organizations and DePauw and Ohio State University, each with two; four additional schools had one organization each. Since 1980, the importance of New York State has been reinforced with the addition of twenty new organizations. At least thirteen were established in the State University System, twelve of them at three schools: Albany, Buffalo, and Binghamton. Six organizations were established in New Jersey, two in Connecticut, and one in Pennsylvania. The Midwest area was also reinforced with the addition of eighteen organizations. The state of Illinois added half of these organizations with the University of Illinois supplying three and the University of Indiana also adding three new organizations.

The fifth region is California, which reached national importance in the 1980s. Prior to 1980, Cal-Berkeley had six organizations originate at this school, the first one in 1909. Other schools included UCLA with two, and USC and San Francisco State, each with one. The latter went inactive in 1946, but was reestablished at Cal-Berkeley in 1988. Since 1980, a plethora of fraternal and sororal organizations emerged in California. From 1981 to 2005, thirty-three national organizations were established. The leading school with five organizations was Cal State-Chico. Three of these organizations were multicultural and two were Latino/a. Cal State Fresno and Cal State Sacramento had three organizations each, while Cal-Berkeley added two more organizations for a total of eight. Other schools with two organizations include UCLA, Cal Poly-San Luis Obispo, Cal State San Jose, Cal-Stanislaus, and Cal State Long Beach. Six other schools had one organization. Outside these five regions the state of Texas stands out with fourteen national organizations established since 1987. The University of Texas was home for eight of these organizations.

Figure 1 identifies, by five-year periods, when national fraternities and sororities originated (see also Appendix I). This chart identifies three waves of establishing new organizations. During the first wave, 1824–74, 17.7 percent of all national organizations were established. These are the traditional Greek-letter organizations with 94 percent of them white, male, and Protestant. In the second wave, 1885 to 1929, 35.7 percent of all national organizations were established. Of this number, nearly half (42 percent) were not the traditional fraternal organization, but rather catered to African Americans, Jews, nonsectarian groups, various religious groups, and ethnic groups. About a third of these new national organizations were sororities.

The third wave, which began in 1975 and ended in 1999, was responsible for 38.1 percent of all national organizations. Only a few of these new organizations were traditional fraternities or sororities as this new group catered to a more diverse student body. The Latino/a and Asian American organizations tied for the most new national fraternities and sororities with thirty-four each, together accounting for just over 50 percent of all the new organizations during this third wave. Of the thirty-four Latino/a organizations, sixteen were established in the east—New York State had ten national organizations while New Jersey had four. There were six Latino/a organizations established in California. Of the thirty-four Asian American organizations, fifteen were established in California, six in New York, and four in Texas, all at the University of Texas.

The other major category of new organizations was the multicultural fraternity and sorority. This group accounted for nearly 24 percent of

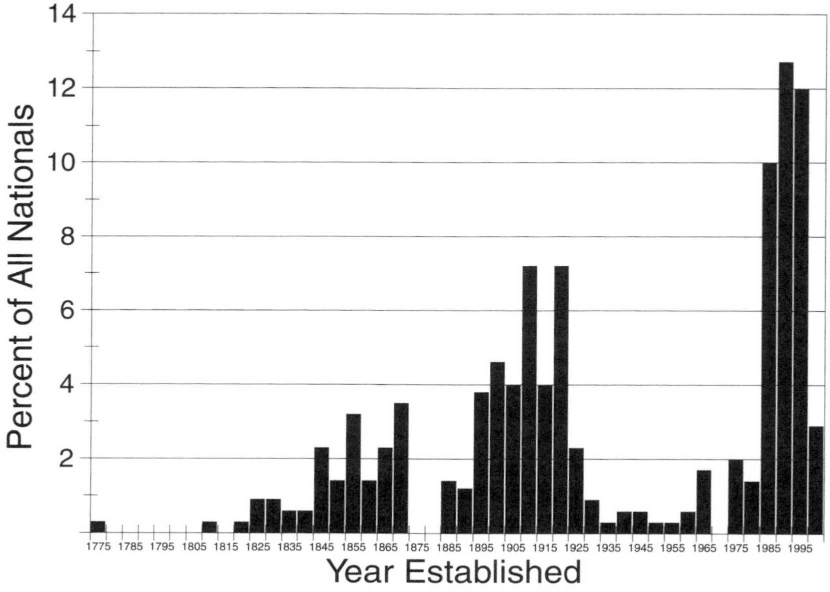

Figure 1

new organizations. California has nine nationals, while New York has eight. The leading schools include the University of Illinois and California State at Chico, each with three organizations. Thus, three-quarters of all new organizations during this third wave were either Latino/a, Asian American, or multicultural fraternities and sororities.

Other types of organizations created or established during this wave included the coed fraternity, alternative organizations for males and females, Native American, additional African American organizations, several with an emphasis on religion, and several general or specific religious fraternities and sororities. These three waves are responsible for 91.5 percent of all national fraternities and sororities established since 1776.

Expansion

Early expansion of a fraternity or sorority could occur in several ways. The first involved personal contact. If one individual was aggressive in spreading the word about his/her organization, that could have a significant impact on growth. For example, Otis Glazebrook, one of the founders of Alpha Tau Omega at Virginia Military Institute, was responsible for establishing chapters at five other colleges. When fraternity members traveled to different colleges for personal or school business, they often advertised for individuals who were interested in establishing chapters. Summer vacation was another vehicle for expansion. When students returned home for the break, they would see old friends and others who attended different schools, expound on the virtues of their fraternity or sorority, and get their friends interested and involved. After returning to their respective schools, these individuals might establish a new chapter. A third aspect of personal contact involved fraternity or sorority members who transferred to other colleges or who graduated and went on to law or medical school. These students often established chapters at their new schools. Another strategy to gain members was to "lift" an individual—in other words, steal an individual from another fraternity.[31]

A second process of expansion involved the several types of local organizations found on college campuses, such as fraternities, sororities, clubs, and literary societies. In one approach, local groups organized with the specific intention of joining a national organization. Once the local organization built up its qualifications, it would apply for membership in a national fraternity or sorority. In a second approach, the national organization would solicit well-established local organizations to become chapters of that fraternity or sorority. The records of many national fraternities and sororities identify numerous chapters that at one time were local organizations.[32]

Today, the method of expansion is called colonization. Usually, the national organization identifies a specific college where it wishes to establish a chapter and sends representatives to the college to recruit members. A second, less common approach involves a local organization becoming a chapter of a national organization. In either case, the chapter is referred to as a colony and is given probationary status before being fully recognized as a chapter.[33]

The expansion of fraternities and sororities can be discussed in terms of adoption and augmentation. The first time a fraternity or sorority is established at a college or university is referred to as adoption. Augmentation refers to the adding of chapters at that particular campus. Both processes illustrate the expansion of this social institution, the first by adding more colleges and universities to the list of those with fraternities and sororities, while the second by enlarging the fraternity system on individual campuses.[34]

The Early Years

Expansion of the first two fraternities, Phi Beta Kappa and Kappa Alpha, is not fully documented. Extant records indicate that chapters of Phi Beta Kappa existed at five schools: William and Mary (1776), Yale (1780), Harvard (1781), Dartmouth (1787), and Union (1817). Kappa Alpha existed at one school, North Carolina (1812). Prior to 1830, only one school had increased its number of fraternities: that was Union College, with its triad of Kappa Alpha Society (1825), Sigma Phi (1827), and Delta Phi (1827).

Besides an early adopter, Union College was the place of origin of six national fraternities, four of them prior to 1840. Union has a unique place in the annals of fraternal history. One explanation for its importance seems to be its curriculum. While most colleges were offering classical courses, Union had expanded the curriculum to include many nontraditional courses. Considered a radical, Union President Eliphalet Nott steered the curriculum away from the classics to include science, engineering, and modern literature; he also accepted students who had been expelled from other colleges. Perhaps another reason for the number of fraternities at this school was that, unlike many other presidents who tried to eliminate these organizations, Nott regarded membership in fraternities as an appropriate student activity.[35]

In the 1820s and 1830s, the majority of schools adopting fraternities were located in New England and New York State. In the 1820s, Princeton (1824) in New Jersey and Bowdoin (1825) in Maine adopted the fraternity system. The chapter at Bowdoin was Phi Beta Kappa, and the chapter at Princeton was a local fraternity, Chi Phi Society. This organization became defunct but was later reestablished and remains active today. Of the eight adopting schools in the 1830s, only the Universities of Georgia and Miami (Ohio) were outside the "Cradle of Social Fraternities." In 1832, Alpha Delta Phi was organized at Hamilton and, in 1833, it established a chapter at Miami (Ohio), the first chapter of any fraternity west of the Appalachian Mountains. Six years later, dissension arose, and eight members withdrew and formed a new fraternity—Beta Theta Pi. Together with Phi Delta Theta (1848) and Sigma Chi (1855), these three came to be known collectively as the "Miami Triad."[36]

During the 1830s, five new fraternities were established, bringing the total to nine. Williams and New York University led the way with three new chapters; Yale, Union, Hamilton, Brown, and Miami (Ohio) each had two. Expansion remained more or less confined to eastern New York State and southern New England. The leading organizations in expansion included Alpha Delta Phi with eight chapters and Sigma Phi with four chapters. Half the Alpha Delta Phi chapters were at schools adopting the fraternity for the first time.[37]

As a fraternity made the transition from a local to a national organization, a system for naming chapters had to be devised. One method was to name the first chapter Alpha for the first Greek letter, the second chapter Beta for the second Greek letter, and so forth. Once the entire alphabet had been used, the next series of chapters would be called Alpha Alpha, Alpha Beta, and so on. A second method referred to the first chapter in each state as Alpha, the second as Beta, and so forth. A third method of identification used Greek letters as initials for certain words in the school's motto.[38]

Generally, faculty members opposed fraternities during this period. Most had been trained for the ministry and had enjoyed few freedoms or responsibilities when they were students. They believed their students should also have to conform. Thus, school administrators and faculty either kept a close watch on fraternities, or some colleges banned them all together. As a result, many chapters went underground and became even more secretive. Members of one chapter, for example, rented the first floor of a dormitory, cut a trap door, and dug out a basement in order to have a secret place to meet. Activities such as this did not enhance the image of the fraternity. Some smaller colleges, however, refused to oppose fraternities because they helped to attract students.[39]

Entrenchment

By 1840, eleven national fraternities had been established, although two were no longer active. During the 1840s, ten new fraternities were founded, bringing the total to nineteen active ones. Four of these established only the parent chapter, while the other six added two or more new chapters. The nine continuing organizations also expanded. For Beta Theta Pi, nearly two-thirds of its chapters were established at schools that previously did not have any fraternities. The same is true for Phi Delta Theta, which established 80 percent of its chapters during the 1850s at first-time adopting schools. This is to be expected, given the relative newness of the institution and the small number of fraternities.[40]

The number of schools adopting fraternities more than doubled from the 1830s to the 1840s, and again from the 1840s to the 1850s. Nearly two-thirds of fraternity expansion during these two decades occurred at first-time adopting institutions. The 1850s saw sixteen new fraternities, two of them female organizations that later became Greek-letter sororities. With the reactivation of Chi Phi Society at Princeton, the number of active fraternities and sororities grew to 36, all of which established new chapters during this decade; 202 new chapters were established at 87 schools, with two-thirds of these schools being first-time adopters.

During the 1850s, expansion shifted to the South, although New England and the Middle Atlantic States were still important.[41]

Prior to the Civil War, the role of a founding chapter was that of a parent. Although most fraternities intended to expand, problems arose because of an inadequate system to administer a national organization. Parent chapters had difficulty controlling other chapters. In several instances a chapter of one national organization switched to a different national organization, sometimes by surrendering its original charter, and sometimes by being "lifted" by the second organization.[42]

The onset of the Civil War saw the adoption process slow considerably. The war disrupted many aspects of American society, including universities and colleges. It also devastated the fraternity in two ways. First, students left college to fight in the war; sometimes an entire chapter would enlist at the same time. Second, fraternity membership naturally declined as college enrollment declined. Many schools nearly ceased to function as their campus buildings were used for barracks, hospitals, and ammunition depots. Many southern colleges suffered damage and took several years to rebuild, and several northern schools closed. One such school, Phi Kappa Sigma Male College (Arkansas), the only example of a college named for a fraternity, was used to store supplies for the Confederacy and was later destroyed by the Union army. It is estimated that 80 percent of chapter losses during the 1860s were a result of the war. There were, surprisingly five new fraternities established, four in the North and one in the South. Of the twenty-seven schools adopting fraternities during the 1860s, seven did so during the Civil War, and three of them were in the South. Adoption, however, went forward more quickly in the North and for the first time, a western school adopted a fraternity when five chapters were established at the University of California–Berkeley.[43]

During the Civil War, many fraternities became inactive, especially in the South. Afterward, the northern fraternities that had chapters in the South were reluctant to reestablish them. This created a void for southern students that resulted in the creation of a number of new fraternities. The first was Alpha Tau Omega (1865) at Virginia Military Institute, followed by Kappa Sigma Kappa (1867) and Sigma Nu (1869). Pi Kappa Alpha (1868) and Kappa Sigma (1869) were established at the University of Virginia; Kappa Alpha Order (1865) was founded at Washington and Lee (Virginia); and Alpha Gamma (1867) at Cumberland College (Tennessee). These new organizations emerged from the conflict trying to "keep alive the spirit of chivalry, self-sacrifice, mutual helpfulness, and comradeship born of their recent experiences." Another goal seemed to be to preserve various aspects of their southern culture. Several organizations used military titles for their officers.

Despite the Civil War, which slowed new chapter growth, 53 chapters were established during the decade, with nearly 70 percent of this growth from 1865 to 1870. Almost half of these new chapters were in the South. During this decade, thirteen new fraternities were established, eight of them after 1865. By 1870, then, a total of forty-nine college fraternities had been established in the United States, but many went defunct during the Civil War.[44]

Beginning in the 1870s, major changes in the college curriculum and student life took place. Led by the president of Harvard and embraced by his fellow educators, an attitude of self-independence spread around the country. Among other things, a degree of freedom emerged whereby students could choose their own course of study. This in turn, "fostered the development of a system of free and competitive enterprises in student affairs." During this decade, six fraternities and six sororities were established. Expansion involved 40 fraternities and sororities, with 270 new chapters at 126 schools. Regional expansion continued to focus on Virginia, with nearly 30 new chapters established.[45]

During the 1880s, the ratio of fraternity chapters to nonmember students was 1:107; a comparative number was 1:580 in 1980. In other words, for every chapter there were 107 non-Greek college students, indicating a high degree of Greek involvement during this decade. Although student enrollments increased by nearly 30 percent, enrollments in fraternities and sororities were at 36 percent. In the 1880s, only two new fraternities and three new sororities were founded, all from 1885 to 1889. In the 1890s, eighteen new organizations were established, the same number as had been founded in the previous two decades combined. Again, half were sororities. More fraternities and sororities were establishing new chapters, but the number of chapters per fraternity or sorority declined. All this occurred at fewer colleges, as the number of adopting schools decreased from the previous decade.[46]

Part of the reason for the decline between the late 1870s and late 1880s might have been an antifraternity movement that swept college campuses. Undoubtedly, it was prompted by the 1874 publication of a book that attacked fraternities for their immoralities and selectivity in membership. From 1875 to 1890, 191 chapters went inactive. Roughly 50 percent of these chapter losses occurred in schools imposing antifraternity regulations. For example, on many campuses, incoming students were required to take a pledge that they would not belong to any fraternity. Purdue University lost a court case when a transfer student, who already belonged to a fraternity, refused to sign such an oath. Fraternities and schools were soon involved in many court cases concerning a student's right to join a fraternity. With this antifraternity regulation, administrators looked forward to the elimination of fraternities and sororities by attrition at their schools. Many chapters, however, went underground, a practice that was not always supported by the chapter's national organization. As a result, many charters were withdrawn. Charters could also be withdrawn for insubordination or low academic standards. During this time around 22 percent of chapter losses were the result of the withdrawal of charters.[47]

Populism took its toll during the 1890s and the first decade of the 1900s. Fraternities came under attack for being exclusive, undemocratic, and promoting unsavory behavior. During this time, the Populist movement influenced the passage of state laws that either banned the fraternity system or reduced its activities at state institutions. For example, the University of South Carolina (1897), University of Arkansas (1901), and the University of Mississippi (1912) passed laws prohibiting fraternities and sororities at these state schools. Seven chapters at South Carolina and six at Mississippi were forced to suspend activities. In Arkansas, however, it was ruled that although the intent of the law was to exclude these organizations, the act actually stated that no fraternity member should receive an honor or class distinction from the university. Thus, members at the University of Arkansas opted to forgo any such honors, and the fraternities and sororities continued to exist. Between 1912 and 1916, legislatures in Texas, Ohio, Wisconsin, Kansas, California, and Missouri also attempted to abolish fraternities and sororities at state institutions. In all these states, however, the proposed legislation was defeated. These examples reflect the degree of bitterness many college administrations and many Americans felt toward college fraternities.[48]

The leading organizations in establishing chapters at first-time adopting schools between 1840 and 1900 included Beta Theta Pi, with twenty-six chapters and Delta Tau Delta and Sigma Alpha Epsilon, both with fifteen. Of the organizations establishing new chapters during this period, Phi Delta Theta and Sigma Alpha Epsilon led with eighty-four and eighty-two chapters respectively. Much of this expansion took place from 1860 to 1890.[49]

This entrenchment phase was one of contrasts. Although growth occurred, the fraternity system was greatly affected by the Civil War, faculty opposition, and the antifraternity regulations of the 1870s and 1880s. Overall, the Civil War was the most damaging, though antifraternity regulations had an impact on individual campuses. However, the proliferation of colleges during the latter part of the nineteenth century greatly increased the possibilities for expansion. Numerous denominational colleges, land-grant schools, women's and coeducational colleges, as well as private schools, offered potential homes for fraternities and sororities. Some organizations established chapters in local communities or at high schools, although these did not survive long. Between 1870 and 1920, 478 new colleges were established around the United States. As students filled these new institutions, many were eager to duplicate the student college life experience of older institutions. As a result, fraternities and sororities greatly benefited.[50]

National Expansion I

By 1900, students attended college for a variety of reasons. Prior to this time, the major reason for attending college was to prepare for the ministry, the law, or one of the other traditional professions. Now, many attended college to better their economic status. Attending college became "the thing to do," with prestige accorded to those who had graduated. As part of the college experience, one became a member of a fraternity or sorority.[51]

During this period, great expansion took place. One notable reason for the rapid growth of fraternities and sororities had to do with student housing. By the end of the nineteenth century, student dormitories were losing money and were being discontinued at many colleges, and fraternities and sororities stepped in to fill this void. Thus, the need for student housing became the primary reason for the dramatic increase in membership. Colleges were eager to help fraternities and sororities construct chapter houses, which solved some of their housing problems and relieved school administrators of the responsibility of watching over students. The rapid increase in new chapters verified that the fraternity system was needed to handle a situation colleges could not or would not address.[52]

From 1900 to 1930, 24 percent of the schools that added fraternities or sororities to their campuses were first-time adopters. Of the top eleven fraternities and sororities to establish chapters at adopting schools, three were black organizations and six were sororities, indicating the increased enrollment of women and blacks at institutions of higher learning. The leading fraternity in establishing chapters at adopting schools was a black fraternity, Phi Beta Sigma, established in 1914. Alpha Phi Alpha, the first black fraternity established in 1906, was tied for fourth with Omega Psi Phi, established in 1911, along with two white sororities. Of the top six leaders in expansion, five were sororities. Chi Omega led with eighty-two chapters while Kappa Delta had seventy-five chapters. Lambda Chi Alpha, the only fraternity, had seventy-six new chapters.[53]

The early editions of *Baird's Manual* classified fraternities as northern or southern based on their place of origin. As the Greek-letter system expanded, however, classification was done on a regional basis. By 1900, regional boundaries were largely irrelevant, because continued expansion meant that chapters of a fraternity or sorority existed in numerous regions or even throughout the country. During this time, some of the fraternities and sororities began to map where schools were located to create target areas for possible expansion. From 1910 to 1919 growth continued as twenty-seven new fraternities and eleven sororities were established. The number of new chapters nearly doubled to a thousand. There were now 114 fraternities and sororities involved in expansion.[54]

The economic prosperity of the 1920s contributed to a rapid increase in college enrollment and a similar rise in fraternity membership. From 1920 to 1925, there were 22 new fraternities and 6 new sororities established. With 134 fraternities and sororities creating more than 1800 new chapters at 309 schools, the 1920s was a decade of growth and expansion unequaled in the annals of fraternity history until the 1970s. Approximately 75 percent of the new chapters were at schools that already had such organizations. Amid this growth, two national associations were formed to serve as umbrella organizations. The initial suggestion for such an organization had been made in 1883, and again in 1893, but it was not until 1909 that the National Interfraternity Conference (NIC) was established, the umbrella organization for most of the traditional national fraternities. The NIC was not the first umbrella organization, for sororities had organized the National Panhellenic Conference (NPC) in 1902, after earlier attempts in 1891 and 1893 had failed. The black national fraternities and sororities were excluded and in 1929, these groups organized the National Pan-Hellenic Council (NPHC) to meet their needs.[55]

Retrenchment

During the 1930s and 1940s nearly 650 new colleges and universities were established in the United States. While college enrollments declined during the thirties, the number increased from 582,000 in 1930 to 1,388,000 by 1950. Certainly the growth of fraternity and sorority chapters on college campuses was greatly affected by the economic events of the 1930s. The spread of fraternities and sororities to new colleges and universities however, continued. Despite the economic hardships of the Depression, sixty-one schools adopted the fraternal and sororal institution. Over half of these schools were located in the South and 21 percent were black colleges. However, during this time only three new organizations were established.[56]

The 1940s only saw four new national organizations. While World War II certainly curtailed fraternity and sorority expansion, the period after the war saw increased numbers of students enroll in college. Fraternities, in particular, took advantage of recruiting servicemen to join their ranks. Seventy-five percent of over the 1,050 new chapters established during the 1940s were done so after the war. During this decade many of the teachers' colleges, or normal schools, catering to females, went coeducational. As these schools made the transition to a four-year college, they offered fertile ground for fraternities and sororities. Many of these schools were located in the Midwest, Southeast, Texas, and California. Growth continued during the 1950s with more than 1,300 new chapters established. The leading organizations for expansion during this period included Tau Kappa Epsilon with 132 new chapters with Sigma Phi Epsilon having 83 new chapters. Alpha Kappa Alpha and Kappa Alpha Psi, a black sorority and fraternity, had 74 and 73 new chapters respectively.[57]

Each decade of this period also had events that had a major impact on chapters going inactive: the economic depression of the 1930s, World War II during the 1940s, and antifraternity legislation again, during the 1950s. The result was some 52 national organizations either went defunct, consolidated with a stronger organization, or merged to create a new national organization. Roughly 25 percent of all chapter losses were a result of consolidation or merger. During the Depression, more than 550 chapters went inactive. Many college fraternities and sororities came upon hard times during the economic crisis as they had overextended themselves during the 1920s by constructing large and expensive chapter houses. Exacerbating the problems of the time for fraternities and sororities was the decision of some colleges to construct dormitories for students. By requiring freshman students to live in the dorms, the colleges had a ready-made clientele and reduced the occupancy in the chapter houses. The construction of dormitories, therefore, also contributed to the loss of chapters during the 1930s.[58]

During World War II, many fraternity chapters closed due to the lack of members, while others operated with diminished numbers. Some fifteen national organizations went defunct during the 1940s.[59] During the 1950s, membership restrictions became an item of contention between fraternities and colleges and universities. Once an institution, like the fraternal and sororal system, becomes sociologically mature, it tries to maintain and preserve itself by resisting changes from within or without.[60] With its black, Jewish, Catholic, and dominant white Protestant fraternities and sororities, these organizations of the 1950s were usually exclusive and segregated. Many national organizations had exclusionary clauses based on racial or religious restrictions.

These restrictions came under attack. Many schools expelled the organizations that would not change membership restrictions. The battle, then, was over who should control the membership of a chapter—the school or the national organization.[61]

This debate over exclusionary clauses was enacted into law in several states. Perhaps the best-known example was in New York. The New York Legislature passed a law prohibiting discrimination based on race or religion. All fraternity chapters in New York had until 1958 to accept the prohibition or to sever themselves from their nationals. Throughout the state there was a substantial closing of chapters as nationals refused to change membership restrictions.[62]

At the other end of the spectrum were schools where students demanded the right of the entire student body to belong to a fraternity or sorority. Thus, in 1953, the administrations at Amherst (Massachusetts), Williams (Massachusetts), and Hamilton (New York) required the entire student body be given the opportunity to belong to a fraternity or sorority if they desired.[63]

The process of consolidation taking place during this phase was probably healthy for the fraternal and sororal organizations as a social institution. The number of fraternities and sororities had become unwieldy and there were too many organizations for the number of students interested in participating.

National Expansion II

After over a decade of consolidation and limited expansion, the fraternity system has mushroomed since the 1960s. While the 1960s and '70s are usually viewed as difficult times for fraternities and sororities, overall expansion continued unabated during this period. During the 1960s, the number of schools adopting fraternities and sororities for the first time reached 105 institutions. That same decade also saw an unprecedented number of new chapters established. While only seven new organizations were founded, more than 1870 chapters were established by 105 college fraternities and sororities.

Despite this growth, chapter losses were also severe. More than 550 chapters went inactive at 236 colleges during this decade. Much of this was due to the social atmosphere on college campuses, epitomized by the "free speech" movement at California-Berkeley. This movement spread to other campuses where students showed their contempt by the lifestyle they led—the "hippie" look, drugs, and "free speech." Others not belonging to this counterculture joined in opposing the Vietnam War and the draft.[64] Although there were exceptions, social fraternities and sororities tended to attract fairly conservative students who were more affluent. With these organizations viewed as part of the "establishment"—traditional, out of style, and prejudiced—they came under attack and lost much of their prestige.

The counterculture movement began in the 1960s and intensified during the early 1970s. With the end of the Vietnam War in 1975, campus life settled down and has remained relatively calm ever since. The seventies, therefore, was a decade of contrasts between the first and second halves. During the first half, fraternity membership was at a low of 149,000 students, but by 1980 this figure had climbed to 230,000. Other aspects that affected the decline of fraternities and sororities during the early 1970s included the changing demographics of the student body. Older students were returning to school and were, for the most part, not interested in student college life. Also, the increase in urban schools resulted in many students commuting to school and not participating in extracurricular activities.[65] Many of these changes helped to lay the groundwork for the explosion of new fraternities and sororities that would take place in the eighties and nineties.

Despite these changes, growth of the Greek system continued during the '70s with more than 2,000 new chapters established at 545 schools. Nearly a quarter of these schools adopted the fraternity system for the first time. This growth accounted for 45 percent of all new chapters established. The greatest expansion occurred in the South—Alabama, Georgia, and northern Florida.

The problems facing this institution in the 1980s were ones of an internal nature: sexual abuse, alcoholism, hazing, and racial and Semitic discrimination. The most visible were the deaths associated with hazing. During the '80s, forty-five fatalities were recorded. The end result was that many schools and fraternities were sued. With increased costs of liability and litigation, as well as the continued deterioration in fraternity behavior, many schools decided to dissociate themselves from these social organizations or reassert their control over them. From 1983 to 1986, the proportion of colleges claiming direct control over fraternity and sorority national organizations doubled from 15 to 32 percent. Even more pronounced was the percentage increase of local fraternities and sororities, which jumped from two in 1983 to thirty-five in 1986.[66]

The popularity of fraternities and sororities steadily increased during the decade of the '80s so that by 1990, fraternity and sorority membership had reached an all-time high of nearly 700,000. Some 400,000 belonged to fraternities at 900 schools, while approximately 275,000 were sorority members at 475 schools.[67] Since 1990, more than 2,200 chapters have been established throughout the country on college campuses. Of the top five organizations for establishing a chapter, all were sororities: Zeta Beta Tau, with sixty-three new chapters; Sigma Lambda Beta, a Hispanic sorority, with sixty chapters; Sigma Lambda Gamma, another Hispanic sorority, with fifty-six chapters; Alpha Kappa Alpha, an African American sorority, with fifty-two chapters; Phi Sigma Sigma with fifty-one chapters.

By the year 2000, the proliferation of new organizations and new chapters around the country had changed the fraternity landscape. Not only were there traditional fraternities and sororities on campus, but a variety of other organizations could be found. Here were Latino and Latina, multicultural, religious, Asian, black, gay and lesbian fraternities and sororities that offered college students options beyond the traditional organizations.

Diversification of a Social Institution

The growth of the Greek-letter fraternity and sorority as a cultural institution on college campuses is reflected in the composition of the student body through time. During the first wave, 1824–74, sixty organizations were established, of which only nine were sororities. During this phase the typical college student was male, white, Protestant, and from a high economic class; fraternities reflected that homogeneity. The creation of new fraternities was often an attempt by students to improve on existing organizations, or many groups sought to get away from social status or wealth as a condition for membership. In addition, the secretive nature of early fraternities alienated many college students. In response, some of these students established "equitable" fraternities, or organizations that were not secret. In 1847, a number of these local "equitable" fraternities formed the nucleus of the Anti-Secret Confederation, the precursor of Delta Upsilon (1864), a national organization today.[68]

Following the first wave of establishment, a period of ten years (1875–84) resulted in no new fraternities or sororities established. As a social institution, fraternities had expanded to a saturation point. This was not true of the sororities, which were only beginning to take hold. After what can be described as taking a deep breath, this social institution embarked on a second wave of establishment (1885–1929). By now the college student body had diversified to include more ethnic minorities, blacks, Jews, and women. Conversely, many of the traditional fraternities reacted by implementing exclusionary clauses, limiting membership to white, male, Protestant students in order to ensure a homogeneous group of individuals of like mind, religion, and race. If the fraternity was to be a brotherhood, it was argued, how could a white Protestant male be compatible with somebody from a different religion or race?[69]

By 1928, more than half the national fraternities had membership rules based on race or religion. In response to these restrictions, nonsecret and nonsectarian fraternities were organized. In 1899, the National Federation of Common Clubs was established, a loosely knit national organization consisting of nonsecret organizations. At its national meeting in 1918, the idea of a fraternity was proposed, and Phi Mu Delta was organized.[70]

Many thought that members of a true brotherhood should come from different religions and races. Thus, nonsectarian and interracial fraternities were created. The first nonsectarian fraternity, Pi Lambda Phi (1895), was established at Yale as a protest against fraternities that excluded Jews. Despite the inclusion of non-Jews, the fraternity remained predominately Jewish until after World War II. Five other nonsectarian fraternities were established between 1895 and 1915. Although officially nonsectarian, many of these groups consisted of mainly Jewish students. Omega Pi Alpha (1901) was organized as an interracial fraternity but was not very successful.[71]

As the enrollments of students from different religious backgrounds increased, many banded together to form a fraternity. Many early fraternities made reference to Christian principles or to a supreme being; however, around the turn of the twentieth century, a couple of organizations implemented ideals and rituals based on the specific teachings of Jesus Christ. Two of these were Alpha Chi Rho (1895) and Alpha Kappa Lambda (1907). Catholic students, who were excluded from traditional fraternities, organized three: Phi Kappa (1889), Theta Kappa Phi (1919), and Alpha Delta Gamma (1924). The first two organizations merged in 1959 to form Phi Kappa Theta. Other religious fraternities included Delta Phi Kappa (1920) for student members of the Church of Jesus Christ of Latter-day Saints (Mormon) and Beta Sigma Psi (1925) for Lutheran students.

Other fraternities were modeled on the many fraternal organizations in the United States. Acacia (1904) was based on the principles of Freemasonry, and membership was restricted to Masons. Square and Compass (1917) and Sigma Mu Sigma (1931) were two other fraternities based upon this fraternal order. Similar organizations included Delta Sigma Lambda (1921), whose members had to be in the Order of De Molay, and Phi Lambda Theta (1920), which was organized for students who belonged to the Independent Order of Odd Fellows.[72]

The greatest number of nontraditional fraternities and sororities established between 1895 and 1920 were for Jewish students, who were attending college in increasing numbers and were excluded from the existing organizations. Jewish students organized some fourteen fraternities and five sororities. The majority of Jewish fraternities and sororities were established from 1900 to 1909. Most were located in New York, reflecting that state's large Jewish population. The City University of New York led the way with four organizations, while New York University, Cornell, and Columbia each had three.[73]

Other ethnic organizations included a Chinese fraternity, Rho Psi (1916), and a Spanish American fraternity, Sigma Iota (1904). The latter organization joined with Phi Lambda Alpha to form Phi Iota Alpha in 1931. Fraternities and sororities also expanded to other countries. In 1867, a chapter of Chi Phi was established in Scotland, but it only survived three years. In 1879, Zeta Psi established a chapter in Canada. Today, many national organizations have chapters in Canada, and a Canadian fraternity, Phi Kappa Pi, was established in 1913.[74]

Beginning in the 1870s, sororities began to proliferate so that by the end of this second wave there were now fifty-two organizations for women. Despite the establishment of several black colleges between the 1860s and 1900s, the first black fraternity was not established until 1906 at Cornell in New York State. As a minority on white college campuses, the ability for blacks to socialize was limited. The second black fraternity, Kappa Alpha Psi was established in 1911 and in 1922, a sorority, Sigma Gamma Rho. The emergence of black fraternities and sororities, however, really unfolded at Howard University, a black college in Washington, DC. Between 1908 and 1920, five national organizations were established at this school. Along with Gamma Tau (1934), which is now defunct, Howard University was home to six black Greek-letter organizations. These included two fraternities, Omega Psi Phi (1911) and Phi Beta Sigma (1914), and three sororities, Alpha Kappa Alpha (1908), Delta Sigma Theta (1913), and Zeta Phi Beta (1920).[75]

For a period of forty-five years (1930–74) a great deal of consolidation and maturation of this social institution occurred after a period of tremendous growth. After 124 new fraternity and sorority organizations were established, there was a pause until the next wave of establishment. This interim period can be viewed as a transition phase. Of the nineteen organizations established, only four can be considered traditional. A variety of new organizations emerged that included interracial, Asian, religious, and several African American organizations.

This proliferation of organizations based on specific religions, races, or nationalities allowed fraternities and sororities to include all types of students and to expand to new campuses. This expansion was, for the most part, locked into the various segregated institutions—Catholic fraternities at Catholic schools, and black fraternities and sororities at black schools. This changed as enrollments increased and student bodies became more diversified. When many of these individuals found themselves excluded from joining established fraternal and sororal organizations, they sought to establish like organizations for their own religious, ethnic, or ideological groups.[76]

By the third wave of fraternity and sorority growth (1975–99), the college student body had grown immensely and further diversified. With increased student enrollments of various ethnic backgrounds, the composition of the student body had drastically changed from its early beginnings. While some fraternities and sororities opened their doors to this influx of different ethnicities, many organizations remained primarily for white college students. Seeking a brotherhood or sisterhood based on similar backgrounds and experiences, numerous students with Latino/a or Asian roots organized a fraternity or sorority to meet that group's specific needs. Thus, while only three Hispanic organizations had been established prior to this wave, thirty-four national organizations were established during this twenty-five year period, along with numerous local organizations. Thirty-two organizations were established for Asian American, Asian, South Asian, or Filipino students. Another thirty-one organizations were established to be more eclectic. These multicultural organizations avoided being traditional organizations as well as focusing on a specific ethnic group. Comprising a diverse chapter membership, these organizations are the best representation of diversity in a student body. Other organizations established during this wave include an additional fifteen African American organizations. Of these five are specifically identified as Christian organizations. Five other religious fraternities and sororities were also established. Four organizations for Native Americans were established from 1996 to 1998.

With the turbulent sixties and seventies and the changes in sexual mores, several coed organizations also emerged. Delta Psi, a traditional fraternity established in 1847, was the first to go coeducational in the 1960s. Several of its chapters opened their doors to females. Another long-standing traditional fraternity, Alpha Delta Phi, established in 1832, had several of its chapters go coed in the sixties and seventies. In 1992 these coed chapters formed Alpha Delta Phi Society. An additional six organizations are classified as coed with two multicultural, two Christian (one African American), and one Latino. During the late 1980s, three national organizations for gay and lesbian members were established; two fraternities and one sorority. Since 1999, however, another seven organizations have been established that cater to different gay and lesbian students. Of the ten national organizations established since 2000, five are classified as gay or lesbian.

Conclusion

As a social organization, the college fraternity and sorority system has experienced three waves of growth followed by a decline in the establishment of new fraternal and sororal organizations. It is estimated that at least 365 national fraternities and sororities have been established since 1776. Not all remain active today as many went defunct, while others merged together. The history of this social institution can be divided into three waves.

The first wave indicates the conditions of origin for this institution along with an initial expansion. As this institution became more formalized and matured, a decline followed. This first wave gave rise to the traditional fraternity along with a handful of sororities. Following a lapse of ten years, the second wave began. During the next forty-five years a number of traditional fraternities were established, but also there was an increase in the number of sororities. These traditional organizations, however, tended to be exclusive, and as the student body diversified, a number of students were excluded from fraternities and sororities based on ethnicity or religion. Thus, this second wave saw the establishment of a number of nonsectarian organizations, organizations for blacks, Jews, and the occasional ethnic organization.

Following the rapid increase of organizations during the second wave, nearly fifty years followed in which this social institution became even more formalized and mature. The student body of the 1980s and '90s was vastly different than the student body of the 1910s. The third wave of twenty-five years opened this institution up to the great social diversity found on college campuses. Thus, organizations for Latinos, Asian Americans, Native Americans, gay and lesbians proliferated on college campuses. The rise of the multicultural fraternity and sorority is another example of meeting the needs of a diverse student body. Few traditional fraternities and sororities were established as each new organization during this wave catered to a specific cultural interest group. Most of the organizations come from the list above, but also included a number of religious and African American organizations.

Currently it seems this social institution is in another period of decline in which the system is consolidating from its rapid growth. Certainly it is too early to see if this pattern will hold over the next decade or two. Given the previous two waves, however, this would seem to be the case.

After this period of consolidation, what will the next wave of organization bring, or has this social institution exhausted its possibilities?

NOTES

1. Information on the early history of college fraternities and sororities was previously published in "The Origin and Evolution of College Fraternities and Sororities," in *African American Fraternities and Sororities: The Legacy and the Vision* (Lexington: University of Kentucky Press, 2005).

2. Oscar M. Voorhees, *The History of Phi Beta Kappa* (New York: Crown Publishers, 1945), 1.

3. John S. Brubacher and Willis Rudy, *Higher Education in Transition: An American History, 1636–1976*, 4th ed. (New Brunswick, NJ: Transaction Publishers, 1997), 3–4.

4. Ibid., 4, 41; Frederick Rudolph, *The American College and University* (New York: Alfred Knopf, 1962), 90.

5. Brubacher and Rudy, *Higher Education in Transition*, 13–14; Henry Sheldon, *Student Life and Customs* (New York: D. Appleton & Co., 1901), 85; Wayne Musgrave, *College Fraternities* (New York: Interfraternity Conference, 1923), 2.

6. Rudolph, *American College and University*, 87–88; Brubacher and Rudy, *Higher Education in Transition*, 42.

7. Brubacher and Rudy, *Higher Education in Transition*, 42, 51; Sheldon, *Student Life and Customs*, 87–8.

8. Brubacher and Rudy, *Higher Education in Transition*, 41, 121.

9. Rudolph, *American College and University*, 96–99; Sheldon, *Student Life and Customs*,110–11.

10. Brubacher and Rudy, *Higher Education in Transition*, 1; Sheldon, *Student Life and Customs*, 83–84.

11. Brubacher and Rudy, *Higher Education in Transition* 46–47; Marianne Rachel Sanua, *Going Greek: Jewish College Fraternities in the US, 1895–1945* (Detroit: Wayne State University Press, 2003), 3–4.

12. Clyde Johnson, *Fraternities in Our Colleges* (New York: National Interfraternity Foundation, 1972), 254.

13. Helen Lefkowitz Horowitz, *Campus Life: Undergraduate Cultures from the End of the Eighteenth Century to the Present* (New York: Alfred Knopf, 1987), 12–13.

14. Johnson, *Fraternities in Our Colleges*, 10.

15. Sheldon, *Student Life and Customs*, 120.

16. Rudolph, *American College and University*, 138, 144.

17. Ibid., 142–43; Brubacher and Rudy, *Higher Education in Transition*, 47–48; Sheldon, *Student Life and Customs*, 132.

18. Rudolph, *American College and University*, 145; Johnson, *Fraternities in Our Colleges*, 6–8.

19. Johnson, *Fraternities in Our Colleges*, 19–20; Horowitz, *Campus Life*, 29.

20. John Robson, ed., *Baird's Manual of American College Fraternities*, 19th ed. (Menash, WI: Baird's Manual Foundation, 1977); Rudolph, *American College and University*, 144, 146–47, 150.

21. William Hastings, *Phi Beta Kappa as A Secret Society* (Washington, DC: United Chapters of Phi Beta Kappa, 1965), 3–4. Perhaps Sheldon is correct that the use of Greek names seems to have been purely by accident. Sheldon, *Student Life and Customs*, 142; Johnson, *Fraternities in Our Colleges*, 14–15; Voorhees, *History of Phi Beta Kappa*, 2.

22. Richard Nelson Current, *Phi Beta Kappa in American Life: The First Two Hundred Years* (New York: Oxford University Press, 1990), 10–11; Johnson, *Fraternities in Our Colleges*, 11; Hastings, *Phi Beta Kappa as A Secret Society*, 6.

23. Musgrave, *College Fraternities*, 9–13; Johnson, *Fraternities in Our Colleges*, 16.

24. Current, *Phi Beta Kappa in American Life*, 53–54; Johnson, *Fraternities in Our Colleges*, 76.

25. Robson, *Baird's Manual*, 5–6, 784; Johnson, *Fraternities in Our Colleges*, 19.

26. Johnson, *Fraternities in Our Colleges*, 23–24; Current, *Phi Beta Kappa in American Life*, 61.

27. Sheldon, *Student Life and Customs*, 220; Marjorie A. Montrose, "Sororities: Present and Potential" (Ph.D. diss., Columbia University, 1956), 46; Johnson, *Fraternities in Our Colleges*, 62.

28. Robson, *Baird's Manual*, 7; Johnson, *Fraternities in Our Colleges*, 57–58.

29. Robson, *Baird's Manual*, 7.

30. Ibid., 448.

31. Robson, *Baird's Manual*, 12; Musgrave, *College Fraternities*, 21; Johnson, *Fraternities in Our Colleges*, 255.

32. Robson, *Baird's Manual*, 12.

33. Ibid.

34. Craig L. Torbenson, "College Fraternities and Sororites: A Historical Geography, 1776–1989" (Ph.D. diss., University of Oklahoma, 1992), 51–54, 87–88. Sources for Figure 1 includes several editions of Baird's Manual of American College Fraternities and web sites for national fraternities and sororities.

35. Brubacher and Rudy, *Higher Education in Transition*, 54; Johnson, *Fraternities in Our Colleges*, 24.

36. Robson, *Baird's Manual*, 250; Francis Shepardson, ed., *Baird's Manual of American College Fraternities*, 12th ed. (Menasha, WI: George Banta, 1930), 2.

37. Torbenson, "College Fraternities and Sororities," 56–58.

38. Robson, *Baird's Manual*, 8.

39. Brubacher and Rudy, *Higher Education in Transition*, 127; Musgrave, *College Fraternities*, 91–93.

40. Torbenson, "College Fraternities and Sororities," 60.

41. Ibid., 93.

42. Musgrave, *College Fraternities*, 32–35.

43. Johnson, *Fraternities in Our Colleges*, 37.

44. Ibid.; Robson, *Baird's Manual*, 7; Jerome V. Reel Jr., *The Oak: A History of Pi Kappa Alpha* (Memphis, TN: Pi Kappa Alpha Fraternity, 1980), 25–26.

45. Johnson, *Fraternities in Our Colleges*, 26–7.

46. Ibid.

47. Sheldon, *Student Life and Customs*, 183; Shepardson, *Baird's Manual*, 17–18; Robson, *Baird's Manual*, 24–26.

48. Brubacher and Rudy, *Higher Education in Transition*, 128; Shepardson, *Baird's Manual*, 17–18; Stephen J. Lourie, "The Historical Development of the Relationship Between the Fraternity and the University in the United States" (master's thesis, University of Missouri-Columbia, 1971), 36.

49. Torbenson, "College Fraternities and Sororities," 60, 93.

50. Johnson, *Fraternities in Our Colleges*, 27–28.

51. Ibid.

52. Brubacher and Rudy, *Higher Education in Transition*, 120–22; Johnson, *Fraternities in Our Colleges*, 29–30; Lourie, "Relationship Between Fraternity and University,"

17–18; Musgrave, *College Fraternities*, 23–25; Oscar and Mary Handlin, *The American College and American Culture* (New York: McGraw-Hill, 1970), 56–57.

53. Torbenson, "College Fraternities and Sororities," 69, 109.

54. Shepardson, *Baird's Manual*, 5; Johnson, *Fraternities in Our Colleges*, 60; Sheldon, *Student Life and Customs*, 218; Robson, *Baird's Manual*, 12.

55. Musgrave, *College Fraternities*, 47–51; Robson, *Baird's Manual*, 37, 39; Jack L. Anson and Robert F. Marchesani Jr., eds., *Baird's Manual of College Fraternities*, 20th ed. (Indianapolis, IN: Baird's Manual Foundation, 1991), 1–42.

56. Current, *Phi Beta Kappa in American Life*, 140.

57. Reel Jr., *The Oak*, 93–94.

58. Lourie, "Relationship Between Fraternity and University," 43–44, 49–51.

59. Robson, *Baird's Manual*, 23.

60. Thomas R. Kessler, "The Logistic Model: A Study of the Growth of Fraternities" (master's thesis, Kent State University, 1963), 2.

61. Brubacher and Rudy, *Higher Education in Transition*, 16; Reel, *The Oak*, 95.

62. Robson, *Baird's Manual*, 24–26; Brubacher and Rudy, *Higher Education in Transition*, 6–7.

63. Robson, *Baird's Manual*, 37; Reel, *The Oak*, 95.

64. Current, *Phi Beta Kappa in American Life*, 250.

65. Susan Tift, "Waging War on the Greeks," *Time*, April 16, 1990, 64–65.

66. Ibid.

67. "New Rules for Fraternities, Sororities," *USA Weekend*, January 12–14, 1990.

68. Shepardson, *Baird's Manual*, 36; Sheldon, *Student Life and Customs*, 179.

69. Johnson, *Fraternities in Our Colleges*, 42, 208; Alfred Lee McClung, *Fraternities Without Brotherhood* (Boston: Beacon Press, 1955), 24: Robson, *Baird's Manual*, 320.

70. Ibid.

71. George Toll, "Colleges, Fraternities, and Assimilation," *Journal of Reform Judaism* (Summer 1985): 94; Johnson, *Fraternities in Our Colleges*, 43–44.

72. Johnson, *Fraternities in Our Colleges*, 39–40.

73. Toll, "Colleges, Fraternities, and Assimilation," 94–97.

74. Johnson, *Fraternities in Our Colleges*, 42.

75. *Baird's Manual*s, various editions.

76. Johnson, *Fraternities in Our Colleges*, 42, 408.

Links, Legacies, and Letters: A Cultural History of Black Greek-letter Organizations

Deborah E. Whaley

AT THE UNIVERSITY OF FLORIDA AT GAINESVILLE THE WHITE FRAternity Delta Tau Delta was suspended for their Mekong Delta Party in 2001. At the party white males dressed as GIs and white sorority women dressed in accordance with their perception of Vietnamese prostitutes. They also decorated their fraternity house with fake barbed wire, sandbags, and grass to replicate their image of a South Vietnam setting. Delta Tau Delta's party resulted in a series of protests by the Asian American student body that was offended by the fraternity's decorations and the insidious ascription to Orientalism inherent in the theme of the party.[1] Delta Tau Delta apologized for the incident by saying: "It never occurred to us [we were doing something wrong], otherwise we would not have done it."[2] In 1997, there was a similar occurrence at the University of Kansas. Among KU's white Greek fraternities, a common ritual went unquestioned until a faculty member of color brought the incident to the attention of other administrators, faculty, students, and staff. This particular incident involved the white fraternity Phi Gamma Delta and the white sorority Delta Delta Delta: "Carrying sticks and wearing grass skirts and body-paint markings on their faces and bare chests, fraternity members rushed into the Delta Delta Delta house and carried a sorority sister outside to the 'Cannibal King.' It was part of an initiation ritual leading up to the Fiji Island Party [they were to have that night]."[3]

The image of the college fraternity and sorority remains mottled by other racist antics as seen with Delta Tau Delta's and Phi Gamma Delta's parties, racial and religious exclusion, and sexual violence. This is because for many members of these white fraternities and sororities, their whiteness is the invisible norm. As explained by cultural critics Annalee Newitz and Matt Wray about the invisibility of whiteness, it becomes "the unraced center of a racialized world . . . where [whiteness] has long held the privileged place of racial normativity."[4] Other racially motivated episodes and discriminatory rites among these groups support this assertion.

Take, for example, a chapter of Zeta Beta Tau fraternity that incorporated acts of bigotry into their pledge process in 1990. Zeta Beta Tau's pledges were asked to find "funny looking Mexicans" to take photographs of as a part of initiation rites. Phi Kappa Psi's chapter at Rider College the same year required pledges to wear costumes imitating their perception of black American youths' clothing at a pledge party they named "Dress Like a Nigger Night." University of Wisconsin at Madison's chapter of Kappa Sigma in 1986 had a Harlem Room party, where white students, in blackface, served watermelon punch, painted graffiti on the surrounding walls of the fraternity house, and placed garbage on the floor to replicate what they believed constituted a ghetto aesthetic.[5] In 1998, white fraternity and sorority members of Pi Kappa Alpha and Alpha Chi Omega at Colorado State University used their university's homecoming parade as a vehicle to display homophobic hate literature, by making a stuffed scarecrow for the event and attaching antigay slogans to it.[6] Insofar as other matters of sexual exclusion are concerned, in the year 2000 a white sorority woman remarked in her school paper after a homophobic incident at the University of Nebraska by a white fraternity that "the Greek system has the right to cross someone off their list if they don't fit the mold of the Greek House."[7] From these few examples, it is clear that the white fraternal system, especially on college campuses, often acts as a social technology of sex and sexualization, which has class and racial implications. As one reporter included in an exposé about the white Greek system: "The Greek system is a sort of apartheid, enabling children from predominately white, upper middle class enclaves to safely attend a messily diverse university . . . without having to mix with those who are different. Presumably, a sorority is a place where a young woman can be 'lavaliered' by a fraternity boy, and they can move on to form their own family in a predominantly white, upper middle class enclave, preferably one that is gated."[8]

White sororities and fraternities have made efforts to embrace other cultures to curtail racial incidents and intolerance. In addition, multicultural and sexually diverse fraternals have formed in response to campus intolerance. Omega Phi Chi sorority at Duke University, for example, is known for its large numbers of Jewish, black American, Latina, Asian American, and Euro-ethnic women. Lambda 10, a gay, lesbian, and bisexual national fraternity, Lambda Delta Lambda, a lesbian and bisexual sorority, and the black American gay fraternity Delta Phi Upsilon in Tallahassee, Florida, have resisted sexual identity barriers by forming their own fraternals and supporting sexual minorities who are Greek-affiliated.[9] White students who pledge black American Greek letter fraternals assert that for the most part, they are welcomed by their black American sisters and brothers.[10] Although these instances describe students who are taking steps toward integrating their fraternals or forming oppositional ones, most universities have pressed the issue by requiring sororities and fraternities to file an antidiscrimination clause in their bylaws. Past and current discrimination in white fraternals is no doubt the reason behind the mandate. In view of this crucial point and the history of exclusion among Greek-letter fraternals, is it possible to see membership in such secret societies as culturally, politically, and socially useful?

This chapter grapples with that question by providing a cultural history of Black Greek-letter Organizations (BGLOs), and by evaluating how black American benevolent and social fraternals shaped their formation. It illustrates how the historical emergence and practices of BGLOs are most similar to eighteenth- and nineteenth-century benevolent societies and social fraternals established by people of African descent. It is the *legacy* of these benevolent and social fraternal groups that would act as *links*—or cultural and social maps—for BGLOs formed at the turn of the twentieth century. Like many organizations, the work and experiences of BGLOs and social organizations changed over time. Different historical moments, region, class consciousness, and in some cases—college affiliation—provided different opportunities and visions of the cultural, social, and political work they undertook. This chapter therefore argues that BGLOs are an example of a body of women and men who skillfully transformed social and academic spaces and utilized them for purposes geared toward social justice for people of African descent living in America. Thus, what follows is an attempt to understand the origins and goals of these organizations while paying close attention to the contours and intersections of race, ethnicity, class, gender, and sexualities. I do this through an *appreciated inquiry* approach, which argues that BGLOs are an example of what is potentially useful within, and multidimensional about, fraternities and sororities as a whole.[11]

Links: Black Benevolent Organizations

In the historical moment of slavery, the United States slave trade and system used men and women of African descent as free labor and as sexual commodities. In the face of adversity, the uprooted populations of Africans re-created cultural practices in memory of their homelands, which included the formation of secret societies. This cultural practice allowed them to create transformed social structures, cultural rituals, and African modalities of spiritual survival that held common characteristics with what they or their ancestors already knew culturally. In the times of United States slavery, secret societies among enslaved men and women served similar functions as those in their homeland, insofar as collective welfare and benevolence was concerned, but the new United States–based secret societies were culturally hybrid. The benevolent organizations in the United States among black Americans were not the same as the secret societies of Africa. Although the newly formed secret societies among them shared ancestry with their forbearers in African secret societies, they faced new cultural, social, and political arrangements that affected the function of their transformed organizations.

As historians and cultural critics Carter G. Woodson, Robert L. Harris, and Jaqui Malone have discussed in their work on African secret societies and black American benevolent organizations, many of these societies focused on mutual cooperation in living arrangements and used African modes of ritual and rites of passage to acculturate members into their secret orders.[12] Throughout the continent, African secret societies often "functioned as powerful agents of social regulation," had political purposes, were religious, culturally centered, and created economic systems of stability for members.[13] In the United States, black benevolent societies and fraternals had to take increased precautions to maintain secrecy, even more so than white fraternals that also faced persecution for their secret composition. The secret component of these orders was not eccentricity or because of exclusivity; rather, it was crucial to their survival. Any gathering among enslaved women and men was illegal and punishable by white slavers with brutal beatings and/or heinous forms of mutilation, for example, lynching and rape, which carried on in the postemancipation years. Thus, to hide and protect the existence of such an organized body among people of African descent was essential in order to continue to meet its organizational goals, which included the uplift work of their collective cultural formation. The fraternals among people of African descent had to be mostly secret in their practices, especially in the early nineteenth century, as they became the site to contemplate and plan freedom for slaves of African descent. Some fraternals were composed of enslaved Africans and others were groups of free black Americans in the North. Fraternal organizations in the North and South, despite regional diversity and bondage status, shared goals of physical and/or political freedom.

The Knights of Tabor, formed in 1846, was an example of a secret society that placed collective freedom at the center of its consciousness.

It was composed of free and enslaved men of African descent, and their creation came about with intents to emancipate African slaves throughout the South. The secret society planned to free Atlanta slaves, for example, in 1857. The fraternal order recruited forty thousand men from slave-holding states to participate in a slave insurrection. Its troupe members, named the Knights of Liberty, stalled their planned insurrection because the Civil War appeared imminent. In memory of the abolitionist secret society, a benevolent secret society of men and women, named the Knights and Daughters of Tabor, formed after the end of the Civil War.[14] This new organization carried on the sentiment of the original order and adapted their cultural and political agenda to serve the new status of black Americans who were legally free, but because of racial discrimination, still held in economic and social bondage. Their efforts resulted in sponsoring a black-run hospital in Mississippi, a much-needed facility during segregation. In the post–World War II years, the hospital served over 135,000 patients, many of those patients being black American sharecroppers in Mississippi.[15]

After the emancipation of black southern slaves, made legal by the Emancipation Proclamation of 1863 and the Thirteenth Amendment, chapters of benevolent groups flourished, as membership grew in large numbers between the years 1890 and 1910. Some of the most prominent benevolent fraternals include the following, and their founding dates are in parenthesis: The Improved Benevolent Protective Order of the Elks (1889), (the "improved" in the title perhaps being a signifying statement on the white order), United Brothers of Friendship (1861), Sisters of the Mysterious Ten (1861), Grand Fountain of the United Order of True Reformers (1881), Mosaic Templars of America (1883), and Sisters of Calanthe (1856). Moreover, there were African American orders of the Freemasons, Odd Fellows, Knights of Pythias, and Order of the Eastern Star.[16] The cultural work of these fraternals included using their lodges as sites for African American musicians to acquire work, by paying them to perform at social functions, and some lodges freely provided rehearsal space for musicians and dance troupes.[17]

Benevolence of these groups within the black public sphere consisted of providing life insurance for members, burial insurance, and financial aid to struggling families in their community and within their organizations. Historian Robin Kelley writes: "Grass-roots institutions such as mutual benefit associations and fraternal organizations . . . not only helped families with basic survival needs, but [also] created and sustained bonds of fellowship, mutual support networks, and a collectivist ethos that ultimately informed black working-class political struggle."[18]

There was a mixture of socioeconomic classes in black benevolent societies, as even the most modest earning members donated a portion of their income to their fraternal in the name of mutual benefit. For the black-established groups there was not a line between secret fraternal and benevolent fraternals. Secrecy allowed them to operate without fear of violence from white vigilantes and the white supremacist fraternal, the Ku Klux Klan. Their benevolence was necessary, too, because the larger communities of which they were a part of continued to experience economic and political disfranchisement. Working and middle-class black Americans were involved in the same benevolent fraternals and secret societies, especially when their end goals were mutual and based on other variables of collectivity. For example, in 1881, a secret society among middle and working-class women emerged to help wage a citywide strike in Atlanta for the rights of washerwomen. Composed of middle-class sororal groups and working-class domestic workers, the group fought for higher wages for women who did wash work. The space in which the two groups of women found solidarity, planned, and executed their activism was a local church.[19]

The economic stability and, later, the slight economic surplus of some fraternals that followed, sought to share wealth with the more disadvantaged members of their community. Philadelphia alone had one hundred black benevolent organizations, sixty of which were women's sororal organizations, wherein fundraising for the economically disadvantaged was the center of their sororal existence.[20] The Philadelphia-based sororal organization the Dorcas Society, for instance, formed because of white Philadelphians' apathy toward poor black American citizens residing in the city. The sororal society provided relief, including clothes to poorer black Americans.[21] In all, between the years 1862 and 1880, 226 fraternal orders existed among black Americans across the United States,[22] wherein there was a demarcation between the lines of social and political, benevolent and secret societies. The subject position of black Americans in these groups demanded that their organizations simultaneously fill all of the aforementioned roles.

Legacies: Black Social Fraternals

At the turn of the century, social fraternals among African Americans, sometimes benevolent, but not formed with the sole intent of providing mutual aid and insurance for members or their communities, emerged within middle- to upper-middle class enclaves in the East and Midwest regions of the United States. One generation removed from slavery, the social fraternals represented and created a space for the emerging black professional class to socialize. The most popular and well-known were the sororal groups the Links and the Girl Friends

(1945, 1927), the fraternal groups the Boulé (also known as Sigma Pi Phi) and Guardsmen (1904, 1933), and the adolescent social club, Jack and Jill (1938), all of which remain active today.[23] The controversy over the early to mid-twentieth-century social fraternal and sororal groups within the black community was rooted in membership barriers based on color and class. In the first half of the twentieth century, physical attributes and class position were important criteria for entrance into chapters of many of these groups.

Allegations of colorism among social fraternities and sororities, especially the aforementioned five, are widespread. Accusations exist that many of these organizations administered "paper bag tests," or other means of color discrimination, wherein the color of a member's skin could not be darker than a beige paper bag. They thus operated much like the blue-vein secret societies among African Americans that were prominent in the South and Eastern regions of the United States, where the veins of potential members had to show through their skin and a comb had to glide through their hair without snarling in order to qualify for membership. These markers of whiteness—fair skin and straight or loosely curled hair—held great aesthetic capital for a number of members and chapters, adding a layer of exclusivity that secret societies already encompassed.[24]

One might explain colorism, classism, and other forms of intracultural prejudice among these groups as internal oppression, where the hailing of an individual into ideologies of self-perception and worth are antithetical to the growth and nurture of the racial, ethnic, gender, and sexual identities they inhabit. The fraternals among black Americans that engaged in the practices of color prejudice and other intracultural prejudices might very well be products of the false consciousness that arises out of exposure to, subconsciously accepting, and acting out the dominant culture's belief system of the inferiority of black Americans. Nevertheless, the reality that one may resist and counteract these ideas and actions requires accountability, rather than merely apologia, by and for social fraternal members who engaged in colorism.

The formation of black social clubs did not come about with the masses of black Americans in mind, or because of a sense of deprivation and alienation among a white majority. Rather, the intent of these sororal and fraternal clubs was to serve as social organizations for a particular class among a still segregated racial-ethnic group. Moreover, while class prejudice among these groups is just as difficult to prove as color prejudice, the socioeconomic standing of members historically and currently, even by members' own admission, is middle to upper-middle class. All four organizations emphasize their members are professionals, (for example, physicians, lawyers, politicians, educators) or, in the case of Jack and Jill, the children of professionals. Caps on chapter membership in many of these social organizations exist, and admission often hinges upon a legacy of familial membership, one member moving to another city or dying, thus opening up a space for others deemed suitable for initiation into a local chapter. Black women, who were not professionals, could gain admission to prominent social sororal groups through the status of their husbands.

The almost incestuous nature of membership based on legacy and long-standing social status would solidify the barriers, including distinctions between new and old money within black communities. Within this socioeconomic matrix, class was determined not just monetarily, but by lineage. These groups thus culturally and socially determined class and equated a familial history of economic surplus with prominent social standing. Did early twentieth-century social fraternals among black Americans patrol the boundaries of skin color and class in their communities? The 1999 president of the Links insists that "for many years people wanted to characterize members of the Links as rich ladies who wore white gloves and sponsored teas and quiet socials, but we are an activist group that takes on important domestic and international projects that assist Blacks, children, and others."[25] In tandem, a member of the Boulé remarks, "It's absurd for Black people to apologize when they are educated, accomplished, and successful, and choose to belong to organizations populated with other blacks *like* them."[26]

The Links, Girl Friends, and Jack and Jill refer to themselves as socially responsible organizations. They also report involvement in and support for health care reform, voter rights, and hunger relief, and many are members of black civil rights organizations.[27] Still, a member of the Links admits that most potential members have to prove they are "rich and important" before they may gain admittance into the organization, and the Girl Friends name their representation in upper-middle-class professions and membership composed of legacies as core to their sororal persona. The Boulé and Guardsmen, too, make no apologies for asserting themselves as a social group for professional men. Initiations and ceremonies are secret for all organizations and closed to outsiders. Only members, too, know handshakes and signals of the Boulé and Guardsmen in particular, which is something they share in common with the secret societies formed among black Americans and among whites in earlier centuries.

Membership criteria into the most well-known social fraternal and sororal groups point to a significant contradiction that provides an understanding of how BGLOs might be situated vis-à-vis these social and, in the case of the Links, Girl Friends, and Jack and Jill, self-proclaimed service-oriented groups. The popular social fraternals among black Americans are yet another chapter in sororal and fraternal history. They were social, at times benevolent, self-avowed elitists, and they perpetuated or concealed color and class prejudice within their organizations. The social clubs would share the experience of being a member of a historically marginalized and disenfranchised group with all black Americans. How they decided to reconcile and act upon what that history meant would differ from member to member and chapter to chapter, but their social formation allowed them to create a space to convene with others who mirrored their socioeconomic class and shared their experiences with racism, which, regardless of class, is an equal-opportunity social poison. Black fraternal members shared the historical experience of racism among themselves and with the men and women who benefited from their benevolence. Yet, the criterion for membership, that is, being a member of the Black Professional Managerial Class (BPMC), insured members of the working class, the strongly economically disadvantaged, and those that did not have a college education could not gain admission. The membership prerequisite of the Links, Girl Friends, Boulé, and Guardsmen, on the one hand, was by their own organizational structure discriminatory in terms of membership intake. On the other hand, they were distinct from other white professional organizations for physicians, educators, lawyers, and the like, in that at least half are engaged in social service to the black American community. While colorism is largely, but certainly not entirely absent from these organizations in modern times, socioeconomic class and legacy remains the criterion that encourages the perception that they are elitist, which often overshadows the cultural work they do for the black community. Benevolent groups' cultural center and commitment to social justice, as well as social fraternals' uplift and aesthetic insecurities, became political, organizational, and social legacies for the practices of BGLOs on college campuses.

Groundwork for Change: The Formation of BGLOs

It is the legacy of African secret societies, black benevolent societies, and social fraternals—white and black—that would act as cultural and social maps for BGLOs formed at the turn of the twentieth century. These organizations emerged in cultural and social opposition to the exclusively white Greek-letter organizations that were in existence. Their Greek letters and identity as Greek-letter societies, like their peers in predominantly white Greek-letter organizations, represented the social options available to students at the time (twentieth century).

It also allowed them to function, in the eyes of white college administrators, as legitimate and recognizable college organizations. Legitimization was not the sole reason for their formation. BGLOs are an example of a body of women and men who utilized an existing social space and skillfully transformed it for their own political purposes. Inasmuch as the newly forming BGLOs are a part of a historical movement among black Americans of cultural and political work through social institutions, fraternals, and secret societies, these organizations were akin to the well-formed cultural fraternals that already existed throughout the African Diaspora. Today, these fraternals fall under the historically black, collegiate, umbrella organization the National Pan-Hellenic Council, and are referred to as the "Divine Nine."

The development of BGLOs was a product of the diverse social and cultural circumstances that faced each group. While Alpha Phi Alpha's, Kappa Alpha Psi's, and Sigma Gamma Rho's formation took place at predominately white colleges (Cornell, Indiana, and Butler Universities, respectively), Alpha Kappa Alpha's, Omega Psi Phi's, Delta Sigma Theta's, Phi Beta Sigma's, and Zeta Phi Beta's formation took place at the historically black college Howard University. The site of their emergence had a direct bearing upon their organizational structure and the ensuing cultural, social, and political consciousness that each developed independently and later, collectively under the National Pan-Hellenic Council (NPHC) formed in 1929.[28] Predominantly white and historically black colleges had different educational goals. Indeed, historical developments and social structures shaped their organizational character. Historically black colleges provided black American students with the opportunity to attain a higher education. This was because many white colleges would not admit black American students due to United States segregation and discriminatory admission policies based

Table 1 The Divine Nine: African American Organizations

Organization	Frat/Sor	Place of Origin	Date
Alpha Phi Alpha	F	Cornell University	1906
Alpha Kappa Alpha	S	Howard University	1908
Kappa Alpha Psi	F	University of Indiana	1911
Omega Psi Phi	F	Howard University	1911
Delta Sigma Theta	S	Howard University	1913
Phi Beta Sigma	F	Howard University	1914
Zeta Phi Beta	S	Howard University	1920
Sigma Gamma Rho	S	Butler University	1922
Iota Phi Theta	F	Morgan State University	1963

solely on race. Historically black colleges were more often than not the only choice for people of African descent in the late nineteenth and early twentieth centuries.[29] White college institutions were used as an apparatus to perpetuate white and, often, male privilege (white women, ethnoreligious groups, and other people of color, too, faced barriers to university admissions policies in the nineteenth and early twentieth centuries). In counter-juxtaposition, historically black colleges opened up educational opportunity structures previously closed to black American women and men. Coinage of black American college institutions as "historically black colleges" came about because they were created for black Americans and their student body was overwhelmingly black.

At the turn of the twentieth century, both college formations encapsulated political ideologies that leaned toward forms of liberal democracy and conservative accommodation. At the historically black colleges such as Howard, where the president was white up until the early mid-twentieth century, these institutions were hardly bastions of radical politics open to the culture and presence of the masses of black Americans. An example of this was in 1922 when the white president of Howard University, J. Stanley Durkee, proclaimed that the theater productions students hoped to bring to campus were culturally inappropriate because of their focus on African folk cultural idioms. Black conservative administrators and professors at Howard shared this sentiment, too, until the mid-1950s.[30] Howard University, founded a few years after the end of slavery, began to serve the growing black American middle to upper-middle classes. Further, until the 1920s, 80 percent of the student population at Howard and many other historically Black colleges, including Wilberforce University (Ohio), Spelman and Fisk Universities (Georgia), and Hampton Institute (Virginia) were reportedly mostly of a light skin complexion. The color makeup of some historically black colleges, at least in the first part of the twentieth century, suggested a dependent relationship between light skin color, class advantage, and higher education.[31]

Historically black colleges such as Bethune-Cookman College (Florida) and Tuskegee Institute (Alabama) did not appear to represent this color and class stigma or stereotype. However, they did prescribe conservative approaches to racism, economic advancement, and cultural politics.[32] The latter colleges encouraged students to succeed in ways and areas that would not threaten or make tides in the chokehold of United States racism and segregation. In contrast, the former colleges insisted students succeed and surpass what their white counterparts thought they could accomplish academically and monetarily; yet, they too did not prescribe radical means to achieve the ends of racial and economic equality. Indeed, political, color, and class divisions in historically black colleges were microcosmic examples of the larger cultural politics within and between assimilation and accommodation, which African America found itself encroached within from the late nineteenth to early twentieth centuries.[33] The two competing prescriptions of accommodation and assimilation in social relations were not exact polar opposites in practice. There were in-between positions for black Americans, characterized by fluctuating and shifting perceptions on what it meant to occupy the subject position of being educated, socially alienated, a racial-ethnic minority, and a part of a diverse culture of people.

For BGLOs, to create a formation radical in its approach to social and cultural discrimination with visible African cultural elements would prove to be a challenge at predominantly white *and* black institutions. Generational schisms would exist at Howard in particular, where five of the eight formed, especially among older white college administrators, the black American professorate, and the emerging social and cultural consciousness of younger students. BGLOs experienced the contradiction of many counter formations that emerge in opposition to the dominant: *while trying to break apart and distinguish themselves from prevailing, hegemonic oppressive social and political structures of the larger culture, they too became susceptible to encapsulating the very ideologies they claimed in collective struggle to resist.* The Greek-letter organizations formed at Howard would toe the line between conservative liberalism and insurgent activism. By contrast, the groups formed at predominantly white institutions would use the seemingly neutral space of the Greek-letter fraternal to carry on, in secret, bonding, social, and cultural work in an environment that was antithetical to the affirmation of their culture and the cultivation of their intellectual pursuits and development. Like many organizations and individuals, the work and experiences of BGLOs changed over time; no single policy or approach would always work, and different historical moments and college affiliations provided different opportunities and visions for their cultural, social, and political work.

Letters of Valor: Black Greek-letter Organizations at Predominately White Institutions

The first national Greek-letter organization founded by Black American college men, Alpha Phi Alpha, sheds light on the historical emergence and social and cultural circumstances of these groups founded at white universities.[34] Alpha Phi Alpha fraternity began at Cornell University to address the toxic social relations of segregation and isolation produced by the modern academy. In 1905, racism threatened the retention of black American students at Cornell, which was prevalent at the time. Black American students experienced ostracization and alienation at the predominantly white campuses where they earned admission. They did not have access to student housing, university public facilities, organized athletics, or white social groups. Predominantly white universities' approach reflected neglect wrapped up in the transparent fabric of "equal access." Politically conservative agendas that claim equal access to institutions, where gender and racial barriers are not written into public and university policy, but nevertheless exist due to the sexist and racially discriminatory practices of individuals that compose institutions, is analogous to the institutional racism explained by writer and activist James Baldwin in 1964.

Baldwin proclaimed at this time that the "impulse in American society, as far as I can tell from my experience in it, has essentially been to ignore me when it could, and even when it couldn't, to intimidate me; and when that failed, to make concessions."[35] The university at this time was thus similar to, and an extension of, the reluctant and painstaking concessions made for black American citizens by the dominant culture and their institutions. In the American context of discriminatory gender, race, sexual, and class relations, the organizational toxicity at universities and their white Greek-letter associations was not unique, but rather represented another manifestation of unequal power relations created through United States institutions and social relations. The access opened up for black Americans in the North and West at select white universities during widespread segregation in the South agreed, or perhaps conceded to admit black American students, but displaced them within an atmosphere of institutional, social, and intellectual neglect.

In the American university, then, black students self-sought and taught academic support, which is what the men of African descent at Cornell would exemplify through their experience. In 1905, the entire incoming class of black American male students dropped out by the beginning of the next year. The men named racism, segregation, lack of support by white faculty, and strained economic resources as the cause of the dropouts. Alarmed by the problem of isolation and retention among the black American male students in particular, the existing seven created a study group organized under the rubric of a literary society. Initially, the small numbers of black American students made arbitrary membership intake impossible and counterproductive. A commitment to graduating from Cornell and education had to be the only criterion, apparently, if the literary society was to survive, and this appeared to be the goal of all the existing black men on campus. In 1906, the literary society adopted the name Alpha Phi Alpha. The change from literary society to fraternity came about because "the students were looking for ways of making their group more purposeful and permanent."[36] A fraternity, the men felt, would allow them to function as an organization acknowledged by the university.[37]

Alpha Phi Alpha's founding was similar to other BGLOs founded at white universities: Kappa Alpha Psi and Sigma Gamma Rho. The idea of Kappa Alpha Psi emerged at Indiana University, another overwhelmingly white college institution at this historical moment, and they too created a fraternal in response to their isolation and lack of academic and social resources. The ten black American men on campus, like Alpha Phi Alpha, were admitted to the university, but not allowed to use public facilities open to white students, including recreational facilities. As an intervention into their social isolation, the ten men, headed by student Elder Diggs and a friend of his, Byron Kenneth Armstrong, began a fraternity, Alpha Omega, to help counteract their social predicament. Elder Diggs and Byron Kenneth Armstrong were working-class students who had formerly been acquainted at and attended Howard University; thus, the formation of BGLOs was not new to them. Both men fled Howard to major in agricultural engineering, which was a major not developed at Howard. The only Greek known to the two men came from their reading of the Bible, where the two Greek words Alpha and Omega are in scripture. At Indiana Diggs enrolled in a course on Greek mythology and Armstrong in Greek heraldry in order to think through what shape Alpha Omega would take as a Greek-letter organization. Alpha Omega later changed its name to Kappa Alpha Nu on January 5, 1911. The new fraternity name lasted until 1914, when they again changed it, this time adopting the name Kappa Alpha Psi. Indiana University's white students taunted Kappa Alpha Nu and nicknamed them 'Kappa Alpha Nig,' an obvious shortcut for the racial epithet, which reportedly influenced changing the name to Kappa Alpha Psi.[38] Replacing the Nu with Psi would also change the Greek translation of their name, one for which there was no translation in racist jest.

Kappa Alpha Psi served vital social purposes that extended to the larger black American communities. Kappa Alpha Psi's social functions, or house parties, became the central space for younger members of the wider black community in the surrounding area of Bloomington, Indiana, to convene and enjoy each other.[39] These parties were often "rent parties" to raise money in order to pay for their living accommodations. The social element of their formation was not to exclude nonfraternity members. Rather, it acted as a recreational space for the wider community. In many respects, then, their fraternal formations became a social safe haven extended beyond Greek-letter membership. Groups and individuals in the dominant culture may take for granted social interaction because of the increased social options within their communities. In contrast, for historically marginalized and racially segregated groups, the social sanctions placed upon them by the university setting and its mostly white students would leave them wanting for ways to round out their academic endeavors. Social interaction at fraternal functions for black Americans became a means to indulge in the specificity of their social lives, which included music, dance, and a forum to discuss issues that concerned them as people of African descent. However, as Robin Kelley notes in his seminal work on social justice and the Black working class, "social links through [fraternal organizations] occasionally translated into community struggles."[40] In this way, the social aspect of BGLOs functioned much like other recreational spaces for black Americans that held the dual role of social interaction and purpose, such as the beauty parlor, barbershop, church socials, and black American social clubs in general.[41]

Whereas black American men faced racial discrimination in the academic context, their female counterparts faced discrimination particular to their subject position as black American women. This is not to say that the gender of men of African descent—being marked not amorphously as men, but as black men, with all the stereotypes and misperceptions associated with maleness and blackness—did not hold racial and gender specific stereotypes.[42] It is to say, however, that for black American women, the weight of sexual, racial, and gender discrimination manifested itself differently for the women. Black American women's gender *and* race made them susceptible to ideologies of gender and racial inferiority. If perceptions existed that Black Americans in general lacked intellectual fortitude, it was even more absurd, in the white supremacist imagination and within general masculinist thinking, that black American women had any intellectual capabilities at all.[43] The discrimination and sexualization targeted at women by men of all races was yet another burden black American women faced when they stepped into the university setting. Sexism had an effect on Greek-letter sorority formation and the additional functions the women chose to incorporate into their organizational structure. The black American sorority addressed the problem of ideas of their intellectual inferiority by outsiders by enforcing strict academic criterion for admission (for example, a high grade point average).[44]

This was the case for the sorority Sigma Gamma Rho, the fourth black American sorority formed, but the first to be founded at Butler University (a chapter of AKA at Butler was chartered the same year).

The seven women that began the sorority already held a commitment to academic life, as they were primary schoolteachers. Their initial membership included a large percentage of the black American female student population at Butler in 1922. Katie Kinnard White, a biology professor at Tennessee State University and former president of the sorority, reveals that in juxtaposition to the sororities formed at Howard, where the cultural climate among students was largely supportive and communal, being among the few black women at Butler forced them to "fight the wilds." Further, the women felt the need to "unite for a common good in order to strengthen their community."[45] There were three other black American sororities for templates when they chartered a chapter on Butler's campus on November 12, 1922: Alpha Kappa Alpha, Delta Sigma Theta, and Zeta Phi Beta, which had all begun at Howard University. These women appeared to be aware of the black American sororities and fraternities that existed before them at historically black colleges, shaping their endeavor to, in the words incorporated into the motto adopted in 1922, create "Better Service, and Better Progress," for black communities. They did not feel it was necessary to begin a chapter of the existing sororities among black American women that were spreading nationally across college campuses and in black communities. The idea of creating better service and progress spoke strongly to their desire to create a sorority different from what they felt presently existed within the black American sororal groups. For them, this would include a heightened focus on academic pursuits and service work in Indiana.

If any similarities exist between Alpha Phi Alpha, Kappa Alpha Psi, and Sigma Gamma Rho, other then the predicament of their development as a way to counteract isolation, racism, sexism, and neglect on predominantly white campuses, it is that all three were not mimics of and did not function in the same vein as white Greek-letter organizations. The Alphas, Kappas, and Sigma Gamma Rhos did not form because they longed for membership in, or did not gain membership into, a white fraternity. In the early years of their formation, the white Greek-letter sites did not meet the cultural, political, and social goals and ends they wished for and created through their own organizations. For example, Alpha Phi Alpha focused their work on the education of black men, by creating their Go to High School—Go to College national and local program in 1922. Through this program, the Alphas organized tutoring and financial support so that young men would have an increased opportunity to obtain a higher educational degree. Kappa Alpha Psi launched its Guide Right Program, also in 1922, for high school seniors, which also mentored and provided monetary relief in the form of scholarships to attend college. During World War II, Sigma

Gamma Rho, targeting black American youth, organized its national Sigma Teen Town to provide housing, career opportunities, and guidance for both genders.[46]

The work performed by the organizations in black communities remained consistent throughout the years. In each decade, the organizations would act as leaders in civil and human rights, and for the sorority Sigma Gamma Rho, women's rights as well.[47] Unlike the black American social fraternals, the three groups did not appear to select members based on color and class; rather, membership included nearly every black American student on the predominantly white campuses. Yet like their sisters and brothers in the perceived elitist social fraternals, their place in the university, and as an academic organization, initially ensured those not matriculated at an accredited university would not gain membership. Lack of membership in the fraternal did not mean the masses of black Americans would not benefit from the fraternals' work, but it did create a socioeconomic line of division which their benevolent, cultural, and community development work was challenged to mend.

Alpha Phi Alpha, Kappa Alpha Psi, and Sigma Gamma Rho were similar to the black American benevolent organizations, inasmuch as their organizations acted as service sites for black Americans. Historian Paula Giddings observes that in the collegiate atmosphere where they were conceived, the focus on academic achievement, strict GPA guidelines, and African American student retention made them closer to, but more socially potent and relevant than, honorary societies such as Phi Beta Kappa.[48] BGLOs formed on white campuses at the turn of the twentieth century may appear to embrace whiteness and white organizational structures because of their existence as Greek-letter societies. In actuality, their identity as Greek-letter organizations allowed them to obtain land grants in the name of the seemingly neutral organizations and to raise funds to build and buy small sorority and fraternity houses close to their respective campuses.[49] Far from the large-scale mansions built by their white peers in suburban areas, their more modest dwellings allowed members of BGLOs to reside near their campuses. This was essential because northern university school dorms, including Indiana and Cornell Universities, did not allow black students to keep residence. Alpha Kappa Alpha sorority, in response to lack of housing or housing segregation on college campuses, made the funding of sorority houses for undergraduates a goal in white suburban areas where their younger sisters could not secure housing because of racial discrimination. Black American fraternity and sorority houses were necessary, then, as they would counteract the problem of long commutes to their respective campuses. Unlike the white fraternal houses, residence was not limited to fraternal members. Rather, fraternal houses became a site for fraternal and nonfraternal members to keep residence near campus during racial segregation. Even if universities did allow black American students to reside in the predominantly white populated dorms, the cultural climate of institutional racism at predominantly White college campuses would likely create a racially hostile and intolerant atmosphere. Black American Greek houses did not form in the name of exclusion; rather, their invention provided people of African descent a residential, cultural refuge.

Letters of Omnipresence: Black Greek-letter Organizations at Historically Black Colleges

The first sorority formed at Howard University, Alpha Kappa Alpha, did not face the type of overt racism by a white student body as seen at Cornell University, Indiana University, and Butler University. Yet, being the first of its kind at Howard created other obstacles. AKA women felt a pressing obligation to set a foundation for what sororal life would entail for black women. Alpha Kappa Alpha sorority was the idea of a Howard University student, Ethel Hedgeman Lyle, and eight other Howard women who shared her vision for academic excellence and political responsibility. Hedgeman, a working-class woman from St. Louis, Missouri, received an academic scholarship to attend Howard University in 1906. She was an active member of the Young Women's Christian Association, the Christian Endeavor, and church choir. All of these affiliations shaped her community-based endeavors once she organized the sorority. Composed of the nine black American women matriculated into the Liberal Arts School at Howard, the women chose the name Alpha Kappa Alpha, because they "are the first letters of three Greek words which form the motto of the sorority, which when translated is 'by merit and by culture.'"[50] Since the idea to have a sorority at Howard was Hedgeman's, the other eight members wanted to elect her as the chapter president of Alpha Kappa Alpha. Yet, as Hedgeman was still a sophomore, the women felt it best to select Lucy Slowe, a senior, innovator, and later recorder of how the organization's internal structure would operate.

At Howard, there were no white sororities for the women to emulate or model themselves after; these women thus seemed to create a sorority in alignment with their culturally specific environment. The women of AKA argue that the sorority was originally designed to "cultivate and encourage high scholastic and ethical standards, to promote unity and friendship among college women, to study and help alleviate problems concerning girls and women, and to be of service to all [hu]mankind."[51] The sorority's goals went beyond nebulous ideas of sisterhood and individual achievement, then, as these women sought to transform the society. Incorporated in 1913, the sorority operates as a business organization out of Chicago, Illinois. Its headquarters, Ivy Center, acts as a structural base and center for the creation and deployment of their political work and ideology. According to members, they are first by merit, driven by culture, and partially sustained through six strands of secret rituals. While on the surface their founding might seem less significant compared to the racism that groups founded at predominantly white colleges would face, AKA women were still among few women at Howard. In addition, as mentioned with the discussion of Sigma Gamma Rho, they were among even fewer numbers of women able to achieve a college education in the early twentieth century. The translation of their sororal name, "by merit and by culture," places culture and education at the center of their sororal identity, which holds great meaning in understanding the defining characteristic of all BGLOs. *Culture* had alienated them from their peers on white campuses, brought them together on historically black campuses, and *merit* is what all sought to redefine through their place in the academy.

Three Liberal Arts majors at Howard University—Frank Coleman, Oscar Cooper, and Edgar Love—followed AKA's founding when they organized Omega Psi Phi Fraternity. The men adopted the theme of "Scholarship, Manhood, Perseverance, and Uplift" as their fraternal ideology. The second fraternity housed at Howard, but the first founded there, the Omegas experienced the antifraternalism prevalent at the time. The negative and suspicious perception of Masonry decades earlier mirrored the administration's position on male fraternals on its campus in 1911. With no specific incident to point to, the male fraternals such as Alpha Phi Alpha and Omega Psi Phi were isolated as potential sites for immorality at Howard because they convened in secret. Further, the fraternity and sorority, in the minds of some Howard administrators and the president, conjured up images of white organizations with which they were familiar, leaving no reference point in which to comprehend the formation of a fraternal space as possibly radical or transformative.

Howard's president announced, "Omega Psi Phi fraternity does not exist" at a university student assembly, asserting his dislike of Greek-letter organizations and displaying his possible reliance on the signifier of white fraternals standing in for the different possibilities black American Greek-letter organizations might engender.[52] In response, members of Omega Psi Phi vowed to the president and other college administrators to disband if caught engaging in, or if there were in substantiated reports of, immoral behavior in their fraternity. While the sorority Alpha Kappa Alpha appeared to draw less concern from Howard's administrators for their formation in 1908, their male counterparts in Omega Psi Phi seemed to suffer from the idea that black American men were predisposed to immoral behavior and aggression. The sexual and racial stereotypes of the masses of black American women notwithstanding, black women's clubs and sororal organizations had already established a history of utilizing these sites for the protection of virtue and morality.[53] In the mind of Howard's president, on the other hand, he viewed black men's social clubs as possible sites of ill virtue and immorality.

Women's social clubs, sororal organizations, and mixed-gender benevolent fraternals established a reputation of benevolence and nurture as a center for their organizational structure. Yet, male secret societies drew great suspicion. Howard's president did not reveal what constituted the alleged immoralities among male college fraternals when he demanded Omega Psi Phi disband. It is reasonable to deduce, however, that in the minds of antifraternalists, college administrators, and the Howard president alike, black men convening in secret would spur the same type of sexually freewheeling and illegal vices and behavior all black American men, despite educational status and class, were thought to partake in during their meetings. In view of these obstacles, Omega Psi Phi began to induct new members, and they were the only black American fraternal organization to charter a chapter for male enlistees in World War I. Omegas reportedly felt social and professional alienation in the United States Army, a sentiment shared by many men of color who fought for freedom overseas, but were less than free in the nation they inhabited. As the decades passed, BGLOs founded at Howard University, Omega Psi Phi included, unlike their peers on the predominantly white campuses, would, and could be more selective in their membership intake. This exclusivity in membership would be one of the long-standing controversies about the organizations.

In juxtaposition to the BGLOs founded at white campuses, such as Alpha Phi Alpha, Kappa Alpha Psi, and Sigma Gamma Rho, fraternal groups founded at Howard had plenty of black students to choose from for membership. Some students did not secure membership into sororities and fraternities at Howard for perceived lack of character and leadership capabilities. Other students, however, experienced rejection for reasons that would appear insignificant. In addition, because of the increased social and political connections such organizations came to represent as they gained popularity among the student body, those not chosen for membership or disenchanted by current organizations on campus were often quite bitter. This disenchantment would take the form of general antifraternalism or some would defy their rejection by creating their own social and political outlets.[54]

A reflection of this was in 1914, the year Omega Psi Phi went from a local to a national organization. This was the same year twenty-two undergraduate women who were members of Alpha Kappa Alpha sorority left under disputed circumstances to start a new sorority, Delta Sigma Theta.[55] DST is the only black Greek-letter sorority to spawn off an existing one. The Deltas quickly asserted their position as activists through their involvement in women's rights. Much to the dislike of Howard University's administration, the Alpha chapter of DST participated in the 1913 march for women's suffrage.[56] DST's political work included academic activism, as in 1937 their first major national project, the National Literary Project, began a crusade to increase literacy in black communities as a whole. In 1938, DST formed the Vigilance Committee, an organization that protested unequal employment opportunities, lynching, and Jim Crow accommodations.[57] The Omegas and the Deltas showed themselves to struggle between an emerging social consciousness and the overseeing of an administration that watched and analyzed their every move. At times, however, such barriers came from within the organizations. In the 1960s, younger members of Kappa Alpha Psi were often at odds with and faced censor and castigation from alumni Kappa members for their participation in Black Power movements.[58]

Langston Taylor laid the foundation for Phi Beta Sigma in 1910. Taylor, then a high school senior in Memphis, Tennessee, wanted to begin a new Greek-letter fraternity when he arrived at Howard University. In the academic year of 1913–14, he chartered Phi Beta Sigma fraternity with the help of a former and a current Howard University student: Leonard Morse, a minister, and Charles Brown, a student. Like all of the black American Greek-letter organizations, Phi Beta Sigma adopted a motto to represent how they would situate their fraternal identity within the existing groups. "Culture for Service and Service for Humanity" became their adage, showing culture, like AKA, and Omega Psi Phi, to be one of the defining aspects of BGLO life for them. The word service implemented in their motto, which is also a key word in the slogan of Sigma Gamma Rho, suggests that for Phi Beta Sigma, culture and service were mutually constitutive. As their fraternity began to solidify through increased membership, Phi Beta Sigma began their "Bigger and Better Business" national program.[59] Bigger and Better Business became an economically conservative venture for them that aided and sought to expand the growth of black American small businesses. Phi Beta Sigma's goal was to influence consumer practices by encouraging black consumer spending to remain within the community. The "buy Black" tactics implicated in their approach were a strategy that would enable black American businesses to prosper and remain secure. Their program did help black American businesses, but American capitalism and its tendency to dislocate the masses and working class from the majority's wealth apparently went unquestioned in their producer-oriented approach.

A friend of Phi Beta Sigma founder Charles Taylor, Arizona Cleaver, started Zeta Phi Beta sorority at Howard University in 1920. Zeta Phi Beta remains the only Greek-letter sorority among black Americans that is an adjoining organization to a male Greek-letter fraternity. Similar to many female auxiliaries, such as the Order of the Eastern Star and Daughters of Rebeka, they modeled their constitution and organizational structure after their brother organization, that is, Phi Beta Sigma. The founders nevertheless began to carve out an independent identity from Phi Beta Sigma. One of the founders, Myrtle Faithful, admitted that initially the Zetas were little more than a social group, but after establishing itself as a sorority, it grew into an institution to "improve humanity overall."[60] Zetas focused on programs reflective of the conservatism and uplift ideology among the black American female intelligentsia of the times: "Scholarship, Service, Sisterhood, and Finer Womanhood" was the mantra they adopted to promote. Zeta's primary program administered in 1943, Zeta Housing Project, was a central clearinghouse for the dissemination of information on, and access to, housing for black Americans during a time of widespread residential housing discrimination.[61]

It would take forty years for Iota Phi Theta, the final NPHC fraternity, to form and later join what members now deem the "Divine Nine" of black Greek-letter membership. Iota Phi Theta established their first chapter at Baltimore, Maryland's Morgan State University in 1963. Unlike the former eight fraternals, Iota Phi Theta came about during the tumultuous sixties and civil rights protest, and on a diverse, urban public university campus. Organized by twelve undergraduate men and guided by childhood friends Lonnie Spruill, Frank Coakley, and Elias Dorsey, Iota Phi Theta's expansion concentrated on historically black and working-class institutions. Instead of transforming its structure to address the times as their predecessors had, Iota Phi Theta came about *because of* the times. The fraternity's composition, similar to the growing class diversification of the former eight in the '60s, did not fit the stereotype of upper-middle and middle-class color-conscious social groups of yesteryear. Several of the men were older in comparison to the average undergraduate college student, a handful married with families, and most were working students.[62] Indeed, their adopted slogan, "Building Upon a Tradition, Not Resting On One," seemed like the same indirect critique Sigma Gamma Rho posed toward earlier BGLOs that began at Howard University.

Iota Phi Theta's motto was strongly suggestive, but their community development still mirrored typical programs of the former eight BGLOs. The Morgan State fraternity initially gathered resources to cultivate and participate in mentorship of young black men, educational excellence, and local benevolence. Notwithstanding their common forms of philanthropy, arising in the mid-twentieth century provided an atmosphere for potential black insurgency. Unlike Kappa Alpha Psi and Delta Sigma Theta, Iota Phi Theta could conceive of their visions for change without coming up against the generational schisms of older leadership's views of working around and within societal constraints versus younger leadership's leaning toward protesting societal constraints. Participation in local desegregation efforts in Baltimore, Maryland, from their conception attested to an agenda that spread beyond their campuses and their communities to encompass hands-on, overt political engagement. As the last BGLO to form and the only one to form midcentury, however, their national agenda and social justice scope would take time to flourish beyond regional borders. Compounding the problem of slower growth and novelty, their lobbying for admission into the NPHC lasted for three decades until their acceptance in 1996, thus affecting the establishment of a strong national and international presence. NPHC leadership, composed of members in the other eight BGLOs, surely found Iota Phi Theta threatening to what for many years was coined "The Great Eight" of black Greek-letter fraternal membership, which no doubt had an affect on the organization's stall to grant the new fraternity NPHC membership.[63] A slogan insinuating other BGLOs were dormant activists while Iota Phi Theta men were producing activists likely antagonized leadership in the established NPHC fraternals that came before Iota Phi Theta. The fraternity's challenge was to catch up to their brothers and sisters in the first eight BGLOs and successfully fulfill a promise of building, rather than resting upon a tradition of activism.

In reviewing the history of BGLOs, it is evident that a consciousness about culture, service, and community development was a part of their fraternal identity formation. Inclusion of this history hopes to emphasize the revered meaning members place on the founders of their organizations. It is also to review, from a historical perspective, the obstacles overcome by these women and men early on in their fraternal formation. The history and founders of all nine organizations, because of their plight in the face of adversity, remain mythical entities of worship for current members. Within a current context, members argue that they are building upon a powerful legacy of determination and change, as represented through the founders' perseverance in the academy. An argument about the relationship between those founders and class, race, collective consciousness, sexuality, and color is included later on in this chapter. For now, a brief examination of BGLOs that are not members of the NPHC hopes to tease out the cultural and organizational nuance in their fraternal structures and assess if being dislocated from the initial nine improves or hinders their shape.

Our Letters Are Equal in Stature: BGLOs Beyond the Divine Nine

While the major nine BGLOs are generally at the center of conversation about BGLOs and seen as the end all to such organizations among black Americans, Greek-letter fraternals outside of the NPHC actually outnumber those within the Greek-letter umbrella organization. Lack of association with the major nine had drawbacks and advantages for the additional Greek-letter societies among black Americans. An advantage for those outside of the NPHC groups included an opportunity to form Greek-letter organizations composed of black men and women of a certain profession, across gender distinctions, and specific to a regional locality. For the Greek groups composed of members of one particular profession, an added common identity through work created an atmosphere for an increase in bonding among members who could provide professional support, aid in the cultivation of empathy, advancement, and longevity in their careers. Sororities such as Chi Eta Phi, established in 1932 in Washington DC, became an outlet of support for black women in the nursing profession. In 1929, Chicago's Iota Phi Lambda, a sorority among black women in business, came about to "stimulate, inspire, foster and give mutual assistance to those persons engaged in business" as a career. Black Greek-letter sororities organized around a specific profession, just as the social groups the Links and Girl Friends enabled social outlets, individual advancement, and class autonomy.

Many non-NPHC Greek-letter groups among black Americans actually predated the original eight's additional chapters on their respective campuses. In other words, whereas the first eight of NPHC had established a national identity as a black Greek-letter society, non-NPHC groups emerged on campuses before the chartering of chapters of the nationally recognized BGLOs in the NPHC. For example, a fraternity for black men, Tau Sigma, dates back to the late nineteenth century. Other professional Greek-letter organizations emerged concurrent with or shortly after the original BGLOs on particular campuses, including Chi Delta Mu (a medical association) and Tau Delta Sigma (law association). These two associations brought black men together in friendship and collegiality at the turn of the twentieth century when the numbers of black male professionals were minute compared to the dominant white culture. Their formations helped to curtail isolation and produced sites of refuge for many college-educated black men who, irrespective of class status, encountered the racism of the day. Their female counterparts included the black sororities Epsilon Sigma Iota (law association) and Rho Psi Phi (medical association). Black students also founded honorary societies such as Sigma Pi, and in the 1940s, multicultural groups such as Beta Sigma Tau (fraternity) and Pi Beta Sigma (sorority) formed in Chicago, Illinois. The latter two sought to create social and professional bonds beyond the barriers of race, but outside of college life and affiliation, membership ended and graduate groups, unlike the NPHC nine, were an exception, rather than a rule.

Organizations where gender was not a criterion for membership opened up possibilities for organizational friendships and community collaborations among black women and men. The NPHC BGLOs always collaborated across gender identities and worked in collectivity for community development on and off campuses, but lifting the gender-specific sanction set the groundwork for mutual respect among black women and men. One such coed fraternal that did not don Greek letters, Order of Akande, joined the move toward Afrocentricism in the post–civil rights era. Nearly a dozen groups that functioned similarly to traditional black fraternities and sororities sprung up that claimed an African-centered fraternal identity, rather than an identity constantly engaged in the negotiation between Greek letters and black consciousness.[64] Among these were Kemet (1988), Auset (1990), Ndugu (1995), and Malika Kambe Umfazi (1995). All of these organizations provided additional identity spaces of maneuver and added attributes in comparison to the nine of the NPHC, but since most black Greek-letter organizations outside of the NPHC were specific to a local, trade, profession, ideological or extracurricular interests, many were unable to sustain beyond a few decades and in many cases, beyond a few years. Whether momentary or long-lasting, Greek-letter organizations and contemporary African-centered fraternities and sororities reveal and fulfill limits of NPHC's black Greek-letter organizations. The former organizations created groups in opposition to the latter, just as the latter organizations formed in counteropposition to Greek-letter societies among white Americans. This intracultural perforation of Greek-letter societies, fraternities, and sororities among black Americans suggests blackness as a, rather than the, force for collectivity. In the larger black public sphere, unity, collaboration, and community interventions would always compete with the struggle to reconcile the multiplicity of differences and prejudices that arise along the lines of color, class, and sexualities in African America.

Linking the Legacies of Distinction: Color, Class, and Sexualities in BGLOs

Color and class distinctions existed within BGLOs, especially at historically black colleges in their early years, which made the specter of elitism difficult to exorcise. Black American Greek-letter fraternals insist that only the most academically sound and leadership-minded individuals gain membership and that color hue was never a criterion. As one member responded to the accusation of elitism and exclusion, "we are elitist in that we strive for academic achievement. We are exclusionary in that our membership is limited to those matriculated in a four-year university."[65] Nonfraternal members, however, argue that black American Greek-letter fraternals' selection process seemed similar to the social fraternals, such as the Links, Girl Friends, and the Boulé. Large numbers of fairer-skinned members in a few of the black American Greek societies at Howard in particular, at least until World War I, left them vulnerable to such accusations.[66] Some later Greek-letter organizations, for example, formed in opposition to what they perceived as membership selection based on color hue. To what degree a large color spectrum was representative of Howard's student population as a whole is difficult to ascertain. The complex intertwines of color, class, and education—at least historically—existed within both camps. The extent to which arbitrary and counterproductive distinctions took place among members lays with an unreachable population, that is, the deceased founders of the organizations. In spite of this, the following oral testimony of members and their collective memories, secondary sources, and hypotheses will help put together this color, class, and sexual puzzle.

Norma Boyd, one of the founders of Alpha Kappa Alpha sorority, claimed that her role and the role of others like her—fair skinned, educated, and wealthy—allowed for a foot in both worlds, black and white. Boyd considered herself a spy in the world of whites, who often passed to "come back and report just how the other half does" so that the "darker people of the race" could strategize with them against the perceived enemy within the dominant culture.[67] Historian Deborah Gray White argues that the position of Boyd, which other fairer-skinned activists shared, suggests they used their position not over, but in solidarity with their black brothers and sisters. Nonetheless, Boyd and others who shared her perception on color advantage heightened the criticism of fraternal members.[68] Boyd's comment may not have been intended as condescending, but it did seem to imply an underlying subtext, that is, that they were inherently special and worthy of praise and celebration for their education, accomplishments, and, sometimes, their color. Many might argue, (as did W. E. B. Du Bois), that these women and men were simply doing, as members of an educated class, what they ought to do: use their position to help to enfranchise the masses of black Americans out of a sense of collective responsibility.

Former president of Zeta Phi Beta, Sojourner Jackson, admitted that in the 1930s, when she graduated from a historically black college, fraternity and sorority membership meant "You were supposed to be above other people. . . . At that time if you didn't have the money—if your parents didn't give it to you—you couldn't get into the organizations."[69] William C. Brown, who is a member of Omega Psi Phi, said that when he pledged in 1939 acceptance into his fraternal meant that he "would be a part of a group of men who were going someplace."[70] Agreeing with Brown, Ozell Sutton, former president of Alpha Phi Alpha, claims that even contemporarily, the black Greek system is "a network that cannot be matched anywhere in the black community."[71] Brown's and Sutton's statements show linkages between the past and present, infering an unapologetic sentiment of social and class distinction. In this social context, BGLOs, like white and black American social fraternals, represent who has cultural capital, social, political, and economic power in their communities. Networking opportunities are surely helpful for members, but for every social circle, those on the margins of that circle exist without access to the professional networking intrinsic to BGLOs. As Deborah Gray White observes, "classism was inherent in the networking strategy that made the [African American] middle class the conduit through which resources flowed *into* black communities."[72]

Cultural critic bell hooks suggests an alternative framework to view the work of black Americans privileged by education and class. Her view is useful in reconsidering the role of the class privileged in the nation's past and present. She contends that it is "possible to gain class power without betraying our solidarity toward those without class privilege, by living simply, sharing our resources, and refusing to engage in hedonistic consumerism and the politics of greed."[73] hooks asserts that wealthy black Americans can reframe their class advantage in solidarity with, rather than at the expense of, other black Americans. The possibilities of Greek-letter organizations may thus hold lessons for social and cultural formations that fail to merge their rhetoric of class consciousness with action in their communities. While a reasonable percentage (though not all) of members initially fell into a middle-class socioeconomic bracket, their community development work, as seen in the former description of their beginnings and cultural work, often spoke as loud as their words.

However, race work, academic excellence, and community development did not mean that members would overcome other forms of prejudice besides colorism and classism, such as heterosexism. Proclaimed solidarity based on the idea that all black Americans are in the same social predicament because of racism alone is problematic and elides other forms of discrimination. Cornel West, a cultural critic, argues that for black Americans, "Racist treatment vastly differs owing to class, gender, sexual orientation, nation, region, hue, and age."[74] AKA member and children's book author Jacqueline Woodson explained this in an introspective autobiographical essay in a 1999 issue of *Essence* magazine. Woodson wrote that she will always defend and affiliate with her sorority and remains close to her sorority sisters, but as an "out" lesbian she often finds the sorority's emphasis on femininity and, by association, heterosexuality, a difficult and privileged criterion. Woodson writes that she and other nonheterosexual women "often feel stereotyped and misunderstood."[75] Fraternals are a social form predominantly characterized by single-sex socialization and organization, and there is a dominant ethos of heteronormativity and heterosexual courtship encouraged within the fraternal framework as a whole. As a result, the possible role of nonnormative sexualities as it intersects with racial identity in BGLOs reveals the limitations and commonalities upon which black Americans identify.

Woodson's commentary is thus descriptive of the reality of the ascription to normative sexual codes by the large majority of sororities and fraternities. To understand this, one might consider the racial and class context in which sexualities emerge. In explaining black American middle-class patrolling of sexuality in general, cultural critic Kobena Mercer writes that "the sexual morality and . . . overly rigid attitudes which have developed amongst some black people is an 'overcompensation' against racist myths of slackness and depravity."[76] Feminist and cultural critic Patricia Hill Collins argues that in a racist and sexist society, heterosexuality, and class advantage for those who identify as heterosexual and economically wealthy acts as one of the few areas in which to acquire power and remain privileged.[77] Nonheterosexual fraternal members may find themselves in a precarious position in relation to the performance of gender and sex in these organizations—a performance that remains safely situated within heterosexual frameworks. Thus, the fraternal apparatus distinguishes itself in other ways beyond the barriers of class, race, and color hue.

Conclusion

An intervention into the celebratory narrative insofar as class is concerned comes from Omega Psi Phi member and 1999 Oakland, California, NAACP director Shannon Reeves. Although Reeves seems to valorize the founders of BGLOs, he states in journalist Lawrence Ross's fraternal history book the *Divine Nine* that black Greek-letter fraternals today need to

> Stop playing clubhouse. I mean, look at what the founders said the organizations were to be about. If you are going to be a part of an organization so that you can go to conventions, so that you can meet and live in these hotels for a weekend, or so that you can get some frequent flyer miles, then say that is what you are about. Don't come out with a ritual; don't come out with a history book. These organizations were established to enhance the quality of life for African Americans in this nation. So every fraternity and sorority has to ask themselves at the end of the day, "Did we do anything to better the quality of life for African Americans?" And if the answer is no, then you are irrelevant.[78]

Harsh words, perhaps, but Reeves's statement reverberates loudly against the potential problem of members relying on past cultural work of founders to circumvent strong community interventions in a current context. In order for their formation to continue to participate in relevant power blocs to the dominant culture's subjugation of black Americans, work beyond the boundaries of Reeves's position is necessary. Without dismissing the cultural, political, and transformative influence BGLOs have, essential elements would further politicize black American cultural formations. Cornel West, who is also a member of Alpha Phi Alpha, argues that black American cultural workers in general "must constitute and sustain discursive and institutional networks that deconstruct earlier modern Black strategies for identity-formation, demystify power relations that incorporate class, patriarchal and homophobic biases, and construct more multivalent and multidimensional responses that articulate the complexity and diversity of Black practices in the modern and postmodern world."[79]

Members of these BGLOs may appear at times to succumb to the dominant conceptualization of aesthetics and the capitalist-driven ethos of what sociologist E. Franklin Frazier called their "conspicuous consumption."[80] Frazier noted that the first eight of NPHC BGLOs spent a total of $2,225,000 in 1952 on cotillions and other social parties. In response, the organizations argue that their lavish parties fund their core civic and community development programs.[81] Few members and chapters would hold enough independent wealth that they could fund their local and national community work without fundraisers, thus the reality of their social aspect and their avowed selfless benevolence no doubt lays somewhere in the middle of both positions. For example, a member of Kappa Alpha Psi noted that he became skeptical of fraternity participation in the late 1970s. After he asked his fraternity chapter to donate money to a scholarship program for black students at his university where he was an athletic coach, the national fraternity granted him $100 out of a substantial treasury of millions.[82]

BGLOs' problematic position within the structures of sexual, color, class, and sexual domination might call into question the possibilities of seeing them as a social-justice collective and counterfraternal movement. I argue, however, that such groups can exist as productive and counterproductive at the same time. When one peels back the mask of propriety that members found necessary, an "innocent Black subject," to borrow phrasing from sociologist Stuart Hall, is unlikely to live underneath the surface skin.[83] There is credence to the accusation of colorism, classism, heteronormativity, and overall elitism; nonetheless, there were and are differences in how these variables of distinction work within the organizations. Therefore, one can make careful generalizations about the specificity of BGLOs' practices. At predominantly white universities, the color and class diversity among members was more apparent. Whereas at historically black colleges, class and color in a seemingly homogenous environment (at least in terms of race) became the way in which they could, and sometimes did, create distinction. Based upon perceived and material differences of gender, class, sexualities, and color, BGLOs held and exercised various amounts of privilege in relation to these shifting identity contexts.

BGLOs remain a cultural enigma to outsiders. Unfortunately, the stereotype of these groups as elitist plagues social and Greek-letter organizations and lumps them together as an exclusive, rather than a potentially transformative site. This organizational lumping ignores their cultural, historical, and specific contextual differences. BGLOs are not immune from the trappings of Greek organizational life that presented challenges to, and stood in opposition to, their avowed intents. BGLOs founded at historically black colleges created formations for service, socialization, and professionalization among black men and women. Like the social fraternals that formed simultaneously along with them or shortly thereafter, they distinguished themselves, and not always in positive ways, from the larger black student body. In juxtaposition, the BGLOs that emerged on predominantly white campuses struggled to assert their academic capabilities and to come together as a racial and cultural collective in the face of racial and gender adversity.

One of the things at stake in the exploration of fraternals in their varied organizational forms, gender, and ethnic compositions, is a struggle over meanings of culture. Within BGLOs' specific cultural configuration, it is essential to see how culture shapes social formation and how these formations reshape their culture. For BGLOs, it is not constructive to disentangle gender, race, sexuality, and cultural restraints, from the gendered, racialized, sexualized, and cultural arrangements they grew out of, resisted, embodied, and perpetuated in their formation. It is only by delving into these problems that true social transformation can occur, which should not imply that the secret societies, benevolent organizations, social fraternals, and Greek-letter organizations among people of African descent do not engage in meaningful community service, cultural and individual development. Like their white counterparts, BGLOs exist as a mixed and often contradictory sign of American cultural politics and social life. However, membership in a BGLO was a marker of race and, by association, blackness. The history of their formation and public record of their cultural work provides evidence of calculated social and political intervention. This reality continues to compete, however, with the popular image of such groups as counterproductive and representative of oppressive class and color-coded politics.

Notes

1. On Orientalism as a stereotype that views Asia, Asians, and Asian Americans within a Westernized, ethnocentric, discriminating framework, see Edward Said, *Orientalism* (New York: Vintage Books, 1979).

2. Author unknown, "U. Florida Greeks Apologize for Mekong Delta Theme Party," *Alligator* April 11, 2001.

3. Tim Potter, "At KU, Painful Lessons In Sensitivity," *Wichita Eagle*, October 3, 1997, pg. 4A.

4. Annalee Newitz and Matt Wray, "Introduction," *White Trash: Race and Class in America* (New York: Routledge, 1997), 3.

5. Jon Weiner, "Racial Hatred on Campus," *Nation*, February 27, 1989, 262.

6. The Rider and Colorado State incidents are described in Hank Nuwer, *Wrongs of Passage: Fraternities, Sororities, Hazing, and Binge Drinking* (Bloomington: Indiana University Press 1999), 219. For more on the connection between white fraternals and homophobia, see Sara Mourra, "Fraternity Life Conflicts with the Image of Homosexuality at UC-Berkeley," *Daily Californian*, May 11, 2001.

7. Julie Narans, "Greeks Can Exclude: They Have That Right," *Daily Nebraskan*, October 24, 2000.

8. Evan Right, "Sister Act: Deep Inside the Secret Life of Sorority Girls at Ohio State University," *Rolling Stone Magazine*, October 14, 1999. To be "lavaliered" is for a fraternity male to give a sorority woman his "fraternity pendant" and declare an exclusive relationship with her. The lavaliered ceremony concludes with the male who has relinquished his fraternity pin being beaten by fraternity members to signify he has given up his autonomous manhood.

9. On sexual minority fraternals and their exclusion in the hetero-dominant ones, see Shane Windemyer et al., *Out on Fraternity Row: Personal Accounts of Being Gay in a College Fraternity* (Bloomington: Indiana University Press, 1998); Benoit Denizet-Lewis, "View Fraternity Life from the Three B-Perspective," *Contra Costa Times*, February 24, 1998; Douglas N. Case, "A Glimpse of the Invisible Membership: A National Survey of Lesbigay Greek Members," *Perspectives* 22, no. 3 (April/May 1996); Stacey Zott, "Out, Proud, Greek?" *Indiana Daily Student Supplement*, February 2, 1998.

10. Author unknown, "Whites in Black Sororities and Fraternities," *Ebony* (December 2000): 172–75; Laurence A. Stains, "Black Like Me: What's Up With White Guys Who Join Black Frats? Are They Trying Too Hard, Or Is It Just a Class Thing?" *Rolling Stone*, March 24, 1994.

11. Appreciative inquiry is a method in social science studies (and the new sociology) where practitioners do not study or present cultural organizations as problems to solve. Rather, this method works under the assumption that cultural organizations, marked by their distinct practices, are cultural enigmas examined for their usefulness and faults. The idea behind this approach is to understand and analyze subculture groups to determine what is best and most problematic about them to the ends of providing a prescriptive vision of change. On this methodology, see F. Barrett, G. Thomas, and S. Hocevar, "The Central Role of Discourse in Large-Scale Change: a Social Constructionist Perspective," *Journal of Applied Behavioral Science* 31 (1995): 352–72; D. Cooperider, F. Barrett, and S. Srivastva, "Social Construction and Appreciative Inquiry: A Journey in Organization Theory," in *Management and Organization: Relational Alternatives to Individualism*, ed. D. Hosking, et al. (Aldershot, UK: Avebury Press 1995).

12. On early African and African American secret societies, see Carter G. Woodson, *The African Background Outlined* (Washington, DC: Association of the Study of Negro Life and History 1936); Robert L. Harris Jr., "Early Black Benevolent Societies, 1780–1830," *Massachusetts Review* 20 (Autumn 1979); Jacqui Malone, "African American Mutual Aid Societies: Remembering the Past and Facing the Future," in *Steppin' on the Blues: The Visible Rhythms of African Dance* (Chicago: University of Illinois Press, 1994); David Fahey, "Introduction" to *Black Lodge in White America* (Lanham, MD: University Press of America, 1994).

13. Malone, "African American Mutual Aid Societies," 169.

14. Ibid., 173. See also Vincent Harding, "Religion and Resistance Among Antebellum Negroes, 1800–1860," in *The Making of Black America*, ed. August Meirer and Elliott Rudwick (New York: Athenaeum 1969), 194–95 and Monore N. Work, "Secret Societies as Factors in the Social and Economical Life of the Negro," in *Democracy in Earnest: Southern Sociological Congress, 1916–1918* (New York: Negro Universities Press, 1969).

15. David Beito, "Black Fraternal Hospitals in the Mississippi Delta, 1942–1967," *Journal of Southern History* 56 (February 1999), 109–40.

16. For a cross-comparison of white and African American Elks, see Charles Edward Dickerson III, *The Benevolent and Protective Order of Elks and the Improved Benevolent and Protective Order of Elks of the World* (Ph.D. diss., University of Rochester, 1981); Malone, "African American Mutual Aid Societies," 167–86.

17. Malone, "African American Mutual Aid Societies," 178.

18. Robin Kelly, "We Are Not What We Seem," in *Race Rebels: Culture, Politics, and the Black Working Class* (New York: Free Press, 1996), 38.
19. Ibid.
20. Johnson and Smith, "Beneficial and Charitable Societies," Teaching Guide for PBS documentary *Africans in America*, http://www.pbs.org/wgbh/aia/part3/3h480.html
21. Ibid.
22. Malone, "African American Mutual Aid Societies," 180.
23. On social fraternal groups and working-class consciousness, see Kelly, "We Are Not What We Seem," 38–39, and for a description of class distinction among social fraternals, see Otis Graham, *Our Kind of People: Inside America's Upper Middle Class* (New York: Harper Collins, 1999).
24. For a discussion of blue-vein societies and colorism among African American fraternals from the revolutionary war to the late twentieth century, see Kathy Russell, Midge Wilson, and Ronald Hall, *The Color Complex: The Politics of Skin Color among African Americans* (New York: Harcourt, Brace, Jovanovich, 1992), 24–25.
25. Graham, *Our Kind of People*, 104.
26. Ibid., 134. Italics mine.
27. Ibid, 101–26.
28. The National Pan-Hellenic Council formed in 1929 to act as a unifying governing body for the eight major African American college fraternals. It serves as the conduit through which the organizations plan, identify, and act upon areas of mutual concern. The National Pan-Hellenic Council is therefore a channel through which they disseminate, discuss, and strategize pertinent ideas to African American Greek life. See *Baird's Manual of American College Fraternities* (Menasha, WI: Baird's Manual Foundation, 1991), 41–42 for a description of the National Pan-Hellenic Council.
29. On the formation of historically black colleges see Julian Roebuck and Komunduri Morty, *Historically Black Colleges and Universities: Their Place in American Higher Education* (New York: Greenwood, 1993).
30. James V. Hatch, "Theatre in Historically Black Colleges: A Survey of 100 Years," in *A Source Book of African American Performance: Plays, People, Movements*, ed. Anna Marie Bean (New York: Routledge Press, 1999), 153, 159–60.
31. Russell, Wilson, and Hall, *The Color Complex*, 24–40.
32. Ibid.
33. The two extremes of assimilation and accommodation were positions attributed to a group of African American intellectuals, including and most notably Booker T. Washington as accommodationist and W. E. B. Du Bois as assimilationist. See Booker T. Washington, *Up From Slavery* (New York: Dover Publications, 1995), and W. E. B. Du Bois, *Souls of Black Folk* (New York: Mass Market Publishers, 1995).
34. The history of the organizations was difficult to piece together. Members' history books (Marjorie Parker, Lawrence Ross, Charles Wesley, and Otis Graham), while useful, contained no footnotes and relied on fraternal archives and oral histories. Paula Giddings's book on Delta Sigma Theta is the only African American fraternal book with citations, and in her citations, she includes the DST sorority magazine and secondary literature on American, African American, and African American women's history. I cull the following history from these members' histories, as well as African American magazines, newspapers, and secondary materials. I have summarized these materials and only cited if I used a direct quote, a substantial amount of material from one source, or if the information was from other nonfraternal initiated secondary materials. For many periodical references, there was no author attributed to what in many cases were short interest pieces. My sources on Greek-letter organizations include:

Lawrence Ross Jr., *The Divine Nine: The History of African American Fraternities and Sororities* (New York: Kensington Publishers, 2000); Tamara Brown et al., *African American Fraternities and Sororities: The Legacy and the Vision* (Lexington: University of Kentucky Press, 2005); Charles Wesley, *The History of Alpha Phi Alpha: A Development in Negro College Life* (Washington DC: Foundation Publishers, 1948); *Kappa Alpha Psi Fraternity Incorporated, San Jose Alumni Chapter Handbook* (San Jose: Kappa Alpha Psi Fraternity Alumni Chapter); Paula Giddings, *In Search for Sisterhood: Delta Sigma Theta and the Challenge of the Black Sorority Movement* (New York: William and Morrow, 1988); Otis Graham, *Our Kind of People: Inside America's Upper Middle Class* (New York: Harper Collins, 1999), Marjorie Parker, *Alpha Kappa Alpha Through the Years* (Chicago: Mobium, 1988); "Zeta Phi Beta: Founded at Howard University, Group Celebrates 71st Anniversary with Innovative Programs," *Ebony* 46, no. 7 (May 1991); "Sigma Gamma Rho: Motto of the Youngest Black Greek letter Organization is Greater Service, Greater Progress," *Ebony* 46 no. 4 (February 1991); "Kappa Alpha Psi: Fraternity Founded at Indiana University Stresses Individual and Group Achievement," *Ebony* 45, no. 7 (1991); "Phi Beta Sigma," *Ebony* 47, no. 5 (March 1992); Rosemary Banks Harris, "College Love Affair for Keeps: Sorority, Fraternity Memberships Often Last a Lifetime," *St. Petersburg Times*, April 14, 1998; Vernon Thompson, "Fraternities, Sororities from Howard: Students Draw Renewed Interest; Clubs Offer On Campus Social Life to Off Campus Commuters," *Washington Post*, November 16, 1978; Denita Gadson, "Greek Power! African American Greek Letter Organizations Wield Massive Influence After School Days," *Black Collegian* 20, no. 1 (September/October 1989); Paula Giddings, "Sorority Sisters," *Essence*, July 1988; Mary Bowan, *Educational Work of a National Professional Sorority of Negro College Women* (master's thesis, University of California Berkeley, 1935).

35. James Baldwin, "Liberalism and the Negro: A Roundtable Discussion," *Commentary* 37 (March 1964), 25–42.

36. Ross, *The Divine Nine*, 6.

37. For more on the history of Alpha Phi Alpha, see Charles Wesley, *The History of Alpha Phi Alpha.*

38. For more on Kappa Alpha Psi, see *Kappa Alpha Psi Fraternity Incorporated, San Jose Alumni Chapter Handbook;* "Kappa Alpha Psi: Fraternity Founded at Indiana University Stresses Individual and Group Achievement," *Ebony;* Ross, *The Divine Nine*, 48. Ross and the Kappa internal publication have two competing stories on the changing of the fraternity's name. I have tried to synthesize the two accounts. Ross presents this story as fact, but the Kappa publication reports this story as unsubstantiated lore among members.

39. On the Kappa's social role in Indiana, see Ross, *The Divine Nine*, 47.

40. Kelly, "We Are Not What We Seem," 38.

41. For a discussion on how the barber and beauty shop functioned as a social site of interaction and political debate, see Noliwe M. Rooks, *Hair-Raising: Beauty, Culture, and African American Women* (New Brunswick, NJ: Rutgers University Press, 1996); bell hooks, "Straightening Our Hair," *Z Magazine* (Summer 1988): 14. Evelyn Brooks Higginbotham discusses the meanings of socialization for African Americans in the black church in *Righteous Discontent: The Women's Movement in the Black Baptist Church, 1880–1920* (Cambridge, MA: Harvard University Press, 1993). For a discussion on the intersection of social organizations and political purpose within the African American middle class, see Graham, *Our Kind of People.*

42. On the resistance and description of stereotypes of African American men, see Don Belton ed., *Speak My Name: Black Men on Masculinity and the American Dream* (Boston: Beacon Press, 1995); Thelma Golden, ed., *Black Male: Representations of Black*

Masculinity in Contemporary American Art (Whitney Museum of Art, 1994); Hazel Carby, *Race Men* (Cambridge, MA: Harvard University Press, 1999); Harry Stecopoulos and Michael Uebel, eds., *Race and the Subject of Masculinities* (London: Duke University Press, 1997); Richard Majors and Jacob Gordon, eds., *The American Black Male* (Chicago: Nelson Hall Publishers, 1994).

43. Misperceptions of African American women as intellectually inferior perpetuated by the dominant culture are discussed in Michelle Wallace, *Black Macho and the Myth of the Superwoman* (London: Verso 1978; 1991 reprint); Nell Painter, "Black Studies, Black Professors, and the Problems of Perception," *Chronicle of Higher Education*, December 15, 2000; Ann DuCille, "The Occult of True Black Womanhood," in *Skin Trade* (Cambridge: Harvard University Press, 1996); bell hooks, *Feminist Theory: From Margin to Center* (Boston: South End Press, 1991).

44. Historian Paula Giddings writes that African American sororities had very strict academic guidelines for membership. See *In Search for Sisterhood*, 20.

45. "Zeta Phi Beta: Founded at Howard University," 80–81.

46. For more on these programs, see Ross, *The Divine Nine*, 8, 48, 279.

47. On the continued cultural work of these groups see Graham, *Our Kind of People;* Parker, *Alpha Kappa Alpha Through the Years;* Harris, "College Love Affair for Keeps"; Thompson, "Fraternities, Sororities from Howard"; Gadson, "Greek Power!"; Giddings, "Sorority Sisters"; and the following articles, "Zeta Phi Beta: Founded at Howard University"; "Sigma Gamma Rho"; "Kappa Alpha Psi: Fraternity Founded at Indiana University"; and "Phi Beta Sigma."

48. Giddings, *In Search for Sisterhood*, 19.

49. Ibid.

50. Ibid., 10.

51. Alpha Kappa Alpha Home page, @http://www.mit.edu: 8001/ activities/ akas /home2.html

52. A description of this incident (Thirkheild's announcement) is in Ross, *The Divine Nine*, 75–76.

53. On African American female representation and the resistance to stereotypes, see bell hooks, *Ain't I A Woman: Black Women and Feminism* (Boston: South End Press, 1981); Darlene Clark Hine and Kathleen Thompson, *A Shining Thread of Hope: The History of Black Women in America* (New York: Broadway Books, 1998); Alice Walker, *In Search of Our Mothers' Gardens* (New York: Harcourt, Brace, Jovanovich, 1983); Gerda Lerner, ed., *Black Women in White America: A Documented History* (New York: Vintage Books, 1972); Wallace, *Black Macho and the Myth of the Superwoman;* Gloria Hull et al., *All the Women Are White, All the Blacks Are Men, But Some of Us Are Brave*, (Old Westbury, NY: Feminist Press, 1982); Paula Giddings, *When and Where I Enter: The Impact of Black Women on Race and Sex in America* (New York: William and Morrow, 1984); Patricia Hill Collins, *Black Feminist Thought: Knowledge, Consciousness, and the Politics of Empowerment* (New York: Routledge Press, 1991).

54. As Paula Giddings wrote about her experience with Delta Sigma Theta, while at Howard "friends of hers would be rejected for petty, even personal reasons, and be devastated by their rejection." Giddings, *In Search for Sisterhood*.

55. In 1912, according to AKA historian Marjorie Parker, there were members of Alpha Kappa Alpha who wanted to vote in a new motto, name, symbol, and colors to represent the organization. One of the former presidents of AKA (Nellie Quander) resisted the proposed changes, as did other sorority members. Quander argued that the proposed changes would dishonor the founders of the sorority; she thus immediately moved toward incorporation, which was a legal action that would ensure the sorority's foundation would remain intact, as the original founders had so conceived. As a result,

the women who suggested the changes left the organization and formed the second African American sorority at Howard University, Delta Sigma Theta (DST). Historian and Delta member Paula Giddings writes a somewhat different version of the discontent among the sorority women in 1912. Giddings, quoting Delta members, writes: "We had broader views. We wanted to reach out in the community. We wanted to be more than just a social group. We wanted to do more, when we graduated, for the community in which we were going . . . we wanted to change some ideas, we were more oriented to serve than to socialize" (49).

Beyond some members wanting to change the motto and sorority colors, as AKA historian Marjorie Parker contends in AKA's member-initiated history book, Giddings implicitly suggests that Alpha Kappa Alpha's scope was not political enough. The women who remained in Alpha Kappa Alpha after the split were and continued to be leaders in the YWCA and NAACP, and they were rallying for women's rights and suffrage. Nonetheless, the rupture between the sorority women should call into question romantic notions of sisterhood, on which sororities often claim to base their identity. See Giddings, *In Search for Sisterhood*, 49. On the early formation of AKA see Norma Boyd, *A Love That Equals My Labors* (Chicago: Mobium Press), 71–92.

56. Ross, *The Divine Nine*, 213–42.

57. Giddings, *In Search for Sisterhood*, 124–98.

58. *Kappa Alpha Psi Fraternity Incorporated;* "Kappa Alpha Psi: Fraternity Founded at Indiana University Stresses Individual and Group Achievement."

59. Ross, *The Divine Nine*, 101.

60. "Zeta Phi Beta: Founded at Howard University."

61. For a description of the Zeta housing project, see Ross, *The Divine Nine*, 248–49.

62. A brief history of Iota Phi Theta is in Ricky L. Jones, *Black Haze: Violence, Sacrifice, and Manhood in Black Greek-letter Fraternities* (Albany: State University of New York Press, 2004), 39–40.

63. Perhaps even more telling, members of the other eight BGLOs and leadership in NPHC openly shared fears that letting another fraternity into the umbrella organization might lead to expansion to nonblacks and other ethnic minorities. On the controversy concerning Iota Phi Theta's struggle for respect among the first eight and admission into the NPHC, see Walter M. Kimbrough, *Black Greek 101: The Culture, Customs, and Challenges of Black Fraternities and Sororities* (Madison, NJ: Farleigh Dickinson University Press, 2003), 91–93.

64. In Kimbrough's study, he cites four dominant eras of Greek fraternal membership: the Maturation Years at the turn of the twentieth century, Black Power Years of the '60s, Afrocentric Era during post–civil rights years, and the Individualist or Multicultural Era, which defines the current moment of black Greek-letter formations.

65. Gadson, "Greek Power," 136–37.

66. Edward Franklin Frazier, *Black Bourgeoisie: The Rise of a New Middle Class* (New York: Free Press 1965). Franklin published his book during a time when fraternal organizations were under attack for creating disunity through their exclusive networks.

67. *Black Women's Oral History Project*, Arthur and Elizabeth Schlesinger Library at Radcliffe College, interview with Norma Boyd, 26.

68. Debra Gray White, *Too Heavy a Load: Black Women in Defense of Themselves* (New York: W.W. Norton, 1999), 96.

69. Thompson, "Fraternities, Sororities from Howard."

70. Kenji Jasper, "A Proud Heritage for Black Greek Groups," *San Diego Union Tribune*, February 24, 1998.

71. Marilyn Freeman and Tina Witcher, "Stepping Into Black Power: Black Fraternities and Sororities Give Their Members Access to a Network of Influence and

Power—and Good Times Too. So What's Wrong With That?" *Rolling Stone*, September 1987.

72. White, *Too Heavy a Load*, 157. Italics mine.

73. bell hooks, *Where We Stand, Class Matters* (New York: Routledge 2000), 108.

74. Cornel West, "The New Politics of Difference," in *Social Theory: Multicultural and Classic Readings*, ed. Charles Lemert (Boulder, CO: Westview Press, 1999), 528.

75. Jacqueline Woodson, "Common Ground," *Essence*, 30 no. 1 (May 1999).

76. Kobena Mercer, *Welcome to the Jungle: New Positions in Black Cultural Studies* (New York: Routledge, 1994).

77. Collins, *Black Feminist Thought*, 123–48.

78. Ross, 311–422.

79. West, "The New Politics of Difference," 528.

80. E. Franklin Frazier argued that middle-class African Americans and their fraternals engage in conspicuous consumption to the detriment of the masses of African Americans. See *Black Bourgeoisie: The Rise of a New Middle Class* (New York: Free Press, 1965).

81. Thompson, "Fraternities, Sororities from Howard."

82. Ross, 311–422.

83. Stuart Hall, "New Ethnicities," in *Critical Dialogues in Cultural Studies: The Stuart Hall Reader*, ed. Kuan Hsing Chen and David Morley (London: Routledge, 1996).

Asian Americans in Sororities and Fraternities: In Search of a Home and Place

Edith Wen-Chu Chen

> Well, shucks, we were outsiders at the time. Awful lot of racism, prejudice, no one (in Panhellenic sororities) ever thought of including any Asians in their group, you know. They were strictly White.
>
> —Shizue Morey Yoshina,
> Class of 1929, Chi Alpha Delta Alumnus[1]

LIVING IN THE DORMS, MAKING FRIENDS, JOINING A SORORITY OR fraternity may seem like part of the quintessential American college experience, but while Caucasian Americans could take leisure and recreation for granted, they were challenges, sometimes not even options for Asian Americans attending college prior to the 1960s. The establishment of early Asian American fraternities and sororities was a consequence of racial exclusion. Mainstream Greek fraternities and sororities could legally discriminate on the basis of race, preserving their upper-class, white, Christian character. After the advent of civil rights, Greek-letter organizations could no longer exclude people on the basis of race, ethnicity, religion, or national origin. Despite the decline of formal racial barriers, the number of Asian American sororities and fraternities have risen in the last fifteen years. Currently, over sixty-four Asian American fraternities and sororities exist, totaling to over three hundred chapters, associate chapters and colonies across the nation.[2]

The examination of Asian Americans in Greek-letter organizations provides a glimpse into another dimension of the Asian American college experience. Most discussions on Asian Americans in higher education focus on their achievements, academic success, and debates about their (over)representation.[3] Little research exists on Asian American student groups and their social lives, a significant component of the college experience. This chapter examines the experiences of Asian Americans in sororities and fraternities. I first provide an overview of the

Asian American educational history in order to provide a context to these experiences. Then I discuss the development of Asian American sororities and fraternities from their origins to their current day and argue that the current dynamics underlying Asian American sororities and fraternities speak to contemporary issues of race and gender for young Asian American men and women.

Asian Americans and Education

The history of exclusion of Asian Americans from mainstream Greek-letter organizations was not isolated to just sororities and fraternities, but must be understood in the larger context of the exclusion, segregation, and marginalization that characterized the lives of Asian Americans prior to the legislation of civil rights. Here, I give a brief overview of the educational history of Asian Americans to provide some insights to the racial dynamics during that period.

Asian Americans have been in the U.S. for over 160 years, beginning with the Chinese who arrived in California after the discovery of gold.[4] Exclusion and isolation characterizes the general pattern of incorporation for Asian Americans prior to the 1960s, especially before World War II. Unlike their European American counterparts, Asian Americans were not given the opportunity to "assimilate" at any level—economically, politically, or socially.[5] Often Asian Americans were excluded from taking jobs that were desirable to whites, paid a significantly lesser wage for the same jobs performed by whites, or imposed with unfair taxes that threatened their livelihoods.[6] Segregation was the norm in which most Asians had little choice but to live in their own communities. Naturalization laws denied Asian Americans citizenship and the right to vote,[7] and antimiscegenation acts[8] further drew the social line between whites and Asians. Exclusion acts were designed to halt and eliminate community formation. The general pattern of incorporation for Asian Americans prior to the enactment of civil rights legislation and especially prior to World War II can be characterized by economic disenfranchisement, exclusion, segregation, and isolation.

Even the schooling experiences of Asian American children were not spared from the hostile racial climate that defines this period. Initially, Chinese American children were not permitted to attend California public schools, despite their parents paying state taxes. The first "Oriental school" was opened in 1885 in San Francisco, followed later by four other Sacramento–San Joaquin Delta communities.[9] These state-funded schools were built with the explicit purpose of keeping Chinese, Japanese, and Korean American children from attending public schools with white children. In Mississippi, *Plessy v. Ferguson* (1896) upheld the principle of racial segregation and was used to justify excluding Chinese children from attending public schools. Hence Chinese children in Mississippi attended schools for "colored" children, along with African Americans, until the 1950s.[10] When Asian American children did attend school with whites, they were not always readily accepted by their fellow classmates or teachers.[11]

Exclusion, antimiscegenation laws, and immigration quotas limited the family formation and community growth of Japanese Americans and more severely Chinese Americans, the two largest Asian ethnic groups prior to World War II. Unlike their representation today, few children of Chinese and Japanese descent attended college.

What was life like for Asian American students when they attended the predominantly white college campuses? While Asian Americans may have been able to sit in the same classrooms with whites, the little work available suggests their social lives were largely segregated. In her historical work on Chinese Americans in San Francisco, Judy Yung notes that Chinese Americans were not permitted to join fraternities and sororities. At Stanford they were expelled from the dormitory by white students and had to establish their own residential Chinese Club house.[12] Similarly, at the University of California, Los Angeles (UCLA), Japanese American women were not allowed to live at the all-women's dormitory. Mabel Ota, who attended UCLA in the late 1930s, recalls "Since I was from out of town, I wanted to stay in the dormitories. But they didn't allow any Japanese. I ended up staying at the Japanese YWCA in Boyle Heights and commuted back and forth every day."[13] The life history of L. Toyama, a second-generation Japanese American, underscores the treatment of Japanese Americans during this period. He recalls, "In going through high school and college, I can't recall how many times I was cast aside just because I am Japanese. I was barred from parties, dances, swimming pools etc."[14] Given the prevalence of overt racism during this time, we can speculate that the need to form ethnic specific clubs was partly a result of a need for Asian Americans to form safe havens.

Asian American Fraternities and Sororities: The Early Years

Few Asian American fraternities and sororities existed in the early years. From 1916 to 1970, only eleven organizations were established. The first Asian American fraternity was Rho Psi (1916) founded at Cornell University by a group of Chinese American men. This fraternity has established chapters throughout mainland China, Taiwan, and Hong Kong.[15] In 1976, the organization changed its name to Rho Psi Society, opening its membership to include women. The organization currently operates as an alumni club.

Aside from Rho Psi fraternity, early Asian American fraternities and sororities were founded in California—specifically either in the Los Angeles or San Francisco Bay areas, reflecting the geographic area in which most Asian Americans lived. Also, few second-generation Asian Americans could afford to attend expensive Ivy League colleges on the East Coast.[16] In contrast, California public universities—where the majority of Asian American sororities and fraternities were founded—charged no tuition. The first of these was Pi Alpha Pi fraternity (1926) at University of California, Berkeley, which was founded by six young Chinese American fellows, all except for one were born in the U.S.[17]

Prior to Pi Alpha Pi's establishment, the founders were friends who banned together, partly as a coping response to racism prevalent during these early years. Asian Americans, even those with college education, had difficulties finding a decent job in the mainstream economy.[18] Most Asians were prevented from other professions such as law, medicine, and other graduate disciplines. These men chose to study science and engineering, since it was considered one of the better paths to employment after graduation.[19]

Beside their field of study, these men also faced housing discrimination, since student lodging was often not rented to those of Asian descent. Three of the founders finally found housing due to the goodwill of "Mother Tusch," a German woman who also had been a victim of racism. Sympathizing with the plight of these men, she rented the students a cabin behind her house. The camaraderie that developed between these men along with other Chinese American friends on campus was the basis for the founding of Pi Alpha Phi fraternity.

Other Asian American fraternities and sororities followed including the Japanese American sorority Chi Alpha Delta (1928) at UCLA, and Sigma Omicron Phi (1930) at San Francisco State Teachers' College. Both Chi Alpha Delta and Sigma Omicron Phi sororities became inactive during World War II. Anti-Japanese hysteria was at its peak, and Japanese Americans—including students—on the West Coast were forced into interment camps. These organizations were later reestablished after the war, as well as new Japanese American Greek-letter organizations such as Sigma Phi Omega sorority (1949) at the University of Southern California and Theta Kappa Phi sorority (1959) at UCLA. Although most of these organizations began as Chinese American or Japanese American specific ones, today they are generally panethnic and include different Asian American ethnic groups.

Recall that discrimination was legal until the late 1960s, and segregation and exclusion was normative in most arenas. Mainstream sororities and fraternities were no different and would routinely deny membership to Asian Americans, along with African Americans, Jews, and the working class,[20] but more than likely most ethnic minorities knew better and did not even consider joining a possibility. Exclusion and segregation was so normative some Asian Americans accepted it as part of their everyday realities. Shirley Lim's *A Feeling of Belonging: Asian American Women's Popular Culture, 1930–1960* is the most extensive and detailed treatment of sorority life during this period.[21] Her work focuses on Chi Alpha Delta, the first Asian American sorority to be established. One of the charter members, Shizue Morey Yoshina recalls they would not even consider joining a Panhellenic sorority, given the all-white membership. She said, "You have no idea. . . . what sort of wall there was between whites and anybody else. And it was pretty bad. And all this persisted until World War II (*until Japanese Americans were forcibly removed to internment camps*). . . . So in the meantime we fought our own battle."[22]

While Asian American fraternities and sororities offered some protection against racism, these organizations still operated in a climate of legal segregation. Members of the Chi Alpha Delta sorority tried to secure a house on "the row" at UCLA from the late 1930s to the 1960s. In 1938, the Chis were initially given the opportunity to purchase the UCLA Religious Conference Building, which was owned by the Janss Investment Company. As Lim's study details, the Chis hopes of owning a house were eventually defeated when one of the owners proclaimed he refused to sell to "Orientals." When the restrictive covenants were finally banned, housing prices had skyrocketed, becoming out of reach for the Chis.[23] To this day, no Asian American sorority or fraternity house exists at UCLA, and it is difficult, if not impossible for most Asian American fraternities or sororities to own a house in the Los Angeles and San Francisco bay areas, where property values are among the highest in the nation.[24]

Subtle and blatant discrimination toward Asian Americans continued well into the 1950s and 1960s. Most fraternities had written policies that privileged some form of Aryanism.[25] For example, the Sigma Nu fraternity included discriminatory clauses against "Negroes" and "Orientals." At the 1954 national convention, the Dartmouth chapter attempted to persuade the other members to eliminate the "Oriental" clause but was defeated by arguments from the West Coast chapters which argued that "their campus prestige would be seriously injured if an Oriental were taken into Sigma Nu."[26]

While it was common for fraternities to contain exclusion policies that were part of their bylaws, most of the sororities' exclusionary policies were unwritten.[27] Margaret Ohara, a Japanese American had applied for a Panhellenic scholarship at UCLA in the late 1950s. Mistaken for being of Irish descent (O'Hara), she initially won the scholarship, but later was denied, once it was realized she was Japanese American. Ohara was denied admittance and membership into all of the Greek sororities on "the row." She later established Theta Kappa Phi, originally an all Japanese American sorority.[28] Hence the establishment of Asian Americans sororities and fraternities was partly a response to racial exclusion as well as a desire to form safe havens to socialize.

Asian American Fraternities and Sororities: 1970s–1980s

Interestingly, despite the end to legalized segregation, Asian American sororities and fraternities continued to grow in the 1970s to the 1980s, with a total of seven new organizations. These groups tended to establish themselves panethnically Asian rather than by specific ethnic group. Prior to the 1960s, Asian Americans identified themselves ethnically such as Chinese, Japanese, and Filipino Americans. As the second and third generation Chinese, Japanese, and Filipinos population began to grow and attend college, they started to realize they had more in common with each other than their immigrant parents. In the late 1960s, Asian American activists coined the term "Asian American" which simultaneously claimed an American identity while at the same time spoke to the shared experiences of racial discrimination and social struggle.[29]

Asian American fraternities and sororities of the 1970s and 1980s were established during the time when the term "Asian American" became popular usage. A review of organizational websites indicate that the organizations included members of Chinese, Japanese, Korean, and of Vietnamese heritage. Lambda Phi Epsilon fraternity (founded in 1981 at UCLA) is currently the largest Asian American fraternity with a total of forty-six chapters, associate chapters, and colony chapters across the nation. It also carries the distinction of being the first and only nationally recognized by the Inter-fraternity Council. The largest Asian American sorority, Alpha Kappa Delta Phi sorority (also known as Kappa Delta Phi), was founded at the University of California, Berkeley in 1989. This sorority boasts thirty-eight chapters and colonies throughout the nation. Like the founding Asian American fraternities and sororities that came before them, organizations established during the 1970s and 1980s were also established in California, followed by expanding chapters and colonies throughout the nation.

Asian American Fraternities and Sororities: Post-1990 Growth

Since 1990, the number of newly established Asian American sororities and fraternities has more than tripled. Before 1990, a total of eight Asian American fraternities and eleven Asian American sororities existed. Today, over thirty-two Asian American fraternities and thirty-two sororities exist, totaling over three hundred chapters, associate chapters, and colonies across the nation.

The growth of Asian American sororities and fraternities in the last three decades is partly due to the increasing numbers of Asian American students on college campuses. Prior to the 1965 Immigration and Reform Act, a number of immigration policies excluded or limited the entry of Asians into the U.S., while local and domestic policies stunted community growth as discussed previously. The Asian American population has grown dramatically since then, from 1.5 million in 1970 to 11.1 million in 2000.[30] Hence, most Asian Americans attending college today are part of the post 1965 wave of migration or children of these immigrants, many of whom are professionals and highly educated. This group includes Chinese, Filipinos, Koreans, and Asian Indians.[31] Other newly arrived groups include Southeast Asians, namely Vietnamese, Cambodians, and Laotians. These new Asian Americans arrived after the passing of a series of refugee acts after 1975 are the result of the U.S. military involvement in Southeast Asia. Many of these refugees had a harder time adjusting to American life and fair worse economically as a group compared to Asians that arrived as immigrants. While earlier Asian American students attending college were primarily Chinese and Japanese and came from working-class backgrounds, today's Asian American students are much more ethnically and socioeconomically diverse.

Noteworthy is that this period is marked with the establishment and growth of South Asian and Filipino fraternities and sororities. Of the forty-five Asian American fraternities and sororities founded since 1990, twelve are South Asian and seven are Filipino. Although South Asians are not new to this country, their numbers were relatively small compared to Chinese, Japanese, and Filipino Americans. Now however, they constitute one of the largest Asian Pacific American populations, with Asian Indians alone ranking the third largest Asian Pacific American ethnic group after Chinese and Filipino.[32] They also have one of the highest college attendance rate.[33] These factors may help explain the remarkable growth of South Asian/Asian Indian Greek-letter organizations. Delta Phi Beta, a coed fraternity, was the first South Asian Greek-letter organization, established in 1992 at the University of California, Berkeley. The founding chapters of the South Asian organizations are more geographically dispersed than their earlier panethnic Asian counterparts, with concentrations in California, Texas, and the East Coast.

In addition to South Asian Greek-letter organizations, Filipino Americans have also established their own organizations. Filipinos are the second largest Asian American ethnic group and also has seen a dramatic increase in their population. They have grown by almost 700 percent from 336,731 in 1970 to 2,364,815 in the year 2000.[34] Filipino Greek-letter organizations include five fraternities and two sororities. The first one to be established was Theta Delta Beta (1990) at the University of California, Irvine. All of the Filipino Greek-letter organizations are in California.

Since the 1990s, we see the growth of both panethnic Asian Greek-letter organizations as well as the establishment of specific Asian ethnic ones, namely South Asian and Filipino. Why have South Asians and Filipinos decided to form their own organizations as opposed to join in panethnic ones? As Kibria has suggested in her research on second generation Chinese and Korean Americans, pan-Asian ethnogenesis may be taking place where there are subgroups of Asian Americans forming such as East Asians (Chinese, Japanese, and Korean Americans), South Asians (Asian Indian, Pakistani, and Bangladeshi Americans), and Filipino Americans.[35] These subgroupings may be based on a combination of cultural similarities, phenotype, religion and history. For example, Filipino Americans are unique from other Asian Americans due to their history of Spanish and U.S. colonization/imperialism. For the South Asian community, the aftermath following 9/11 held special significance as members were at higher risk for hate crimes.[36] While in the past, different Asian American ethnic groups have often come together as under the label "Asian American" as a political or economic strategy, these groups may feel more comfortable socializing with people who are more similar to them in experience.

Race and Gender Still Matter

Little research is available on the contemporary experiences of Asian Americans in sororities and fraternities. What little research has been conducted on Asian American Greek-letter organizations has focused on pan-Asian ethnic ones. Unfortunately, at the time of this writing no research had been conducted on the more ethnospecific South Asian and Filipino organizations.

This section focuses on the research of pan-Asian ethnic fraternities and sororities. The evidence available suggests these arenas are important sites for Asian American college students to explore young womanhood and manhood and define what it means to be Asian in America. In short, race and gender continue to shape the lives of Asian American college women and men as it plays out in their experiences with sororities and fraternities.

It should be remembered that Asian American fraternities and sororities continue to persist despite the fact that traditional sororities and fraternities have eliminated the discriminatory clauses and policies that once barred people of color. The rapid growth of Asian American sororities and fraternities in the late 1980s, at the very least, suggests the needs of Asian American students are not fulfilled in mainstream Greek organizations. At worst, a climate of white hegemony continues to exist in these arenas and on university campuses. In Mitchell Chang's study, "Race Identity and Race Relations in Higher Education: Fraternity and Sorority Membership among Students of Color," he examined the participation of students of color in mainstream fraternities and sororities. Chang found that generally white students are still overrepresented in these organizations.[37] Based upon a sample of 300,000 students from 365 four-year colleges and universities across the country, he suggests that white students find shelter in these organizations during times of racial tension or use these clubs as vehicles to perpetuate racial intolerance. Students of color joining these organizations tend to share conservative values with the white students in these groups, including an interest in sports, partying, and believing that one can do little to change society. Therefore, mainstream sororities and fraternities may allow students of color to participate, as long as they do not disrupt the conservative values and structure of these organizations.

My own work, "The Continuing Significance of Race: A Case Study of Asian American Women in White, Asian American, and African American Sororities," is one of the rare studies that includes an in-depth look into experiences of Asian American women in Panhellenic sororities.[38] This qualitative study took place at a large public West Coast university, one of the most diverse in the nation. Consistent with Chang's work, I found that Asian American women were underrepresented in Panhellenic sororities and white women were overrepresented compared to their numbers on campus. Specifically, there were proportionally over four times fewer Asian American women in Panhellenic sororities than at the university. These results are especially shocking given that the university is one of the most diverse in the nation, with a heavy Asian American student population. Similarly,

Julie Park's study, Asian American women were also underrepresented. This study was based at a midsized private university in the Southeast, one of the least diverse in the nation. It should be noted that Park's results are similar to mine, despite the difference in geographic location, size, and type of university.[39] Also, in both studies, the more popular houses or "top houses" tended to be "Whiter," and Asian Americans along with other women of color tended to be located in less popular houses, which had a harder time recruiting members and maintaining quota.[40]

Some may view the integration of Asian American women in traditionally white sororities as a sign of racial progress; however, I argue the participation of Asian American women in these arenas is *not* based upon principles of multicultural democracy, but is conditioned upon submitting to an elite white cultural model of womanhood and definition of American. My study found that Asian American women in mainstream sororities were careful to construct a non-Asian identity in front of their white sisters as a strategy of accommodation. This strategy can be seen when the women spoke of their feelings about Asian American sororities vs. Panhellenic ones. Reasons for not joining an Asian American sorority include, "I was kind of trying not to be Asian," "I didn't want to be seen as just another Asian girl in an Asian sorority," or "I wasn't in tune with my culture yet." Growing up in predominantly white neighborhoods, a couple of women stated they would feel uneasy being around "all Asians," and felt more comfortable around whites. A few others did not see the need for an Asian American sorority, declaring "You're in America now," "Why separate yourself? You should just integrate." Distancing themselves from their immigrant, non-Western roots, several other women spoke more condescendingly of Asian American sororities, citing that they were "too FOBish."[41] These women may have been able to participate in Panhellenic sororities, but not in the way that allowed them to explore issues of race and ethnicity that would critically examine the normative definition of American.

On the other hand, Asian American sororities and fraternities offer safe spaces that allow Asian American students to affirm racial pride and "Asian" cultural values. Asian American women's sense of belonging in their sorority should be understood in the context of feeling out of place in many arenas that are predominantly white. Libby, a Chinese American who grew up in a predominantly Asian American and minority community speaks about her feelings of insecurities in predominately white arenas. "I've never been really fully comfortable in a dominant White environment. I mean, most of my friends have always been Asian. It's not that I can't hang around them. But it's hard for me to identify with them and to feel fully comfortable. I do tend to feel a little inferior."[42]

While it is somewhat expected that Asian American women from Asian and minority communities would feel marginalized in white settings, interestingly, some of those most self-conscious of their "difference" were ones that grew up in predominantly white neighborhoods. Specifically, a third of the women spoke about experiences of being stereotyped, exoticized, denigrated, or subjected to other forms of racial harassment. Part of the appeal of being in an Asian American sorority was they would be among others sharing their minority status. Lydia, a second-generation Korean American, stresses the importance of the sorority being Asian American to her sense of well-being and belonging: "I remember thinking another reason why I would want to go into an Asian American sorority was the fact that because everyone was Asian American, that the issue of being Asian American wasn't an issue. So therefore, you could just be yourself and talk one on one without looking at each other's eyes or color and be like conscious of the fact that they're Asian. It's just not there anymore. You could be yourself. It was just . . . maybe actually feeling like you were normal. I think that's another important thing why I think I joined."[43] Similar results were found in Deborah Lou's study, "We're All Sisters Here: Asian American Women's Experiences from Leftist Politics to Sorority Membership," which took place at a midsized public California university. These women's reasons for joining an Asian American sorority reflected their craving for diversity in an otherwise white-dominated campus environment consisting of "hippie, surfer, and partying cultures." In my study, many of the women, however, were unable to pinpoint exactly why they did not feel comfortable in mainstream settings. Upon probing, they stated they were often ignored and felt excluded in these arenas despite their efforts to assimilate.

Asian American sororities may not be political in the traditional sense; nevertheless they provide a space for Asian American women to come together to act collectively as a racial and gendered minority. Lou's study compares the membership of one Asian American sorority to those in an Asian American student political activist organization. Unlike the activist women, the sorority women rarely discussed racism and sexism as systemic problems. However, they did talk about their personal experiences with these issues. Similar findings were discussed in my work. Lou argues that sororities can be political since they do make claims about Asian American women's specific and discriminated position in society, especially in terms of mainstream Greek culture.[44] The political underpinnings of these Asian Greek-letter organizations then allow Asian American women to explore issues of race, raise their consciousness about the varying needs of the Asian American community, and thereby better serve them.

While Asian American sororities may provide a sense of belonging in a society that otherwise defines them as a stranger or an "other,"[45] this is not to say they are completely alternative from mainstream sororities. Asian American sororities may also be guilty of subscribing to a larger system of sexism, like their mainstream counterparts. This is partly due to the close relations that many Asian American sororities have with Asian American fraternities.

To some extent, Asian American fraternities may help define the popularity of Asian American sororities. In my study, one of my informant's stated, "Well, no one wants to be known as the ugly sorority," which suggests a notion of beauty that emphasizes looks as defined by their attractiveness to men. Browsing the websites of some of the Asian American fraternities, the invitations often feature scantily clad Asian American women in sexually suggestive poses, reminiscent of the cover of the men's magazines *Maxim* or *FHM*. It may be difficult to generalize the nature of Asian American sororities, since sororities can vary in their mission, goals, and activities. At the campus of Lou's study, two Asian American sororities existed—one which had a reputation for being more "down to earth," emphasizing sisterhood and community, while the other seemed more concerned with "image" (partying, social status, clothes, and attracting men).[46] The research thus far suggests that Asian American sororities may struggle between being a source of empowerment for young Asian American women or falling into a disempowering system of (hetero) sexism and elitism.

Like Asian American sororities, the fraternities are important spaces for men to explore issues of race, ethnicity, and masculinity. Having a racialized, gendered space may be especially important for Asian American men, given the dominant images of Asian American men as asexual, emasculated, and nerdy. On the one hand, Asian American men may share stereotypes with their women counterparts of being forever foreign, inferior, nerdy, all looking alike. However, Asian American women are often seen as sexually desirable by the mainstream, albeit often with racialized overtones.[47] Men, on the other hand are not seen as desirable romantic/sexual partners. It has been argued that this mainstream depiction of Asian American men has also psychologically influenced women in how they view Asian American men, leading many to prefer to date and marry white men over their own ethnicity.[48]

Fraternities, then, are a site where Asian American men can redefine their own definition of manhood in a society that defines them as less than so. The only research study on fraternities is Jachinson Chan's work, "Asian American Interest Fraternities: Competing Masculinities at Play."[49] Based on observations and interviews with members of Lambda Phi Epsilon at University of California, Santa Barbara, Chan documents how fraternity members were well aware of the emasculating stereotypes of Asian men. However, as Chan argues, "At the house, a fraternity brother is no longer a minority and he does not have to deal with the stereotypes associated with Asian American men. Indeed, the fraternity house provides a context for normality for the Lambdas." This includes performing male rituals such as gambling, smoking, drinking, playing video games, playing sports, as well as theme parties (Vegas, '50s gangsters, Togas, Pajamas), which create friendship opportunities and meeting potential girlfriends. Also, they organize parties at five-star hotels, drive expensive cars, and spend money generously. The fraternity provides a context for Asian American men to define themselves as well-assimilated, fun-loving, and (hetero)sexual, countering the mainstream image of the nerdy model minority.[50] These kinds of activities are not unique to Lambdas but are common among Asian American fraternities as one can see by perusing the various organizational websites.

While fraternities may offer an alternative outlet for Asian American men, they may also reinforce the status quo through acceptance of (hetero)sexism, much like mainstream fraternities. Markers of this kind of manhood are revealed in Lambda Phi Epsilon's *forLife* magazine in which one can see young Asian American men stylishly dressed with their arms draped around their girlfriends. Another page reveals a full-page photo of a proud Lambda brother posing with Sung Hi Lee, a Korean American model and actress famous for her multiple appearances in *Playboy* magazine.[51] The elevation of male masculinity may reject the racial imagery imposed upon Asian American men, but at the same time it conforms to mainstream notions of masculinity in its complicitness, if not embracement of the objectification of Asian American women. Chan eloquently sums up the contradictory space that fraternities, such as the Lambdas, occupy: "While mainstream fraternities do not necessarily recruit or welcome Asian American men, the Asian American interest fraternity replicates the activities and rituals of mainstream Greek fraternities. This tension reflects the dilemma that many Asian American men face. Although they recognize that stereotypes and glass ceilings limit their opportunities to compete with their White male counterparts, the desire to be a part of a normative model of manhood overrides the critique of a system that seeks to exclude Asian American men in the first place."[52]

Ultimately, this kind of masculinity, defined by competitiveness, physical toughness, and heterosexism can be destructive as seen in the death of Alam Kim. For years, Lambda Phi Epsilon and Pi Alpha Phi had been competing for dominance in terms of "members, prestige and girls."[53] This rivalry escalated on January 21, 2003, in San Jose, California. Tensions had been building between the two groups when a fight broke out between the San Jose State chapters of Pi Alpha Pi and Lambda Phi Epsilon that had the backing from their brothers of the UC Santa Cruz chapter. The fight led to the death of Alam Kim, a member of the San Jose State chapter of Lambda Phi Epsilon, who was trying to stop the fight. A number of others were seriously injured and went to the hospital.[54] These two groups were known to openly haze their new members, in which pledges of the two fraternities would walk around with cuts and bruises. At one point, "Death Row Lambdas," as they called themselves, had featured in their website a wooden electric chair with leather straps, with the words, "Have a seat, buckle up, enjoy the ride." Other incidences involving the organization include a drug raid in Riverside, California, and gunshots during a fight at the Austin, Texas, fraternity house.[55] Also at the University of Texas chapter, one young member died of alcohol poisoning during a celebration of the induction of new members in 2005.[56]

In another fatal incident, Kenny Luong, a nineteen-year-old pledge died after a football game in Irvine, the final initiation ritual of nine weeks of pledging.[57] The football game, which was a "rough, no-pads, no helmets tackle contest for pledges" left other pledges injured on the sidelines, while Luong and the remaining three others on the field battled it out with the opposing team of twenty, members of the Irvine chapter of Lambda Phi Epsilon. Luong eventually died of head injuries suffered from the game.

Many Asian American fraternity members have argued that these isolated incidents do not represent the overall mission and goals of Asian American fraternities, which they say emphasize community service, academics, and brotherhood. For example, the chapter of Lambda Phi Epsilon at UC Santa Cruz has participated in the Santa Cruz AIDS Walk, bone-marrow drives for Asian Americans, and a campus multicultural festival.[58] The chapter also received a Greek Service award from the chancellor. By providing community service, Asian American students become aware of the different needs of the Asian American community that otherwise may have gone unnoticed. Additionally, many members know little about their cultural heritage before becoming members, explained Brian Gee, former national president of the Pi Alpha Phi fraternity.[59]

Like Asian American sororities, Asian American fraternities may also struggle between defining themselves in a liberatory way—one that emancipates them from the racialized images by the mainstream—and reconnecting to the larger Asian American community; and reinforcing normative notions of masculinity that stresses material wealth, physical aggressiveness, (hetero) sexual prowess, and competitiveness. Some Asian American fraternities may be making steps toward freeing themselves from negative aspects of Greek life by providing alternative ways of socializing, such as forbidding drinking and smoking at their functions.[60]

Conclusion

The research on Asian Americans in sororities and fraternities speak to the need for more research on this group's social experiences in college. Despite the prevalence of Asian Americans in colleges and universities throughout the country, there is still little written about the social experiences of Asian Americans in higher education. The majority of the work focuses on their academic achievement, reinforcing the idea that Asian Americans are the model minority. Academics is only one aspect of the college experience. The social experience should not be overlooked.

Exclusionary race-based policies propelled the formation of Asian American Greek-letter organizations. Today, with the decline of formal barriers, Asian Americans are increasingly found in traditionally white Greek organizations, as well as minority-dominated ones. However, research and available evidence suggest that Asian Americans are still limited from fully participating in mainstream Greek organizations quantitatively and qualitatively. Quantitatively, the studies show that their numbers are dramatically lower than their representation on universities. Qualitatively, the participation of Asian Americans in predominately white arenas often requires them to conform to notions of Anglo-Saxon cultural superiority. In the case of Asian American women in Panhellenic sororities, the acculturation of Asian Americans women may entail accepting/adopting racist notions of Asians as homogeneous, "FOBish," inferior, and "nerdy." In other words, while Asian Americans may be allowed to "assimilate," this will not necessarily "set them free."[61]

The growth and persistence of Asian American–specific sororities and fraternities suggests the need for spaces that allow young Asian American men and women to explore issues of race, ethnicity, and gender and to define themselves on their own terms. In today's social climate where minority focused organizations are seen as examples of "reverse racism," these stories reveal that the persistence of minority-specific organizations, such as Asian American sororities and fraterni-

Table 2 Asian American Fraternities, 1916–2005

Fraternity	Place of Origin	Date	Original Ethnic Focus
Alpha Iota Omicron	Illinois	2003	South Asian
Alpha Kappa Omega	Cal State-Hayward	1996	Filipino
Alpha Psi Rho	San Diego State	2000	Pan-Asian
Alpha Rho Pi*	San Diego	1998	Filipino
Alpha Sigma Lambda	Cal State Poly	1993	Pan-Asian
Alpha Xi Omega	Cal-Berkeley	1997	Pan-Asian
Beta Chi Theta	UCLA	1999	South Asian
Beta Kappa Gamma	Texas	1999	South Asian
Beta Omega Phi	USC/Cal State-Los Angeles	1965	Pan-Asian
Chi Rho Omicron	Cal State-Fresno	1995	Filipino
Delta Epsilon Psi	Texas	1998	South Asian
Delta Epsilon Sigma Iota*	SUNY-Buffalo	1997	Asian Indian
Delta Phi Beta*	Cal-Berkeley	1992	South Asian
Delta Sigma Iota*	Penn State	2000	South Asian
Gamma Epsilon Omega	USC	1963	
Iota Nu Delta	SUNY-Binghamton	1994	South Asian
Lambda Phi Epsilon	UCLA	1981	Pan-Asian
Lambda Theta Delta	Cal-Irvine	1983	Pan-Asian
Nu Alpha Phi	SUNY-Albany	1994	Pan-Asian
Omega Phi Gamma	Texas	1995	Pan-Asian
Omega Sigma Tau	UCLA	1966	Japanese
Pi Alpha Phi	Cal-Berkeley	1926	Chinese
Psi Chi Omega	Cal-San Diego	1992	Pan-Asian
Pi Delta Psi	SUNY-Binghamton	1994	Pan-Asian
Rho Psi	Cornell	1916	Chinese
Sigma Beta Rho	Penn	1996	South Asian
Sigma Chi Alpha	Penn	1996	Pan-Asian?
Theta Delta Beta	Cal-Irvine	1990	Filipino
Xi Kappa	Georgia	1997	Pan-Asian
Zeta Chi Epsilon	San Francisco State	1991	Pan-Asian
Zeta Epsilon Tau	USC (relocated to Cal State-Long Beach in 1988)	1971	Pan-Asian
Zeta Phi Rho	Cal State-Long Beach	1995	Filipino

*indicates coed fraternity

Table 3 Asian American Sororities, 1928–2005

Sorority	Place of Origin	Date	Original Ethnic Focus
Alpha Delta Kappa	USC	1977	Pan-Asian
Alpha Kappa Delta Phi	Cal-Berkeley	1989	Pan-Asian
Alpha Kappa Omicron	San Francisco State	mid '90s	Filipina
Alpha Phi Gamma	Cal State Poly	1994	Pan-Asian
Alpha Sigma Rho	Georgia	1997	Pan-Asian
Chi Alpha Delta	UCLA	1928	Japanese
Chi Delta Theta	Cal-Santa Barbara	1989	Pan-Asian
Chi Sigma Alpha	Washington	2002	Pan-Asian
Chi Sigma Phi	Cal State-Fullerton	2000	Pan-Asian
Delta Chi Lambda	Arizona	2000	Pan-Asian
Delta Kappa Delta	Texas A & M	1999	Asian Indian
Delta Phi Kappa	USC	1960	Pan-Asian
Delta Phi Lambda	Georgia	1998	Pan-Asian
Delta Phi Omega	Houston	1998	South Asian
Delta Sigma Psi	San Diego State	1998	Pan-Asian
Kappa Phi Alpha	Baruch-CUNY	1997	Pan-Asian
Kappa Phi Gamma	Texas	1998	South Asian
Kappa Phi Lambda	SUNY-Binghamton	1995	Pan-Asian
Kappa Psi Epsilon	Cal State-Long Beach	1996	Filipina
Kappa Zeta Phi	Cal State-Los Angeles	1960	Pan-Asian
Omega Tau Zeta	Ohio State	2000	Pan-Asian
Phi Zeta Tau	California-Irvine	1983	Pan-Asian
Pi Theta Kappa	Cal State-Northridge	1988	Pan-Asian
Rho Delta Chi	Cal-Riverside	1991	Pan-Asian
Sigma Alpha Phi	San Jose State	1995	Pan-Asian
Sigma Kappa Chi	Cal-Santa Barbara	1993	Pan-Asian
Sigma Lambda Kappa	Parsons School of Design	1999	Pan-Asian
Sigma Omicron Pi	San Francisco State (re-established at Cal-Berkeley in 1946)	1930	
Sigma Phi Omega	USC	1949	Japanese
Sigma Psi Zeta	SUNY-Albany	1994	Pan-Asian
Sigma Sigma Rho	St. John's	1998	South Asian
Theta Kappa Phi	UCLA	1959	Japanese

ties, is often times the result of continuing white hegemony, as well as the search for places where their participation is meaningful. Asian American sororities and fraternities are like a home, a place that provides some protection against racism, where Asian Americans can develop self-definitions of themselves as Asian American, nurture their ethnic and racial identities, and provide comfort and joy for one another. However, the evidence also suggests that they are not completely free of problems. While these systems somewhat acknowledge racism, Asian American Greek-letter organizations may tolerate, if not actively promote, sexism, class hierarchies, and homophobia. To be truly oppositional, these organizations will need to contend with these issues as well.

Notes

1. Shirley Jennifer Lim, "Girls Just Wanna Have Fun: The Politics of Asian American Women's Public Culture, 1930–1960" (PhD diss., University of California, Los Angeles, 1998). Also see her book, *A Feeling of Belonging: Asian American Women's Public Culture, 1930–1960* (New York: New York University Press, 2005), which is based upon her dissertation.

2. Research on the current number of Asian American sororities and fraternities was compiled based upon information from Association of Fraternity Advisors, *Related Links*, http://fraternityadvisors.org/links.htm and htttp://en.wikipedia.org/wiki/Cultural_interest_fraternities_and_sororities#Asian.

3. For a more complex analysis on the representation of Asian American students in higher education, see Shirley Hune and Kenyon S. Chan, "Special Focus: Asian Pacific American Demographic and Educational Trends," in *Minorities in Higher Education, 15th Annual Status Report*, ed. Deborah Carter and Reginald Wilson (Washington, DC: American Council on Education, 1997), 39–67, 103–7. Also see Dana Takagi, *The Retreat from Race: Asian-American Admissions and Racial Politics* (New Brunswick, NJ: Rutgers University Press, 1992) for a provocative account on how Asian American students were viewed by faculty and admission officers.

4. For a comprehensive historical treatment of the Asian American experience, see Sucheng Chan, *Asian Americans: An Interpretive History* (Boston: Twayne Publishers, 1991).

5. Probably one of the most traumatic events in recent U.S. history that illustrates the racial divide between whites and people of color is the internment of 120,000 Japanese Americans, most of whom were U.S. citizens, during World War II. At war with Japan, the U.S. justified the internment of Japanese Americans because they were deemed to be "an enemy race," whose "racial affiliations [were] not severed by migration" (General John L. DeWitt cited in Chan, *Asian Americans*, 125).This treatment was not imposed upon German and Italian Americans despite the fact that the U.S. was also at war with Germany and Italy.

6. Sucheng Chan details the difficult economic lives of the Asian Americans in chapter 2, "Immigration and Livelihood, 1840s to 1930s," as well as "Hostility and Conflict, " (Chan, *Asian Americans* 25–42, 45–56).

7. In 1870, Congress amended the Nationality Act of 1790, which had limited citizenship through naturalization to "free white persons," specifically excluding African Americans and Native Americans. The 1870 amendment extended the right to naturalize to persons of African ancestry while deliberately denying the Chinese and later other Asian immigrants this right. Consequently, Asian immigrants were not allowed to vote or become members of the body politic. Not until 1943, when Congress rescinded the Chinese Exclusion Act, were the Chinese able to become naturalized citizens. Filipina/os and Asian Indians gained naturalization rights in 1946, under the Tydings-McDuffie Act, and other Asian groups in 1952 under the McCarren-Walter Act. See Bill Ong Hing, *Making and Remaking Asian America through Immigration Policy, 1850–1990* (Stanford, CA: Stanford University Press, 1993), 23, 36–37, 45.

8. Antimiscegenation laws were especially detrimental to the formation of Asian American communities, given that restrictive immigration led to the development of primarily male communities, also known as "bachelor societies" Chan, *Asian Americans*, 103–11. Asian-white marriages were prohibited in California by various antimiscegenation laws beginning in 1880. Not until 1948 were California's miscegenation statutes declared unconstitutional, and not until 1967 were all such statutes in the United Stated eliminated. See Dick Osumi, "Asians and California's Anti-Miscegenation Laws" in *Asian and Pacific American Experiences*, ed. Nobuya Tsuchida (Minneapolis: Asian/Pacific American Learning Resources Center, University of Minnesota, 1982), 1–37 and Chan, *Asian American*, 59–61.

9. Chan, *Asian Americans*, 57–58.

10. Ibid., 58.

11. Judy Yung, *Unbound Feet: A Social History of Chinese Women in San Francisco* (Berkeley: University of California Press, 1995), 127; David K. Yoo, *Growing Up Nisei: Race, Generation, and Culture among Japanese Americans of California, 1924–1949* (Urbana: University of Illinois Press, 2000), 161.

12. Yung, *Unbound Feet*, 128.

13. *Pacific Ties*, May/June 1982, 15, cited from Lim, "Girls Just Wanna Have Fun," 33.

14. Part of the Survey of Race Relations (1924–1927)—directed by Robert Park, discussed in Yoo, *Growing Up Nisei*, 26–27.

15. www.rhopsi.org; www.lamdaphiepsilon.edu; Office of Workforce Diversity, Equity and Life, Quality, "The Cornell University Story: A Holistic Approach to Diversity and Inclusiveness," at www.ohr.cornell.edu/commitment/ publications/ Cornell_Story_2005.pdf.

16. Chan, *Asian Americans*, 179

17. Pi Alpha Phi fraternity, www.pialphaphi.com.

18. Ronald Takaki, *Strangers from a Different Shore: A History of Asian American.* (New York: Penguin Books, 1989), 218–20; Chan, *Asian Americans*, 113–15.

19. Pi Alpha Phi fraternity, www.pialphaphi.com.

20. Helen Lefkowitz Horowitz, *Campus Life: Undergraduate Cultures from the End of the Eighteenth Century to the Present* (Chicago: University of Chicago Press, 1988), 275; Alfred M. Lee, *Fraternities Without Brotherhood: A Campus Report on Racial and Religious Prejudice* (Boston: Beacon, 1955).

21. Lim, *A Feeling of Belonging*, chapter 1.

22. Ibid., 27.

23. Ibid., 31–32.

24. Lauren Bonifacio, "Minority Greeks Lack Row Home," *Daily Trojan Online*, June 29, 2005. Available at www.dailytrojan.com/media/paper679/previousarchive/ V150/N66/01–minor.66c.shtml.

25. Lee, *Fraternities Without Brotherhood*, 78–79.
26. Lee , *Fraternities Without Brotherhood*, 93–94 cited in Julie Park, "Melting Pot or Greek Salad: A Study of Asian American Women and sororities at a Predominantly White Institution" (Unpublished Undergraduate Thesis, Vanderbilt University, 2004), 1.
27. Lee, *Fraternities Without Brotherhood*, 77, cited from Park, "Melting Pot or Greek Salad," 21.
28. Theta Kappa Phi, http://www.thetakappaphi.com.
29. Yen Le Espiritu, *Asian American Panethnicity: Bridging Institutions and Identities* (Philadelphia: Temple University Press 1992), 27, 30–32.
30. See Shirley Hune, "Demographic and Diversity of Asian American College Students," *New Directions for Student Services: Working with Asian American College Students* 97 (2002): 13.
31. Ibid., 13
32. Jane Singh, "South Asians: New Communities and New Challenges" in *The New Face of Asian Pacific America: Numbers, Diversity & Change in the 21st Century*, ed. Eric Lai and Dennis Arguelles (Asian Week and UCLA's Asian American Studies Center Press, 2003).
33. K.V. Rao, "Instant Identity: The Emergence of Asian Indian America," in *The New Face of Asian Pacific America: Numbers, Diversity & Change in the 21st Century*, ed. Eric Lai and Dennis Arguelles (Asian Week and UCLA's Asian American Studies Center Press, 2003).
34. Melany Dela Cruz and Pauline Agbayani-Siewert, "Filipinos: Swimming with and against the Tide," in *The New Face of Asian Pacific America: Numbers, Diversity & Change in the 21st Century*, ed. Eric Lai and Dennis Arguelles (Asian Week and UCLA's Asian American Studies Center Press, 2003).
35. Nazli Kibria, *Becoming Asian American: Second-Generation Chinese and Korean American Identities* (Baltimore: John Hopkins University Press, 2002), 204–5.
36. See National Asian Pacific American Legal Consortium, "2001 Audit of Violence Against Asian Pacific Americans, Ninth Annual Report" (February 2003), Available at http://www.advancingequality.org/dcm.asp?id=50.
37. Mitchell Chang, "Race Identity and Race Relations in Higher Education: Fraternity and Sorority Membership Among Students of Color" (paper presented at the Association for the Study of Higher Education National Conference, Orlando, Florida, November, 1995).
38. Edith Chen, "The Continuing Significance of Race: A Case Study of Asian American Women in White, Asian American, and African American Sororities" (PhD diss., University of California, Los Angeles, 1998).
39. Park, "Melting Pot or Greek Salad," 29–30.
40. Ibid, 77–82.
41. American born and raised Asian Americans will sometimes derogatively refer to Asian American immigrants or those Asian Americans who are not attuned to Western cultural aesthetics and behavior as "FOBs." While Asian American sororities do have some 1.5 generation Asian Americans, the overwhelming majority of them are American born. The term "FOBish" used by Asian American women in Panhellenic sororities to describe Asian American sororities may reflect these women's own insecurities about being mistaken as foreign born and the need to conform to mainstream definitions of "American," which includes being born in America (rather than in Asia), speaking "American" accented English (rather than Asian accented English), and embracing Western cultural traditions (rather than Asian cultural traditions).
42. Chen, "The Continuing Significance of Race," 88.

43. Ibid., 88–89.
44. Deborah Lou, "We're All Sisters Here: Asian American Women's Experiences from Leftist Politics to Sorority Membership" (master's thesis, University of California, Santa Barbara, 1998), 121.
45. Takaki, *Strangers from a Different Shore;* Alice Hom, "In the Mind of An/Other," *Amerasia Journal* (1991): 41–42.
46. Lou, "We're All Sisters Here," 77.
47. Some may suggest that Asian American women may have an easier time being accepted into the mainstream, as seen in the greater outmarriage rates and their representation in mainstream media. However, I argue that this acceptance often times is based upon a relationship that sees Asian American women as ultrafeminine and inferior to white heterosexual males. Evidence includes the overrepresentation of Asian American women in mainstream porn, their depiction in mainstream media as sex objects for white men, and the prevalence of the "Asian fetish." The greater acceptance of Asian American women is not because race does not matter for Asian American women, rather it reveals the necessity of looking at the intersectionality of race and gender when examining the experiences of Asian American women and men. In other words, the pairing of Asian American women and white men does not disrupt the normative heterosexual, white dominant, patriarchal hierarchical order. Darrell Y. Hamamoto offers a provocative discussion on the construction of Asian American male and female sexuality in "The Joy Fuck Club: Prolegomenon to an Asian American Porno Practice," in *Countervisions: Asian American Film Criticism*, ed. Darrel Y. Hamamoto and Sandra Liu, (Philadelphia: Temple University Press, 2000).
48. This is a very popular topic among Asian American youth as demonstrated in the number of Asian American online discussions such as modelminority.com. For an excellent overview of Hollywood's depiction of Asian American women and men, see *Slaying the Dragon*, dir. by Deborah Gee; executive producer, Asian Women United; 60 minutes, National Asian American Telecommunications Association, film, 1988.
49. Jachinson Chan, "Asian American Interest Fraternities: Competing Masculinities at Play," in *Asian Pacific American Genders and Sexualities*, ed. Thomas K. Nakayma (Tempe, AZ: Arizona State University, 1999), 65–73.
50. Ibid., 68–70.
51. Ibid., 68.
52. Ibid., 69.
53. http://nationamaster.comn/encyclopedia/Pi-Alpha-Phi
54. Suzanne Herel et al., "Fraternity Feud's Unlikely Victim: Friends Say Man Tried to End Rivalry," *San Francisco Chronicle*, January 26, 2003.
55. Roy Rivenburg, "Asian Frat in Spotllight After Death," *Los Angeles Times*, September 7, 2005.
56. http://en.wikipedia.org/wiki/Lambda_Phi_Epsilon.
57. David Reyes and H. G. Reza, "Fraternity Held Edge at Fatal Ballgame," *Los Angeles Times*, September 1, 2005.
58. Jondi Gumz, "UCSD suspends fraternity involved in fight," *Sentinel*, January 25, 2003.
59. May Chow, "San Jose State Frat Brawl Ends in Death of 23–Year-Old APA," *AsianWeek*, January 31–February 6, 2003.
60. Rivenberg, "Asian Frat in Spotlight."
61. Edward Iwata, "Race without a Face," *San Francisco Focus*, May 1991, 50–53, 128–30.

Nuestra Historia y Futuro (Our History and Future): Latino/a Fraternities and Sororities

Susana M. Muñoz and Juan R. Guardia

THE EFFORTS OF LATINO/A[1] STUDENTS TO FORM GREEK-LETTER organizations at the turn of the twentieth century marks an auspicious beginning. Not only were they pioneers on the part of Latino/a college students in forming their own organizations, they represent Latino/a students' ability to take a traditionally white institution—college fraternities and sororities—and reshape it for their own interests and needs. Although there were only a scattering of Latino/a Greek-letter organizations (LGLOs) founded in the 1970s, it was not until the 1990s that LGLOs became prominent on many college campuses across the nation. Today, there are over thirty-five established LGLOs. Their development offers a tremendous catalyst for promoting Latino and Latina student success and cultural awareness.

In many cases, institutions fail to understand the complexities and history of why these organizations exist. The history of LGLOs may provide institutions a peek into the values and mission that guide them. This knowledge may provide Greek advisors, campus activities directors, and vice-presidents a sense of how institutions can meet the needs of and support LGLOs. Additionally, lack of institutional knowledge of the Hispanic/Latino culture is a factor that facilitates Latino/a perceptions and reports of racial tension and discrimination on campus.[2]

In this chapter, we pull together the paucity of research on LGLOs. In an effort to provide a better understanding of these groups, we begin with the roots of Latino/as in higher education, followed by the early activism and the foundation of Latino student organizations. Then we discuss the history of LGLOs, the establishment of a national Latino/a Greek umbrella organization, and perspectives from founding sorority and fraternity members, and we share our personal reflections as members of our respective LGLOs. Finally, we discuss research conducted on LGLOs and share some thoughts on working with LGLOs.

Early Activism and the Foundation of Latino Student Organizations

One cannot discuss the historical perspectives of Latino student organizations or LGLOs without including a brief history of Latinos in higher education. In 2003, the United States (U.S.) Census Bureau announced that Hispanics are the nation's largest minority group. Latinos represent 37.4 million people in the U.S., which constitutes 13.3 percent of the total population.[3] "Although Hispanics are the fastest-growing minority in the U.S., their numbers at all levels of the educational system in this country have not kept pace with their population growth."[4] MacDonald and Garcia discussed how "the pipeline to college for Latinos has generally been blocked at the lowest levels of schooling . . . as a result, it was not until the last quarter of the twentieth century that Latinos entered higher education in significant numbers."[5] By 2002, Hispanics had only earned 11.1 percent of bachelor's degrees and the breakdown was: Mexican 7.6 percent, Puerto Rican 14.0 percent, Cuban 18.6 percent, and Central and South American 17.3 percent.[6]

Early student activism can be traced back to Chicano[7] and Puerto Rican students with "a concrete agenda to change the role of Latino students on campus as other than privileged exceptions." The goal for these students was to demand a variety of services, specifically geared to aide in access and retention for their respective community.[8] We will discuss these two separate communities individually.

Most agree that Chicano/a student activism began on college campuses in the 1920s when Ernesto Galaraza, a Stanford University graduate student in history, spoke in support of oppressed Mexican immigrant workers in California during a National Conference on Social Work. Without the support of any social, academic, or cultural organization, Galaraza rebuked racist notions and perceptions of Mexicans as lazy and inassimilable. Contrary to public opinion, Galaraza stated that "the very economic structure of the United States rests on the blood and sweat of the [Mexican] immigrant without any true commitment for the well being of the people."[9] Galaraza wanted society to recognize that Chicanos/as and other Latinos/as had contributed to the building and growth of the United States through hard labor.

Chicanos were treated like second-class citizens, and the majority Eurocentric culture tried to systematically transform them into a product of mainstream society through acculturation. The public and private school systems gave Mexican-American children a large dose of white-American traditional values, which contributed to the erosion of indigenous cultural pride. Mexican-American youth were confused about their self-identity because the schools promoted one set of traditional values, while individual families remained loyal to Mexican virtues and values. These issues with Chicano youth became an important stepping stone for creating community support systems. Thus, during the 1940s and 1950s, Chicanos directed their energies toward gaining power by creating community and political organizations to address Chicano issues. These organizations included the Mexican American Movement (MAM), the Association of Mexican American Educators (AMAE), the Political Association of Spanish Speaking Peoples (PASSO), and the League of United Latin American Citizens (LULAC).[10]

During the late 1960s, the quest to diversify college campuses began at various institutions across the nation. In 1968, the first Latino protest on a college campus occurred at San Jose State College in California. Graduating seniors and audience members "walked out of commencement exercises to protest the underrepresentation of Chicano students and lack of bilingual and cultural training for professionals who worked in Latino communities.[11]

In Colorado, Rodolfo "Corky" Gonzales led and hosted the first National Chicano Youth Liberation Conference in Denver, Colorado.[12] This conference set the stage for dissemination of information about civil rights, nationalist ideology, and Chicano self-identity to youth on college campuses and throughout Chicano communities. Students began to understand the purpose of taking a revolutionary stance by making their college education beneficial to the overall Chicano community, rather than using education as a stepping stone to increased individual socioeconomic mobility—an accepted core value of American society. This motivated Chicanos to enter their colleges with a nationalist and revolutionary attitude toward attaining their degrees. Chicano student activism was born.

This conference is known in Chicano history as the "founding" of the Chicano Student Organizations, and it also served as the impetus for Chicano students to take an active role in addressing the needs of Mexican Americans at institutions of higher education. In addition, El Movimento Estudiantil Chicano de Aztlan, or the Chicano Student Movement of Aztlan (MEChA) formed as an organization at many campuses and advocated educational civil rights and equal access.[13]

The Puerto Rican student experience has different beginnings. In 1898, the United States acquisition of Puerto Rico "resulted in the introduction of American schools and the English language in Puerto Rico" and "by 1905, almost five hundred Puerto Ricans were attending American institutions as a means of building pride in the United States and educating officials to staff the colonial government."[14] Thus began the Americanization of Puerto Ricans on the island and attending mainland schools in order to better their country.

Puerto Rican students began to form their own student organizations in response to their population increase in the mid-twentieth century. One organization, ASPIRA (aspire) was formed in 1961 by educator and leader Antonia Pantoja, "to empower the Puerto Rican and Latino community through advocacy and the education and leadership development of its youth."[15] Organizations such as ASPIRA and others assisted Puerto Rican students to raise awareness and issues confronted in their community, including the Puerto Rican Student Movement at City University of New York, the Puerto Rican Alliance at Brooklyn College, and the Puerto Rican Student Union at Hunter College.

As Mexican-Americans chose Chicano/a to signify pride in their culture, Puerto Ricans chose the term "Boricua"[16] as a symbolic term of endearment to describe their homeland and became the chosen ideology for many student organizations during the 1960s.[17] The lessons learned from student activism during the 1960s continue to resonate with many LGLOs. It is when Latinos/as face micro- and macroaggressions on college campuses that they turn to each other for solutions. The principles of unity and organization emphasized during the civil rights movement is once again applied on college campuses in order to gain voice and basic acknowledgment of the needs of Latino/a students.

The History of Latino/a Greek-letter Organizations (LGLO)

There are four phases that describe the history of LGLOs. The "principio" (the beginning) phase consisted of "secret societies" that existed across the nation in the late 1800s and later merged into one fraternity in the East Coast.[18] During the "fuerza" (force) phase, LGLOs were established based on the necessity for survival and to have a stronger voice on college campuses. The "fragmentación" (fragmentation) phase saw the rapid expansion of LGLOs to form a national umbrella group in an effort to unite all LGLOs. Currently, in the "adelante" (moving forward) phase, Latino Greeks are moving forward with well-developed national infrastructures.

Phase I: Principio (1898–1980)

As mentioned previously, Latino student organizations have been in existence since the late 1800s, but due to limited research and historical documentation, one may argue otherwise. Phi Iota Alpha Fraternity, Inc. can trace its roots to 1898 when a group of elite Latin American men organized the Union Hispano Americana (UHA) organization at Rensselaer Polytechnic Institute in Troy, New York. Although not a Greek-letter organization, UHA conceptualized the values of a fraternal organization by providing a cultural and intellectual safe haven for its members. UHA proceeded to operate outside its New York parameters and connect with similar groups across the nation. These "secret societies" connected with comparable organizations at other universities to discuss the possibility of forming a well-rooted organization. UHA later merged with Pi Delta Phi (founded at Massachusetts Institute of Technology in 1916) and Phi Lambda Alpha (founded in 1919 at the University of California Berkeley) to form Phi Lambda Alpha in 1921. Phi Lambda Alpha merged with Sigma Iota (founded in 1904 as the Sociedad Hispanio-Americana and in 1912 became the first Latin American fraternity) at Louisiana State University and formed Phi Iota Alpha Fraternity on December 26, 1931.[19] Phi Iota Alpha was incorporated in Louisiana in 1936 and in New York in 1953. The mission of Phi Iota Alpha operates under the ideology of Pan-Americanism, which is "the unification of all Latin American nations and all Latin American people."[20] This reference denotes that the brotherhood of Phi Iota Alpha identified with their Latin American lineage and formed an intellectual group to discuss the social, economic and political problems of their native countries and how these factors were affecting their educational experiences in the United States.

In fall 2004 we had the pleasure of interviewing Phi Iota Alpha Fraternity, Inc. Trustee Tiberio C. Faría, a member of the fraternity since 1956. He provided anecdotal stories of his time in the fraternity and it was very clear that he is proud member of the organization. He went on to describe the membership of the organization at what was then Alpha Chapter at Louisiana State University:

> At that time I attended college, mid 1950s, from its foundation, Phi Iota Alpha had deep political beliefs and criteria. Our members ranged from being very wealthy to not having much money at all, but the organization provided an equalitarian process; no one man was better or worse than another. The prestige that attracted Latino men to the organization was the prestige that followed it: members included ex-presidents and political figures of various Latin American countries, including Colombia, Chile, Honduras and Panama, and many Cabinet Ministers in several other countries. One of our members from Cuba, in time, became the CEO of Bacardi Rum, a large USA based corporation of international fame and projection. Thus, what attracted men to the organization was very different from what the traditional Greek organizations offered: lifelong fellowship and brotherhood, and the motto is: Once a Phi Iota Alpha, always a Phi Iota Alpha.[21]

Mr. Faría's highlights the importance of his fraternity experience as a college student and the lifelong connections he made with his fraternity brothers fifty years ago.

During the 1930s through the early 1950s, there was no expansion of LGLOs in the United States. However, on the island of Puerto Rico, Phi Zeta Chi Fraternity (1958) formed at the University of Puerto Rico-Mayaguez and its sister sorority Eta Phi Zeta (1969) was founded in Arecibo, Puerto Rico. Both of these organizations strive to develop leadership and fellowship, but it is not clear how these organizations function within the realms of the university system. Some writers have also speculated that the University of Havana in Cuba had "secret societies" similar to fraternities. Due to government communism, documenting such activities could have had lethal consequences during that time.[22]

Meanwhile, Phi Iota Alpha Fraternity, Inc. continued to flourish on college campuses across the nation. In addition to the chapters at Louisiana State University and Rensselaer Polytechnic Institute, chapters were established at Tulane University, Indiana Technical College, Tri-State College (now Tri-State University), the University of Michigan, and Columbia University. Many of the members from this period went on to become influential leaders in Latin America. Phi Iota Alpha is the only Latino fraternity whose members have been presidents of three Latin American countries: Colombia—Mariano Ospina Pérez (1946–50) and Carlos Lleras Restrepo (1966–70); Honduras—Carlos Roberto Flores (1998–2002); and Panama—Eric Arturo Delvalle (1985–88).

The year 1975 saw the founding of two new Latino fraternity and sorority organizations in the United States. Kean University (formerly Kean College) in New Jersey witnessed the formation of two organizations: Lambda Theta Alpha Latin Sorority, Inc., the first Latina-based sorority in the nation, and Lambda Theta Phi Fraternidad Latina, Inc., the first Latino fraternity at Kean University. During that time, Kean University was in the midst of establishing a Latino and Caribbean Studies program and like other institutions, students were at the vocal forefront of these developments. As the students organized, Latinas were still underrepresented and struggled for equality. Lambda Theta Alpha founders recognized this concern and created a united sisterhood in order to "compete, collaborate, and assist with any student run programs, thus making their voices as loud and profound as the majority voice."[23]

Meanwhile, the men of Lambda Theta Phi were also working to establish themselves at Kean University. Jesus Peña, a brother of Lambda Theta Phi, wrote about the historical events that led to the formation of his fraternity in *The History of Lambda Theta Phi Latin Fraternity, Incorporated*, the only published history of an LGLO. Peña discussed the disunity among Latino students at Kean University, particularly between

Cubans and Puerto Ricans, and the chilly environment for Latinos in general. He also described a Latino college professor and college administrator, known as the Fraternal Fathers, and how they played an important role in the formation of the organization. The Fraternal Fathers knew that uniting two groups of Latinos could potentially provide a powerful force on campus. One specific event that politicized the fraternity was the student council elections. The group wanted to encourage Latinos to vote in mass numbers but as the fraternity members soon learned, Latino students at the time did not cast their votes simply because they could not understand the voting directions. The fraternity petitioned the student council to provide bilingual instruction in Spanish. When the petition was agreed upon but ignored in the following election, it ignited a series of protests. Instead of filing a legal suit against the university for infringement of civil rights, the Latino students worked within the university system and the student council constitution's bylaws were successfully amended to provide bilingual signage and instructions at every voting booth.[24]

Although political activism was the foundation of the fraternity in 1976, some brothers plunged into developing the ideals and fundamental values of the organization. Throughout the formation of Lambda Theta Phi, the Fraternal Fathers continued to offer guidance and mentorship. In addition, two allies played a role in assisting the fraternity including Sigma Theta Chi Fraternity (a traditional fraternity) and the Veterans' Fraternity, an organization dedicated to support returning Vietnam War veterans. The two organizations shared their constitutions and other documents to aid the Latino fraternity in its development. The Fraternal Fathers challenged the brothers of Lambda Theta Phi to think outside the realms of the university walls and to envision a fraternity that could have a societal impact. The Founding Fathers knew that their fraternity had to be unique and exemplify Latino culture and heritage. Peña stated: "Our brotherhood would be foremost a fraternity of Latino college men—initially undergraduates, eventually alumni. The organization would encourage its members to interact with non-Latinos in every aspect of college life: academic competitions, athletics, cultural events, social functions, and charitable endeavors. In being a well-round, exceptional student, a Lambda could best represent the inherent excellence of Latino manhood."[25]

Although the fraternity acknowledged that it was not separating itself from the university's traditional Greek system, they were also adamant about not assimilating the customs and traditions of traditional white fraternities. The men of Lambda Theta Phi, like many LGLOs, were not going to compromise their Latino culture to be Greek: instead they were adding Latino values and ideals to the Greek system.

In 1976, the last undergraduate chapter of Phi Iota Alpha Fraternity, Inc. closed its doors when Jorge Beal, the last active president, graduated from Louisiana State University. Although the undergraduate chapters were inactive, Phi Iota Alpha alumni remained active with the fraternity in the United States and in Latin America. In 1984, Ivan Moreno, the 1973 fraternal national secretary, passed the torch to an interest group of Latino students at Rensselaer Polytechnic Institute. These men revived the undergraduate spirit of Phi Iota Alpha. Since then, Phi Iota Alpha's undergraduate chapters and alumni chapters have grown nationwide.

In 1978, Latino males began to discuss the idea of forming a Latino fraternity at Rutgers University as a result of controversy between students of color and the university administration. As stated in Lambda Sigma Upsilon Fraternity, Inc. history, "Minority students, in particular, Latinos, felt that they were not getting the attention they so desperately need to succeed in their academic endeavors."[26] In the midst of protests and sit-ins, a group of Latino men met regularly to discuss what they could do to better serve their needs: "these men decided that a Social Fellowship would best provide a support group to other students and also provide a family away from their own." Thereafter, twenty men founded Lambda Sigma Upsilon (1979), which stands for "Latinos Siempre Unidos" (Latinos Always United); this group became the catalyst for the change between the students and the university administration at Rutgers University. The *principio* phase exemplifies the critical role LGLOs played in bringing change to their college campuses. The creation and growth of these LGLOs brought new and complex issues to Greek life on college campuses.

Phase II: Fuerza (1980–90)

The *fuerza* (force) phase brought a new kind of energy to the expansion of LGLOs. Chi Upsilon Sigma Sorority, Inc. (1980) which stands for "Corazones Unidos Siempre" (United Hearts Forever) joined other newly formed organizations at Rutgers University. The main reason this organization was established was because of its "desire to create a sisterhood—a place away from home in which the members could feel the strong sense of family, which is such a strong force in the Latino culture."[27] It is important to recognize that nature of having an extended family in college was, in fact, a mechanism for Latino/as on many college campuses.

Three significant events occurred during this period. Lambda Upsilon Lambda Fraternity, Inc. (1982) was the first LGLO to be founded at an Ivy League institution (Cornell University). Hernando Londono,

Founding Father, established his fraternity because Latino males only had the choice of joining a traditional white or historical black fraternity. In addition, "the existing Latino organizations did not provide enough sense of unity among the Latino population." Londono and twelve other men wanted to form an organization that produced brothers "that will become the leaders of our people, that will make great sacrifices for the benefit of our people, that stand for and live up to the best of the Latino culture."[28] This statement implies that forming a Latino fraternity was a selfless act. No other entity had the Latino community's interests at heart, so these college students took matters into their own hands and provided an avenue to empower and become role models for their communities.

Up to this point, the formation of LGLOs were primarily in the New York and New Jersey region. The second significant event was the establishment of Alpha Psi Lambda National Inc. (1985) at the Ohio State University and Lambda Theta Nu Sorority, Inc. (1986) at California State University—Chico. Alpha Psi Lambda was founded by thirteen men and women making the organization the "nation's first and largest co-ed Latino fraternity."[29] Lambda Theta Nu was the first LGLO to be established on the west coast.[30] Founding Mother Lisa Saldano's testimony on the formation of Lambda Theta Nu described a less than positive climate for Latina college students. Due to the nature of the campus culture, Latinas gravitated toward one another for solitude and support. Saldano spoke about a particular location on campus where sisters could find a friend or a familiar face in uncharted territory:

> Lambda Theta Nu Sorority, Inc. had humble beginnings. Planning meetings on a concrete slab. The same concrete slab where we sat proudly, wearing our letters, even though at times we were chastised, ridiculed, doubted, and told we would never last. The same slab where we knew we could find a sister sitting there and find refuge from our bad day and support to face the new one tomorrow. Where we could always share a triumph, no matter how big or small, with another Latina, a sister, a friend, and confidant, who knew how hard it was to get there. We loved that concrete slab, our corner of the world on campus, our true beginning, our pedestal, our stage. Humble beginnings. We have been through lots together, we've laughed together, we've cried together, but most importantly, we've done it . . . *together* . . . and you all should find comfort in knowing that once you join our family, never again will you stand alone.[31]

This is a revealing statement about why these Latinas bonded together. Many of them were sharing the same experiences and since family support was how many Latinas/os accomplished many of their goals, students attempted to emulate a support system similar to a "family unit" to enhance their chances of success in college.

The third significant event was the establishment of two organizations in two new regions. Sigma Lambda Beta International Fraternity, Inc. (1986) was founded at the University of Iowa, and Kappa Delta Chi Sorority, Inc. (1987) was founded at Texas Tech University. The establishment of LGLOs in these two regions brought more national awareness of LGLOs on college campuses. This was especially the case for Sigma Lambda Beta, since it was founded in Iowa, which does not have a significant Latino population. Sigma Lambda Beta is the only Latino fraternity or sorority to use "international" as part of its formal name. Although they do not have a chapter in another country, the founding fathers represented many countries, such as Bolivia, Cuba, Cambodia, and Mexico.[32]

In closing the *fuerza* stage of Latino Greek history, Omega Delta Phi Fraternity, Inc. (1987) became the first Latino fraternity founded at Texas Tech University, and two more fraternities were founded on the west coast: Gamma Zeta Alpha Fraternity, Inc. (1987), the first Latino fraternity in California, and Nu Alpha Kappa (1988), founded at California Polytechnic State—San Luis Obispo. The women added four more Latina sororities, which were all located in the East Coast region: Señoritas Latinas Unidas/Sigma Lambda Upsilon, Inc. (1987) at Binghamton University, Latinas Promviendo Comunidad/Lambda Pi Chi Sorority, Inc. (1988) at Cornell University (the first Latina sorority founded at an Ivy League institution), Lambda Phi Delta Sorority, Inc. (1988) at University at Buffalo, SUNY, and Omega Phi Beta Sorority, Inc. (1989) at University at Albany, SUNY.

This stage brought an enormous amount of *fuerza* (force) in the expansion of LGLOs across many different regions. The majority of the organizations were still in the infancy stage of developing a national infrastructure. Organizations tended to focus on undergraduate development and often times "national headquarters" were student dormitories or student activities offices instead of actual office buildings. Finally, there was little communication and collaboration among LGLOs outside of their regions. Latino Greek-letter organizations were expanding, but it was still to be determined how they were going to work together.

Phase III: Fragmentacion (1990–2000)

The *fragmentacion* (fragmentation) stage brought a significant amount of expansion that produced both positive and negative results. In some cases, Latino students were arriving on campuses in search of a Latino fraternity or sorority.[33] During this period, only two Latino fraternities were founded: Gamma Phi Sigma (1992), founded at Temple University, and Sigma Delta Alpha (1992), founded at San Jose State University. On the other hand, Latina sororities added seventeen more organizations across the country. Three were established in the state of California: Alpha Pi Sigma Sorority, Inc. (1990), Phi Lambda Rho Sorority, Inc. (1993), and Sigma Omega Nu Latina Sorority, Inc. (1996). Sigma Lambda Gamma National Sorority, Inc. (1990) was the first Latina sorority to be founded in the Midwest at the University of Iowa, followed by two other sororities established in Indiana, Gamma Phi Omega International Sorority, Inc. (1991) and Delta Phi Mu Sorority, Inc. (1991), and Delta Tau Lambda Sorority, Inc. (1994) in Michigan. The East Coast also saw the establishment of five new Latina sororities, including Alpha Rho Lambda Sorority, Inc./Alianza de Raices Latina (1993) at Yale University. The other states in which new Latina sororities were formed were Arizona, Colorado, Florida, and Texas.

One of the reasons that Latina sororities expanded so quickly was because there was unsuccessful communication among existing LGLOs and because founders wanted to start a Latino fraternity or sorority unique to their institution. Founding mother of Sigma Delta Lambda Sorority, Inc. (1996), Christina Daniels, elaborated on her experience:

> Established Latina sororities did not appeal to us primarily because we were not completely aware of what they offered. We researched a few via websites and attempted at contacting a couple, but no one returned our messages fast enough. We wanted to do something now, and not wait until someone maybe returned our emails and phone calls. In addition, we are very proud Tejanas (Texans) and we wanted a sorority that was Texas based and to our limited knowledge and experience, there were not Latina sororities established in Texas. Soon after our founding (as first a student organization), a group of Latinos followed our lead and initiated a chapter of Omega Delta Phi. Since we were not simply chartering from an already established Latina Greek organization and since there was not a Greek council who would recognize us, we had to first establish ourselves as a student organization until our incorporation.[34]

It is important to note that Kappa Delta Chi Sorority, Inc. was in existence at that time but limited research informed Sigma Delta Lambda otherwise. This group of women wanted to establish an organization they could identify with as Texans. Some established LGLOs had no interest in expanding to other campuses, or just wanted to focus their expansion to regional areas. Nevertheless, this vast expansion process across the nation caught the attention of many community and university administrators.

The astonishing growth of LGLOs presented some challenges to college administrators and to the LGLOs themselves. How would these organizations work within the existing Greek system? Many were the only LGLOs on campus, while others operated with several other LGLOs present. Nonetheless, administrators had to find new answers to solve the challenges that faced many college campuses. The Greek system on many college campuses included the National Panhellenic, National Inter-fraternity, or National Pan-Hellenic Councils. Although these councils can amend their bylaws to include LGLO, none of these councils directly address the needs of LGLOs. The Latino Greek community looked toward each other for support and guidance during this particular situation.

Forming a national umbrella organization was a vision that started in the early 1990s on the campus of University at Albany, SUNY when members of Phi Iota Alpha Fraternity, Inc. and Omega Phi Beta Sorority, Inc. established the first national Latino Greek Council in 1991, after negotiating the campus bureaucracy.[35] This organization set the format for creating a larger platform for greater national collaboration and was renamed the Concilio Nacional de Hermandades Latinas (National Council of Latino Brothers and Sisters).[36] Another umbrella organization, the National Association of Latino Fraternal Organizations, Inc., was established in 1998 to unify and improve communication among LGLOs. The two Latino Greek umbrella organizations existed simultaneously and in theory promoted similar goals and objectives. The dividing factor between the two was the national criteria required by the Concilio Nacional de Hermandades Latinas (CNHL). Concilio Nacional de Hermandades Latinas required LGLOs to have ten recognized chapters and have representation of chapters in two different states. The tenth chapter must be at least a year old and the organizing chapter must be at least five years old. During the late 1990s, this singled out the smaller and younger chapters from gaining acceptance into the CNHL. On the other hand, the National Association of Latino Fraternal Organizations (NALFO) criteria was more inclusive of smaller, regional organizations by requiring only a minimum of two chapters, which must be in existence for at least a year. During the NALFO Summit Meeting during the summer of 1999, an Exploratory Committee was created and charged with the mission of creating a plan to unite both umbrella councils through five options: 1) merge under CNHL, 2) merge under NALFO, 3) merge CNHL and NALFO, 4) retain the status quo, and 5) create a new umbrella council from scratch.[37]

A committee of an equal number of CNHL and NALFO representatives reviewed the five proposals and recommended that a merger occur under the NAFLO organization because "it brings together the largest number of LGLO's (in terms of overall numbers) and keeps intact the operating structure of a fully functional and operating umbrella council."[38]

Although this recommendation was supported by the members of the committee "the actions were not."[39] CNHL never merged with NALFO and ceased to exist; however, NALFO continued to operate with the clear purpose "to promote and foster positive interfraternal relations, communication, and development of all Latino Fraternal organizations through mutual respect, leadership, honesty, professionalism, and education."[40] NALFO unites Latino Greek voices and provides empowerment and support to its membership. Currently, twenty-one organizations are under the NALFO umbrella.

Locally, Latino Greeks and other Greek-letter organizations entertained the option of creating the councils on their respective campuses. It was found that creating Multicultural Greek councils benefited both LGLO chapters and university administrators. For current culture-based fraternities and sororities, it is a great way to develop relationships with other Greek organizations, collaborate on programming topics, and share resources. It also provides the university a forum to disseminate important information on policy and regulations. Creating a Multicultural Greek council can also serve as a catalyst for gaining visual presence on campus, but it does not necessarily resolve issues of Greek unity and trust.[41]

The *fragmentacion* stage was characterized by rapid expansion of Latino Greek organizations and new challenges for universities. NALFO was formed to answer the call for unity, and Multicultural Greek councils offered students an alternative resource for support on college campuses.

The state of Latino Greek-letter organizations during this period saw the formation of a stable national infrastructure, which included a sound financial plan, increase of liability insurance, and the establishment of a national headquarters.[42] There was a significant emergence of alumni activity and organizations became more interested in building leadership among alumni members. Larger organizations divided the nation into regions and assigned one person to govern those chapters.

Phase IV: Adelante (2000–present)

The *adelante* (moving forward) stage presents a great surge of excitement for LGLOs. The creation of Latinogreeks.com and other individual Latino/a fraternity and sorority websites allowed the Latino/a community to learn about each others' history and purpose. NALFO continues to increase its momentum and facilitate discussions that are pressing issues in the Latino Greek community. During this time, NALFO launched its first annual Latino Greek awards gala in 2000, which recognized undergraduates, organizations, and alumni for their accomplishments. Additionally, NALFO collaborated with the National

Order of Omega to create its own Order of Omega chapter "which recognizes individuals who exemplify the ideals of Greek Life, and has adopted St. Jude's Children's Hospital as its national philanthropy."[43] Currently, NALFO is working on developing local NALFO councils for regional areas.

As NALFO continues to spearhead the national agenda for LGLOs, many organizations are moving toward operating as business corporations rather than student-driven entities. LGLOs are establishing educational foundations in order to create scholarship awards for college students, Latino step teams are becoming nationally visible, and as membership increases, organizations are focusing on risk management and liability issues. Finally, established alumni associations are increasing in numbers and provide leadership development and professional growth.

LGLOs can find optimism in the *adelante* stage. The increase of communication and collaboration among these organizations demonstrated strength and national unity. NALFO has been instrumental in creating a vision and advocating for Latino Greeks on a national front. Latino Greeks will no longer be "unknown," and thanks to NALFO, colleges and universities are able to call upon a national entity that can assist them in working to construct better environments for Latino Greek success. Through the voices of two founders, the next section of this chapter will illustrate how and why LGLOs were formed.

"Nuestra Voz": Voices from Founding Mothers and Fathers of LGLOs

In order to fully understand the history and experiences of Latino Greeks, it is important to share the voices of members who started these organizations. Two founders, Dr. Irma Almirall-Padamsee of Latinas Promoviendo Comunidad/Lambda Pi Chi Sorority, Inc. and Mr. Ricardo Zamudio of Sigma Lambda Beta International Fraternity, Inc. provided information on the beginnings of their organizations, what has changed since their inceptions, and where they believe the organization is headed. Before sharing their stories, background information about each organization is provided.

The history of Latinas Promoviendo Comunidad/Lambda Pi Chi Sorority, Inc. dates back to 1988 when the organization was established as the first Latina-based sorority at an Ivy League institution, Cornell University. The five founding Hermanas (sisters) were Patricia Rivera, Maria Caban, Eva Marie Sosa, Migdalia Franklin, and Dr. Irma Almirall-Padamsee. These five women "strove to establish an organization that would transcend their collegiate experience and consolidate their strength as responsible members of the community."[44] As the mission statement of Lambda Pi Chi states:

> We, Las Hermanas de Latinas Promoviendo Comunidad/ Lambda Pi Chi Sorority, Inc., founded at Cornell University on April 16, 1988, pledge to promote the distinguished ideals of La Comunidad, La Cultura Latina, y La Hermandad [The Community, the Latino/a Culture, and Sisterhood]. Through the support and strength of Nuestra Hermandad, we aim to advance the Latino Community through dedicated service, as well as foster an appreciation for Nuestra Cultura Latina [Our Latina Culture]. It is through the sincere knowledge that La Hermandad Nunca Termina [The Sisterhood Never Ends] that we will accomplish all we have set out to do.[45]

Since 1988, the organization has grown to twenty-one undergraduate and professional chapters spanning the eastern United States and is a member of the NALFO.

Lambda Pi Chi is committed to the three ideals on which the organization was founded—*La Comunidad, La Cultura Latina, and La Hermandad*—namely, the community, the Latina culture, and sisterhood. These ideals seek "to empower women by providing a supportive network dedicated to their personal and professional advancement. Our special sisterhood is further enhanced by our shared dedication and promotion of public service and cultural awareness, with an emphasis on Latinos."[46] Thus, Latinas Promoviendo Comunidad/ Lambda Pi Chi Sorority, Inc. has been effective in uniting women from all ethnic and racial backgrounds to achieve the common goal of the organization and *La Comunidad* [The Community].

Sigma Lambda Beta International Fraternity, Inc. was established in 1986 at the University of Iowa. The "Lambda Betas," nickname of the organization, began with eighteen founding fathers from various countries, including Cambodia, Cuba, and Mexico, as well as Puerto Rico. As the history states: "Our Founding Fathers had a dream and vision that our Honorable Fraternity could promote a positive image of the Latino Community in the University of Iowa and other Universities located throughout the Nation by scholastic achievements, eternal Brotherhood, the dissemination of our unique and rich culture, and service to our community."[47] Since its inception, the organization has expanded to seventy-one undergraduate chapters, fifteen colonies, and twelve alumni chapters. Sigma Lambda Beta is a member of the North-American Interfraternity Council and in 2003 became a member of NALFO.

The fraternity was established with the following principles: Brotherhood, Scholarship, Cultural Awareness, and Community Service.

Brotherhood is described as promoting a family-oriented atmosphere. Scholarship revolves around academic success in higher education and graduate and professional programs. Cultural awareness refers to programmatic events on campuses, including El Dia De Los Muertos, Cinco de Mayo, and Puerto Rican Day Parade to name a few. Community service is an important part of Sigma Lambda Beta. Chapters perform a minimum of two community service events per semester, but often perform more.[48]

The following six questions were asked of each individual: (1) Why did you and others decide to start a Latino fraternal organization? (2) Describe the racial climate at your institution at the time of your attendance. (3) What were some of the challenges with regard to starting your organization? (4) Who were your biggest allies in assisting you to start your organization? (5) Looking at the expansion of Latino Greeks today, is this what you and others envisioned? (6) Would you have done anything differently back then with the information you know now?

The first question provided the founders an open door to share their views about how and why their organizations were started. Dr. Almirall-Padamsee shared her story:

> The community of Latino students and staff at that time (1988) at Cornell was very small. Although there was a student association, which two of the other founders and I started (La Associacion de Latinas Universitarias) [The Association of Latina University Women], it became clear that what many women really wanted and needed was a means by which to foster lifelong, deep friendships. Having a formal means by which women, who were especially interested in the richness of the Latino heritage, perceived themselves as leaders for their communities and were committed to making positive change for the Latino community at the university and after graduation seemed to make sense. We did reflect for a long time whether we should start a Greek organization focused on third-world women's issues, but decided that the challenges facing the Latino community in the U.S. because of historical, economic, and educational reasons was a big enough focus.[49]

Because there were no other Latina Greek-letter organizations at Cornell, the women sought to establish a network in which they could communicate and contribute knowledge and information about the Latino culture, in addition to forming lifelong friendships. Mr. Zamudio explained how Sigma Lambda Beta was founded:

> We decided to start Sigma Lambda Beta [SLB] at The University of Iowa because there were no other fraternal organizations there that had a significant number of members "like us." There were the predominantly white fraternities, the predominantly black fraternities, but there were no predominantly "brown" fraternities. Those organizations did not appeal to

> most of our founders (although there were a couple founders that were already members or considering membership in other fraternal organizations). To the best of my knowledge none of SLB's original founders were aware of existing Latino fraternal organizations, so we decided to go ahead and start our own.[50]

The founders felt that they needed an organization that represented "brown" men, specifically Hispanic or Latino. Of interest is that sixteen of the eighteen founders of Sigma Lambda Beta are of Latin American or Hispanic descent.

The racial and ethnic climates at colleges and universities across the country contribute to the development of students, in and out of the classroom. Climate also proved to be an important factor contributing to the formation of these two organizations. Dr. Almirall-Padamsee said:

> The racial climate at Cornell was difficult because the number of undergrads were small and "misaligned" as compared to the national demographics. That is, of the average 1,700 undergrads of color during those years, over 1,000 were of Asian decent and were counted for Admissions Office information but not included, for example, within the population directly serviced by the Minority Affairs Office on campus. The diversity of the staff and faculty was very limited and only added to the perceived alienation of the students of color. The curriculum was overwhelmingly Eurocentric and although of top caliber theoretically, left much to be desired by students who wanted to learn about the history, experience, and contributions of non-European communities.[51]

Dr. Almirall-Padamsee explained further: "Our university had experienced various building takeovers, sit-ins, and eventually a hunger strike, which were directly triggered by Latino and black student dissatisfaction with the university's inability and seeming unwillingness to meaningfully address the financial, educational, and social needs of the students of color on campus."[52] Because the university was not fostering relationships with its students of color, the students decided to take action themselves. For Lambda Pi Chi, this was yet another reason for women to establish an organization that would suit their needs.

Mr. Zamudio's experience at the University of Iowa was very different. He explained: "At the University of Iowa during the middle to late 80s, I don't know if there was such a thing as a "racial climate." It was an institution with a very small minority enrollment. There were, of course, established organizations that catered to different racial/ethnic groups, but I do not remember a larger amount of controversy in terms of the racial climate. So if I had to describe it, I guess I would describe it as calm, if only because there wasn't a large amount of diversity within the university student population to make it any different."[53]

Although the racial climate at the University of Iowa was opposite of Cornell University, Mr. Zamudio and the other founders of Sigma Lambda Beta felt their organization would serve the needs of Latino men (and men of other racial/ethnic backgrounds) at the University.

Many student organizations face various challenges when starting from the ground up. Whether it is institutional support, financial, or recruitment, new organizations have to overcome many hurdles before they are recognized by a university. Latino Greeks are no different. Dr. Almirall-Padamsee discussed the challenges of Lambda Pi Chi: "Because our organization was the first Latina Greek organization on campus, there were few to whom we could turn as we worked to better develop and implement its structure, premises, and traditions. University staff more knowledgeable of the white Greek and even black Greek systems, although supportive, had limited advice they could offer. Funds were nonexistent. Technology wasn't advanced enough at that point for us to easily find other similar organizations across the country."[54]

Dr. Almirall-Padamsee also described the importance of relationships with other organizations. Personal friendships with Latino Greek and some black Greek fraternity members became pivotal as was their willingness to share whatever they could about how their organizations were started, how they defined their uniqueness and university official standing, and how they programmed. Building trust, working as colleagues via joint programming, finding staff and faculty willing to help them, and aggressively learning university procedures for programming and fund-raising helped define success for Lambda Pi Chi.[55] The connections among various Greek-letter organizations assisted Lambda Pi Chi with their initial efforts to develop their organization. In addition, collaboration among the organizations also allowed for the development of cross-cultural programming.

Sigma Lambda Beta also faced several challenges. The first was how the organization had to learn, understand, and take the appropriate actions to establish the group. Assistance in establishing the organization came from University of Iowa's college administrator Mary Peterson. Mrs. Peterson had extensive knowledge of the fraternal system, both on the Iowa campus and throughout the country. As such, Mr. Zamudio stated not only has Mary Peterson been the biggest ally for the fraternity, but "she is the single most important reason why Sigma Lambda Beta has remained in existence since 1986. She continues to serve as our Executive Director."[56]

The second challenge for Sigma Lambda Beta was maintaining membership. Although the organization was founded with eighteen members, three years later only four remained. At the University of Iowa during the late eighties, there was not a large number of Latino men on campus. In addition, there were few men who wanted to join a predominately Latino fraternity. Since 1986, there has continued to be spurts of high and low membership in the fraternity.

The third challenge was to get men from other college campuses interested in joining Sigma Lambda Beta. Zamudio stated: "There was a lot of travel involved in going to other campuses to talk with men who were potentially interested, and having them come to our campus to learn more about our organization. From there it slowly became easier to expand to other campuses, as our network of members available to talk to groups at different campuses continued to expand."[57]

As mentioned earlier, support from other organizations is an important step when forming a new one. For Lambda Pi Chi, support came from organizations such as the existing Latino Fraternity, La Unidad Latina/Lambda Upsilon Lambda Fraternity, Inc., Alpha Chapter, Alpha Phi Alpha Fraternity Inc., Alpha Chapter and especially the women in the Latino umbrella group, La Asociacion Latina [The Latino/a Association]. In addition, the staff of the Office of Minority Educational Affairs were invaluable as were various faculty members from the Africana Studies and Research Center.[58]

Many years have passed since Lambda Pi Chi and Sigma Lambda Beta were formed. We asked the founders if the current state of their organizations is what they envisioned. Dr. Almirall-Padamsee shared four points regarding Lambda Pi Chi:

1. Systematic identifying of hard money within a university budget and within the broader community. For example, having sustained alliances with those on campus who control those funds and believe in the good work of the organization,
2. Defining a vehicle by which to better translate the goals and philosophy of the organization via current challenges and issues faced by undergrads at an institution. For example, a training program at a yearly conference for current undergrads to better understand and use the different forms of activism in order to make the needs of the Latino undergrads known to the administration in 2004 vs. how it might have been done in 1988,
3. Systematizing a formal way to keep attracting alumni. For example, expecting each chapter to set up job shadowing or mentoring programs with the alumni from that chapter, and
4. Building one physical place where all records, notebooks, and histories for all chapters and the National Group. These materials would be archived and available to lend for educational purposes to chapters or members.[59]

Mr. Zamudio shared his thoughts:

> When we started Sigma Lambda Beta, we didn't envision the expansion of Latino Greek organizations. We focused on establishing and building our organization without much regard to what other organizations were doing around us. Of course, in the Midwest during 1986 we did not have competition from other Latino Greek organizations. To see the expansion of Latino Greek organizations in the last decade is truly amazing. I would like to believe that SLB had a tremendous impact on that expansion, as we grew out from the Midwest to the East Coast to West Coast and eventually to the southern states. Our expansion made other Latino Greek organizations take notice. I also believe our expansion was a catalyst for other groups to decide to start their own organizations.[60]

The views shared by Dr. Almirall-Padamsee and Mr. Zamudio shed light on the historical beginnings of two Latino/a Greek-letter organizations. The challenges faced by these organizations are also highlighted by the successful work they have done in their communities and in keeping the Latino culture alive at colleges and universities across the country. These are just a few of the rewards that come with membership in a Latino Greek-letter organization.

Personal Reflections from the Authors

Susana's Story. Joining a Latina sorority was a foreign concept for me during my undergraduate years. I was a freshman in college and received a phone call from a student encouraging me to attend a sorority meeting. I immediately dismissed the invitation and thought that there was no way anyone would consider me "sorority material." After the urging of another friend who received the same phone call, I reluctantly attended the informational meeting. I was pleasantly shocked that the room was filled with Latinas; in fact, I couldn't remember a time when I was surrounded with so many Latinas all at once on campus. I thought to myself "where have you all been and boy, have I needed you this past year!" I pledged my organization and felt that I could "breathe" again. I noticed my self-esteem was heightened, and because of the confidence I gained from my sorority I noticed that I was participating more in class discussion, I was taking on leadership roles on campus, and I started to become less passive about creating change on my college campus.

Fifteen years later, I continue my involvement with my sorority by mentoring other young women to make the most out of their college experiences. The popularity of LGLOs has increased since my undergraduate years, and I am filled with joy that these organizations continue to have an impact on young people. Yet I am disheartened that

LGLOs continue to face the same issues and problems of the early 1990s. I believe that institutions of higher education must first value and practice the concept of diversity for LGLOs to be fully accepted by their campus community.

Juan's Story. I was not a member of Greek-letter organization during my undergraduate career. In the mid-1990s at Florida State University, the only Greek organizations on campus where the traditional white and black Greek letter fraternities. My first experience working with LGLOs was at George Mason University (GMU) as a student affairs administrator. In that position I worked with the only Latino fraternity and Latina sorority on campus, although I was not the advisor to either organization. It was clear that the Latino/a culture played an important part in the cultural, social, and educational programs they contributed to the GMU campus. This sparked my interest in becoming a member of a LGLO.

A year after I began the doctoral program at Iowa State University, I decided that I would look into joining a Latino fraternity. After researching the various Latino fraternities, I chose Phi Iota Alpha Fraternity, Inc. as the organization that I wanted to join. After contacting them and speaking with various members, my decision was reaffirmed after they advised me that their organization has a graduate educational process. It was an interesting experience going through the educational process as a married, thirty-one-year-old, full-time doctoral student. In addition, my own ethnic identity was enhanced as a result of the educational process.[61] Nevertheless, I completed the educational process and successfully "crossed" into the fraternity in spring 2005. Since then, I have become an active lifetime member of the organization.

Research of Latino/a Fraternities and Sororities

The majority of recent research available on LGLOs stems from individual research conducted by graduate students. A dissertation by Gabriel Reyes investigated whether an ethnic fraternity encourages persistence in college.[62] His findings show that students view participation in an ethnic fraternity as a means of support, as a source of empowerment to participate in other facets of student life, and as an entity that provides a comfortable "family" unit in which students' cultural backgrounds are valued. John Hernandez's dissertation addressed the environmental factors that contribute to Latino student retention. His findings indicate that involvement in extracurricular activities was a factor that assisted in longevity in college for Latino students. Additionally, individuals in his study who participated in a LGLO gained long lasting friendships, empowerment, and self-esteem, academic and emotional support, a shared understanding of cultural language, and strength from the support and power of a large united voice. Also, one of his participants spoke of having an "awakening" moment when he met Latino fraternity brothers from other schools who shared his same ethnic and socioeconomic background and were succeeding in college. This experience inspired him to make the most of his college experience by dedicating more effort to academics.[63]

In terms of Latina sororities, Jennifer Gray Nuñez's recent research found that Latinas gained a heightened sense of ethnic identity development through their participation in a Latina based sorority. One of her participants noted that she was not raised in a household where Spanish was the primary language. This particular college student concluded that not knowing Spanish often communicates to other Latinos that you do not know your culture. Joining a Latina sorority gave her more confidence to practice and learn her native language which enhanced her identity as a Latina. While Nunez's primary focus was on ethnic identity development,[64] her findings are similar to other researchers that conclude that Latina sororities aid in maintaining one's cultural identity, serve as a family unit as a mean of academic and social support, and enhance one's comfort level in terms of "fitting in" a large university.[65]

Gina Garcia's thesis explored the relationship of campus climate and social support to adjustment to college by Latina sorority and nonsorority members.[66] She found that members of a Latina sorority had positive perceptions of their campus environment and received higher level of support from their sisters, which contributed to higher levels of adjustment to college compared to the nonsorority members. In addition, Latina sorority members felt more satisfied with their academic, social, and personal lives than nonsorority members did. Moreover, Garcia discussed that although membership in a Latina sorority assisted the women with their adjustment to college, sorority membership may not do much to combat the negative perceptions of the campus racial climate.

In 2006, I (Juan R. Guardia) completed my dissertation on the ethnic identity development of Latino fraternity members at a Hispanic-serving institution.[67] In my study, Latino fraternity members described how their involvement in a Latino fraternity enhanced their ethnic identity development. Specifically, they sought an organization that embraced the Latino culture and provided them with a familial (*hermandad*-brotherhood) atmosphere on campus. In addition, members also described how speaking Spanish was reinforced and supported by fraternity brothers. Moreover, the members discussed how the educational process also made a significant impact on their ethnic identity development. As Joe noted, "I would say that our educational process kind of helps you bring out the Latino in you."

My own study and the others discussed suggest that LGLOs have a positive influence on the lives of Latino/a students. If the research indicates that LGLOs create meaningful and positive college experiences for Latino/a students, perhaps institutions can utilize these groups as part of their retention planning and assessment. Much like, incorporating diversity efforts on college campuses, LGLOs should not be kept on the marginal sidelines by the institution but rather interwoven into the fabric of the university culture.

Working with Latino/a Greek Organizations

Many times, Latino Greeks arrive on campus without any regard to how institutions plan to include them in the Greek Life culture. The following are a few suggestions for providing an inclusive transition for Latino Greeks:

- Colleges and universities can begin to review current institutional policies on establishing Greek organizations on campus. Are the policies inclusive of Latino Greeks?
- Institutions can develop an installment ceremony for any new Greek organization, which is a practice that can also bind the Greek community together. Additionally, Greek advisors and other university officials can make a Latino Greek organization feel valued by learning their history, mission, principles, and national policies.
- Many advisors of LGLOs are Latino/a faculty and staff that do not have much experience with Greek Life. Greek Life can provide training to these individuals, especially with issues of liability and risk management.
- The administration can foster a working partnership between the Office of Multicultural Affairs and Greek Life by developing strategies for collaboration. Also, when planning IFC, NPHC, NPC, LGLO student retreats, it is important to include the Office of Multicultural Affairs in the planning process and to encourage all Greek organizations to support each others' events.

Conclusion

Latino Greek-letter organizations have come a long way from secret societies to student-directed entities to large business-savvy corporations. Documenting the history of LGLOs is one way to strengthen the unity and longevity of the Latino Greek community. It is also important that all LGLOs formally document their past struggles and triumphs of starting an organization so that it can be shared among all Greek organizations.

LGLOs were formed out of a need to academically and socially thrive at predominantly white institutions, to organize a united voice to combat anti-Latino agendas, and to provide a safe haven where Latinos could be themselves. Unlike many other campus organizations, membership in a Latino fraternity or sorority does not end at graduation. Latino Greek members know that joining an organization is a lifelong commitment. This history of Latino Greeks provides a glimpse into struggles that Latinos have endured and continue to endure to have access to higher education. The stories of our founding fathers and mothers inspire us to continue their legacy and to lift up other brothers and sisters as they attempt to enter the gates of higher education. Phi Iota Alpha Trustee Fraternity, Inc. Tiberio C. Faria, eloquently states, "My parting thoughts on this are that every generation has the opportunity of doing what is demanded of them at their own time, and it's up to them to face their challenges and opportunities, make mistakes, have achievements, and live their moments of glory and despair, and learn by both, and grow by both, in the process of becoming better citizens of the world, for a better world, and that is what this [Latino Greeks] is all about, I humbly believe."[68] Latino Greek organizations can be catalyst for recruiting and retaining college students across the country. Together—as familia (family), they can change the world.

Table 4 Latino/a Organizations

Organization	F/S	Place of Origin	Date
Phi Iota Alpha Fraternity, Inc.	F	Rensselaer Polytechnic Institute	1931
Lambda Theta Alpha Latin Sorority, Inc.	S	Kean University	1975
Lambda Theta Phi Latin Fraternity, Inc.	F	Kean University	1975
Lambda Sigma Upsilon Latino Fraternity, Inc.	F	Rutgers University	1979
Corazones Unidos Siempre/Chi Upsilon Sigma National Latin Sorority, Inc.	S	Rutgers University	1980
La Unidad Latina/Lambda Upsilon Lambda Fraternity Inc.	F	Cornell Unviersity	1982
Alpha Psi Lambda National Inc.	Coed	Ohio State University	1985
Latino America Unida/Lambda Alpha Upsilon, Fraternity, Inc.	F	University at Buffalo, SUNY	1985
Lambda Theta Nu Sorority, Inc.	S	Cal State University Chico	1986
Sigma Lambda Beta International Fraternity, Inc.	F	University of Iowa	1986
Omega Delta Phi Fraternity, Inc.	F	Texas Tech University	1987
Gamma Zeta Alpha Fraternity, Inc.	F	Cal State University Chico	1987
Kappa Delta Chi Sorority, Inc.	S	Texas Tech University	1987
Sigma Lambda Upsilon/Señoritas Latinas Unidas Sorority, Inc.	S	Binghamton University, SUNY	1987
Nu Alpha Kappa Fraternity, Inc.	F	Cal Poly State University-San Luis Obispo	1988
Latinas Promoviendo Comunidad/Lambda Pi Chi Sorority, Inc.	S	Cornell Unviersity	1988

Latinas en Progreso y Desarrollo/Lambda Phi Delta Sorority, Inc.	S	University at Buffalo, SUNY	1988
Omega Phi Beta Sorority, Inc.	S	University at Albany, SUNY	1989
Alpha Pi Sigma Sorority, Inc.	S	San Diego State University	1990
Sigma Lambda Gamma National Sorority, Inc.	S	University of Iowa	1990
Hermandad de Sigma Iota Alpha, Inc.	S	University at Albany, SUNY	1990
Gamma Phi Omega International Sorority, Inc.	S	Indiana University	1991
Delta Phi Mu Sorority, Inc.	S	Purdue University	1991
Lambda Pi Upsilon Sorority/Latinas Poderosas Unidas, Inc.	S	SUNY Geneseo	1992
Gamma Phi Sigma Hermanos Unidos Fraternity, Inc.	F	Temple University	1992
Sigma Delta Alpha Fraternity, Inc.	F	San Jose State University	1992
Gamma Alpha Omega Sorority, Inc.	S	Arizona State University	1993
Alpha Rho Lambda Sorority, Inc./Alianza de Raices Latinas	S	Yale University	1993
Phi Lambda Rho Sorority, Inc.	S	Cal State University-Stanislaus	1993
Pi Lambda Chi Latina Sorority, Inc.	S	University of Colorado	1994
Gamma Eta Sorority, Inc.	S	University of Florida	1995
Sigma Delta Lambda Sorority, Inc.	S	Texas State University	1996
Sigma Omega Nu Latina Interest Sorority, Inc.	S	Cal Poly State University-San Luis Obispo	1996
Alpha Sigma Omega Latina Sorority, Inc.	S	Syracuse University	1997
Alpha Beta Sigma Sorority, Inc.	S	University at Buffalo, SUNY	1998
Delta Psi Alpha Fraternity, Inc.	Coed	Northern Illinois University	1998

Notes

1. Although considerable debate revolves around social, economic, and political baggage that accompanies the use of various racial/ethnic labels, this is not the purpose of this paper. Nevertheless, a clarification of terminology is in order to help clarify any confusion among readers. The term "Latino" and its plural derivative "Latinos" are used much like the term "Hispanic"—an umbrella term for those individuals who trace their ancestry from Latin American countries. The feminine forms of the terms, "Latina and Latinas," will be used when specifically referring to females who trace their ancestry from Latin American countries. The terms "Latino/a" and "Latinos/as" are used to refer emphatically to a male/female experience.

2. Sylvia Hurtado, "The Institutional Climate for Talented Latino Students," *Research in Higher Education* (1994): 21–41.

3. Ramirez and de la Cruz, *The Hispanic Population in the United States, 2002*, Washington, DC: U.S. Census Bureau.

4. Margarita Benitez, "Hispanic-Serving Institutions: Challenges and Opportunities," in *Minority-serving Institutions: Distinct Purposes, Common Goals*, ed. Jamie P. Merisotia and Colleen O'Brian (San Francisco: Jossey-Bass, 1998), 58.

5. Victoria Maria MacDonald and Teresa Garcia, "Historical Perspectives on Latino Access to Higher Education," in *The Majority in the Minority: Expanding the Representation of Latina/o Faculty, Administrators, and Students in Higher Education*, ed. Jeanette Castellanos and Lee Jones (Sterling, VA: Stylus, 2003), 16.

6. Ramirez and de la Cruz, *Hispanic Population in the United States*, 4.

7. The term "Chicano" and its derivatives are used to differentiate U.S. born Latinos/as who trace their ancestry from Mexico.

8. MacDonald and Garcia, "Historical Perspectives on Latino Access," 28.

9. Carlos Muñoz, *Youth, Identity, Power: The Chicano Movement* (London: Verso, 1989), 21.

10. Ibid., 25–26, 43.

11. MacDonald and Garcia, "Historical Perspectives on Latino Access," 30.

12. Muñoz, *Youth, Identity, Power*, 75.

13. Ibid., 81–82.

14. MacDonald and Garcia, "Historical Perspectives on Latino Access," 23.

15. ASPIRA Association. http://www.aspira.org/about.html.

16. The term "Boricua" is a symbolic term of endearment to describe their homeland. Santiago defined Boricua from the word "Borinquen" or "Land of the Brave Lord," which is what the Arawak Indians called the island before the arrival of Columbus. See Roberto Santiago, *Boricuas: Influential Puerto Rican Writings—An Anthology* (New York: Ballantine, 1995), vxiii.

17. MacDonald and Garcia, "Historical Perspectives on Latino Access," 31.

18. Roberto Rodriguez, "Hermandades on Campus: Elite Latino Secret Societies and Fraternities of the Past Gives Away to Today's Brotherhoods and Sisterhoods," *Black Issues in Higher Education*, December 14, 1995, 26–29.

19. Howard J. Baily, ed., *Baird's Manual of American College Fraternities* (Menasha, WI: George Banta Publishing, 1949), 315.

20. Phi Iota Alpha Fraternity, Inc., "History." http://www.phiota.org/history.html

21. Interview with Tiberio C. Faria, September 21, 2004. Tiberio is a Trustee for Phi Iota Alpha Fraternity, Inc.

22. Latino Greek-lettered Organization—Fraternal Societies. http://www.lglo.com/modules.php?name=News&file=pring&sid=1.

23. Lambda Theta Alpha Latin Sorority, Inc. *History*. http://www.lambdalady.org/prn-history.htm.

24. Jesus Peña, *The History of Lambda Theta Phi Latin Fraternity, Incorporated* (New York: Vantage Press, 1994), xiii, 12–14.

25. Ibid., 16–20, 31.

26. Lambda Sigma Upsilon, Incorporated, "About History." http://lsu79.org/about_history.

27. Chi Upsilon Sigma Sorority, Incorporated, "History." http://www.justbecus.org.

28. La Unidad Latina, "A Movement Starts at Cornell University: The Story of La Unidad Latina." http://www.launidadlatina.org/story.htm.

29. Alpha Psi Lambda, "History." http://www.alpha-psi-lambda.org/.

30. Lambda Theta Nu Sorority, Inc. "History." http://www.lambdathetanu.or/Assets/welcome.htm.

31. Ibid.

32. During a conversation, Susana asked Sigma Lambda Beta brother Juan A. Rodriguez why his organization's name included "international."

33. Teresa Puente, "Special Report: Hispanics on Campus—Getting Organized," *Hispanic*, (1992): 31–32.

34. Interview with Tina Daniels, August 24, 2004. Tina was the founding mother of Sigma Delta Lambda.

35. University of Albany—Greek Life. "Latino Greek Council at SUNY Albany." http://www.albany.edu/~lgc/history.html

36. Monica Miranda and Martin De Figueroa, "¡Adelante Hacia El Futuro! (Forward to the future) Latino/Latina students: Past, present and future," *Perspectives* (Summer 2000), 6–9.

37. Exploratory Committee, Concilio Nacional de Hermandades Latinas and National Association of Latino Fraternal Organizations Joint Exploratory Committee Report and Proposal, September 1999, 2.

38. Ibid., 14.

39. Miranda & Martin De Figueroa, "¡Adelante Hacia El Futuro!" 8.

40. National Association of Latino Fraternal Organizations, "Home & News."

41. Michelle Espino, "Joining a Council or Creating Your Own," *La Mensajera* (Summer 2003): 3

42. Presentation by David Oritz, Susana Muñoz, and Dennis Camacho.

43. National Association of Latino Fraternal Organizations, at http://www/nalfo.org

44. Lambda Pi Chi Sorority, Inc. "About Us: History & Mission."

45. Ibid.

46. Ibid.

47. Sigma Lambda Beta. "Information—Fact Sheet."

48. Ibid.

49. Interview with Dr. Irma Almirall-Padamsee, October 15, 2004. She is a founding mother of Latinas Promoviendo Comunidad/Lambda Pi Chi Sorority, Inc.

50. Interview with Ricardo Zamudio, August 6, 2004. He is a founding father of Sigma Lambda Beta International Fraternity, Inc.

51. Interview with Dr. Irma Almirall-Padamsee.

52. Ibid.

53. Interview with Ricardo Zamudio.

54. Interview with Dr. Irma Almirall-Padamsee.

55. Ibid.
56. Interview with Ricardo Zamudio.
57. Ibid.
58. Interview with Dr. Irma Almirall-Padamsee.
59. Ibid.
60. Interview with Ricardo Zamudio.
61. Juan R. Guardia, "Latino/a Fraternity-Sorority Ethnic Identity Development," *Hispanic Outlook in Higher Education*, September 10, 2007.
62. Gabriel Reyes, "Does Participation in an Ethnic Fraternity Enable Persistence in College" (PhD diss., University of Southern California, 1997).
63. John Hernandez, "En Sus Voces (In Their Voices): Understanding the Retention of Latino/a College Students" (PhD diss., University of Maryland College Park, 1999), 162–63.
64. Jennifer Gray Nuñez, "The Empowerment of Latina University Students: A Phenomenological Study of Ethnic Identity Development through Involvement in a Latina-Based Sorority" (master's thesis, Iowa State University, 2004).
65. Carolyn Layzer, Strategic Sisterhood in a Latina Sorority: Affiliation, Recognition, and Solidarity," Education Resources Information Center (ERIC), ED 441887 (2000), 13–21; Margarita Olivas, "Latina Sororities and Higher Education: The Ties that Bind," Education Resources Information Center, ED 407194 (1996), 28–30; Marcella Mendoza Patterson, "Latina Sisterhood: Does it Promote or Inhibit Campus Integration?" (PhD diss., University of Southern California, 1998) were are all resources that provided similar conclusions.
66. Gina Ann Garcia, "The Relationship and Perceptions of Campus Climate and Social Support to Adjustment to College for Latina Sorority and Non-Sorority Members" (master's thesis. University of Maryland, College Park, 2005).
67. Juan R. Guardia, "Nuestra identidad y experiencias (Our identity and Experiences): Ethnic Identity Development of Latino Fraternity Members at a Hispanic-Serving Institution" (PhD diss., Iowa State University, 2006)
68. Interview with Tiberio C. Faria.

Preserving and Creating Traditions: A Native American Emergence in Greek Organizations

Linda Kelly

A POSITIVE HIGHER EDUCATIONAL EXPERIENCE HAS BEEN CLOUDED by discrimination and prejudice for many Native Americans. A strong cultural capital for college aspirations has been thwarted by poverty, geography, lack of information, and other factors. It is no surprise that it took until 1994 before Native Americans became involved with the Greek organization phenomenon on campuses across the United States.

Higher education administrators have had many concerns about Greek organizations that revolve around the abuse of alcohol as it relates to physical violence, regretted sex, and academic failure.[1] Problems related to hazing and alcohol still have not been adequately solved.[2] A related concern is that fraternities tend to prolong adolescence and at the same time act as substitution for home.[3] College administrators have not taken the authority to prevent discriminatory practices[4] and organizations have not been accountable for institutional standards.[5] With these concerns as part of the history of Greek organizations, it is noteworthy that all of the Native American organizations have taken a strong stance against the use of alcohol. These organizations are also concerned about being part of the larger student campus and community.

Rich traditional beliefs, values, and traditions have been woven into the fabric of each Native American Greek organization, making them innovative and exemplary. Self-determination and traditional heritage have carved a unique place for these fraternities and sororities among other Greek organizations. Six organizations have risen to the challenge of being committed to education, have developed community, fought against the negative stigma that is sometimes felt toward Greek organizations, and created positive images of Native Americans on campus. As more Native Americans enter the higher education environment, some noted that they were not included in all aspects of the college experience. Insightful leaders recognized the importance of being represented in traditional college culture, which included Greek organizations. Although there has been tension between embracing a new culture and maintaining traditions, there was the recognition that the voice of Native Americans in these organizations was imperative for a place of power in the student world. Resolution came through creating new traditions, rejecting offensive practices, and developing a unique vibrant identity in the Greek world.

To appreciate the arena into which Native American fraternities and sororities have emerged, a much abbreviated history of Native American higher education will provide the background for general Native American inclusion in the higher education environment. Next, a look at the state of North Carolina, the University of North Carolina-Pembroke, and the Lumbee Tribe will provide background to understand the rise of the Native American fraternity and sorority. Of the six Native American fraternities and sororities, four of them originated in North Carolina. The history of UNC Pembroke (UNCP) includes its mission to educate Native Americans. This school is located in the part of North Carolina dominated by the Lumbee Tribe, the largest tribe in the state.

Finally, a snapshot of each of the fraternities and sororities that exist will describe their beginnings, mission or principles of organization, values and beliefs, symbols, community service, and membership. For each of these organizations there is a mission congruency with the institution of higher education with which they are affiliated.

Brief History of Native American Education

Federal policies have shaped educational priorities for Native Americans throughout the history of the United States. Attitudes initially were patronizing and based on religious zeal. Values shifted from a need to Christianize, to "civilize," to exterminate, assimilate, terminate, and finally to encourage self-determination. Each era changed the educational goals that were desired for Native Americans by the school founders or the U.S. government. When the Indian Self-Determination and Education Assistance Act passed in 1975, it created a national policy that recognized the government's obligation to promote services and programs to Native American communities in order to foster growth and development. Since 1975, the climate has been conducive to nurturing education and campus life to meet the needs of Native Americans.

Within the first decade of U.S. colonization there were plans to educate Native Americans. Colonial beliefs and values centered around

Christianizing the "savages." Civilizing the natives had the implication of trying to teach them agriculture and to till the land. Harvard College was founded in 1636 and included in its goals higher education for Native Americans. The first president of Harvard, Henry Dunster, worked with the Indians and established a school for Indians. He obtained funds from the Society for the Propagation of the Gospel in New England to allow the building of a residence hall for Native Americans.[6] Acculturation was the goal.

It was not until 1665 when an Algonquian, Caleb Cheesehateaumuck, became the first Native American graduate from Harvard. He did not have immunity to the diseases of the colonists, and he died within months of his graduation.[7] Cultural lifestyles collided and contributed to tragedy and failure during the first century of education.

The charter for the College of William and Mary included a Christian education for Native Americans. The Bafferton building was built in 1723 for this purpose. Only five or six students ever attended this school. Elders of the tribes refused to send their children to strangers while chiefs sent their captured enemies instead. Native attendance was mainly by force.[8] The goal of educating Native Americans was abandoned and no longer part of the mission.[9]

Native American education was the primary goal of Dartmouth College when it was established in 1769.[10] Dr. Eleazer Wheelock felt the Indians in the area were entitled to his services, with the General Court of the province of Massachusetts Bay providing support for this goal. Six Iroquois children were funded for one year. Dartmouth's goals included Christianizing as well as teaching liberal arts and sciences. The school had no patronage in America and no help from abroad. The Continental Congress in 1775 and 1776 appropriated five hundred dollars for the support of Indian students at Dartmouth with a goal to maintain friendship or prevent hostility among the tribes.[11] Since 1970, Dartmouth has enrolled students from over 111 different tribes. Annual powwows are part of celebrating this heritage.[12] Of all the Eastern colleges with an early mission to educate Natives, only Dartmouth has a chapter of any of the Greek organizations that are organized solely for this population.[13]

The College of New Jersey, now Princeton, provided support to three Delaware Indians in 1779. Only one student graduated, yet was murdered about nine years later. Almost fifty years passed before other Native Americans attended Princeton, and only three attended during the first half of the nineteenth century.[14]

Several tribal groups took their own initiative to educate their population. The Cherokee and Choctaw organized a higher education system comprised of over two hundred schools. Several of their graduates went to eastern colleges, such as Ohio University, Jefferson College, Indiana University, Asbury University, and Lafayette College.[15]

Cultural understanding was centuries away from these early attempts at education. Misinterpretations, lack of understanding, and intolerance were rampant. The current policy era of self-determination created a catalyst for the growth of tribal colleges, which have been created to meet the unique needs of this population. Navajo Community College, now Dine College, was founded in the 1960s to bring a cultural perspective to education planning. Thirty-six institutions are located primarily in the Dakotas, Montana, and the southwest. To date none of these institutions support Greek organizations.[16]

Continued Alienation

How Native Americans are included into the fabric of the university setting will contribute to retention. Assimilation of students into the campus depends on their perceptions of how they fit into the college as well as their goals for their educational experience. Even today alienation and discrimination are still felt when attending college.[17] An additional characteristic that contributes to the ultimate success of the Native American experience in the higher education arena is resilience, both as an individual trait and as cultural resilience.[18] Tierney and Kidwell state that it is the resistance to the assimilation policies that dominated Native American education for centuries that has left cultural integrity intact.[19]

Reasons for these perceptions continue to be investigated to provide strategies to assist minorities so they feel more a part of the college experience. The informants from personal interviews concurred with these perceptions.[20] For these and other reasons, a community of supportive Native Americans was desired to guide students through the higher education process. The campus climate opened for the creation of Native American Greek organizations to meet previously unmet needs. The founders of these organizations have the characteristic of being resilient both as individuals and as representatives of their respective tribal groups. A summary of the names of the organizations and institutions which support them is listed in Table 5.

North Carolina and Native Americans

Students are surprised that Native Americans are in North Carolina. These students often make such comments as "Aren't the Native Amer-

Table 5 Native American Greek Organizations

Organization	F/S	Place of Origin	Date
Alpha Pi Omega	S	–UNC Chapel Hill (Alpha Chapter)	1994
		–UNC Pembroke (Beta Chapter)	1996
		–Oklahoma State (Gamma Chapter)	2004
		Graduate Chapters:	
		–Alpha Pi (Orange County, NC)	
		–Beta Pi (Robeson County, NC)	
		–Gamma P (Columbus County, NC)	
		Provisional Chapters:	
		–New Mexico	
		–Arizona	
		–Wisconsin-Madison	
		–Dartmouth	
Epsilon Chi Nu	F	North Carolina State/East Carolina	1996
		–Pitt Community College	
Phi Sigma Nu	F	UNC Chapel Hill	1996
		–UNC Pembroke	
		–Oklahoma State	
Sigma Omicron Epsilon	S	East Carolina	1997
		North Carolina State	2004
Gamma Delta Pi	S	Oklahoma	2001
		–Bacone College	
Beta Sigma Epsilon	F	Arizona	2000
		Northern Arizona	2004

icans in the West?"[21] This group in North Carolina experienced the horrors of the Indian Removal Act of 1830 that forced many local tribes to move to Oklahoma. This removal is called the Trail of Tears. Even with this history, North Carolina is one of the states with the largest number of Native Americans. As a state, 131,736 individuals identify themselves as Native American either as one race or in combination, which is about one quarter of the population.[22] The Lumbee are the largest group in the state. UNC Pembroke is located where a majority of the Lumbee live today. It is the political and cultural center of this tribe.[23] It is not surprising, then, that North Carolina has a unique place in the history of Native American Greek organizations. Of the six organizations, four began in North Carolina. Alpha Pi Omega, a sorority, and Phi Sigma Nu, a fraternity, began at the University of North Carolina-Chapel Hill. Today both organizations have chapters at UNC Pembroke. East Carolina University in Raleigh is the home of the fraternity Epsilon Chi Nu and the sorority Sigma Omicron Epsilon.

The Lumbee

The name Lumbee originates from the Lumbee Tribe, the largest Native American group in North Carolina. Numbering over forty thousand, the Lumbee have lived in the area of Robesen County since the 1700s. This tribe is the largest Native American group east of the Mississippi River and the ninth largest tribe in the United States.[24] In spite of this fact, the group is not federally recognized, partially because of the language requirement.[25] Therefore, there are no federal dollars to support tribal members. The tribe takes its name from the Lumbee River, although its name has changed several times. More distant ancestors were known as the Cheraw. In the 1900s they were known as the Croatan, then called the Cherokee of Robeson County. They have been called the Lumbee since 1956. Throughout the history of the United States, the Lumbee have had to fight for recognition. Still today they seek federal recognition.

University of North Carolina at Pembroke

Pembroke is located in Robeson County, the largest in North Carolina. This school has the longest history in its delivery of education to Native Americans. As early as 1887, Native Americans petitioned for a school to train Native American teachers. The General Assembly of North Carolina responded by enacting legislation to create the Croatan Normal School. Local Native Americans built Croatan, which was located approximately a mile from the current UNC Pembroke campus. Over the years the name of the school has changed, but its emphasis on Native American education did not. In 1911, the school was called the Indian Normal School of Robeson County. Two years later it became the Cherokee Indian Normal School of Robeson County. In 1941, another name change created Pembroke State College for Indians and eight years later the school became Pembroke State College. In 1969 the school became a university and in 1972 joined the University of North Carolina campus system.[26]

UNCP's mission states a commitment to academic excellence and to instill in the students a continuing appreciation for the diverse cultures and an active concern for the well-being of others. The UNCP also continues to expand its leadership role to enrich the cultural life of the region, which since its inception included the Native American community.[27]

Landmarks on campus provide visual evidence of the proud Native American influence and history at this institution. Several are in prominent places throughout the campus, such as the Old Main building and sculptures titled the "Font," "Tommy," and the "Arrowhead." Old Main was built in 1923 and is the oldest brick building on campus. Originally it housed administrative offices, classrooms, and an auditorium. A fire in 1973 burned the building, but it was restored in 1979. Today it houses the Multicultural Center and the Native American Resource Center. The American Indian Studies department is located on the second floor. The "Arrowhead" is a sculpture built by J. Hampton Rich which is in the shape of an arrowhead with Chief Sequoia depicted on one side and a buffalo trail marker on the other. A black sculpture, "Font," represents the Lumbee River and is located in Lumbee Hall. "Tommy" is the sculpture of the Red Hawk, the university's mascot.[28]

While university athletic mascots with Native American references have been under attack for many years, Pembroke has supported the Braves since the 1940s. Since this institution was created solely for Native American students, the name was appropriate. Today the term Braves is the nickname for the athletic team and the red-tailed hawk is used as the mascot. This bird is indigenous to Robeson County and is a companion to the term Braves. The logo depicts the hawk behind the image of a Native American male warrior.[29]

In 1953, the Board of Trustees approved admission of non-Indians for up to 40 percent of the student body in response to the Supreme Court's desegregation initiative. Up until this time Pembroke was the only state-supported four-year college for Native Americans in the United States. The school continues to support education for Native Americans. In the spring of 2005 enrollment was at an all time high with 1,019 Native American students. In fall semester 2003, 4,722 students were registered at Pembroke, 21.2 percent were Native American, around 1,000 students.[30] Clearly Pembroke stands behind Native Americans in all aspects of their educational experience.

New recognition of the Native American tradition from this campus has been recently noted. UNC Pembroke has been declared North Carolina's historic American Indian serving institution. House Bill 371, sponsored by Representative Ron Sutton of Pembroke, was passed and signed by Governor Mike Easley on July 5, 2005. The university is officially recognized as an institution that has served Native Americans historically. Representative Sutton believes that the declaration of the historic mission to educate Native Americans will be positive for the college and will help recruit students, both regionally and nationally.[31]

Hok Nosai

Serendipitously both the first Native American sorority (Beta chapter of Alpha Pi Omega) and the first Native American fraternity (Phi Sigma Nu) at UNC Pembroke were created in 1997. This factor precipitated a unique initiative from Pembroke to create a council that embraces both Native American Greek organizations. Hok Nosai, taken from a Tutelo-Saponi phrase that means "all one," is the name the council selected. The goals of this council are to promote unity, cooperation, and friendship between Native American sororities and fraternities at UNC Pembroke. At this time there are only two organizations under this council.[32]

Hok Nosai's mission is to promote harmony between the members of Hok Nosai as well as between members of other Greek organizations at UNC Pembroke and to facilitate active involvement of member organizations in the local community and on campus. Hok Nosai develops strategies for action on matters of mutual concern to the member organizations. The council has as a goal to create a positive image of Greek life on campus. Social, recreational, public service, and any activity in a nonprofit agency is encouraged as long as there is no violation of the guidelines provided by the Inter-Greek Advisory Board and/or conflict with the mission of UNC Pembroke.[33] The Hok Nosai requires all activities to be congruent with the mission of the college, as well as with Inter-Greek Advisory Board.

Native American Fraternities and Sororities

Alpha Pi Omega

The University of North Carolina (UNC) at Chapel Hill is home to the first Native American Greek organization and sorority, Alpha Pi Omega, established in 1994.[34] It is interesting that this campus, which has a small minority of Native Americans, is the home of the first Native American sorority. In the fall of 2003, UNC Chapel Hill enrolled 26,359 students, of which 0.8 percent were Native American.[35] It is perhaps this paucity of supportive faces that created a need for fellowship among Native American women.

From the beginning, influences of Native American culture have shaped this organization. As an example, the number four is a sacred number, which coincidentally is the number of women who founded Alpha Pi Omega. Four Lumbee women, known as the Four Winds, represented one of the four elements; Jamie Goins represented air, Shannon Brayboy water, Christina Strickland fire, and Amy Locklear earth.[36]

Retention of Native Americans at UNC Chapel Hill was a concern of the founders of the sorority. Danielle Mclean, President of Alpha Pi Omega for the 2005–6 academic year, provided insight into the organization and its symbols. She indicated that many Native Americans attending UNC Chapel Hill are originally from Pembroke and had desires to pursue their education away from home. This proved to be too much for some when there was a lack of a supportive community. For some students, after frustration and disappointment, their choice was to return home. One explanation for this attrition is often that this is the first time many Native American students are away from home. They have not been prepared for campus life and academic rigors and become homesick. Frequently Native American students are the first generation to attend college. The founders were concerned about this attrition pattern and desired to keep Native American women attending UNC Chapel Hill on campus until graduation. One of Alpha Pi Omega's goals was to support these women in a Native American sisterhood in order to keep them on campus. Alpha Pi Omega began because of a felt need and was created because it was the right place at the right time.[37]

As a group, the original founders consulted with elder Native American women from different tribes in North Carolina to receive advice about creating Alpha Pi Omega. Continuing with the sacred number four, the founders then developed four main principles: spirituality, education, contemporary issues, and tradition, the cornerstones of the organization. With a focus on education and service to others as part of the mission at UNC Chapel Hill,[38] this sorority's principles are congruent with University. Four symbols represent the sorority: the queen bee, cedar tree, dogwood flower, and amethyst.[39]

It is the bee that describes the pledging process, which occurs in the spring. Initiation is known as the honey process. The theme of the bee is continued in the identification of officers such as the grand dean of honeycombs and the grand busy bee. Fourteen members comprise the Board of Directors and are know as the Grand Keepers of the Circle.

Several foci are the intent of pledging. One is to build up the individual. Another is to learn about others. Each sister must provide four hours of community service per month. Overall the goal is to keep young women in school. It simultaneously becomes a growing-up and learning process. Concerns about alcohol are addressed by the sorority. Fighting a double negative image is a concern to the sorority, one in which Native Americans are viewed as drunks and the other as people of color. Rules of the sorority include no alcohol use at all during pledging, as pledging is viewed as a purification process. Alcohol brings people down, and being in the sorority is about building people up. Members may not use cups or glasses with the sorority emblem for alcohol or they may be expelled.[40]

Once sisters have joined the sorority they become more involved in campus life. The bond that develops between them as a group is different than what is experienced in the Native American Association, as it tends to be deeper and at a higher level. Even without a chapter house on campus, camaraderie is still present among the women. Consistent contact is made with all members through a mandatory weekly chapter meeting. All of the sisters must clock in fifteen hours of study time. Alpha Pi Omega is serious about putting education first.[41]

In the spring of 1995 the first class was pledged and became the Alpha chapter. They are referred to as the fifteen warrior women. A graduate chapter formed the following academic year with three women. A Beta chapter was established in 1996 at UNC Pembroke. A second graduate chapter was established at this school. Several graduates of UNC Chapel Hill returned to Pembroke and desired to remain active in the sorority. Subsequently three graduate chapters have been formed in Orange, Robeson, and Columbus Counties in North Carolina.[42]

A Gamma chapter was created at Oklahoma State University in 2004. In addition, several provisional chapters at the University of Arizona, University of New Mexico, Dartmouth College, and the University of Wisconsin-Madison have started.[43]

Eleven years after the inception of Alpha Pi Omega, there are over two hundred sisters who have gone through the honey process.[44] Alpha Pi Omega has been innovative on a number of levels and has reached far across the United States to reach Native American women and support them during the higher education process.

Alpha Pi Omega can claim a variety of firsts. It is the first Native American Greek organization, first Native American sorority, creator of the first graduate chapter, first organization to have a chapter at an Ivy league school (Dartmouth), and first Native American Greek organization at Chapel Hill and Pembroke.

Sigma Omicron Epsilon

A second Native American sorority was established at East Carolina University (North Carolina) in 1997. It is predominantly a Native American sorority, though anyone who has a general love and respect of American Indians will be considered. Seven Native American women desired a local community to combat a homesickness they felt while away from home. Traditionally Native Americans are encouraged not to go away to school, but rather to stay at home. The women in Sigma Omicron Epsilon believe they can bring more resources into the Native American communities with higher education. One of the driving forces for establishing this sorority was to create a network for Native American women. Seven women became the founders and include Jolena Bullard Locklear, Berna L. Chavis, Cabrina Cummings, Candance Hammonds, Patrice Henderson Oxendine, Deidra Arlene

Jacobs-Blanks, and Una Gail Locklear. Six of the founders are members of the Lumbee tribe and Deidra is Waccamaw-Siouan.[45]

It is not surprising that Native Americans felt a need for support at East Carolina. Minorities represented 20.7 percent of the 21,756 students in 2003. Only 0.7 percent of this group was Native Americans. North Carolina State has a similar percentage at a larger student body of 29,854.[46] Native Americans are the minority of the minorities at both institutions. Various tribes represented at these colleges include the Lumbee, Cherokee, Waccamaw-Siouan, as well as Plains tribes.[47]

The mission of the organization is built around Native American beliefs. The pledging rituals are also based on these beliefs. Smudging, the burning of herbs used for purification, is part of the ceremony as well as learning traditional crafts such as making shawls and dream catchers. Holding on to traditional Native American values and utilizing them for personal growth and leadership are integral to Sigma Omicron Epsilon.[48]

Pledging is also an educational process as sisters learn about other Native American tribes. Each of the young women are different but similar in being Native American. It is this similarity and community that are the focus. When pledging is complete, the result is a changed person; one is totally different.

The significance of the number seven continues through the mission of the organization. Seven objectives were created to support the vision of the organization of these seven women. The objectives are 1) to provide sisterhood and fellowship for women, 2) to provide the university and community with programs and services that will expose them to the riches, culture, and traditions of Native American/American Indians, 3) to involve women in learning experiences about the culture and history of Native Americans/American Indians, 4) to increase the university's and community's awareness of challenges faced by Native Americans/American Indians in everyday life, 5) to increase the enrollment of Native American/American Indians at the university, 6) to provide support for the East Carolina Native American Organization (ECNAO), and 7) to provide the university and community with programs about Native Americans'/American Indians' contributions throughout history.[49]

A Beta chapter began in fall of 2004 at North Carolina State University. Four women were part of this chapter; Ericka Locklear, Christine McArthur, Samantha Locklear and Ashley Lowery. Objectives for this chapter are similar, yet worded slightly differently: to provide fellowship for Native American women, to learn about the culture and history of Native Americans, to provide programs that will expose the university and community to Native American contributions in American history and culture, to increase the university's awareness of challenges faced by Native Americans, to increase enrollment of Native American women at North Carolina State, and to provide support for the North Carolina State Native American Organization.[50]

Sigma Omicron Epsilon perceives that it needs to fight in its own way as a Greek sorority as it belongs to no umbrella organization on campus.[51] While East Carolina University is trying to develop an umbrella organization for black, Hispanic, and Asian students, North Carolina State established the Collaborative Greek Council in 2000 to be a home for organizations not belonging to any national umbrella organizations for fraternities or sororities. This organization is supportive of the diversity represented on campus.[52]

Annually, the sorority supports powwows and a variety of services and programs to promote education and Native American culture for both the university and the community. The sorority is involved with community organizations such as the Susan B. Anthony Association which supports research for breast cancer, a disease that disproportionately affects Native Americans. Other organizations include Habitat for Humanity, a diabetes association, the Boys and Girls Club, and the Little Willie Center, an after-school tutorial program.[53]

Several layers of significance surround the choice of the butterfly to represent Sigma Omicron Epsilon. The butterfly represents growth. The Beta chapter's web site has a butterfly moving through the Web page as a cursor. It was chosen because the butterfly represents the process an individual goes through in life, just as one does in pledging with a sorority. When the butterfly begins its life, it is not the beautiful and developed insect we think of. It begins as larva and goes through change over time to become the beautiful butterfly we adore. Native American women come in all sizes and colors, like butterflies. In comparison to women who pledge, many women change and develop just as the butterfly does in life. People skills are developed during the pledging process, and many of the women are aware of qualities they possess that were previously unrecognized.[54]

Three colors have been chosen out of the seven sacred earth colors given from the Creator that are symbolic to this organization. The earth representation is especially significant as the common name for Sigma Omicron Epsilon is Sisters of the Earth. Blue represents "Father Sky," the Creator. White stands for the purity of women. Yellow represents the earth and the East. The East represents the beginning, the direction the sun arises each day. It is also the direction where Native Americans enter the powwow arena when dancing to honor ancestors. Yellow is also for the sun that shines on Mother Earth.[55]

The yellow rose has been chosen as their flower, which again has the reference to the earth and the East. This rose signifies many emotions which include strong feelings of pure joy, gladness, happiness, delight, and friendship. Fun and freedom can also be symbolized through yellow roses. After embracing a new beginning through the pledging process and the sorority in general, the yellow rose is chosen to represent and remember this life changing experience.[56]

Gamma Delta Pi

A third, and currently the youngest, Native American sorority was launched at the University of Oklahoma at Norman in 2001. Gamma Delta Pi was established by five women from various tribes and are known as the Five Changing Women. These women and their tribal identity are: Jennifer Nez-Blanchard, Navajo; Sedelta Oosahwee, Cherokee/Mandan/Arikara/Hidatsa; Joyce Shield, Comanche/Osage/Chippewa-Cree; Robin Williams, Kiowa/Apache/Nez Perce/Assiniboine/Sioux/Umatilla; and Shema Yearby, Seminole/Creek/Mississippi Choctaw.[57]

Toni Tsatoke, Clan Mother of Gamma Delta Pi for the year 2004–5, provided background information on the history and structure of this organization. A campus organization, the American Indian Student Association (AISA) is one in which many Native Americans at the University of Oklahoma are involved to seek community support. What was lacking was an opportunity to build a sisterhood for the Native American women. While other sororities existed on campus, the founders believed these other sororities would not be conducive to supporting the collective culture which Native American women were struggling to maintain. Joining an already existing sorority would, by design, further assimilate the Native American women into the larger campus life. The collective beliefs of Native American women, the founders believed, would have been lost in this type of organization. For these reasons a sorority was born.[58]

Although there is a perceived stigma in all Greek organizations, the founders of Gamma Delta Pi wanted to be able to be equal and recognized among other organizations.[59] Through creating an unique sorority, they would not compromise their own needs and still be able to maintain, promote, and strengthen their cultural identity while being a Greek organization. Gamma Delta Pi is committed to creating a lifelong bond among sisters, as it strives to instill character, develop an appreciation for native culture, unity, respect, scholarship, and provide a sisterhood of Native American women. This sorority provides a transition for the women who come from reservations and need a family, comfort, and general support. Any person who is matriculated at a college or university, meets the requirements, and is committed to the mission of the sorority can apply.

The student body at the University of Oklahoma represented 27,146 students in fall of 2003, of which 7.4 percent or about 2,008 were Native American. Native Americans are the largest represented minority on campus.[60] It is understandable this minority desired a support system.

There are seven points in the mission of the organization: 1) to provide a sisterhood to Native American women and all other women interested, 2) to act as a guide and mentor to those who seek cultural strength, knowledge, courage, and importance in their lives, 3) to provide a forum for exchanging information, concerns, ideas, experiences, resources, support, and questions relating to the broad spectrum of Native American culture, 4) to become actively involved in civic, educational, and cultural programs to enhance both the Native American communities and the image of the represented higher education institution, 5) to influence a climate to stimulate positive multicultural relations conducive to achieving education, personal, and community goals, 6) to promote the establishment of local chapters at various colleges and universities in the United States and Canada and provide for their proper organization, installation, and maintenance, and 7) to have and protect a distinctive and exclusive badge.[61] As stated in the organization's mission, they are tied to the mission and image of the University of Oklahoma.

Symbols steeped in traditional Native American culture are also an integral part of this sorority and begin with the pledging procedure. New members engage in the pledging process for four weeks during the spring semester. Activities surround the four stages of the butterfly, representing the metamorphosis a pledge undergoes and the growth that occurs. At the end of pledging, the women exhibit a greater strength and inner beauty demonstrated through the spirit of the butterfly. This makes Gamma Delta Pi the second Native American sorority to choose this symbol with which to identify.

Turquoise has been selected as the jewel because it represents Native American culture. This jewel has been used as money, an object for trade, for spiritual reasons, and for creating jewelry. Native Americans in the Southwest are best known as creators of turquoise jewelry. Since one of the Changing Women is Navajo, this connection was made and selected to represent Gamma Delta Pi.

Cedar and sage were chosen because they are sacred plants and are medicines for which women are responsible. Sage is used for purification, introspection, and direction. Courage, growth, and the ability to express feelings are enhanced with the use of cedar. Cedar and sage are both used in blessing ceremonies, as the smoke carries the request through prayer to the Creator. Respectful attention to these plants is expected by new members.[62]

Medicine wheels, which represent the wheel of life, traditionally have four colors, red, black, yellow, and white, that relate to the four directions. Different tribes may use different colors that represent different ideas associated with the directions. For Gamma Delta Pi, North is represented with White, where wisdom, logic, air, animals, mentality, energy, and the elders are defined. Yellow stands for the East where definition of the sun, fire, spirituality, enlightenment, and children can be found. The South is represented by red, which reflects and defines water, plants, emotions, trust, and innocence. Black represents the West. It is in the shadow of black that Mother Earth, the physical aspect of life, is defined providing insight and stability. Gamma Delta Pi views the stages of life as corresponding to the colors in the medicine wheel. The natural cycles of birth, growth, death, and regeneration are similar to the new member process, which is why these colors represent the sorority. These colors also represent the councils of leadership.[63]

Beauty and strength coupled with youth and innocence are symbolized through the white rose. Thorns on the rose are reminders of the challenges which all people experience in the world. Inner beauty, which is present in each individual, is symbolized through the pale and spotless perfection of the petals on a rose. Beauty can overcome the difficulties in life.[64]

Although not designated as a specific symbol, the number four is repeated several times within the structure of the organization. The pledging process is divided into four stages to coincide with the transformation of the butterfly in the egg, caterpillar, cocoon, and butterfly stages. This number is reflected also in the choice of the four colors of the medicine wheel and the four directions.[65]

The designation of the officers is led by the Clan Mother. Other offices are divided into four councils, each with the name of the four colors of the sorority, white, yellow, black, and red.

Service is embedded into the sorority. Native American Hoops is an annual all-Indian women and men's basketball tournament sponsored by Gamma Delta Pi. Through time this tournament has become one of the largest basketball tournaments in the state.[66] Other fundraisers are supported during the year, such as a buffet where various traditional foods are offered. One of the charities to which the sorority donates is Mikela's Miracle. The sisters promote awareness of sudden infant death syndrome (SIDS).[67]

As of fall 2005 there are twenty active sisters in Gamma Delta Pi. They are the only organization that commented on wanting to reach out to the

Tribal Colleges to begin a new chapter. This goal is consistent with their mission in trying to promote the development of new chapters.

A Beta Chapter formed at Bacone College, one of the few institutions with a historic mission to educate the Native American population. Bacone is an independent Baptist college created to serve Native Americans in 1880. One of the college's missions is to emphasize curricular and cocurricular programs to the voice and culture of American Indians.[68] The student population in the fall of 2003 was 918, of which 39.1 percent or 358 students were Native American.

Epsilon Chi Nu - EXN

Epsilon Chi Nu was founded at East Carolina University in 1996 and incorporated in 2003.[69] This organization claims to be the first Native American fraternity, yet Phi Sigma Nu makes the same claim. The Community Advisor states that it does not matter who was first, the bond between the men and the community is the most important fact.[70] Two Lumbee men are the founding fathers of this organization, Matthew Chavis and Quinn Lowry.[71]

Chavis and Lowry were active members of the East Carolina Natives Organization (ECNO). They were involved in drumming groups and tried to bring a Native American presence on campus through powwows. Both wanted to teach and share with others the Native American culture. Crutchfield wrote the constitution for ECNO and was chosen as the Community Advisor and Elder Chief.[72]

Mr. Crutchfield explained that one of the problems Native Americans experience on campus is they feel like they are in a goldfish bowl. Native culture is not understood and the Native people stick out in the crowd continually and reinvent themselves for others. The experience is often overwhelming. When one is at home on the reservation or within the Native American community, one's identity is understood. A brotherhood of Native American men would fulfill this need for a shared identity and supportive community during the college experience. Native Americans are an invisible minority to the majority, and they usually come from small rural areas and can get lost in the larger cities.[73]

The first Alpha class was pledged in 1997. Although primarily composed of Native American men, it is not exclusive. Non-Natives are welcome as long as they embrace the embodiment of the goals and mission of the organization.[74] The name Epsilon Chi Nu (EXN) was chosen as it comes from The East Coast Natives, the original name of the group.[75]

To become a member the following three criteria had to be met: the individual must be male, have an overall GPA of 2.0, and be enrolled in an institution of higher learning. East Carolina University's mission is dedicated to educational excellence and values contributions of a diverse community.[76] This organization supports educational excellence and contributes to the cultural diversity on campus. This organization is located at East Carolina University, but those attending Pitt Community College are also welcome. Pitt is the first community college to have brothers on their campus.[77] Graduate chapters have been established at Duke University.[78] As of fall 2005, there were over thirty members who claim brotherhood with fraternity.

Goals of the organization are to encourage each other and develop an understanding of one another. A strong spiritual sense is part of this organization and a respect for the environment is paramount. The purpose is to encourage a Native American way of thinking which includes a balance in the world and for the self.[79]

During the pledge process a sweat is an option and other Native American traditions are utilized. Alcohol use is strongly discouraged, and if it is used at sponsored meetings or functions, one can be dismissed. Epsilon Chi Nu believes that using or abusing alcohol further reinforces the negative stereotype that Native American men are drunks.[80]

Three colors are used for their symbolism in Epsilon Chi Nu: turquoise, black, and red. Turquoise represents the richness of the Native Cultures, black indicates having crossed over, and red signifies blood and honor. The eagle is used as it is sacred to many Native people.[81]

One of the requirements of this fraternity is to support other minority organizations. Another goal is to support the Native American sorority at East Carolina University. In the initial years of the fraternity, more interaction was planned for with Sigma Omicron Epsilon. The constitution of the fraternity stated there would be interaction with Sigma Omicron Epsilon. During the last three years, however, there has been a disconnect. The advisor would like to see both groups be more interactive. Several events, such as a tailgate party and travel together for the Gathering of Nations in Albuquerque, briefly brought them together.[82] Several organizations are supported by the brothers including tutoring with Big Brothers. The brothers also speak in classes in the Native American community.[83] These activities support the university's mission to serve (East Carolina University), which they do in the Native American community.

Phi Sigma Nu

In 1996, Phi Sigma Nu was established at the UNC Pembroke. The founders are seven young men: Earl Evans, Bo Goins, Chad Hedgepeth, Sandon Jacobs, Greg Richardson, Marty Richardson, and James Worriax.[84]

Two Native American clubs already existed on campus, ACES and NASA, with interest in these groups fluctuating from semester to semester. Each of these clubs had a cultural focus and were run by the college, while the founders desired more including a sense of ownership and belonging. They felt a fraternity was more personal, so this is the route they pursued. Many Native American students attend Pembroke who are not from Robeson County and the founders wanted to find a way to make a bond stronger between these Native American men.[85] Many tribes are represented in the fraternity including the Coharie, Eastern Band of the Cherokee, Haliwa Saponi, Lumbee, Shawnee, and the Waccamaw Siouan.[86]

Choosing to become a member of a fraternity is not an easy decision. Many of the men who might be interested are discouraged by their parents. This relates to all of the negative stereotypes associated with fraternities.[87]

Cultural diversity is one of the goals of the fraternity as they are committed to promoting self-awareness and self-respect. Through the fraternity they develop individual character, promote opportunity and justice, and strive for excellence in education. Other qualities endorsed through brotherhood include leadership, community, honesty, wisdom, pride, and unity.[88] The values that are part of the organization reflect the mission of UNCP which also supports academic excellence, appreciation for cultural diversity, and concern for the well-being of others.[89]

Anyone with a desire to support the Native American tradition, has a cumulative GPA of 2.0, a GPA no less than 2.0 the previous semester, has completed 12 credit hours, and submits transcripts and an application two weeks prior to interviews may be considered eligible for initiation.[90]

The initiation process is secret, but Native American traditions are used from various traditions of the founders. Initiation reinforces Native American beliefs. No alcohol is used at all as this process is viewed as purification.[91]

The turtle has been embraced by Phi Sigma Nu to represent the fraternity. This symbol was chosen because of its symbolic characteristics and traditional importance in Native American cultures. The turtle is viewed as a gentle warrior, one who is silent and passive, but defensive when provoked. The symbol is constant and unchanging, similar to the continuation of Native Americans on this continent. Turtles move from place to place with the most dangerous time in its life being when it hatches, as it is vulnerable to predators. This is likened to how a pledge feels initially until he becomes enlightened and made to know the divine power that brought him to the brotherhood. Turtles can live more than a hundred years, similar to how the fraternity desires to prosper for generations to come. Turtles also have the ability to survive when wounded, which is similar to the strength the fraternity will need through adversities, challenges, and changes.[92]

Seven is also a sacred number for Native Americans and has a special significance for this fraternity, since there are seven founders. Four colors have been chosen by the fraternity, red, yellow, black and white, representing the four directions.[93]

After-school tutoring and involvement in the Boys and Girls Club are the agencies that Phi Sigma Nu chooses to support. After nine years of existence, there are over sixty members of this fraternity. As of this date there is not a graduate chapter, but the fraternity is looking into how to make this work.[94]

Beta Sigma Epsilon

The University of Arizona (UA) is home of the youngest Native American fraternity, Beta Sigma Epsilon. This fraternity was established in 2000 by two Navajo cofounders, Nathan Pryor and Eric Riggs. Pryor reviewed the retention trends of Native American males at this institution, which showed a decrease of 20 percent from 1989 to 1996 as well as a lack of involvement in organizations and general campus life. This fraternity was created to be an effort to counteract these trends.[95]

The student body at UA in fall 2002 was 36,847, with 724 or almost 2 percent being Native American. Native Americans enrolled 526 or 1.96 percent of all undergraduates (28,278) at Arizona. Of these, 337 were female and 189 male. Of the 1998 Native American freshman, 35 percent graduated and 6 percent were still enrolled, for a 45 percent retention rate. Native Americans are one of the groups that have the lowest retention of all students at UA. Only African Americans had a slightly lower retention rate at 43 percent.[96]

Enrollment for fall 2004, including graduate, undergraduate, and professional programs, was 36,932 students. Of this number, 763 were Native American, 2.1 percent of the total.[97] These enrollment figures represent an increase in the Native American percentage of students. This increase was primarily female students, as the male enrollment only increased by one. While one may still have a concern about Native American men and their representation on the UA campus, the fraternity is still too young to note any overall impact on retention. Individual stories may be of more importance.

The purpose of Beta Sigma Epsilon is to serve the Native American community by developing multiple dimensions of young Native American men. A mission was created around their view of the organization, the members, and what they strive to achieve and do. Pryor developed what he described as the Circle of Honor to unite several of the founding concepts into schemata that represent the beliefs of the fraternity. In the visual representation, the circle encloses four boxes that outline the goals of the organization. Excellence is represented in the first section. Each member strives for excellence in brotherhood, academia, professional goals, community service, and cultural awareness. To achieve excellence in these areas, the second box is wrapped around and called Course of Action. Action is mandated in leadership, unity, prudence, determination, truth, and respect.[98]

How these goals are achieved is listed in a third box which indicates what the organization promises to provide. Resources, tools, experience, opportunities, and a supportive environment are what Beta Sigma Epsilon provides for the men. In return, the fourth outlines what is expected of the members such as participation, growth and development, achieving personal goals, helping others, and having better than a 2.5 GPA.[99] The mission of UA is to discover, educate, serve, and inspire.[100] As indicated in the mission of Beta Sigma Epsilon, their goal is also to strive for academic excellence and leadership in the community, a strong congruency with the University's mission.

A shield is the emblem of this fraternity, taken from Native America tradition. An eagle is spread around the shield with five feathers suspended from the circle. The Circle is divided into four sections, each with its own symbol. In each section, one of the following is placed; an arrowhead, an Oak leaf, a gila monster, and a book with 2000, the year the fraternity was established.[101]

The Alpha class was inaugurated in the fall 2000 and consisted of three men, Garret Curley and Craig Wood, both Navajo, and Josh Lucio a Zuni. In 2004, a Beta chapter was established at Northern Arizona University. Recent figures indicate a membership of thirteen, which includes three graduate students and four non-UA members. The Inter-fraternal Council (IFC) recognizes the fraternities that are supported by the University of Arizona and Beta Sigma Epsilon is recognized by this council.[102]

Conclusion

While many fraternities receive negative press about hazing and drinking rituals, Native American Greeks have forged a proactive role to present the opposite image. Ingenuity appears to have come naturally for the Native American Greek organizations as can be noted in the images they have created to represent their organizations. A strong heritage is present at all levels of each of the organizations.

Although each Native American Greek organization has its unique character, there are several overlapping elements. Each organization utilizes, preserves, and honors Native American culture, which is etched strongly into the mission of each organization, the pledging process, the structure of the offices, the symbols of the organization, the special events they sponsor, the community organizations they are involved in, and generally everything they do.

Representatives from every Native American fraternity and sorority indicated that rules against alcohol are foremost in their principles. They are strongly committed to the college mission and education excellence and to creating a positive image for their organization and Native Americans in general on campus. Each organization is involved in the community at large to support agencies that affect Native Americans.

A late entrance into the Greek world has not deterred the determination of the Native American students who have shaped and nurtured the growth of sororities and fraternities that meet their needs. Each organization has been crafted to support Native Americans in the college environment by bringing a community of people together to strive for excellence in education. All these Native American organizations are exemplary organizations for their college and community. Native American Greek organizations fit an ideal of combining culture, education, and community.

Notes

1. B. G. Riorden and R. Q. Dana, "Greek Letter Organizations and Alcohol: Problems, Policies and Programs," in *New Challenges for Greek Letter Organizations: Transforming Fraternities & Sororities into Learning Communities*, ed. W. G. Whipple, New Directions for Student Services 81 (San Francisco: Jossey-Bass, 1998), 49–59; M. D. Shonrock, "Standards and Expectations for Greek Letter Organizations," in *New Challenges for Greek Letter Organizations: Transforming Fraternities & Sororities into Learning Communities*, ed. W. G. Whipple, New Directions for Student Services 81 (San Francisco: Jossey-Bass, 1998), 79–85; Alfred Lee McClung, *Fraternities Without Brotherhood: A Study of Prejudice on the American Campus* (Boston: Beacon Press, 1955).
2. Shonrock, "Standards and Expectations," 79–80.
3. McClung, *Fraternities Without Brotherhood*, 9.
4. Ibid., 55.
5. Shonrock, "Standards and Expectations," 79, 83.
6. D. H. DeJong, *Promises of the Past* (Golden, CO: North American Press, 1993), 25.
7. B. Wright and W. G. Tierney, "American Indians in Higher Education," *Change* 23, no. 2 (1991): 11.

8. J. Brudvig, (n.d.). The College of William and Mary. White Dove's Native American Indian Site Eastern Universities and Indians. Available at http://users.multipro.com/whitedove/encyclopedia/eastern-universities-and-indians.html.
9. Wright and Tierney, "American Indians in Higher Education," 12–13.
10. M.C. Szasz, *Education and the American Indian; The Road to self-Determination since 1928*, 3rd ed. (Albuquerque: University of New Mexico Press, 1999), 134.
11. DeJong, *Promises of the Past*, 25.
12. J. Daniell. Dartmouth College. White Dove's Native American Indian Site Eastern Universities and Indians. http://users.multipro.com/whitedove/encyclopedia/eastern-universities-and-indians.html
13. Alpha Pi Omega. Alpha Pi Omega Sorority, Inc., http://geocities.com/alphapiomegasorority
14. A. Bush. Princeton University. White Dove's Native American Indian Site Eastern Universities and Indians. http://users.multipro.com/whitedove/encyclopedia/eastern-universities-and-indians.html
15. Wright and Tierney, "American Indians in Higher Education," 13–14.
16. T. Tastoke, personal communication, July 4, 2005.
17. C. M. Loo and G. Rolison, "Alienation of Ethnic Minority Students at a Predominantly White University," *The Journal of Higher Education* 57, no. 1 (1986): 64–65; J. S. Taylor, "America's First People. Factors Which Affect their Persistence in Higher Education" (ERIC Document Reproduction Service No. ED437874), 1999; S-M. R. Ting and A. Bryant, "The Impact of Acculturation and Psychosocial Variables on Academic Performance of Native American & Caucasian College Freshman," *Journal of College Admission* 171 (2001): 22–38.
18. I. HeavyRunner and K. Marshall. "Miracle Survivors," *Tribal College* 14, no. 4 (2003): 14–19.
19. W.G. Tierney and C.S. Kidwell, "The Quiet Crisis," *Change* 23, no. 2 (1991): 4.
20. J. Crutchfield, personal communication, July 31, 2005; D. McLean, personal communication, July 28, 2005; T. Tsatoke, personal communication, July 14, 2005.
21. Alicia Hunt, personal communication, October 31, 2005.
22. U.S. Census 2000.
23. J. Crutchfield, personal communication.
24. Lumbee Tribe. The Offical Site of the Lumbee Tribe of North Carolina. http://www.lumbeetribe.com/lumbee/indes.htm
25. J. Locklear, personal communication, July 24, 2005.
26. University of North Carolina at Pembroke, Welcome to UNCP, About UNCP. http://www.uncp.edu
27. University of North Carolina Pembroke Mission Statement, http://www.uncp.edu/uncp/about/mission.htm
28. University of North Carolina at Pembroke Web site.
29. Ibid.
30. Ibid., National Center for Educational Statistics, 2005.
31. University of North Carolina at Pembroke Web site.
32. J. Crutchfield, personal communication.
33. University of North Carolina at Pembroke Web site.
34. Alpha Pi Omega Web site.
35. National Center for Educational Statistics, 2005.
36. Alpha Pi Omega Web site.
37. D. Mclean, personal communication.
38. University of North Carolina-Chapel Hill Mission statement. http://www.unc.edu/about

39. D. Mclean, personal communication.
40. Ibid.
41. Ibid.
42. Ibid.
43. Alpha Pi Omega Web site.
44. D. McLean, personal communication.
45. A. Hunt, personal communication.
46. National Center for Educational Statistics, 2003
47. A. Hunt, personal communication.
48. A. Hunt, personal communication, October 28, 2005.
49. Sigma Omicron Epsilon (n.d.). Sigma Omicron Epsilon Beta Chapter. http://soebetachapter.tripod.com/id17.html
50. Ibid.
51. A. Hunt, personal communication, October 28, 2005.
52. Sigma Omicron Epsilon Web site.
53. A. Hunt, personal communication, October 28, 2005.
54. A. Hunt, personal communication, November 1, 2005.
55. Ibid.
56. Ibid.
57. Gamma Delta Pi (n. d.). Native American Indian Sorority. http://students.ou.edu/W/Robin.S.Williams-1/homegage.htm
58. T. Tsatoke, personal communication, July 29, 2005.
59. Ibid.
60. National Center for Educational Statistics.
61. Gamma Delta Pi Web site.
62. Ibid.
63. Ibid.
64. Ibid.
65. Ibid.
66. C. Good Voice, Native Sisterhood. http://www.reznetnews.org/student041203_sisterhood
67. T. Tsatoke, personal communication, July 14, 2005.
68. Bacone College Mission Statement. http://www.bacone.edu/information/mission.html
69. Epsilon Chi Nu, Epsilon Chi Nu, Inc. http://www.epsilonchinu.org
70. J. Crutchfield, personal communication.
71. Epsilon Chi Nu Web site.
72. Ibid.
73. J. Crutchfield, personal communication.
74. Ibid.
75. Epsilon Chi Nu Web site.
76. East Carolina mission. Part II. University Organization, *East Carolina University Faculty Manual.* http://www.ecu.edu/cs-acad/fsonline/customcf/facultymanual/part2/22.htm
77. Epsilon Chi Nu Web site.
78. J. Crutchfield, personal communication.
79. Ibid.
80. Ibid.
81. Epsilon Chi Nu Web site; J. Crutchfield, personal communication.
82. J. Crutchfield, persoal communication.
83. J. Crutchfield, personal communication.

84. Phi Sigma Nu. Phi Sigma Nu: Native American Fraternity. http://phisgmanu.com
85. J. Locklear, personal communication.
86. Phi Sigma Nu Web site.
87. J. Locklear, personal communication.
88. Phi Sigma Nu Web site.
89. University of North Carolina Web site.
90. Phi Sigma Nu Web site.
91. J. Locklear, personal communication.
92. Phi Sigma Nu Web site.
93. Ibid.
94. J. Locklear, personal communication.
95. Beta Sigma Epsilon. Beta Sigma Epsilon, Alpha Chapter, University of Arizona. http://clubs.asus.arizona.edu/~bse
96. Decision and Planning Support (DAPS) (n.d). University of Arizona Website. http://daps.arizona.edu
97. University of Arizona. Students by Ethnicity and Gender, Headcount Enrollment, Fall 2004. Office of Institutional Research & Evaluation.
98. N. Pryor. Beta Sigma Epsilon Web site. http://clubs.asua.arizona.edu/~bse/mission_circleof
99. Ibid.
100. University of Arizona Web site. Mission statement. http://www.arizona.edu/home/aboutua.php
101. Beta Sigma Epsilon Web site.
102. Ibid.

Multicultural Fraternities and Sororities: A Hodgepodge of Transient Multiethnic Groups

Amy E. Wells and Mark K. Dolan

AMERICAN COLLEGES AND UNIVERSITIES ARE NOW MUCH MORE diverse in terms of student race and ethnicity today than they were in the nineteenth and early twentieth century—the heyday of the fraternity and sorority movement. However, as student demographics have changed on campuses, membership diversity in the long-standing North American Interfraternity Conference (IFC) and National Panhellenic Conference (NPC) organizations has grown at a snail's pace. Greek life at the University of Southern California (USC) exemplified this slow growth in 2004 when the white student population numbered only 47.5 percent; among the twenty-eight IFC and NPC groups, white membership still comprised 76.3 percent of total membership—a pace requiring thirty years to catch up with overall student diversity at the university.[1] The key social aspects of Greek life that promote traditionalism, elitism, and exclusion despite increasing student heterogeneity cause fraternities and sororities to stand out as a puzzling feature of American campus life—a phenomenon explored over time in scholarship and the popular press.[2]

Multicultural Greek-Letter Organizations (MGLOs) have appeared continuously on the collegiate landscape for twenty-five years. Yet even the professionals who work with Greek-letter organizations lack an informed understanding of these unique fraternities and sororities.[3] To some, MGLOs are mistaken with the long-standing African American, Asian, or Latino Greek-letter organizations. While specific ethnic or ethnic-interest fraternal groups have increased in number and popularity,[4] historically they were not established for the purpose of bringing about multiethnic, multiracial organizations and promoting multicultural awareness. Fraternities and sororities that expressly identify themselves as multicultural are the focus of this chapter. The central questions behind this initial history and first scholarly exploration of these groups include: How do MGLOs express organizational identity and purpose? What significant patterns, complexities, and nuances emerge in the history of MGLOs? And finally, how do these groups fit into the larger historical and organizational structure of American campus life and the collegiate cocurriculum?

A Prelude to MGLOs: The Case of Beta Sigma Tau

The origins of multicultural and multiethnic fraternities and sororities can be traced to incidents of single-race fraternity and sorority chapters "with ideas of inclusiveness" pledging outside racial bounds.[5] These incidents began during an unprecedented period of social protest on American college campuses in the late 1920s and 1930s[6] and grew to a bona fide movement through the 1940s and 1950s,[7] coalescing with the demands of World War II veterans returning to discriminatory social practices as well as the report of President Truman's Commission on Civil Rights (1947) that called for expanded educational opportunity in a democratic society.[8] In 1948 one upstart fraternity, Beta Sigma Tau, "attracted wide attention" as it came together at a Roosevelt College (Chicago) conference from twenty-four separate "intercultural and interracial fraternities" as a "new style fraternity with no discriminatory barriers." Eventually Beta Sigma Tau expanded to eight chapters and sparked a new sorority, Pi Beta Sigma.[9]

Following another period of campus unrest among college students in the 1980s and 1990s[10] and in the wake of an expanded and contested formal curriculum dubbed "the canon or culture wars,"[11] nearly a half-century later, another fraternity, also Beta Sigma Tau, claimed to have made "waves" of its own at the University of Toledo. Reportedly pledging "ninety-four men from all walks of life" since 1997, the Beta Sigma Tau roster boasted of "African Americans, Caucasians, Asians, Buddhists, Catholics, Atheists, and many other races, nationalities, and religions." A local upstart organization, Toledo's Beta Sigma Tau fashioned itself as capturing the "true attitude and meaning behind a social fraternity," with the intention to "level, not raise, barriers among people . . . and provide a foundation that transcends racial, national, and religious differences."[12] Despite its strength in 1997, however, Toledo's Beta Sigma Tau subsequently swayed from its multicultural mission and folded as its founders and core leaders graduated.[13]

Thus, the case of Beta Sigma Tau is an interesting starting point for this history of the multicultural fraternity and sorority movement—a movement largely, but not exclusively, characterized by the worldviews of founders and a hodgepodge of multiethnic local or single chapter groups. Beta Sigma Tau of 1948 represents the movement's genesis but false dawn over fifty-five years ago. Toledo's Beta Sigma Tau of 1997, unrelated to the 1948 group, represents the movement's contemporary momentum but also its impermanence, lack of cohesion, and amorphous nature. Together these snapshots of Beta Sigma Tau highlight the challenge of researching and writing about a collection of disparate groups with the aim of creating a larger, national story for the contemporary multicultural Greek organization movement.

MGLOs: The Contemporary Movement

Between 2002 and 2007, nearly thirty multicultural fraternities (twelve) and sororities (twenty-two), with 264 combined chapters—205 women's; 55 men's—have been identified on college campuses across the country.[14] Although each organization has its own identity with distinct characteristics, for the most part multicultural fraternities and sororities are structurally similar to North American Interfraternity Conference (IFC), National Pan-Hellenic Council (NPHC), and National Panhellenic Conference (NPC) chapters. They have established philanthropies, symbols, colors, mottoes, and mascots. Some closely follow NPHC traditions incorporating hand symbols and step shows.[15] Recruitment also varies among these groups, with chapters adopting styles similar to either the NPHC intake process or IFC and NPC recruitment. In fact, some chapters have created a membership recruitment style that *combines* intake processes with traditional recruitment practices. Some recruitment practices even vary from chapter to chapter within the same organization. Regulating or governing these organizations with such a deliberate array of traditions and practices proves to be challenging and hence, the National Multicultural Greek Council (NMGC), an advisory board, provides leadership and support for established multicultural fraternity and sorority member organizations.

Contemporary MGLOs began in 1981 when five female students at Rutgers University (New Brunswick, New Jersey) founded the first national multicultural sorority, Mu Sigma Upsilon, Inc. Mu Sigma Upsilon was not only the first, but also became one of the largest national multicultural sororities with twenty-eight chapters and an alumni association represented in seven states. Although the majority of Mu Sigma Upsilon chapters reside in the East, one chapter resides at the University of Kansas. Other sororities identified that rival Mu Sigma Upsilon in number of chapters and organizational development include Lambda Sigma Gamma, a sorority founded at California State

Table 6 Multicultural Sororities

Organization	Year Est.	Campus Established	No. Chapters	States Represented	NMGC Member
Mu Sigma Upsilon	1981	Rutgers	28	CT, FL, KS, NJ, NY, PA, VA	Yes
Lambda Sigma Gamma	1986	Cal State-Sacramento	22	CA	No
Lambda Tau Omega	1988	Montclair State	14	FL, IL, NJ	Yes
Omega Phi Chi	1988	Rutgers	10	FL, NJ, NY	Yes
Eta Omega Tau	1988	Pace University	4	NY, KY, TX	No
Phi Gamma Theta	1990	Cal State-Chico	3	CA	No
Sigma Theta Psi	1991	San Jose State	9	CA, NV	No
Zeta Sigma Chi	1991	Northern Illinois	11	IL, IN, MD, MI, PA, TX, WI	No
Sigma Alpha Zeta	1992	Cal State-Fresno	5	CA	No
Chi Sigma Upsilon	1993	New Jersey City University	2	NJ	Yes
Upsilon Kappa Delta	1993	Cal State-Chico	3	CA	No
Delta Xi Phi	1994	Illinois	15	AL, CA, IL, KS, MA, MD, MI, MS, NY, WI,	Yes
Zeta Sigma Phi	1994	USC	1	CA	No
Iota Psi Phi	1995	Cal State-Fresno	3	CA, ID, WA	Yes
Delta Sigma Chi	1996	City Un. New York	7	NY	Yes
Lambda Fe Usöñ	1996	SUNY-Stony Brook	2	NY	No
Sigma Iota Sigma	1996	SUNY-Buffalo	4	NY	No
Lambda Psi Delta	1997	Yale	10	CT, FL, NJ, TX	Yes
Theta Nu Xi	1997	North Carolina	37	AZ, CA, FL, GA, IN, IL, MI, NC, NM, NJ, NY, PA, TX, UT, VA,	No
Delta Gamma Pi	1998	Towson	11	CA, IN, LA, MD	No
Alpha Delta Sigma	2003	Alabama	1	MI, NY, PA, SC AL	No
Zeta Chi Phi	2003	Texas-San Antonio	3	FL, MN, TX	No

University at Sacramento in 1986, with twenty-two chapters solely in California, and Theta Nu Xi, founded at the University of North Carolina in 1997. Additionally, Theta Nu Xi stands out as a particularly fast-growing organization with thirty-seven chapters located in fifteen states and has garnered attention from campus newspapers across the nation. Table 6 lists contemporary multicultural sororities in order of establishment with additional information depicting the campus where the fraternity or sorority originated; the total number of chapters including active, colonies, alumni, and "eternal" or memorial chapters; states represented, and status of NMGC membership.

Psi Sigma Phi Multicultural Fraternity, Inc., cofounded in 1990 at Montclair State University and Jersey City State College is the largest continuously operating national multicultural fraternity. Psi Sigma Phi has several chapters in New Jersey colleges and universities as well as chapters at Utah State University, Penn State University, and the University of North Carolina at Chapel Hill. Rivals for designation as the oldest contemporary multicultural fraternities include Epsilon Sigma Rho, a California-based fraternity with six chapters, and Delphic of Gamma Sigma Tau which traces its own history to the late 1800s but has experienced several periods of inactivity and moved in and out of NMGC membership during the past five years. Table 7 portrays contemporary multicultural fraternities in order of establishment with additional information depicting the campus where the fraternity or sorority originated; the total number of chapters including active, colonies, alumni, and eternal chapters; states represented, and status of NMGC membership.

Both Mu Sigma Upsilon and Psi Sigma Phi have national executive officers, and along with ten other Multicultural Greek-Letter Organizations (MGLOs) comprise the membership of the National Multicultural Greek Council, Inc. (NMGC). Established in 1998, the NMGC exists as an advisory council to encourage the exchange of ideas between member organizations, promote multicultural awareness, and support membership achievements. In order to apply for membership in the NMGC, Greek Letter Organizations (GLOs) must be a multicultural or multiethnic organization in existence for a minimum of five years or have a minimum of five chapters/colonies. The interested GLO must also function as a legal and incorporated body under laws set forth by one of the fifty states of America. The NMGC Executive Board conducts an annual conference at a host university in order to meet with members and discuss the future goals of the association.

The insights and personal experiences of NMGC President, Denise J. Pipersburgh, Esq., a founding member of Lambda Psi Delta Sorority, Inc. provide historical context for understanding the development

Table 7 Multicultural Fraternities

Organization	Year Est.	Campus Established	No. Chapters	States Represented	NMGC Member
Delphic of Gamma Sigma Tau	1986	SUNY-New Paltz	2	NY	Yes
Epsilon Sigma Rho	1986	Cal State-Sacramento	6	CA	No
Psi Sigma Phi	1990	Montclair State& Jersey City State	10	NC, NJ, PA, UT	Yes
Gamma Omega Delta	1992	SUNY-New Paltz	5	NY	Yes
Tau Phi Sigma	1992	Illinois	7	IL, IN	No
Sigma Chi Omega	1993	Cal-Santa Barbara	1	CA	No
Chi Delta Beta	1994	Cal State-Stanislaus	3	CA	No
Delta Omega Epsilon	1994	College of Staten Island	6	NY	No
Phi Sigma Chi	1996	City U. of New York	3	NY	Yes
Beta Gamma Nu	1997	USC	4	CA	No
Omega Delta	1997	Illinois	4	IL	No
Sigma Delta Phi Epsilon	1997	SUNY-Buffalo	4	NY	No

of some MGLOs.[16] An African American woman with a strong Belizian cultural heritage, Pipersburgh pledged a Latina group at first during her undergraduate study at Yale (1992–98). While her sister looked into participating in an African American sorority at Howard University and Pipersburgh appreciated the lifetime commitment perspective expressed by members of those groups, she found the pledge process for African American groups unappealing and worried that her Belizian cultural heritage would not be adequately expressed or appreciated. Unsatisfied by her experience in a Latina group, however, Denise and other Lambda Psi Delta founders "broke off" to create something new and different.

Pipersburgh explained that many multicultural fraternities and sororities broke away from established ethnic or ethnic-interest groups, briefly thrived, went defunct, and even got revived as they grappled with the task of carving an identity apart from the original ethnic center. As a result, MGLOs have depicted a wide array and mixture of traditional elements in the expression of mottoes, colors, and rituals. For example, Lamda Psi Delta founders adopted a sorority hymn and kept the group's actual name secret—much like African American Greek groups, according to Pipersburgh. Furthermore, she explained that this decision contrasted with the practices of Latina groups which often, but not exclusively, spelled out group meanings in group names. However, the task of articulating how diversity was recognized and appreciated and what it meant to be multicultural required a good deal of work and a thoughtful approach.

According to Pipersburgh, the NMGC has received at least two new member applications per week for several years. Nevertheless, NMGC membership and recognition did not come easily for member groups; their recognition attained only after a thorough review by the NMGC's membership council. In sum, membership required organizations to demonstrate a meaningful amalgam of ideals and activities that truly promoted diversity and multiculturalism. In other words, an NMGC member cannot just be a group that has a diverse membership; it has to be "more than that," according to Pipersburgh. So while numerous "organizations that don't fit anywhere come to us," the NMGC President explained, a holistic approach to diversity and multiculturalism must be found in organizational mission statements, membership, and activities.

This history confirms that NMGC's scrutiny before bringing groups into their fold is understandable. Quite clearly, the expression of organizational purpose related to multiculturalism, diversity of membership, level of sustained activity, and overall organizational quality among MGLOs comes off as uneven or uncertain at best. The narrative that follows next is organized around the central research questions and seeks to provide an initial history of MGLOs as well as to generate questions for future research.

How Do MGLOs Express Organizational Identity and Purpose?

When exploring the identity, purpose, structures, and activities of Greek organizations, outsiders or nonmembers can only get so far.[17] Inspired by popular culture rather than antiquity, MGLO interior cultures are guarded literally by password protection devices and figuratively by a cinematic display of mermaids, knights, black panthers, white Bengal tigers, dragons, diamonds, "D.I.V.A.S." and "GQ" gentlemen.[18] Nevertheless, this interior landscape conveys important distinctions about MGLOs from other Greek organizations primarily through mission statements and community-oriented philanthropic activities that affirm diversity, promote education (most often for first generation college students), and advocate social change.

Multicultural fraternities expressed their distinct identity through various statements that affirmed diversity and countered previous incarnations of brotherhood that did not display or affirm diversity. Omega Delta defined itself in contrast to IFC groups: "While other groups are content with staying in their own ethnic groups and comfort zones, we pushed forward to bring multiculturism [*sic*] into prominent view." In addition to the statements articulated by Beta Sigma Tau about capturing the "true attitude and meaning behind a social fraternity," Delphic of Gamma Sigma Tau boasted that it did not "base brotherhood on the surface of the skin, but on what is beneath it in the heart and soul." Epsilon Gamma Rho espoused a "philosophy of acceptance of any and all people" and Sigma Chi Omega pledged itself to not only accept differences but also assured that the group "embraced" differences and vowed to "teach others to do the same."

Furthermore, multicultural fraternities also encouraged membership as a form of social activism and thereby an important part of MGLO identity. For example, Gamma Omega Delta invited site visitors to "make a difference" with this quote from anthropologist Margaret Mead (1901–78): "Never doubt that a small group of thoughtful and committed citizens can change the world; indeed, it's the only thing that ever has." Phi Sigma Chi mission charged itself "to direct members toward a consciousness of their lifetime responsibility of helping others." Psi Sigma Phi revealed a goodwill mission: "We believe that men, meeting in a spirit of goodwill, in an honest effort of understanding, can live together on this earth in peace and harmony." And finally, Phi Sigma Chi at Arizona State University expressed a "common goal to improve the state of our communities through leadership development." Table 8 presents a list of mottoes or essential ideals for multicultural fraternities.

Multicultural sororities expressed their distinct identities through various statements that affirmed diversity, womanhood, and education as well as countered previous manifestations of unity and sisterhood. Similar to the articulated purpose of the multicultural fraternity Delphic of Gamma Sigma Tau, the sorority Sigma Alpha Zeta underscored the "modern need for multicultural thinking" and confirmed that true "sisterhood, not race" stood out as the group's essential ideal. Zeta Sigma Phi asserted its identity in the statement: "some girls define their lives by a sorority, but this sorority is defined by our lives." Two multicultural sororities identified their goal to embody multiculturalism through their membership. The first, Lambda Sigma Gamma, sought

Table 8 Multicultural Fraternities' Mottoes and Foundational Ideals

Fraternities	Mottoes/Ideals
Delphic of Gamma Sigma Tau	Friendship, fellowship and fidelity & Unity Amongst All
Epsilon Sigma Rho	Education, Strength, and Respect
Gamma Omega Delta	Gentlemen of Quality and Diversity / Service, Brotherhood, and Education
Tau Phi Sigma	As Humans Always United, As Brothers Never Defeated
Psi Sigma Phi	Dedicated to the causes of education, community service and multiculturalism
Sigma Chi Omega	Strength through Diversity / Mind, Body, & Brotherhood
Chi Delta Beta	Higher Education, Multiculturalism & Brotherly Love
Delta Omega Epsilon	Unavailable or missing information
Phi Sigma Chi	We are bound by nothing, for Phi is the limit!
Beta Gamma Nu	Pride in Culture, Brotherhood in Arms, & Respect for Life
Omega Delta	Building Brotherhood through Professionalism
Sigma Delta Phi Epsilon	Family, Individuality, Culture, Education, Respect, Community Service, Leadership, and Co-Education

to attract "women of different creeds, ethnicity's [*sic*], cultures, socio-economic backgrounds, physical talents, mental abilities, and sexual preferences. The second, Theta Nu Xi, vowed to be a "living" model for "sisterhood across different races, cultures, religions, backgrounds, and lifestyles." And finally, four multicultural sororities, namely, Mu Sigma Upsilon, Delta Xi Phi, Zeta Sigma Phi, and Lambda Psi Delta, expressly addressed women's empowerment through unity either in their mottoes or tenets.

Multicultural sororities also expressed aspirations for individual activism through membership and the possibility of social change through education. In addition to the mottoes and ideals presented in Table 9, some additional examples highlighted group purpose and identity related to inspiring social change. For example, Iota Psi Phi claimed it "recognizes the many ills of this world however, we also recognize the strength and power of people themselves" and added, "we know that with true unity we can make changes, for education surpasses ignorance." Theta Nu Xi desired to use "our sorority as a vehicle to educate the campus and community on issues of diversity."[19] And finally, Delta Xi Phi expressed its mission modestly, "we are working diligently to ensure that we continue growing in a positive fashion that will impact the society in which we live."[20]

Scant evidence existed that any one MGLO, or the NMGC for that matter, has fully arrived at integrating each of the dimensions of multicultural educational theory wholesale as articulated by scholar James A. Banks.[21] The five dimensions of his theory involve: content integration (the extent to which content includes a variety of cultures and groups to illustrate key concepts); the knowledge construction process (the extent to which the implicit cultural assumptions and biases in the knowledge construction process are investigated and understood); an equity pedagogy (involves modification of teaching practice to facilitate learning and achievement among members of various cultural, ethnic, and social-class groups); prejudice reduction (seeks modification of students' racial attitudes); and empowering school cultures and social structures (seeks to examine and reorder commonly accepted practices that disempower students from diverse groups). More often, these organizations and their members wore their multicultural identity with a good portion of eighteen- to twenty-four-year-old optimism and in a far less cerebral fashion. Hence, ideas and images depicting multiculturalism primarily but not exclusively represented two aspects of Banks's model, namely "content integration" and "prejudice reduction."[22]

Toward "content integration" multicultural groups used "a variety of cultures and groups to illustrate key concepts and principles." For example, the previously mentioned use of a quotation from Margaret

Table 9 Multicultural Sororities' Mottoes and Foundational Ideals

Sororities	Mottoes/Ideals
Mu Sigma Upsilon	Mujeres Siempre Unidas (Women Always United) / Academic Excellence, Unity Among All Women, & To Be Active in the Community
Lambda Sigma Gamma	Unity Through Sisterhood
Lambda Tau Omega	Excellence Through Unity, Knowledge & Dedication
Omega Phi Chi	Honesty, loyalty, respect, responsibility, academic excellence, and involvement in community service
Eta Omega Tau	Sisters of the Heart / Service, Professionalism, and Sisterhood
Phi Gamma Theta	Strength and Honor are Her Clothing
Sigma Theta Psi	Honesty, Loyalty, Respect, Open-Mindedness, Leadership, and Academic Excellence
Zeta Sigma Chi	Keeping the Dream Alive
Sigma Alpha Zeta	Sisterhood, academic excellence, and community service
Chi Sigma Upsilon	Solidarity Through Respect for Individuality
Upsilon Kappa Delta	Academics, Community Service, Multiculturalism, and Sisterhood
Delta Xi Phi	Advancement of Women through Higher Education; Increasing Multicultural Awareness; Community Service; Sisterhood, & Friendship
Zeta Sigma Phi	Knowledge, Color, Beauty, Power
Iota Psi Phi	Diversity, Integrity, and Education
Delta Sigma Chi	A Sisterhood of Multiculturalism / Persistence is the key to success in life, our sisterhood is the lock.
Lambda Fe Usöñ	D.I.V.A.S. (Diversified, Intelligent, Valiant, Authentic Sisters) / Unity, Faith, Strength
Sigma Iota Sigma	Multiculturalism, Sisterhood and Unification of Women to Achieve Individual Goals, Education, and Community Service
Lambda Psi Delta	Sovereignty to the Community/Intellectual Development, Empowerment of Women, Leadership, Cultural Awareness, and Upliftment of the Community
Theta Nu Xi	Sisters of Diversity, Together as ONE
Delta Gamma Pi	Live it, Love it, Show it! *And* Sisterhood bound together by Diversity, Unity, and Friendship, serving our Community.
Alpha Delta Sigma	The brilliance of our sisterhood shall be a light for the world
Zeta Chi Phi	Nothing, absolutely nothing can stop a truly committed person

Mead on a fraternity web site suggested an integrated approach to gender for the male organization, Gamma Omega Delta. While Delta Xi Phi Sorority sported a different color on each section of its web site "to represent diversity,"[23] the Lambda Psi Delta Sorority web portal took visitors through a fast, flashy series of various national flags showing international identity as an aspect of its membership and approach to diversity. Iota Psi Phi Sorority drew on a Chinese proverb, "A journey of a thousand miles must begin with a single step," for inspiration and diversity. In addition, the group selected the "neutral" tones of black, brown, and white to represent itself in the Greek community.

Toward the task of "prejudice reduction," multicultural groups also gave their idealism and energy. For example, at the University of Michigan, Zeta Sigma Chi Sorority sponsored the event "Homophobia in the Greek Community" not only to challenge Greek members about the community's collective homophobia and low tolerance for nonheterosexuals but also to discuss the harmful effects of "hyper-masculine" and "hyper-feminine" stereotypes of Greeks by non-Greeks in the campus community.[24] Theta Nu Xi Sorority at the University of Arizona sponsored two forums to advance nonviolence. The first in 2003, "Create a Hate Free Zone," sought to increase awareness of derogatory language —to let students know that "phrases like 'that's gay' or 'that's retarded' offend and hurt people.[25] The second, in 2004, discussed communication problems and reported constraints in male/female relationships and lesbian/gay relationships that intensify sexual abuse and domestic violence.[26] And finally, the Indiana University chapter of Theta Nu Xi, along with Delta Sigma Theta Sorority (NPHC) and the Office of Diversity Education, facilitated a panel discussion on "four major civil rights movements and their continued relevance" to help participants understand the "cycle of oppression."[27] In this way, MGLO activism "can be viewed as a form of resistance to oppressive social relationships."[28]

Through philanthropic activities and community service, MGLOs further differentiated their identity and purpose. Members of multicultural fraternities sought to build leadership and improve the lives of others through their community service efforts. Although multicultural fraternities lent their support to large, national organizations such as the American Cancer Society, Big Brothers of America, and the Juvenile Diabetes Foundation, a few fraternities exhibited a notable focus upon "grassroots" activism and service.

Other MGLOs elevated group and member consciousness while providing support for younger males in various ethnic groups; especially populations that have not thrived in postsecondary educational institutions. Along these lines Beta Gamma Nu's program called "The

College Experience" stood out. Beta Gamma Nu claimed that through this program the group reached young students from middle school to high school and exposed them to college life through the success stories of people that came from similar neighborhoods and schools. Seeking to "motivate and create a connection between aspiring students," Beta Gamma Nu introduced young men, presumably first-generation college students, from diverse, underrepresented communities to college student life as well as "the importance of giving back to their communities."

Mentioning its efforts to "mobilize those with similar interests," Phi Sigma Chi members aimed their efforts at community improvement, listing in addition to its beautification project the arming of at-risk youth for success in a youth leadership program. Similarly, members of Sigma Chi Omega tutored students at the San Marcos High School in Santa Barbara and completed a holiday project with elementary school students. In giving food to the Food Bank of New Jersey and working at the Newark Soup Kitchens, for example, members of Psi Sigma Phi learned about a wide range of social issues and different populations as well as the importance of giving time, service, and financial support. Table 10 highlights specific philanthropic activities for multicultural fraternities found during review of multicultural fraternity websites.

A similar emphasis on improving the lives of others through enhanced self-awareness, education, political activism, and community-based service existed among the wide array of philanthropic activities of multicultural sororities. Toward this end, Lambda Psi Delta espoused its community-oriented motto and philosophy among its five tenets, namely, "upliftment of the community," as well as boasted of the most comprehensive list of activities in which it not only "Rocked the Vote," for example, but also helped the homeless, abused, and the terminally ill. Lambda Psi Delta also supported the education of nonmembers in the community through programs like America Reads; the AMIGOS Tutoring Program; Leadership, Education, and Athletics in Partnership; the Community Solutions Mentoring Program, and the New Haven Adult Education Center. Chi Sigma Upsilon also advanced education through its support of an African American and Latino Male Retention Conference and the provision of tutorial services to Public School #5. One initiative, the New York Public Interest Research Group (NYPIRG), exemplified the community-based or "grass roots" political activism approach to improve quality of life in neglected neighborhoods espoused as a goal of multicultural groups and attracted support from Delta Sigma Chi and Lambda Fe Usöñ. And finally, two groups support explicit goals of multicultural education, including Zeta Sigma Chi with its support of the National Association of Multicultural Education (N.A.M.E.) as well as Theta Nu Xi whose philanthropic sup-

Table 10 Multicultural Fraternities' Philanthropy and Community Service Activities

Fraternities	Philanthropy and Community Service
Delphic of Gamma Sigma Tau	American Foundation for Suicide Prevention
Epsilon Sigma Rho	The Fight Against Prostate Cancer
Gamma Omega Delta	Disadvantaged Children; Learning Leaders Program of New York City
Tau Phi Sigma	American Diabetes Association; American Cancer Society; Boys and Girls Club; Purdue Latino Cultural Center
Psi Sigma Phi	Kidney Urology Foundation; City Year; Multiple Sclerosis & AIDS Walks; Juvenile Diabetes Foundation; Food Bank of New Jersey; American Cancer Society; Valerie Fund; Newark Soup Kitchens; Dove Services; Adopt A Highway Program
Sigma Chi Omega	Isla Vista street & beach clean-ups; Project Santa at IV Elementary School; Tutoring at San Marcos High School in Santa Barbara
Chi Delta Beta	Specific activities not provided
Delta Omega Epsilon	Unavailable or missing information
Phi Sigma Chi	Multicultural Awareness; 363 Campaign; Beauti-phi-cation Project; Network for Success (Youth leadership)
Beta Gamma Nu	Big Brothers of America; The College Experience
Omega Delta	Members complete 15 hours of community service each semester
Sigma Delta Phi Epsilon	Community service projects that benefit the university and surrounding communities where the group is established

port reached the National Conference for Community and Justice. Table 11 provides additional elaboration on some of the philanthropic activities culled from multicultural sorority web sites.

Considered together, and in context with more immediate activities such as providing relief to Hurricane Katrina and tsunami survivors as well as victims of domestic violence, the community service dimension of MGLOs represented a diverse and community-centered identity. In addition to comforting the sick and providing roofs for homeless, MGLOs also gave high levels of support to prospective first-generation college students and their own college and university communities. To

Table 11 Multicultural Sororities' Philanthropy and Community Service Activities

Sororities	Philanthropy and Community Service
Mu Sigma Upsilon	Ovarian Cancer National Alliance; AIDS Walks NY & NJ; Thanksgiving dinner at the Lakewood Baptist Church; Adopt-A-School; Tsunami Relief; Boys/Girls Club; Soups for Troops; Breast Cancer Research; Yard clean-ups
Lambda Sigma Gamma	Head Start
Lambda Tau Omega	AIDS & AIDS Awareness; Child Abuse Prevention; Breast Cancer Awareness; American Heart Association; March of Dimes; Easter Seals; Meals on Wheels
Omega Phi Chi	Adopt-A-School/Highway; American Red Cross; Diabetes, AIDS, Breast Cancer, and Multiple Sclerosis Walks and Runs; Elijah's Soup Kitchen; Hurricane Relief; Neighborhood Relations; Special Olympics; Toy Drives
Eta Omega Tau	Toys for Tots; Covenant House; Catholic Charities of NYC; Rap Da' Vote; Hug—Don't Hit 1998
Phi Gamma Theta	Clothing and toy drives; AIDS Walks; Domestic Violence Prevention; Cinco de Mayo Festival at Brett Harte Elementary School
Sigma Theta Psi	Breast Cancer Awareness; American Cancer Society/Relay for Life & Making Strides Against Breast Cancer; Susan G. Komen Race for the Cure
Zeta Sigma Chi	The Ronald McDonald House; National Association for Multicultural Education
Sigma Alpha Zeta	Unavailable or missing information
Chi Sigma Upsilon	Rape, Abuse, and Incest National Network (RAINN); AIDS Research Foundation for Children; AIDS Walk NY & NJ; Public School Tutoring; African American & Latino Male Retention Conference; American Diabetes Association; Hurricane Mitch Relief; Making Strides Against Breast Cancer; March of Dimes; Seniors Columbus Day Luncheon & Thanksgiving Dinner
Upsilon Kappa Delta	Unavailable or missing information
Delta Xi Phi	American Cancer Society; American Red Cross; Habitat for Humanity

(continued)

Table 11 Continued

Sororities	Philanthropy and Community Service
Zeta Sigma Phi	Project Angel Food; The Amanda Foundation
Iota Psi Phi	YWCA/Marjaree Mason Center; Centro Bellas Artes; American Veterans; Valley Children's Hospital Kid's Day; Cross Cultural Leadership Retreat; Central California Blood Bank; Women's Herstory Month; Spirit of Woman House; Association of College Unions International
Delta Sigma Chi	Safe Horizon Domestic Violence Shelter; The Stay Strong Foundation; New York Public Interest Research Group (NYPIRG); Little Sisters Club
Lambda Fe Usöñ	Big Brothers/Big Sisters; Blood Drives; Special Olympics; NYPIRG
Sigma Iota Sigma	City Mission; Cornerstone Manor; Vive la Casa; Compass House; March of Dimes; Linda Yalem Run
Lambda Psi Delta	Operation Santa; Multiple Sclerosis, American Heart Walks; 9–11, Hurricane Katrina, and Tsunami Relief; Hunger, Homeless, and AIDS Awareness Events; America Reads; AMIGOS Tutoring Program; Asian Refugee Health Project; Charter Oak Cultural Center; Community Solutions Mentoring Program; Domestic Violence Services; Great American Cleanup; Habitat for Humanity; Juvenile Probation Tutoring Program; Leadership, Education, and Athletics in Partnership; The Leukemia Society of America; Light the Night; Little Hearts Inc.; New Haven Adult Education Center; Nichols School Annual Fund Drive; American Red Cross; Rock the Vote; Ronald McDonald House; Salvation Army; SCADD (Halfway House for Women recovering from Drug and Alcohol Abuse); Trinity Café; Young Voices Initiative, Inc.; Youth Together
Theta Nu Xi	The National Conference for Community and Justice
Delta Gamma Pi	Members select a community organization and devote 15 hours of service/semester
Alpha Delta Sigma	American Cancer Society
Zeta Chi Phi	SAM Ministries (Support for the Homeless)

elaborate, one major project listed in the roster of annual events for USC's Sigma Chi Omega fraternity included cosponsorship of the USC "Multicultural Show" where community members star in various ethnic and cultural performances. In addition, MGLOs also supported numerous speaker's bureaus, Women's History Month and Martin Luther King Jr. activities, and campus leadership retreats that benefited their larger campus communities.

What Significant Patterns, Complexities, and Nuances Emerge in the History of MGLOs?

White Greek-letter organizations flourished in the late 1980s.[29] Since that time, fraternity membership declined while sorority membership remained healthy overall.[30] In the face of changing student demographics and besmirched by numerous incidents of hazing, alcohol abuse, ethnic and racial hostility, and violence, membership in IFC groups plunged to Vietnam War levels—a historic low point.[31] Accordingly, IFC fraternities lopped off weak chapters and offered up reforms such as alcohol-free housing and new member development programs.[32]

Although membership in ethnic and ethnic interest fraternities subsequently "exploded" according to some observers,[33] multicultural fraternities have lagged behind multicultural sororities in terms of organizational growth and development.[34] For example, only three organizations, all sororities, have established over twenty chapters, namely, Mu Sigma Alpha, Lambda Sigma Gamma, and Theta Nu Xi. Only one fraternity, Psi Sigma Phi, has established at least ten chapters. While the recent advance of multicultural women's groups across the American South, namely in Alabama, Georgia, and Mississippi where IFC and NPC groups had pledged very few, if any, persons of color appeared noteworthy, researchers found no multicultural fraternities outside of eight states: California, Illinois, Indiana, New Jersey, New York, North Carolina, Pennsylvania, and Utah.[35] Definitively, multicultural sororities have achieved wider appeal with chapters existing in twenty-five states.

MGLOs have been founded at many different kinds of higher education institutions, including regional universities, technical colleges, and flagship universities. To some extent, MGLO establishment and development has occurred on campuses with some of the incidents of protest or unrest during the 1980s and 1990s described by Rhoads in *Freedom's Web*. Thus, in the contemporary MGLO movement, multicultural groups first cropped up at Rutgers and have been established at Columbia University (Theta Nu Xi Sorority), Penn State (Psi Sigma

Phi Fraternity), and Michigan State (Zeta Sigma Chi Sorority), for example. However, no causal link existed between these incidents of protest and the birth of MGLOs on those campuses because in the case of Rutgers and Mu Sigma Alpha Sorority, for example, the sorority preceded the incidents of campus unrest described by Rhoads by fourteen years.[36] More likely, the establishment and growth pattern of MGLOs happened in larger states with high levels of population diversity, and hence, student diversity, such as California, Illinois, Florida, New Jersey, and New York. Then, too, the types of students attracted to Greek organizations as founders and members are more likely to be traditionally minded and socially conservative, and hence, less prone to campus protest.[37]

While MGLOs expressed lofty ideals in their missions and mottoes, they also reflected the trappings and trouble of their Greek predecessors. In fact, one season of the television show, "Sorority Life: Los Angeles" followed sixteen new members of USC's multicultural sorority, Zeta Sigma Phi. While the show depicted "catty, shallow, and superficial girls," according to one USC senior, it also depicted hazing as the show fixed its cameras upon new members who had moved into the "Pledge House" and were required to perform "certain duties" to join the sorority.[38] Outside of Zeta Sigma Phi, photographs of multicultural group members holding wooden paddles, veiled references to recruitment practices of other groups on MGLO web sites with accompanying firm antihazing statements, implied to researchers that incidents of hazing have occurred among MGLOs and other Greek groups on MGLO campuses.

In 2007, a coed multicultural Greek organization at the University of Mississippi gained attention from the national media.[39] Espousing a mission of "spreading the multicultural, multiethnic, multiracial message of unity and love for all" and comprised of eighty students, predominantly international, this new student group sought to bring international students into the tradition of football tailgating in the Grove during the fall as a primary activity. Thus, despite its promise for enhancing cultural diversity on the Greek-dominant University of Mississippi campus, the downside of the Awesome Dudes of Alpha Delta is that the group also espouses a philosophy that "we all party the same regardless of color or creed."[40]

So rather than break the mold as promised in MGLO rhetoric, behavioral patterns and gender relations among MGLOs fit familiar patterns. For example, some MGLOs, akin to NPHC groups, claimed formal association with opposite gender groups and provided Internet links to their web sites.[41] Accordingly, MGLO web sites prominently displayed photographs from mixers and service projects with these intimates and implied a ready-made "complement" of acceptable social partners.[42] In most cases, this association appeared innocent enough, and to a large extent, the opposite-gender groups expressed an identity apart from the opposite-gender group. However, the downfalls of association also came through. In one example, a woman's group was created solely as an auxiliary group "to promote and assist the fraternity in all its endeavors."[43] A second group recognized as the "Omega Delta Sweeties" provided photographs and testimonials that documented sexual bravado and incidents of alcohol abuse.[44]

Although this "social complement" function[45] assisted in growing the Greek system over time, traditional gender relationships can be troublesome when they distract women with "romance" and constrain academic aspirations.[46] In the worst-case scenario, traditional notions of gender relationships have perpetuated sorority women's acceptance of submissive relationships and exposed them to sexual exploitation and abuse.[47] While use of the terms "herstory" and "womyn" on several multicultural sorority web sites as well as inclusion of inspirational poems such as Chi Sigma Upsilon's "Resilient Women" poem articulated an increased understanding of feminist ideas among some group founders and members, the balance of gender conceptions for sorority members weighed toward the traditional.[48] In fact, the vehement declaration of "Independence" of one exceptional gender-aware multicultural sorority, Lambda Tau Omega (LTO), illustrated one's group take on the problem of men and fraternity association in shaping women's and the sorority's identity—even while their organization Web site displays women on the beach in bikinis. The LTO web site proclaimed with great emphasis, "Since the inception, Lambda Tau Omega Sorority began her journey alone and vowed that LTO shall NEVER be affiliated with any fraternity. Lambda Tau Omega Sorority, Inc. shall remain independent, she will NEVER have fraternity brothers."[49]

Even as MGLOs communicated consensus around increased activism, broad acceptance of diversity, and "prejudice reduction," the number of opposite-gender complement groups and activities predominantly communicated heterosexual identities for multicultural fraternities and sororities. The level of inclusion of gay, lesbian, bisexual, and transgender members appeared contested because in some instances, homosexuality or "lifestyles" as it is often conveyed, remained conspicuously absent from narratives about diversity represented in group membership. Furthermore, on one campus, the opportunity to affiliate with a national group rejected by a fledgling local group and the addition of another multicultural group on the campus fueled speculation by observers that a shared "but conservative" perspective against the possibility of same-gender-loving members prevailed among members of the original "multicultural" group.[50]

How Do MGLOs Fit into the Larger History and Organizational Structure of American Campus Life and the Collegiate Cocurriculum?

Issues related to advising and the proper placement of multicultural fraternities and sororities within the larger Greek community has challenged students, colleges and universities, and the NMGC for some time.[51] Thus, practices have varied widely, with some MGLOs participating as members of local IFC, NPC, or NPHC councils,[52] while other MGLOs have joined with other ethnic or ethnic-interest groups to form local multicultural Greek councils.[53] Still other MGLOs have been advised by offices of multicultural affairs, answering primarily to the general rules for campus student organizations while under the watch of an administrator.

Again, NMGC President Denise Pipersburgh explained that the NMGC has fielded many requests from campus multicultural Greek councils seeking membership but has declined them because many local multicultural Greek councils are comprised of a collection of single ethnic or ethnic-interest groups and subsequently do not have a mission of multiculturalism suited to the NMGC.[54] As a perfect solution has not filled this void, the task of guidance and support has fallen largely to campus administrators to create institution-specific strategies and structures. Nevertheless, this research has confirmed that efforts to offer or restructure advising and governance must be comprehensive and well contemplated in order to preserve the identities of MGLOs, improve the overall campus climate for racial and cultural diversity, and promote effective multicultural educational experiences among white students in general.[55]

The promise of MGLOs looms larger than their influence thus far. Because the preexisting arrangement of Greek groups into predominantly white and ethnic or ethnic-interest groups presents the possibility of building "ethnic enclaves" and increasing perceptions of victimization among whites and members of various ethnic groups,[56] MGLOs may be the type of formal multicultural educational activity that, in concert with policy and practice designed to promote diversity, may increase intercultural interaction among students and improve overall campus climate.[57] In addition, MGLOs may give members of student populations previously excluded from higher education an important sense of belonging and university identity[58] while promoting brotherhood and sisterhood as well as community among members of increasingly diverse campus environments.[59] Futhermore, MGLOs promise the possibility of moving beyond the limitations of monoracial identities and spaces by promoting individual exploration and support for college students of mixed race and/or mixed cultural heritages to honor all the portions of their identities and communities even as they grow and develop through the college experience.[60]

Yet this history argues that for the most part, multicultural fraternities and sororities have constructed a collective identity of diversity awareness and blended it with various Greek forms, structures, and activities. Though the contemporary movement has expanded to a significant national presence, it has been shaped largely by the worldviews of energetic, idealistic founders banded together in a hodgepodge of transient multiethnic groups. Thus, because MGLOs have emerged as familiar expressions of the collegiate cocurriculum, fitted for an era of increased student diversity, multicultural fraternities and sororities have expanded rather than fundamentally altered or transformed the nature of American undergraduate student culture.

While a shared identity exists among MGLOs related to increased diversity in membership, the need for prejudice reduction and community-based philanthropy, heretofore, the movement has exhibited unevenness in group quality and development—not unlike the roughness in quality and competition among IFC, NPC, and NPHC groups in an earlier era that brought about a movement for enhanced self-regulation and governance. For MGLOs, we see two positive forces capable of challenging MGLOs to realize their true potential: 1) the NMGC as it continues to hone its mission and craft incentives to attract new members thereby expanding its educational mission and scope, and 2) the stable active alumni chapters that have taken root and proliferated among some organizations that may offer guidance and ongoing support through a network of dedicated professionals genuinely committed to multicultural education.

Notes

The authors acknowledge the research of Pam K. Vrana, University of New Orleans, as instrumental in sustaining the project in its early stages.

1. Aaron Burgin, "USC Struggles With Diversity," *Daily Trojan*, September 1, 2004.

2. See William J. Crotty, "Democratic Consensual Norms and the College Student," *Sociology of Education* 40, no. 3 (Summer 1967): 200–219; M. G. Lord, "The Greek Rites of Exclusion," *Nation* 4, no. 11 (July 1987), 10–13; Alvin J. Schmidt and

Nicholas Babchuk, "The Unbrotherly Brotherhood: Discrimination in Fraternal Orders," *Phylon* 34, no. 3 (3rd Quarter 1973): 275–82; John Finley Scott, "The American College Sorority: Its Role in Class and Ethnic Endogamy," *American Sociological Review* 30, no. 4 (August 1965): 514–27; William S. Scott, *Values and Organizations.* With the Collaboration of Ruth Scott (Chicago: Rand McNally, 1965); Helen L. Horowitz, *Campus Life: Undergraduate Cultures from the End of the Eighteenth Century to the Present* (Chicago: University of Chicago Press, 1987). See also David O. Levine, *The American College and the Culture of Aspiration, 1915–1940* (Ithaca, NY: Cornell University Press, 1986); Frederick Rudolph, *The American College and University* (New York: Vintage, 1962); and John R. Thelin, *A History of American Higher Education* (Baltimore: Johns Hopkins University Press, 2004).

3. In fact, a popular handbook published in 2003 for campus administrators working with Greek organizations does not even mention the type of multicultural fraternities discussed in this chapter in the discussion entitled "understanding emerging fraternal organizations," Dennis E. Gregory and Associates, *The Administration of Fraternal Organizations on North American Campuses: A Pattern for the New Millennium* (Asheville, NC: College Administration Publications, 2003).

4. Leo Reisberg, "Ethnic and Multicultural Fraternities Are Booming on Many Campuses," *Chronicle of Higher Education,* January 7, 2000, A60.

5. A comprehensive description of these activities is found in Anthony Wayne James, "The Defenders of Tradition: College Social Fraternities, Race, and Gender, 1945–1980" (PhD diss., University of Mississippi, 1998), 12–44.

6. Frederick Rudolph, *The American College and University: A History* (Athens: University of Georgia Press, 1990 [1962]), 464–68.

7. Some organizations, not many, articulate this history. One example is http://www.orgs.bucknell.edu/chiphi/historyDiversity.html. See also Jim H. Smith, "Breaking the Fraternity Color Bar: UConn Led the Way," *Journal of Blacks in Higher Education* 28 (Summer 2000): 114–15.

8. Richard Hofstadter and Wilson Smith, eds., *American Higher Education: A Documentary History* (Chicago: University of Chicago Press, 1961).

9. James, "The Defenders of Tradition," 38. See also Carey McWilliams, "Toward Real Fraternity," *Nation,* August 12, 1950, 144.

10. A comprehensive journalistic account is offered by Tony Vellela, *New Voices: Student Activism in the '80s and '90s* (Boston: South End Press, 1988). A comprehensive scholarly analysis is offered by Robert A. Rhoads, *Freedom's Web: Student Activism in an Age of Cultural Diversity* (Baltimore: Johns Hopkins University Press, 1998). In this work, Rhoads compares ostensibly unrelated incidents of campus protest in the 1980s and 1990s with democratic struggle articulated in the Students for a Democratic Society (SDS) Port Huron Statement (1962), and the larger legacy of student activism during the civil rights movement, Vietnam War era, and free speech movement. Rhoads uses the new thread of identity politics to explain the increased agitation and agency from the students of "marginalized groups" and their advocates to "elevate diverse communities and cultures" (17). Specifically he traces contemporary cultural diversity-related protests to the Divestment Movement—and a student blockade at Columbia University in 1985 and activities at Mills College (1990), UCLA (1993), Penn State (1993), Rutgers (1995), and Michigan State (1995). These latter cases related respectively to feminist identity and women's college education, support for Chicano Studies, gay liberation, the genetic heritage and academic potential of African Americans, and tuition waivers for American Indians at a land-grant university.

11. Clifton F. Conrad and Jennifer Grant Haworth, eds., *Revisioning Curriculum in Higher Education* (Needham Heights, MA: Simon & Schuster Custom Publishing,

1995) contains articles, reprints, or chapters from representative voices and arguments in this debate including but not limited to: William J. Bennet, *To Reclaim a Legacy: A Report on the Humanities in Higher Education* (Washington, DC: National Endowment of the Humanities, 1984); James A. Banks, "The Canon Debate, Knowledge Construction and Multicultural Education," *Educational Researcher* 22 (1993); Dinesh D'Souza, "Victim's Revolution of Campus," in *Illiberal Education: The Politics of Race and Sex on Campus* (New York: Free Press, 1991); and Henry Giroux, "Decentering the Canon: Refiguring Disciplinary and Pedagogical Boundaries," in *Border Crossings: Cultural Workers and the Politics of Education* (New York: Routledge, 1992).

12. "Beta Sigma Tau—University of Toledo." http://www.betasigmatau.com, (site discontinued). To highlight the transient nature of these groups and/or web documents, in March 2006, this same page could not be found.

13. This was confirmed by Lori Edgeworth (Director of Student Judicial Affairs and Greek Life, University of Toledo) in a telephone interview May 24, 2006.

14. Association of Fraternity Advisors, Related Links, [WWW document] http://www.fraternityadvisors.org/links.htm, accessed March 21, 2005. The number of Multicultural fraternities and sororities identified by the Association of Fraternity Advisors (AFA) in March 2005 numbered fifteen for fraternities and twenty-one for sororities. We found this to be inaccurate. For example, the 2005 AFA list did not contain the names of four multicultural Greek groups holding membership in the National Multicultural Greek Council (NMGC). Our count was derived from an effort to triangulate the data when possible. Data searches were conducted to verify the existence of chapters through active and/or recent postings on organizational Web sites, listings on college and universities Web sites for records of registered and active student organizations, various newspaper articles, and through interviews.

15. For example, stepping is featured as an important activity for Mu Sigma Upsilon Sorority and Psi Sigma Phi Fraternity. See also Zach Levine, "Sororities 'Step and Stroll' for Charities at Rutgers," *Daily Targum*, November 22, 2004.

16. Denise J. Pipersburgh, Esq. (president, National Multicultural Greek Council) interview with Amy E. Wells, March 2005 and March 2006.

17. The Web sites for IFC, NPHC, and NPC groups are similar in that nonmembers can only visit certain pages or layers of the site. While some scholars of fraternities and sororities point out that the Web sites provide only a surface depiction of Greek life and do not account for the "real lived experience," other scholars, particularly those in cultural and media studies who make their work of studying communication in American culture, underscore the value of analyzing and interpreting new media. Because MGLOs definitively share common ideals and attributes apart from other IFC, NPHC, and NPC groups as portrayed through their Web sites, we offer up the work of James W. Carey who describes two views of communication, transmission vs. ritual, to consider a "ritual" view of communication as an interpretative framework for viewing MGLO media. "Ritual communication" is communication directed not toward the extension of messages in space but toward the maintenance of society in time; not the act of imparting information but the representation of shared beliefs," or "a sacred ceremony that draws persons together in fellowship and commonality." See James W. Carey, *Communication as Culture: Essays on Media and Society* (New York: Routledge, 1992), 18. The example of an "oppositional culture" that "shrinks" rather than "expands" individual influence to promote social change could be found in Josh Adams and Vincent J. Roscigno, "White Supremacists, Oppositional Culture and the World Wide Web," *Social Forces*, 84, no. 2: 760–78.

18. For example these include but are not limited in some example to mermaids (Lambda Tau Omega Sorority), knights (Psi Sigma Phi Fraternity), black panthers (Iota

Psi Phi Sorority, Sigma Theta Psi Sorority), white Bengal tigers (Delta Xi Phi Sorority, Delta Sigma Chi Sorority, Lambda Psi Delta, and Lamda Fe Uson), dragons, diamonds (Lamda Psi Delta Sorority and Delta Xi Phi Sorority), "D.I.V.A.S." (Lambda Fe Usöñ), and "GQ" gentlemen (Gamma Omega Delta Fraternity).

19. Theta Nu Xi Multicultural Sorority, Inc. http://www.thetanuxi.org

20. Delta Xi Phi Multicultural Sorority, Inc. http://geocities.com/~deltaxiphi/index2004.html

21. See James A. Banks, *Cultural Diversity, and Education: Foundations, Curriculum, and Teaching*, 4th ed. (Boston: Allyn and Bacon, 2001), 5.

22. Ibid. This is a "common interpretation," by those who are new to multicultural education and do not see it "as directly connected with political struggle," according to Christine Sleeter. For these proponents, they see multicultural education "as a means of reducing prejudice and stereotyping among individuals." See Christine E. Sleeter, *Multicultural Education as Social Activism* (Albany: State University of New York, 1996), 10–13.

23. Delta Xi Phi Multicultural Sorority, Inc. Web site.

24. Andres Kwon, "U. Michigan Greek Organizations Homophobic, LGBT Students Say," *Michigan Daily*, April 12, 2005.

25. Alexis Blue, "U. Arizona Students Find That 'Words Hurt,'" *Arizona Daily Wildcat*, November 14, 2003.

26. Jennifer Amsler, "Sorority Holds Sexual Abuse Forum at U. Arizona," *Arizona Daily Wildcat*, November 18, 2004.

27. Eboni Gatlin, "Forum Discusses Race, Civil Rights at Indiana U.," *Indiana Daily Student*, January 25, 2005.

28. Christine Sleeter, *Multicultural Education*, 10.

29. Ezra Bowen, "New Look for Thriving Greeks," *Time*, March 10, 1986, 77.

30. Leo Reisberg, "Fraternities in Decline," *Chronicle of Higher Education*, January 7, 2000, A59.

31. Ibid. See also Christopher Shea, "Racist Acts Roil Nation's Campuses, Igniting Protests," *Chronicle of Higher Education*, November 25, 1992.

32. Ibid. See also Elizabeth Farrell, "Four Rules for Saving a Fraternity," *Chronicle of Higher Education*, December 3, 2004, A35.

33. Leo Reisberg, "Fraternities in Decline," A60. George Washington University exemplifies this growth adding six ethnic or ethnic-interest groups in 2003. See Elizabeth Chernow, "Greek Life Expands at George Washington U.," *GW Hatchet*, July 8, 2003.

34. This difference stands out in the ongoing, longer-term visiting of Web sites too whereby comprehensive organizational development and momentum favors the women's groups.

35. Timothy Roche and Leslie Everton Brice, "Blacks Need Not Apply," *Time*, June 11, 2000, 104; "The Racially Segregated Fraternity Row at the University of Alabama," *Journal of Blacks in Higher Education* 19 (Spring 1998): 44–45; Patrik Jonsson, "South Wrestles With Segregated Sororities," *Christian Science Monitor*, September 18, 2001, 4; "Greek Life Still Segregated at the University of Alabama," *Journal of Blacks in Higher Education* 19 (October 2002): 17; "Black Student Gets Bid to White Sorority at University of Alabama," *Black Issues in Higher Education* 20 (September 2003): 17; "Changing World New Sororities Lead Way For UA Greek System," *Birmingham News*, May 21, 2003.

36. Rhoads, *Freedom's Web*, 189–218.

37. For an in-depth exploration of sorority women's preferences and beliefs, especially the penchant toward traditionalism and careerism, see Barbara J. Bank with Har-

riet M. Yelon, *Contradictions in Women's Education: Traditionalism, Careerism and Community at a Single-Sex College* (New York: Teachers College Press, 2003).

38. Christina Wakayama, "'Sorority Life' Garners Mixed Reactions on USC Campus," *Daily Trojan*, September 30, 2003. In one study of twenty-five thousand new freshman in 1985, Astin found that as seniors, Greek members were "more likely than nonmembers to be conservative in their sociopolitical identification and views," see Ernest T. Pascarella and Patrick T. Terenzini, *How College Affects Students Volume 2* (San Francisco: Jossey-Bass, 2005), 307.

39. Richard Fausset, "A Frat for Misfits at Ole Miss; Cheers! A Motley Band of Foreign Students and Domestic Square Pegs Has Created Its Own Fraternity: The Awesome Dudes of Alpha Delta," *Los Angeles Times*, September 16, 2006, A1.

40. Ibid.

41. For example, this is the case for Phi Sigma Chi Fraternity and Delta Sigma Chi Sorority, Sigma Chi Omega Fraternity and Zeta Sigma Phi Sorority, and Mu Sigma Upsilon and Lambda Sigma Upsilon, a Latino Fraternity.

42. From images and texts available on their websites, MGLOs appear, at least to a limited extent, to sanction interracial and intercultural dating. In this way, the multicultural philosophy of MGLOs does represent itself as a form of "resistance to white supremacy and also (for many) to patriarchy" (Sleeter, *Multicultural Education*, 10), and the stricter notions of dating and mating adhered to possibly by family members or members of IFC, NPC, and NPHC groups—for a historical treatment see John Finley Scott, "The American College Sorority: Its Role in Class and Ethnic Endogamy."

43. The "Gamma Rubies" of Delphic of Gamma Sigma Tau Fraternity were identified as an "auxiliary." See http://delphic-gst.org/auxilary.html

44. See http://www.omegadelta-alpha.com/page.php?page_id=133. While the OD Sweeties did not appear to be a "little sister group" per se, some of the problems long associated with "little sister groups" surfaced in their narratives. As a point of information, the North-American Interfraternity Conference adopted a resolution in 1987 encouraging "elimination" of such groups among member fraternities. See Gregory and Associates, *The Administration of Fraternal Organizations on North American Campuses*, 389. See also Mindy Stombler, "'Buddies' or 'Slutties': The Collective Sexual Reputation of Fraternity Little Sisters," *Gender and Society* 8, no. 3 (September 2004): 297–323.

45. Susan Carole Malone, "Gender Role Attitudes and Homogamy Preferences of College Greeks" (PhD diss., University of Florida, 1996). Abstract in *Dissertation Abstracts* International, Publ., nr. AAT 9709272, DAI-A 57/10 (April 1997): 4546.

46. Dorothy C. Holland and Margaret A. Eisenhart, *Educated for Romance: Women, Achievement, and College Culture* (Chicago: University of Chicago Press, 1990).

47. L. Kalof and T. Cargill, "Fraternity and Sorority Membership and Gender Dominance Attitudes" *Sex Roles* 25 (1991): 417–23.

48. This supports the findings of Bank with Yelon, *Contradictions in Women's Education.*

49. Lambda Tau Omega Sorority, Inc. Web site. In addition, this group used feminist language including "Herstory" and "womyn" to further differentiate its identity. Interestingly, the group's web page also features four to five bikini-clad women spelling out LTO on the beach.

50. Interview with a Student Affairs Administrator, March 22, 2005. This interview was conducted in confidentiality with Amy E. Wells, and the name has been withheld in mutual agreement.

51. This was confirmed by Denise Pipersburgh in her interview with Amy E. Wells. This situation was also confirmed by Christine McGill (Greek Advisor, University of

Virginia) in discussion with Amy E. Wells, March 25, 2005. See Natasha Altamirano, "U. Virginia Holds First 'State of the Greek System' Address," *Cavalier Daily*, October 22, 2003.

52. Omega Delta Fraternity elected to stay with the IFC instead of join the newly formed United Greek Council, one of four Greek governing councils. See Kari Alexander, "U. Illinois Greek System Expands With New Council," *Daily Illini*, January 26, 2004. See also Megan Nichols, "U. Alabama Multicultural Sorority Vying to Join Panhellenic," *Crimson White*, September 12, 2003.

53. For example, Rutgers multicultural groups participate in the Rutgers Pan-Hellenic Council along with historically black and Latino/a groups. See Brittany Mendenhall, "Rutgers Sororities, Fraternities Show Pride to Hopefuls," *Daily Targum*, February 15, 2005. For additional examples of multicultural Greek councils see University of Florida: http://grove.ufl.edu/~ufmgc/; University of Southern California: http://www-scf.usc.edu/~mcgc/; and University of Virginia: http://www.student.virginai.edu/~mgc-uva/.

54. Baylor University exemplifies this situation, as they have a Multicultural Greek Council but no MGLOs. See Yuan Sheng, "Minority Greek Council Created at Baylor U.," *Lariat*, February 24, 2004.

55. Thoughtful approaches must involve curricular and cocurricular activities and are particularly challenging to create in order to counter the negative effects of Greek membership particularly for white students. See Linda Kay Robinson, "The Influence of Curricular and Co-Curricular experiences on Students' Openness to Diversity at a Predominantly White, State Supported University in the South" (PhD diss., Union Institute, 2000) and Gregory Kazou Tanaka, "The Impact of Multiculturalism on White Students" (PhD diss., University of California, Los Angeles, 1996).

56. Jim Sidanius, Colette Van Laar, Shana Levin, and Stacey Sinclair, "Ethnic Enclaves and the Dynamics of Social Identity on the College Campus: The Good, the Bad, and the Ugly," *Journal of Personality and Social Psychology* 87, no. 1 (2004): 96–110.

57. Sylvia Hurtado, "The Campus Racial Climate: Contexts for Conflict," *Journal of Higher Education* 63, no. 5 (1992): 539–69; A. Chavez, F. Guido-DiBrito, S. Mallory, "Learning to Value the 'Other': A Framework of Individual Diversity Development," *Journal of College Student Development* 44 (2003): 453–69; Sylvia Hurtado, Jeffrey F. Milem, Alma R. Clayton-Pederson, and Walter R. Allen, "Enhancing Campus Climates for Racial/Ethnic Diversity Through Educational Policy and Practice," *Review of Higher Education* 21, no. 3 (1998): 279–302. See also "Multicultural Classes Should Be Required," *Lariat* (Baylor University), November 6, 2003 and "Studies Show Dividends of Diversity," *Academe* (November-December 1999): 13.

58. Gabriel Allan Reyes, "Does Participation in an Ethnic Fraternity Enable Persistence in College?" (PhD diss., University of Southern California, 1997); Jesus G. Trevino, "Participation in Ethnic/Racial Student Organizations" (PhD diss., University of California, Los Angeles, 1992). For student opinion see Yvonne Wingett, "Minorities Find Connection in Ethnic Greek Organizations," *Arizona Republic*, October 31, 2004.

59. S. Hurtado, J. F. Milem, A. Clayton-Pederson, and W. R. Allen, "Enhancing Campus Climates," 279–302.

60. As a community of scholars, we have just begun to explore the complexities of how individuals live out their identity and race in American culture. For more see Mary C. Waters, *Ethnic Options: Choosing Identities in America* (Berkeley: University of California Press, 1990); David R. Harris and Jeremiah Joseph Sim, "Who Is Multiracial? Assessing the Complexity of Lived Race," *American Sociological Review* 67, no. 4 (2002): 614–27; and Kristen A. Renn, *Mixed Race Students in College: The Ecology of Race, Iden-*

tity, and Community on Campus (Albany: State University of New York Press, 2004). Nor have we begun to adequately understand the complexities or politics around white identity in American culture and what motivates white students to join or create such organizations. See Jennifer L. Eichstedt, "Problematic White Identities and a Search for Racial Justice," *Sociological Forum* 16, no. 3 (2001): 445–70.

Multicultural Fraternity Web Addresses

Delphic of Gamma Sigma Tau: http://www.delphic-gst.org/

Epsilon Sigma Rho Fraternity, Inc.: http://www.epsilonsigmarho.org/

Gamma Omega Delta Fraternity, Inc.: http://www.gamma-omega-delta.org/

Psi Sigma Phi Multicultural Fraternity, Inc.: http://www.psisigmaphi.org/php/begin.php

Sigma Chi Omega Fraternity, Inc.: http://www.sigmachiomega.com/

Chi Delta Beta Fraternity: http://www.chideltabeta.com/

Phi Sigma Chi: http://www.phisigmachi.com/home.html

Beta Gamma Nu, Inc.: http://www.betagammanu.com/

Omega Delta: http://www.omegadelta.org/index.php

Multicultural Sorority Web Addresses

Alpha Delta Sigma Sorority, Inc.: http://www.alphadeltasigma.org/?pg=history

Delta Xi Phi Multicultural Sorority, Inc.: http://www.geocities.com/%7Edeltaxiphi/

Delta Sigma Chi Sorority, Inc.: http://dsc1996.org/history.html

Iota Psi Phi: http://www.csufresno.edu/StudentOrgs/IOTAPSIPHI/

Lambda Psi Delta Sorority, Inc.: http://www.lambdapsidelta.org/

Lambda Tau Omega Sorority, Inc.: http://www.geocities.com/CollegePark/Lab/8874/

Mu Sigma Upsilon Sorority, Inc.: http://www.musigmaupsilon.org/

Chi Sigma Upsilon Sorority, Inc.: http://www.angelfire.com/nj/csu93/

Omega Phi Chi, Inc.: http://www.omegaphichi.org/

Lambda Sigma Gamma Sorority, Inc.: http://www.lambdasigmagamma.org/

Sigma Theta Psi Multicultural Sorority: http://www.sigmathetapsi.com/page/page/2375754.htm

Zeta Sigma Phi Multicultural Sorority, Inc.: http://www.zetasigmachi.com/

Sigma Alpha Zeta Sorority, Inc. http://orgs.sa.ucsb.edu/saz/

Lambda Fe Uson Sorority, Inc.: http://www.sinc.sunysb.edu/Clubs/divas/

Upsilon Kappa Delta: http://www.upsilonkappadelta.org/

Theta Nu Xi Multicultural Sorority, Inc.: http://www.thetanuxi.org/

Challenging the Heterosexual Model of Brotherhood: The Gay Fraternity's Dilemma

King-To Yeung

College students can organize themselves in multiple ways, ranging from informal reading groups or social clubs that have open membership to formal student organizations with highly selective memberships. A group's organizational model defines its size, decision-making processes, types of members, and patterns of interaction. Each model also places different demands on participants and offers various levels of privileges and benefits to those who commit to the organization. As a thought experiment, we can imagine that students would organize themselves in as many ways as they want depending on their needs, goals, and aspirations, but casual observation of any college campus in the United States may force us to conclude that there are only a limited number of organizational forms that students would adopt as part of their college life. Organizational forms that can provide significant cultural meaning and facilitate a sense of legitimacy on campus, as well as in society at large, are even fewer. With their historical significance in the social organization of American life, collegiate fraternities undoubtedly offer the much-desired legitimacy and prestige that few other organizational forms may provide, even though their presence in contemporary student life is not free from controversy.[1]

As one of the dominant forms of student organization, fraternities explicitly use a familial metaphor to construct solidarity within a single sex (hence brothers), and neutralize the potential divisions among members in terms of class, race, or sexuality.[2] To achieve an often idealized familial relationship, these groups depend on rituals, secrecy, and numerous symbolic constructions to create an environment in which members play the role of brothers *in a family*. The commitment to the group through symbolic construction of intimacy thus helps members to discard their differences and break boundaries across social divides. This idealized image, however, is often partially fulfilled in practice.

Homogeneity rather than diversity typically characterizes the composition of fraternity membership on American campuses. Even though legal barriers no longer exist to support segregation of any kind (besides that based on biological sex), homogeneity of race, ethnicity, and social-class backgrounds persists in a majority of fraternal organizations.

While there is an increased sensitivity to racial diversity in college fraternities, differences in sexual orientations have less frequently been addressed. Cutting across various racial- and ethnic-based fraternities is the blanket presumption that members are heterosexual.[3] Tacit in its nature, this heterosexual model of brotherhood is never consciously cultivated through group policy; rather, members are expected to fulfill certain cultural expectations as to how they should express and present themselves according to heterosexual norms. Numerous studies on fraternities, for example, have shown how interactions within fraternal settings construct the meaning of masculinity defined by "compulsory heterosexuality,"[4] which ultimately devalues femininity and contributes to the oppression of women.[5] A collection of testimonies of gay members in college fraternities, *Out on Fraternity Row*, also reveals that even though some gay men had no trouble revealing their sexuality to other brothers, the organization continued to operate as if all members are heterosexuals.[6] One can say that heterosexual norms define the very essence of the fraternal model, just as the same norms govern familial relationships in the larger society.

Since the late 1980s, several Greek-letter organizations have emerged to address specific questions regarding alternative sexualities within the fraternity and sorority institution. Some of these organizations not only emphasize members' sexualities but their ethnic identities, and all of them bring the diversification of identity to the forefront of the groups' collective missions. Table 12 lists some of these burgeoning collectives.

This chapter will focus on how a group of gay college men from a particular fraternity sought to challenge the heterosexual model of fraternities while preserving key elements of the tradition. Using a case study of the national gay fraternity Delta Lambda Phi (DLP), one of the fastest-growing gay fraternities in the country, this chapter investigates how DLP members attempted to redefine the fraternal model by constructing a fraternity that, from the perspective of its members, can best realize a true ideal of brotherhood divorced from homophobia and conventionalized gender practices. The essential goal of DLP was to overturn the rather arbitrary assumption that all brothers are heterosexual and that gay men are unfit for fraternal organizations.

But if entrenched heterosexual norms truly define the fraternity organizational form, DLP would need to do more than just modify sexual ideologies within the group. Embracing the fraternal model, for

Table 12 Greek Organizations Catering to Students with Alternative Sexualities

Organization	Year Est.	Place of Origin	Identities Stated by the Group*
Delta Phi Upsilon Fraternity	1985	Tallahassee, FL	Gay men of color
Delta Lambda Phi Fraternity	1987	Washington, DC	Gay, bisexual, and progressive men (all races)
Lambda Delta Lambda Sorority	1988	Cal-Berkeley	Lesbians of multicultural backgrounds
Gamma Mu Phi Fraternity	1999	Richmond, VA	African American and Latino men; same gender loving, bisexual and affirming men
Alpha Lambda Tau Fraternity	1999	Las Vegas, NV	Gay, bisexual, transgender, and alternative lifestyle-friendly male college students
Iota Lambda Pi Fraternity	2000	Tallahassee, FL	Stud, butch, and dominant lesbian women
Beta Phi Omega Sorority	2000	Tallahassee, FL	National Feminine Minority Lesbian Sorority
Kappa Psi Kappa Fraternity	2001	Tallahassee, FL	Noncollegiate organization for men of all colors and sexual orientations (but has been working on being chartered on three campuses)
Phi Nu Kappa Sorority	2002	Tallahassee, FL	Feminine bisexual and lesbian women
Alpha Psi Kappa Fraternity	2002	Tallahassee, FL	Bisexual studs, doms, and butches
Gamma Rho Lambda	2003	Arizona State University	Woman of alternative lifestyle
Sigma Phi Beta Fraternity	2003	Phoenix, AZ	Gay and bisexual college men (all races)
Gamma Alpha Upsilon Professional Fraternity	2003	Baltimore, MD	Lesbian, pansexual, and same-gender loving women
Kappa Alpha Lambda Sorority	2003	Atlanta, GA	Lesbian, bisexual, and heterosexual women
Kappa Xi Omega Sorority	2004	Tampa, FL	Educated, professional, and cultured lesbian women
Sigma Nu Omega Sorority	2004	Detroit, MI	Lesbian, Gay, Bi-sexual, Trans, Questioning, and Allied Community
Lambda Phi Theta Fraternity	2005	Jacksonville, FL	Gay and bisexual men of color

* This column indicates the social categories and terminologies used by the organizations.

DLP brothers, also meant exclusion of women, being apolitical, and perhaps being elitist. These commitments to a fraternal form would challenge the brothers' sexual identity, as being gay may imply a subcultural norm that resists, or at least questions, any rigid and exclusionary boundary between social categories, particularly, the men/women distinction. This apparent contradiction prompted both fellow students and members of the gay community suspicious of any exclusive organization to ask DLP members, "Why have a fraternity at all?"

The dilemma of DLP brothers is thus primarily a contention over their choice of organizational forms. As they simultaneously constructed a fraternity that is different from but also inspired by an idealized model that embraces both equality (as family) and oppression of differences, brothers found themselves caught between gay and straight worlds. Because choices of organizational form always convey cultural meanings that in turn shape how members in an organization make decisions and interact,[7] the adoption of any particular organizational model is not arbitrary. The key to a sociological analysis is to place social actors' experience within the larger cultural and institutional environment in which they navigate possibilities and constraints. Once we acknowledge how few organizational models are available to American college students to organize meaningfully, we can make sense of the institutional logic of DLP's group practices, even if they seem contradictory.

In the following sections, this chapter discusses how some gay men came to adopt the fraternal form in order to challenge the heterosexual assumption entrenched in traditional fraternities. Simultaneously, it shows how the adaptation of a fraternal form helped DLP members construct a haven for gay men that encouraged brotherly, nonerotic relations lacking in mainstream gay culture. Also examined is that DLP's challenge to the fraternal tradition had only been partial and selective. While brothers had modified many fundamental (perhaps infamous) elements of the fraternal model, they fell short in questioning its single-sex premise that excludes membership based only on candidates' biological sex. The question that needs to be addressed is not whether DLP should include women as members, but why DLP brothers had defended a single-sex model while modifying, reforming, and arguably subverting nearly every other "traditional" aspect of the fraternal form.

The answer provided here is an institutional one. Given the limited number of legitimate organizational models available to American students, the choice of a fraternal model may appear obvious for stigmatized groups, such as gay men, as a means to formulate meaningful relationships they perceive lacking in the larger society. Defending a single-sex fraternal model also helped DLP brothers distinguish their organization from all-inclusive gay and lesbian student groups, which the brothers perceived as too political and pragmatic, or, to use a term some brothers used, too "business-like." Broadening the repertoire of organization options on campus can therefore resolve some of the dilemmas DLP faces. Imaginatively expanding organizational possibilities allows students to organize in ways that fit their needs, without submitting to the social restrictions of entrenched, traditional organizational models.

Delta Lambda Phi National Social Fraternity

Recognizing the lack of venues for young gay men to form meaningful social relationships beyond those of dance clubs or organizations motivated toward political or service goals, a small group of men in Washington, DC, began to recruit the first Delta Lambda Phi (DLP) pledge in the end of 1986. Their efforts intended to counteract what they saw as the limitation of gay organizations at the time: internal divisions, deviant sexual activities, and lax membership standards.[8] The founders of DLP adopted a traditional collegiate fraternity model but stressed the fraternity's openness for "men of all races, colors, creeds, irrespective of sexual orientation."[9] Twenty-four men were initiated into active brotherhood and the Alpha Chapter of DLP was born in 1987. By 1998—the year when this research was completed—the fraternity had significantly grown to a nationwide organization with sixteen active chapters and four colonies based mostly on numerous state and private universities across the country.[10] The research materials presented in this chapter report the fraternity's ideology, activities, and identity formation during the late 1990s, when the group had passed its tenth anniversary—an appropriate time for members to reflect on the group's goal and evaluate its collective performance.[11]

Critiquing the Fraternal Model: Creating a Gay Brotherhood

To DLP brothers, the founding of a fraternity offered more than an alternative social venue for gay men to interact. In an attempt to combine the ideal of brotherhood with the acceptance of sexual diversity in an all-male organization, DLP brought together the best part of the fraternal institution and the gay community. To show how these aspects of the straight and gay worlds may complement each other, it is useful to compare how the DLP's sexually diverse model of brotherhood is both different from and similar to the traditional fraternity, which assumes all members as heterosexual.

DLP members shared many similarities with members of straight fraternities, from the commitment to creating intimate, long-lasting social bonds among members, to an involvement in campus and community life, to the construction of a nationwide network of alumni. Structurally, DLP also modeled itself after the collegiate fraternities that assume a formal structure of positions and relationships. All DLP chapters were run by elected officers who occupied formal positions (for example, president, vice president, secretary, treasurer, sergeant at arms) and committees consisting of active members. Members were divided into cohorts of pledge classes, and standards were implemented to determine whether a pledge brother would be initiated. Furthermore, big-brother-little-brother relationships were constructed out of the differential seniority of members, and it is from these relationships that many brothers found their fraternity experience most rewarding.

From the perspective of the brothers, DLP was a real fraternity that welcomed members with stigmatized identities and alternative lifestyles.[12] While gay members in traditional fraternities are often reticent in disclosing their sexual orientation to their fraternities, DLP fostered an environment where being gay was accepted and embraced as a natural part of selfhood. For example, brothers would help each other in the coming out process with words of assurance: "Don't be ashamed of who you are. If your parents don't approve of you, fine, that is who you are."[13] Since coming out is an essential process in the development of a gay identity,[14] it gave DLP brothers a major venue through which they could actualize the meaning of brotherhood, as they supported each other in a process that is often filled with uncertainty and pain. This support was both emotional and material, as some might be rejected by their parents and end up homeless; brothers at such times would provide shelter and some financial support for one another. DLP also fostered a social sense of community by bringing gay men together in a safe environment. Some brothers who had never participated in the gay community or interacted with any significant number of self-identified gay men came out through the very act of joining DLP. For those brothers who were out at the time of joining, they could become "more out" and more comfortable about their sexuality with the support of other brothers, as evidenced by one brother's transformation: "He is older and had just come out. . . . Maybe he was uncomfortable about the whole situation, but felt comfortable enough to join or rush, and then two years later, you know, he's here now, and he's hugging everybody. He's Mexican and he bleached [his hair] blond, so we're like: 'peroxide is not a toy,' and now he can joke about it. He's okay with it. I remember before if we had made a joke like that he would be so mad and run away. But now he's like, whatever. . . . That's like a positive thing that people get out of the fraternity."

Because of the recognition that "most of us have felt like outsiders all of our lives," DLP members found common ground upon which members can express their self-identity in an organizational structure that gave them a sense of legitimacy in college life and reconnected them to the larger society, both straight and gay. Sometimes there was a dissonance between how "out" the chapter intended to be and how comfortable individual members felt about their sexuality being displayed in public. Since DLP claimed to respect individuality, closeted members were not forced to participate in public events if they did not desire. However, collectively organized events (for example, participating in the gay pride parade) often became an opportunity for closeted members to try out their courage.

Socializing brothers about the meaning of being gay not only reinforced the common thread linking the brothers—that is, their sexuality—but also built bridges joining the brothers to the larger gay community. In one chapter, part of this socializing process was to teach members the "essential gay history" as a component of the pledge program: "I have noticed the younger gay men who have come out at the age of, like, eighteen, nineteen, twenty, or who are in the process of coming out, lack the gay history. . . . There's a reason why [gay men] idolize Joan Crawford; there's a reason why they love Marilyn Monroe. . . . We teach gay history in a coming out group. Everybody is supposed to know gay history.

The gay fraternity further moved beyond simply serving as a site where young men could learn what it means to be gay—something brothers could have gotten in other venues such as gay, lesbian, bisexual, and transvestite (GLBT) student groups on campus.[15] The unique quality of the gay fraternity lay in its ideal of brotherhood, which DLP brothers saw as a necessary complement to the oversexualized and alienated gay cultures: "I think that there is a gay culture but I don't necessarily believe that there is a gay community. . . . Gay men are very alienated from each other. We go around, we walk around on the streets and see each other, but at the same time there seems to be a lack of a real—there is just this lack of feeling that we are a community . . . there is a substantial amount of rejection of gay men toward each other."

Building a brotherhood was thus a serious critique to the gay community, where, as one brother pointed out, "people tend to have a lot of acquaintances or 'friends' but they don't seem to be that intimate with these people." DLP counteracted this alienating culture through a commitment to the kinds of long-lasting and intimate bonds among brothers that are proposed in the traditional (heterosexual) fraternity institution. The brothers also perceived such a bond as a unique feature vis-à-vis other GLBT student groups, a distinction to which we will return later in this chapter. For now it suffices to note that emulating a heterosexual fraternal model has helped DLP brothers to straddle a gay culture whose sexuality they shared but whose values they did not, and a heterosexual institution with other problematic values that, as will be seen next, can only be partially redeemed by the actualization of brotherhood.

Mirroring DLP's critique of the gay community was its defiance of the homophobia prevalent in some straight fraternities. As homosexuality is often equated with femininity,[16] issues of homophobia could be tackled by redefining the conception of masculinity in the fraternity's group practices. In contrast to the hegemonic notion of masculinity that defines the relationship among men by competition, dominance, the suppressing of femininity and the oppression of women,[17] DLP returned to men their "feminine" side, with particular attention to the gendered representation of the self in the fraternity's private spaces. For example, the above chapter that taught gay history also organized a "shopping committee": "[The shopping committee's] sole purpose is to schedule the next shopping spree. It's a hoot . . . you get five to ten queens together it's a riot. We all go to Neiman's and other stores. . . . Then we go to PayLess or Shoe Rack. . . . We go in there and see if we can find pumps in everybody's size. That's fun because most of us are not drag queens but we do it just to cause a stir."[18]

Depending on the degree of tolerance on particular campuses, chapters would assume different levels of radicalism. In one chapter, members dressed up in full drag to publicize a fraternity party at the school's student center. According to one witness, his DLP brothers "were just all outrageously dressed. They went straight to the middle [of the Center] and just had a great time. I was like: Oh my god, I would never have done that. It would scare me too much." Of course, these acts were more memorable simply because they were rarer than other routinized practices having incorporated gay cultural elements that challenged the masculine conception of fraternity men, such as calling each other "girls" or "girlfriends," adopting stereotypical effeminate mannerisms, and just interacting in a "queeny" fashion. From playing the "gay Monopoly" in a group retreat to hosting a drag show on campus, DLP fostered a safe space in which hegemonic masculinity can be challenged.[19]

Another DLP modification of the masculine conception of fraternal men was its strict prohibition of hazing—an infamous group practice of some traditional fraternities that construct masculinity through dominant-submissive relationships among members.[20] For DLP brothers who had struggled with social stigma and discrimination against their sexual orientation, hazing simply had no place in the gay fraternity because "gays have been hazed enough by society." Another brother said plainly, "DLP will not haze. Period. End of sentence!" DLP's no-hazing policy was not simply rhetoric because the fraternity brothers carefully monitored their pledge training mechanism to ensure they were not violating the hazing policies they themselves supported.[21] Brothers expressed serious concerns over even the slightest hint of violation, as a brother described the following event:

> For [the pledges'] initiation journey they go from place to place on their way to their initiation site. If they get an answer wrong they get blindfolded until the next stop [along the journey]. There has never been a problem with that except this last time when one of our pledges did not know any of his information so he ended up being blindfolded the entire trip. Well, one of other brothers got all up in arms because this guy was blindfolded the whole trip. . . . I explained to him that if they get it wrong they get blindfolded and it just happens to be that this person ended up being blindfolded the entire trip. So he asked, "Is this alright with all the brothers?" I'm like "yeah, and this is alright with the pledges."

Hazing was so obviously inappropriate in a gay fraternity that pledges sometimes even joked about being hazed just to challenge (in a teasing way) the burden imposed on them in the pledge process. In practice, DLP brothers made a conscious effort to keep pledging a demanding process without resorting to hazing. For example, one brother suggested that his chapter could ask the pledges to "do incredibly difficult things that don't cross the line into hazing. You can ask them to plan a giant service project or a giant party, or you can have them learn songs for a serenade together . . . going on a retreat together, doing teamwork-building exercises." Thus, the brothers did not equate a challenging pledge period with hazing. In essence, DLP redefined what "toughness" could mean to a fraternity man and, as one brother put it, allowed its members to "fit into the Greek system without all of the bad stuff that goes along with it . . . like Hell Week and hazing and everything else . . . making people parade through campus with a marshmallow stick up their butt or anything else like that." DLP pledges were "tested" in their symbolic and literal "journey" toward initiation, but were not hazed.

With their rejection of dominant-submissive relations among brothers, DLP further redefined how members could relate to each other with emotional openness. For example, in the ritual of "warm fuzzy," brothers in one chapter were encouraged to express their emotional feelings toward one another in a nonerotic context:

> In our warm fuzzy exercise, we have a ball of yarn, or we have a warm fuzzy pillow or something. And then one person starts and throws the pillow at somebody and gives that person a warm fuzzy. Like, "Oh, thank you for helping me out, you're one of the nicest [people] I've seen." And that person has to throw it at somebody else in the fraternity. We did this like for two hours, until we're all like really comfortable and tired. It's all sappy, and then a box of Kleenex gets passed around. It's like, "boo hoo [weeping] . . . you're so wonderful to me." You know, a big drama, but it's great: it really pulls us altogether.

As scholars of the sociology of emotion have suggested, emotional rules are gendered—that is, there are social norms guiding how men and women should feel and express their emotions.[22] On the one hand, allowing inner feelings to be an important part of group activities, DLP rejected the (heterosexual) gender norms that defined men by their competition and "toughness."[23] On the other hand, such rituals also allowed gay brothers to establish intimacy with other gay men without engaging in the eroticism that the brothers believed was the hallmark of gay culture at large. Overall, this example of an "emotional work" also illustrates how the gay fraternity combined a gay cultural element (the drama) and a new definition of men (emotion) and applied them in a new context (the gay brotherhood), thereby reappropriating the meaning of fraternal men together.

By simultaneously adopting and modifying the fraternal model, DLP enacted an integrated criticism of both gay and straight norms. However, given the persisting homophobic campus environment in which DLP chapters found themselves, the two worlds DLP tried to incorporate could at times come into conflict. To consolidate the meaning of brotherhood meant that DLP would have to situate itself more firmly within the larger fraternity institution, but to be a part of the gay community the group must also reflectively rethink the many restrictions imposed by the fraternal model. Essentially, the challenge for DLP members was to balance how "gay" and how "Greek" they wanted to become.

The Limits of the Critique: Gayness Toned Down

DLP members adopted various strategies to cope with their stigmatized status in the traditional fraternity institution. Adopting the traditional fraternity structure led DLP brothers to feel that they were not very different from other college fraternities except for the fact that members were self-identified gay men. Brothers felt that the only difference between DLP and other straight fraternities was members' sexual identities; as one brother said, "We have a national [organization], we have the same types of criteria . . . we're all men, and even though we're gay men there's really not anything that really differentiates us from other men down the block in the other fraternities." In achieving their goal of emulating traditional fraternities, DLP brothers tended to deemphasize their collective sexual identity—the essential element that brought them together in the first place—and emphasize the "traditional" aspects of their organization. In a chapter founded within a conservative community, one brother advised his chapter to shift its focus from being a "gay fraternity" to being the "best fraternity" on campus: "Right now anything we do will get press coverage because we are the gay fraternity. I want that to change so that we are not the gay fraternity but that we are the best fraternity—that we have the highest GPA, have the most service work for a social fraternity, that we have the biggest impact on campus . . . the gay thing is just one of the things that makes us . . . but that is not the primary thing. I want the fraternity to get to the point that straight people will not have problems coming to our rushes and pledging." Here we see a common strategy of overcompensation when groups with stigmatized status attempt to gain legitimacy by overrealizing certain ideals that are usually unmet even by groups with "normal" status.

Attempting to minimize their stigmatized status, DLP members endeavored to eliminate the negative stereotypes implied by a gay fraternity, particularly the presumption that gay fraternities must be a highly sexualized space where young gay men gather for group sex. To debunk this stereotype, DLP often imposed some sort of self-censorship in the ways the group publicly expressed its sexual identity. For instance, a chapter decided to ban suggestive references to body parts after some members used the phrase "Gilbert's Grapes"—obviously a reference to male genitalia—to name a flavor of snow cone sold in a fund-raising booth. One brother explained why such a decision was important to the group: "It bothered me a lot that they would want to show one's affection for someone's 'grapes' during a public event. . . . I don't want to belong to an organization that promotes or encourages sexual innuendo or perception that straight people may have of us. . . . I just don't want people to think of me as [being like] all these gays . . . and all that they do is have sex, you know, because I am not like that."

Since the fraternity received no complaints from the public, this incident illustrates that censoring public images indeed came from DLP itself, often with the anticipation of how the public would have viewed the group had DLP deviated from the conventional image of a legitimate fraternity. This self-censorship also extended to DLP's image within the gay community. When one of the fraternity's recruiting advertisements accidentally appeared in the sexually explicit classified section of a national gay magazine, the chapter immediately pulled the advertisement within two issues. One brother pointed out the need for DLP to demonstrate a clean reputation within the gay community: "I mean if we were to put an ad in any gay publication, we would put it in an area where ads are normally like: joining the square dancing club, or gay swimmers' league, those kinds of things where they're reputable. . . . This way we are proving to the gay community that we are reputable." Despite the fact that sexual innuendo was not necessarily a problem in DLP's private interaction, and that sexuality was a key feature that would attract membership,[24] the gay fraternity often sought to downplay its "gayness" in the public, a strategy that could potentially normalize the group as a "real" fraternity.

Toning down its feminine character was another strategy used by the gay fraternity chapters to cope with the homophobic campus and community environment. Since the entrenched culture understands male homosexuality as the opposite of masculinity, and thus the opposite of brotherhood, typically feminine behaviors were suppressed. While enjoying (or not stigmatizing) acting feminine within the private space of the fraternity, brothers were aware that, in order to gain acceptance on campus, they should not act like "flaming queens." In an interfraternity function—a volleyball competition with straight fraternities—this concern over feminine mannerisms became a sore spot for some members in the DLP collective: "The queeny guys sometimes don't want to tone it down, you know? It becomes really uncomfortable . . . to the more butch guys. I guess it's because [the butch guys] don't mind, but they don't want to be stereotyped as queeny. So when we're in public, it becomes a problem when the queeny guys just go off: 'Girl Friend! Oh he's got a nice ass.' And the straight-acting guys are like: "Uh-oh . . . let's, let's tone it down there. We don't want to draw too much attention to ourselves. We just like to keep a low profile.'"

Devaluing femininity is certainly common in certain segments of gay male culture,[25] but at least within the private space of DLP, a diversity of gendered performance was acceptable. In social settings where a "reputable image" was called for, brothers collectively pursued a masculine image they felt as the "appropriate" or legitimate image of the fraternity. However, this pursuit could potentially create a rift between the "butch brothers" and "femme brothers"—a challenge to the intimate brotherhood DLP members intended to build.[26]

Certainly, the problem of group presentation is not unique to DLP. Most GLBT student groups confront a similar challenge as they struggle to legitimize themselves when facing hostility from other individuals or groups on campus. But unlike many GLBT student organizations that adopt more confrontational tactics to challenge homophobia, DLP assumed a strategy of mainstreaming, a coping mechanism that emphasizes the *commonalities* between the brothers and the outside world rather than their differences.[27] This coping tactic echoed the brothers' desire to be "simply another fraternity down the block" or "the best fraternity on campus." Although not always successful, the active involvement of DLP in legitimizing itself within the fraternity institution reflects a common strategy many "deviant" social groups adopt in order to be considered "normal" within the larger society.

Defending the Single-Sex Fraternal Model

Not only was DLP's challenge to the traditional fraternity institution partial, it was also selective. This selectivity is particularly clear when we consider how the gay fraternity drew its membership boundaries. Despite its various deviations from the fraternal form, DLP held onto a single-sex organization model that implies the exclusion of women from full membership.[28] As a collective, DLP brothers made a conscious effort to defend their single-sex model by claiming equality vis-à-vis other straight men, as shown in the following official statement: "Delta Lambda Phi has visited the topic of women members several times. In 1992, the Fraternity's governing body decided to remain exclusively male rather than going coed. The reasoning being, if straight men can have a 'traditional' (i.e., non-coed) Greek experience, gay men should be able to have it as well."[29] Consistent with its mainstreaming strategy, DLP drew parallel comparisons with straight fraternities regarding how membership should be determined. DLP assumed that the gay brothers' needs for the "traditional" Greek experience—if such a thing really exists—were similar to the needs of straight men. Furthermore, there was also a degree of commonality among all gay men based on their presumably shared experience, as the official statement continues: "gay men, by virtue of their being gay men, go through a unique, shared social experience. Delta Lambda Phi is a way for gay men of varying backgrounds (sometimes radically varying backgrounds) to find common ground in that experience. Those who claim that our lesbian friends, as much as we love and support them as comrades-in-arms, have the same social experience as gay men, are, frankly, deluding themselves. Our lesbian friends have the option of pledging our 'sister' sorority, Lambda Delta Omega."

Here DLP constructed a clear distinction between men and women, and not between sexualities. If straight men and gay men are similar through inescapable biology, and if all gay men share some common experiences, then a single-sex organizational model seems inevitably appropriate and justifiable. In fact, there was no formal proscription against straight male membership, and two straight men were DLP members at the time of this research.

To many brothers, a single-sex organizational model was the most essential component of fraternity identity. When asked what would happen when the fraternity were to follow the example of other GLBT groups and accept lesbian membership on the assumption that the similarities between gays and lesbians are greater than those between gay men and straight men, many brothers said that DLP "wouldn't be a fraternity anymore." For them a fraternity is a place of boys and/or men; incorporating women would alter the organizational foundation of DLP. Another brother concurred: "They [members of the GLBT community] are thinking that we are being exclusionist. . . . Well, of course we are. It's a fraternity. That's the point. It's men dealing with men things."

The exclusion of women, however, was never a conscious program of DLP to perpetuate the institutional oppressions against women; brothers did not reject women membership simply for the sake of excluding them. Rather, it was the idealized value of "male bonding" that the brothers perceived as a distinguished element in a fraternal form. According to one brother, "a bond among men is different than the bond among people." Even though DLP brothers had attempted many ways to redefine what such a bonding could mean—for example, it could mean men sharing their emotional feelings with each other or dressing up in drag together—the brothers clung to an almost mystical ideal wherein a bonding experience is possible only for a male group who may share nothing more than biological sex. One brother described his bonding experience as "something magical you carry with you always . . . that almost transcends words."

The gay fraternity's defense of a single-sex organizational model thus reveals the arbitrariness and persistence of gender boundary in the fraternal model. Brothers further supported these entrenched boundaries through a rigid but vaguely articulated understanding of gender differences in their discourse. As one brother said: "I'm not trying to sound chauvinistic or anything. I just don't think we should allow women to join DLP primarily because men and women are obviously different. Men and women also have different needs and different ideas, and I think that would actually cause more problems than be good because there are [already] so many differences on various levels." The "difference" brothers often pointed to, however, was unspecific, often relegated to the notion that "there is a different kind of energy when men are around." Whether this is true or not is beyond the scope of this chapter, but when the fraternal form is legitimized in a particular social environment, it is readily available for some to adopt it in order to justify the exclusion of membership based on biological sex.

A puzzling question remains regarding DLP's selectivity in its challenge to the fraternity tradition. While brothers had modified—albeit only partially—almost every other traditional component of the fraternal form, why could they not let go of the single-sex model? With the rise of many coed fraternities across American campuses, there is no reason to believe that a single-sex membership is a more essential ingredient to defining the fraternal model than, for example, the use of "toughness" to define a bond among men—an element that DLP had modified. The answer to this question may be found in the institutional logic that constrains how student organizations operate on American campuses. This requires us to situate DLP with other similar student organizations in the multiple-organizational environment in college campuses. We need to ask how much power students have to create innovative organizational models capable of achieving novel goals and disrupting old forms.

The Institutional Constraints and Dilemma of DLP

Even though in principle social actors, including students, can experiment and develop new styles of organizing beyond existing models, complete innovations of this sort rarely occur. Rather than constructing new organizational models from scratch, actors combine and reconfigure existing organizational templates and reappropriate cultural meanings in new contexts. In studying how special-interest groups emerged as a dominant organizational form in nineteenth-century American politics, Elizabeth Clemens argues that novel organizations tended to conjoin unfamiliar faces with familiar organizational formats, or culturally inappropriate templates with familiar faces. In other words, new organizational forms come from breaking the norms that guide "what sorts of people *should* or *could* master what sorts of organizational competence."[30] For instance, in the nineteenth century women negotiated new public roles by organizing themselves as clubs: "Neither 'clubs' nor 'women's organizations' were unfamiliar; what was novel was women organizing as clubs. The significance of this innovation may easily escape a modern reader, but it involved a precedent-setting claim by women to appropriate heretofore masculine organizational forms. And once organized as men, would it not be appropriate for them to engage in public affairs and politics?"[31] DLP certainly fits within this pattern of organization innovation because the fraternal model is a familiar template for student organizing. By conjoining gay membership with the fraternal model and diverging from its oft-noted homophobic content, DLP reappropriated the cultural meanings that determine what it means to be a fraternal man. DLP brothers often recounted stories of people being shocked upon hearing that a gay fraternity even exists. They were well aware of their challenge to the college scene and believed that they were on a mission to enact social change, particularly in conservative regions where gay organizations are rare: "I think by virtue of calling ourselves the gay fraternity was making a statement nationally, especially down here [in a political conservative state]. In San Francisco or Washington DC or New York, gay fraternities might not be such a huge statement, but in the Bible Belt, forming any kind of gay organization is making a statement." Similar to the nineteenth century women's clubs described above, DLP posed a challenge to the heteronormative world and asked whether it is appropriate for young gay men to organize as a fraternity.

The selectivity of DLP's challenge, however, begs the question about the alternative models available to brothers so they can make a difference on campus. Unsurprisingly, one finds rather limited choices. In general, two familiar organizational models have dominated how American students organize themselves in the post–student movements era after the mid-1970s.[32] One the one hand, students organize around particular academic, professional, political, religious, or sociocultural interests. These may be called the "special-interest model" of student organization. Under this model, some pragmatic or activist interest defines membership, and sometimes a common social identity brings the group together. This is usually the case with most GLBT groups and various identity-based student groups. In contrast to the "special-interest model," fraternities and sororities represent what may be called the "solidarity model" of student organization. This model focuses on the construction of a "social bond" among members, with their identity anchored in the specific group to which they belong. Through a familial metaphor advocated by the solidarity model, members' identities toward a group often override other special interests or social categories.

Exclusivity of group membership is predictably high in groups using the solidarity model. For example, a transfer of membership between two GLBT groups may not cause a serious identity crisis for an individual, since any two GLBT groups can be said to be equivalent if they worked on similar issues with comparable goals. However, groups adopting a solidarity model are relationally different from one another —"relational" because it is the relationships among members that define the unique identity of a solidarity-based group. The transfer of membership between two fraternities may be considered an act of disloyalty. Member selection in fraternities and sororities is thus more exclusive, often guided by an evaluation of whether an individual is worthy enough to assume the role of brothers or sisters.

Given the dichotomy in the organizational models available to college students, building a gay fraternity using the solidarity model entails distinguishing similar groups using the special-interest model. For DLP brothers, the gay fraternity's difference from GLBT groups defined DLP's identity and worthiness. For example, brothers thought that GLBT groups were too lax in their member selection, and the lack of a discerning selection procedure was linked to the inability of GLBT groups to build intimate relationships among members: "to become a member of DLP you can't just sort of walk in and say, 'I want to be a member.' With every other gay organization you just walk in and say 'I want to be a member,' and maybe there is a membership fee, and usually there is not even that. So you are not investing in it, and so the relationship formed there—sometimes they exist not necessarily in the context of an organization, whereas in a fraternity the relationships do exist within the context of the organization."

The degree of exclusivity was assumed to produce group cohesion, and brothers took pride in the intimate relationship they build vis-à-vis other GLBT organizations: "[in other gay organizations] you always know maybe the first name and almost never their last name, and you clearly almost never know anything about them. So you tend to have a lot of people who are acquaintances rather than friends." In contrast, "even though DLP itself is business-like, it is also a very close-knit group. It is more than just an organization."

To be distinguished from a purely "business-like" organization with special interests is also to avoid being political. Brothers believed that political activism is the key goal of many GLBT groups, but for DLP, "it has not gotten involved in any political involvement whatsoever. That is not our goal." As another brother put it, "we don't participate in any political activities because we think it is not our duty to be politically active." Most frequently, brothers differentiated their activities by their "social" or "political" nature, as if the terms were diametrically opposed and mutually exclusive. If a brother raised a political issue that requires DLP's collective involvement, other brothers might invoke the "social" purpose of the fraternity in order to avoid forthcoming debate: "[Being non-political] is one thing that we pretty much agree to. If it comes up, we're not going to discuss it, because we are not a political organization. We are here to have fun and we are here to be supportive. . . . Sometimes, a brother who likes the liberal causes brought issues up. I mean, sometimes it's a legitimate concern, like should we be involved in [a political action]. We have to sit down and say, 'No, we can't because that's not what we do.'" In informal settings, discussions of political issues were generally silenced. As one brother said, "At our last party, myself and another brother were discussing finances and taxes in the kitchen. Once the other brothers realized what we were talking about, they chastised us for discussing it. It is true; we keep our brotherhood very social."

Although DLP brothers viewed their nonpolitical stance as a way to diminish in-group conflicts among brothers, avoiding political obligations could sometimes be at odds with the dissenting position DLP took in the larger fraternity institution. As a challenger to a traditional model, the very existence of DLP already conveyed a particular political message, which brothers referred to as "making a statement" or "letting ourselves known" in the straight world. The unstated politics of DLP might, therefore, bring it inevitably closer to GLBT groups, despite brothers' constant attempt to differentiate the gay fraternity from these groups.

Furthermore, when we look at the actual practices of DLP, these similarities become even more apparent. In many chapters, both groups joined interorganizational events on campus; they participated in gay rights and sometimes women's rights rallies; they fundraised for AIDS; and they both aimed at dismantling stereotypes and prejudices against gays and lesbians. The practical redundancy between DLP and GLBT student groups was therefore high. However, DLP brothers usually found no difficulty in distinguishing themselves from groups with similar practices. For example, DLP brothers framed their participation in political activities as a "social" mission. They highlighted the individual nature of their actions and deemphasized their collective character, as reflected by a brother who described a fundraising event that most would consider political: "We had [an honorary member] who ran for secretary of the state in Y state. We did gala for him; we did voluntary screaming for him [i.e., cheerleading]; we did fund raising for him, and we endorsed him in a manner . . ., which we could, yet we didn't want to use our name, even though he knew that we're all members of the gay fraternity, Delta Lambda Phi. And he thanked us as Delta Lambda Phi, even though we didn't ask him to. He said, 'I would like to thank the brothers of Delta Lambda Phi for coming over here.' *And we didn't go there as Delta Lambda Phi; we went there as individuals*" (my emphasis). By backgrounding the collective nature of their actions, brothers were able to practice politics *as if* they were acting individually without violating the fraternity's "social" imperative. Reframing what collective action could mean, DLP thereby permitted the involvement of the many activities similar to that of GLBT groups.

With this degree of practical redundancy in the college institution, the same-sex model had become a major, if not the only, character through which DLP could distinguish itself from other GLBT student groups. Brothers frankly noted that if DLP included women, "it would become just another GLBT student organization." And we have seen that the brothers do not aspire to be just another "business-like" group, even though many of their activities were just as pragmatic and potentially political as other GLBT organizations.

The defense of a single-sex model by DLP, as arbitrary as it is, indeed embraced an institutional logic that reflects how American campuses work. The exclusion of women allowed DLP brothers to claim uniqueness as a collective within an institutional environment that offers limited organizational models for stigmatized students to cope with homophobia and simultaneously garner legitimate status in the college environment. The choice of a fraternal model thus appeared obvious to young gay men who aspired to intimate and meaningful social relationships that they thought were lacking in the larger gay community.

Certainly, other organizational forms, such as communal groups, also stress the development of meaningful relationships among constituents, and they do so without drawing a rigid gender boundary among members.[33] What this organizational form lacks is the familiarity—at least for American college students in the post-1970s era—that can allow participants to accrue a sense of legitimacy in the larger college environment. Constructing a communal group for gay and lesbian students may create further marginalization. And legitimacy is perhaps all the more important for some students with a stigmatized identity.

However, seeking legitimacy by flirting with a traditionally homophobic institution can create a dilemma that cannot be resolved by simply modifying some of the elements of the fraternal model. For example, it is questionable whether DLP had ever advanced a legitimate status in the eyes of other members in the Interfraternity Council (IFC), an umbrella organization for fraternities within a college. One DLP brother explained that other fraternities on campus regarded DLP as a "joke fraternity": "They have IFC games during the homecoming week, and you know there are all these queens out there. . . . Of course we got our butts kicked most of the time, but we were still out there. We are like the joke fraternity. There have been a couple of members of our chapter who actually were in other [straight] fraternities, and they told us all about how they bad-mouthed us."

Although a few chapters immersed themselves in gay culture and functioned as full members of the Greek community on the IFC, DLP as a whole seems to have retreated on its goal of seeking a legitimate status within the traditional fraternal institution. In 1996, DLP terminated its pursuit for National Interfraternity Conference (NIC) membership, the national organization for all college fraternities. Even though adhering to many traditional practices, conjoining the fraternal model with gay membership might still prove to be too risky and culturally inappropriate to the traditional fraternal institution in which homophobia persists.

In relation to the larger gay world, members of the gay community sometimes accused the fraternity of being "too Greek" because of its exclusionary practices in choosing members. As one brother summed it up: "We are the outcasts. In reality, we offer a support group for the young gay male. However, in the eyes of many gay political leaders, we are discriminating because we do not allow [just] anyone in; you must be accepted. And of course, we're sexist in their eyes [referring to the exclusion of women]." Even though DLP brothers had challenged many problematic practices, such as hazing, and actively redefined the meaning of masculinity in the traditional conception of fraternity men, their defense of a single-sex model remained too conservative in the eyes of the gay community, which often viewed (at least theoretically) biological sex as fluid as sexuality. In attempting to take the best of both straight and gay worlds, DLP seems to be rejected by both.

Implications

While organizational models are not freshly created but adopted from preexisting schema, we must consider the possibility of imagining, manufacturing, and making available new organizational models for students caught between the culture of sexual conformity proposed by traditional fraternities and the paradoxes of cultural legitimacy that plague the phenomenon of the gay fraternity. Given the limited number of prestigious organizational forms available on American campuses, stigmatized groups such as the gay fraternity would have to choose between a fraternal model that assumes an arbitrary notion of gender difference and a GLBT model that fails to foster meaningful relationships among gay men in a noninstrumental format. This chapter thus urges college administrators to promote campus policy to expand the range of legitimate organizational models and embrace those who are brave enough to build organizations that appear completely—and not partially—different.

To facilitate more organizational imagination on university campuses, we must first challenge the persistent privileges granted to the traditional fraternity and sorority, institutions that reinforce arbitrary notions of gender difference and reproduce entrenched gender barriers and inequalities in society at large.[34] The examination of the gay fraternity in this chapter has shown that there is nothing really "magical" about fraternities' time-honored tradition of "male bonding"; insofar as gay men were often rejected in traditional (or homophobic) fraternities, what is at stake for the established fraternity structure is not "male bonding" per se but, more accurately, a "heterosexual bonding" whose value is derived from the careful maintenance of sexual difference. Despite their own critique of this heterosexist model, however, the gay fraternity brothers of DLP continued to take the single-sex fraternal form for granted. Even though DLP brothers redefined the meaning of fraternity men by adopting cultural strategies usually associated with femininity, the gay fraternity rejected lesbian membership on the assumption that lesbians' experiences as a sexual minority were insufficient grounds for social solidarity. At the same time, however, DLP erased all differences among men by welcoming heterosexual men into the gay fraternity. Accepting the gender-exclusive fraternal form as a given, gay fraternity members then reconstructed the experience of male bonding through collective activities and rituals, as if to argue that similarities among men prefigure and exist prior to DLP's organization that seeks to foster the possible meanings of male bonding.

We can attempt to understand DLP's struggle using an institutional analysis that looks at how different organizational models interact within a specific social environment. If students are given more autonomy and encouragement to innovate new organizational forms, those with a stigmatized status, such as gay men, may seek to invent collectivities specifically addressing their needs without falling into the dichotomous choice between a special-interest model (which may be "too business-like") and an exclusive solidarity-based fraternal model (defined by received and arbitrary notions of biological sex). For example, university administrators can give financial and administrative incentives to groups who might support nontraditional or nonprestigious student organizations, just as administrators now provide such support for conventional fraternity/sorority organizations. These incentives should include granting charters and financial priorities to groups that address new ways of challenging and dissolving boundaries of race, class, gender, and/or sexual orientation; indeed, we should remember that the practice of fraternal legacies often ensures that exclusivities of race and class interconnect with the exclusivities of male privilege.

We can imagine a new student organization built, for instance, on the principle of familial relationships and intimacy, one that assumes a horizontal decision-making process, and/or one that advocates social justice and equality by adopting an egalitarian, nonhierarchical organizational model for itself. Given the current constraints of the university environment, students seeking to create nontraditional, nonhierarchical campus organizations surely would require a great deal of energy, persistence, and even political courage. Likewise, administrators will need to demonstrate an equal degree of energy, persistence, and courage as they help promote alternative organizational models—which may be less immediately prestigious than long-established fraternities—and support unconventional students whose needs are unmet by the limited number of available campus associations. Further, administrators must be willing to engage in educational programs (for example, workshops) that encourage students to organize themselves autonomously rather than depend on preexisting, arguably antiquated organizational structures (including but not limited to fraternities/sororities). Creating a university culture that is critical of organizational models can also help students to reflect on issues of identity, belonging, and community.

Future research on alternative fraternities will require comparative analyses conducted along multiple vectors of organizational difference. First, while the voices of gays and lesbians within traditional fraternities and sororities have been heard,[35] we lack systematic comparisons of the ways in which traditional institutions incorporate or reject members who do not conform to their heterosexist assumptions. Second, an empirical comparison between gay fraternities and lesbian sororities does not, to my knowledge, exist thus far. In order to refine our understanding of DLP's reproduction of gender difference within a gay fraternal model, we need to ask whether lesbian sororities face problems of exclusivity, self-identity, and public representation analogous to those of their somewhat more privileged gay male counterparts. As long as gender inequalities remain ingrained in the university system, which privileges fraternities over sororities, we may expect that lesbian organizations might not resort to the traditional sorority model to construct legitimacy in campus environments. Or if they do, lesbian sororities might organize according to a different logic than that of gay fraternities, perhaps by declaring themselves as more politically radical than the brothers of DLP, or by eliminating gender boundaries by accepting males into their fold. For example, in 2000, Iota Lambda Pi Fraternity was established in Tallahassee, Florida to cater to the needs of "butch, stud and dominant" lesbians. Thus, rather than calling themselves a sorority, the group adopted the "fraternity" label.[36] Future research can seek to understand the reasons why such groups transgress the rigid gender boundary established by the fraternity/sorority model. Was this an action trying to be subversive, to shock the fraternity community, or merely to serve as a form of seeking legitimacy? The ways lesbian sororities participate in crossing the gendered border may be indicative to the resilience and rigidity of the fraternity institution.

Finally, the goals of DLP, as presented in this chapter, cannot be necessarily generalized or made applicable to all gay fraternities on U.S. campuses. For instance, Delta Phi Upsilon, a gay fraternity for men of color established two years earlier than DLP, makes political activism a much more integral part of their agenda than do the DLP brothers. While DLP members assume that emphasizing political activism could foment in-group conflicts among radical and more sociopolitically moderate brothers, Delta Phi Upsilon actively engaged in political actions designed to call attention to race and class injustices. If DLP rejected a political platform because it would appear "too-business like" and too close to the organizational style of other GLBT groups, do brothers of Delta Phi Upsilon face the same dilemma? We may assume that, as a gay fraternity for men of color, Delta Phi Upsilon's members would view civil rights activism as a certain source of unity rather than a possible cause for dissension. However, we must still ask whether a more socially acceptable, race-conscious civil rights activism could be meant to legitimize them in the eyes of homophobic cultures unwilling to accept the notion of gay Latinos and African Americans.

Notes

1. Leon Jackson, "The Rights of Man and the Rites of Youth: Fraternity and Riot at Eighteenth-Century Harvard," in *The American College in the Nineteenth Century*, ed. Roger Geiger (Nashville, TN: Vanderbilt University Press, 2000); Anthony W James, "The Defenders of Tradition: College Social Fraternities, Race, and Gender, 1845–1980" (PhD diss., University of Mississippi, 1998); Wilson C. McWilliams, *The Idea of Fraternity in America* (Berkeley: University of California Press, 1973).

2. Mary Ann Clawson, *Constructing Brotherhood: Class, Gender, and Fraternalism* (Princeton, NJ: Princeton University Press, 1989).

3. Andi O'Conor, "The Cultural Logic of Gender in College: Heterosexism, Homophobia and Sexism in Campus Peer Groups" (PhD diss., University of Colorado-Boulder, 1998).

4. Compulsory heterosexuality is the notion that all human beings are naturally heterosexual and hence should be expected as such in all social environments and relationships. For Adrienne Rich, in a patriarchal society, this norm coerces women into heterosexual relations that support the domination of men over women; see Adrienne Rich, "Compulsory Heterosexuality and Lesbian Existence," *Signs* 5, no. 4 (1980): 647–50.

5. Sharon R. Bird, "Welcome to the Men's Club: Homosociality and the Maintenance of Hegemonic Masculinity," *Gender & Society* 10 (1996): 120–32; A. Ayres Boswell and Joan Z. Spade, "Fraternities and Collegiate Rape Culture: Why Are Some Fraternities More Dangerous Places for Women?" *Gender & Society* 10, no. 2 (1996): 133–47; Linda Kalof and Timothy Cargill, "Fraternity and Sorority Membership and

Gender Dominance Attitudes," *Sex Roles* 25 (1991): 417–23; Peggy Reeves Sandy, *Fraternity Gang Rape: Sex Brotherhood, and Privilege on Campus* (New York: New York University Press, 1990); Mindy Stombler and Patricia Yancey Martin, "Bring Women IN, Keeping Women Down: Fraternity 'Little Sister' Organizations," *Journal of Contemporary Ethnography* 23 no. 2 (1994): 150–84; Mindy Stombler and Irene Padavic, "Sister Acts: Resisting Men's Domination in Black and White Fraternity Little Sister Programs," *Social Problems* 44, no. 2 (1997): 257–75.

6. Shane L. Windmeyer and Pamela W. Freeman, eds., *Out on Fraternity Row: Personal Accounts of Being Gay in a College Fraternity* (New York: Alyson Books, 1998).

7. Elisabeth S. Clemens, *The People's Lobby: Organizational Innovation and the Rise of Interest Group Politics in the United States, 1890–1925* (Chicago: University of Chicago Press, 1997).

8. Delta Lambda Phi, Chapter Handbook, II-6 (date not listed).

9. Ibid., III-8.

10. A few chapters were community-based chapters, and accepted noncollege men for active membership. Other chapters were multi-university based. By 2004, the gay fraternity had gained significant growth with twenty active chapters and ten colonies.

11. The detail of the research methodology is documented in King-To Yeung and Mindy Stombler, "Gay and Greek: The Identity Paradox of Gay Fraternities," *Social Problems* 47, no. 4 (2000): 134–52. Briefly this project is a collective research effort under the supervision of Mindy Stombler, who directed two studies on the DLP's construction of gender and political ideology. We depend primarily on forty-two open-ended in-depth interviews, two years of participant observation in a community-based chapter in a state university, the attendance of the national convention in 1996 (by Stombler), and extensive archival data. All names of members and locations are changed to protect the identity of the research participants.

12. Elizabeth Cohn, "A House With No Closets," *Rolling Stone* 30 (September 1993): 87–95.

13. Stephen Whitlock, "The Rise of Greek Civilization," *Equal Times* (Fall 1995) (Archival Data).

14. Gilbert Herdt, "Coming Out as a Rite of Passage: A Chicago Study," in *Gay Culture in America*, ed. Gilbert Herdt (Boston: Beacon Press, 1992), 29–67.

15. The variety of student groups for sexual dissents or individuals with alternative sexualities is lumped together in this article as the Gay, Lesbian, Bisexual, and Transgendered (GLBT) groups.

16. Michael S. Kimmel, "Masculinity as Homophobia: Fear, Shame and Silence in the Construction of Gender Identity," in *Theorizing Masculinities*, ed. Harry Brod and Michael Kaufman (Thousand Oaks, CA: Sage, 1994), 119–41.

17. R. W. Connell, *Gender and Power: Society, the Person and Sexual Politics* (Stanford, CA: Stanford University Press, 1987).

18. I consider this event a "private event" because it did not involve other straight fraternities or student organizations on campus.

19. This does not mean all DLP brothers engaged in feminine behavior. Indeed, as we will see below, display of femininity in public was a question for some "butch brothers." The important point here is that DLP did not stigmatize femininity at least in its private setting. See King-To Yeung, Mindy Stombler, and Reneé Wharton, "Making Men in Gay Fraternities: Resisting and Reproducing Multiple Dimensions of Hegemonic Masculinity," *Gender & Society* 20, no. 1 (2006): 5–31.

20. Ricky L. Jones, *Black Haze: Violence, Sacrifice, and Manhood in Black Greek-letter Fraternities*, (Albany: State University of New York Press, 2004); Hank Nuwer, *Broken Pledges: The Dead Rite of Hazing* (Atlanta: Longstreet Press, 1990).

21. This part of the paper regarding no-hazing policies of DLP is adopted from Mindy Stombler, Renee Wharton, and King-To Yeung, "A House with No Closets: Exploring the Structure of and Dynamics within Gay Fraternities," paper presented at the annual meeting of the Society for the Study of Social Problems, Toronto, Canada, August 10, 1997.

22. Arlie Russell Hochschild, *Managed Heart: Commercialization of Human Feeling* (Berkeley: University of California Press, 1984).

23. Peter M. Nardi, "Sex, Friendship, and Gender Roles among Gay Men," in *Men's Friendships*, ed. Peter M. Nardi (Newbury Park, CA: Sage, 1992), 173–85; Scott Swain, "Covert Intimacy: Closeness in Men's friendships," in *The Gendered Society Reader*, ed. Michael S. Kimmel (New York: Oxford University Press, 2000), 364–82.

24. It should be pointed out, however, that sexuality is not the only element that defines a gay identity. See Barry D. Adam, *The Rise of a Gay and Lesbian Movement* (Boston: Twayne, 1987); Jeffrey Escoffier, *American Homo: Community and Perversity* (Berkeley: University of California Press, 1998).

25. For discussions on how hypermasculinity culture was adopted in the American gay culture, see Martin P. Levine, *Gay Macho* (New York: New York University Press, 1998); Gregg Blachford, "Male Dominance and the Gay World," in *The Making of the Modern Homosexual*, ed. Kenneth Plummer (Totowa, NJ: Barnes & Noble, 1981), 184–210.

26. However, in our research, we did not observe any heated debate over the public image DLP brothers should present in front of other fraternities. This is largely because all brothers, butch or femme, tended to agree with a normalized image as an appropriate presentation for the fraternity. When the queeny brothers were asked to tone it down, they succumbed to the request without any complaints.

27. See Urvashi Vaid, *Virtual Equality: The Mainstreaming of Gay and Lesbian Liberation* (New York: Doubleday, 1995) for a discussion on whether mainstreaming strategies are effective for stigmatized groups to establish legitimacy in the larger society.

28. Partial membership, coded as "little sister," is available to women in some fraternities. See Mindy Stombler, "'Buddies' or 'Slutties': The Collective Sexual Reputation of Fraternity Little Sisters," *Gender & Society* 8, no. 3 (1994): 293–96.

29. From the "Frequently Asked Question About Delta Lambda Phi," *Delta Lambda Phi National Social Fraternity*, <http://www.dlp.org/national>.

30. Clemens, *The People's Lobby*, 53; emphasis original.

31. Ibid., 54–55.

32. During the heydays of student movements, American college students not only questioned the authoritative university culture, they also experimented the different ways in which student collectives could be formed. For groups such as Student Nonviolent Coordinating Committee (SNCC), organizational form was more than just a means to the activist goals members sought. The very form of organizing is an end to itself—how decisions were made and how power was distributed constituted an essential identity and purpose of the group's existence. See Francesca Polletta, *Freedom Is an Endless Meeting: Democracy in American Social Movements* (Chicago: University of Chicago Press, 2002).

33. For an extensive comparison across different kinds of communal groups in America during the 1970s, see Benjamin D Zablocki, *Alienation and Charisma: A Study of Contemporary American Communes* (New York: Free Press, 1980).

34. The critique of the fraternity institution has been well established by Bird, "Welcome to the Men's Club"; Boswell and Spade, "Fraternities and Collegiate Rape Culture"; Clawson, *Constructing Brotherhood*"; Sandy, *Fraternity Gang Rape;*" Stombler and

Martin, "Bringing Women IN, Keeping Women Down"; and Stombler and Padavic, "Sister Acts."

35. For lesbians in college sororities, see Shane L. Windmeyer and Pamela W. Freeman, eds., *Secret Sisters: Stories of Being Lesbian and Bisexual in a College Sorority* (Los Angeles: Alyson Books, 2001); for gay men in traditional fraternities, see Shane L. Windmeyer and Pamela W. Freeman, eds., *Out on the Fraternity Row* (Los Angeles: Alyson Books, 1998).

36. "The Beginning," Iota Lambda Phi Fraternity, Inc., <http://www.truegentlewomen.org/herstory.htm>.

Praising God and Maintaining Tradition: Religious Diversity within College Fraternities and Sororities

Craig L. Torbenson

THE PERCEPTION OF A COLLEGE FRATERNITY AND SORORITY MAY be the antithesis of a religious organization. While social fraternities and sororities focus on a variety of character-building traits, religious organizations include a spiritual aspect that most social organizations do not. For those who join a religious fraternity or sorority, religion is a very important element in their life. Based on their religious principles, members of religious organizations feel it is morally wrong to engage in the activities of drinking, sex, and drugs, activities unofficially associated with many social fraternities and sororities. While those of the Jewish faith strive to maintain their customs and traditions, for members of Christian Greek-letter organizations it is their depth of commitment to Jesus Christ that is their guiding principle. For Christian organizations, the sentiment expressed by Jason Willoughby, National Chaplain for Alpha Gamma Omega, provides insight into the social-religious fraternity and sorority. He said: "What makes us unique as a social fraternity is our connection to the Person of Jesus Christ. He is the brains of our operation. He is the glue that holds us together. He is the teacher that shows us how to live life, have friends, work hard, and make a lasting difference in other people's lives. There's something bigger than all of us at work, something better that's happening than human organization can produce."[1]

This chapter examines three areas in which religion has had a role in adding to the diversity or variety of college fraternities and sororities. The first area examines the role of religion in the creation of early fraternities. Since most institutions had ties to religion during the first 150 years of higher education, it was only natural to find religion widespread on college campuses. As such, early college fraternities and sororities reflected the religious nature of the university or college and student body. While this did not create much diversity, it is important to understand the role of religion in these early fraternal organizations, for it sets the stage for the other two areas that follow.

A second area looks at the exclusion of students of different religions from the established traditional fraternities and sororities. While most college students during the nineteenth century were professing Christians, establishing such a brotherhood should not have excluded anyone from consideration. That was not the case with the Catholics and Jews. Around the beginning of the twentieth century, a number of Jewish and nonsectarian fraternities and sororities emerged, along with several organizations that were denomination specific.

The third area examines a number of religious fraternities and sororities, as well as coed organizations, formed for those serious in practicing their religion and thus creating a bond between students through a social and intellectual exchange. While traditional organizations were available to join, they did not meet the needs of a group of students seeking the fraternity experience with individuals that shared the same religious values. Thus, while the religious fraternity or sorority may not have a diverse membership, it does, however, add to the overall variety, and hence diversity, of this social institution.

Religion in Early Fraternities

The early beginnings of the fraternity, as a social institution, are wrapped in the religious setting of the early colonial college experience. Nearly all colleges had been established by various religious denominations for the purpose of training young men to become missionaries or ministers. A religious itinerary was followed by those attending school that included morning and evening prayers, compulsory attendance at church meetings, and the formation of student religious groups. Another event that occurred on college campuses was the religious revival. A revival could be sparked by any number of events, including a rousing sermon, the death of a classmate, or prayer. The result was a confession of sin and of their religious experience. If a college did not have at least one revival in the four years a group of students attended school, then the faculty of the school felt "they or—God—"had failed that group of students.[2]

Given the role of religion in the colonial college, it was only natural that early student organizations incorporated various religious aspects into their group. With the establishment of the first fraternity in 1776, Phi Beta Kappa, the creation of a new type of student organization was realized. While not religious in nature, this organization set the pattern for fraternities to follow by having individuals desiring to join their organization to "acknowledge only The Deity, a Supreme Being, or a Creator."[3] Thus, those desiring to become a member of Phi Beta Kappa had to take the following oath of fidelity. Certainly other early fraternities had similar types of oaths: "I ____ , do swear on the Holy Evangelists of Almighty God, or otherwise as calling the Supreme Being to attest this my oath, declaring that I will, with all my possible efforts, endeavor to prove true, just, and deeply attached to this our growing Fraternity."[4]

While Phi Beta Kappa's ritual made no reference to Christianity, the group did debate several religious topics including Athe Advantages of an established Church" and "Whether Religion is necessary in Government." The group participated in the intellectual mileau of the time and although not antireligious or denomination specific, the group leaned to the deistic. In fact, Phi Beta Kappa had written into its constitution "that in every design or attempt, whether great or small, we ought to invoke the Deity, by some private sacrifice or devotion, for a fraternal prosperity." Certainly religious influence did not escape the organization as it kept "on hand a copy of the New Testament."[5]

With the emergence of various student organizations and in particular, the literary society, the battle between the religious piety of the college and the intellectual enlightenment of the student took place during the latter 1770s and into the early 1800s. The literary society provided students with the intellectual stimulus they were not receiving under a college curriculum that included rote memorization. Thus, shedding the religious dogma of the college, the literary society "respected reason, nurtured intellect, and subjected much that was established to scrutiny and debate."[6]

While the literary society filled the intellectual vacuum that students encountered at early colleges, the fraternity filled the social vacuum by shifting the emphasis of a college education from the next world to this world. Instead of preparing students for success in the afterlife, the fraternity prepared its members with the "attitude and skills necessary for success in this world." Instead of having status as a Christian, one had social status. Instead of one's prestige coming from spiritual grace, it came from worldly skills. Instead of having "Christian grace, humility, equality, and morality," the fraternity institutionalized new values of prestige. The decline in the religious emphasis of the college was facilitated by the fraternity which recognized "secular values, . . . good friendship, good looks, good clothes, good family, and good income." The fraternity fostered the cultivation of polished manners, certainly a skill necessary for success in this world. The fraternity, then, became a school of accomplishment that prepared its members "to take their place among men, not among the angels."[7]

While the founding principles of early fraternities included a focus and belief in brotherhood, all shared a "common religious heritage" based on the "moral foundations" of Judeo-Christian ethics. Although not specifically mentioning a religion, the ideals of most of these early organizations included characteristics that a well-rounded gentleman would have. Such characteristics, or values, would include friendship, courage, service, morality, academic excellence, service, leadership, self-sacrifice, good judgment, self-esteem, and bodily health.[8]

Although early fraternities and sororities were not affiliated with any specific religious organization, many implemented religious concepts or symbols into their constitution, rituals, or insignia. This is not surprising given the religiosity that permeated college campuses from 1825 to 1874. Several examples of fraternities that implemented some aspect of religion include Sigma Chi (1855) with its crusader's cross on its badge along with the motto "In Hoc Signo Vinces," translated as "Conquer Under the Sign of the Cross." Sigma Alpha Epsilon (1856) included the cross as part of its coat of arms while Phi Kappa Sigma (1850) used a cross and Alpha Tau Omega (1865) a Maltese cross as their insignias. Kappa Alpha (1865) also displayed a cross on its badge.[9] The twelve founders of the Hobart Order of Chi Phi (1860) were called "Apostles" and the preamble to their constitution reads, "and may God in his infinite mercy, look down with favor upon us and assist us in the undertaking."[10]

Thus, the founders of a fraternity tended to be young men who had a belief in a Creator and who used prayer to help them in formulating a new fraternal organization.[11] For example, the six founders of Phi Delta Theta (1848) were all churchgoing individuals. Although they attended three different religions, each had a deep faith in Christ. These beliefs were manifested in the way each lived his life and certainly influenced the early beginnings of this fraternity. This scenario was typical of many of the early fraternities.[12] This religious influence was often manifested through an organization's rituals or symbols. The editor of the first edition of *Baird's Manual of American College Fraternities*, published in 1879, described a graduate of a fraternity as, "First of all, believers in their Creator; they may not be agnostics, pagans, or atheists; and they must be loyal students of their college, so long as their college is itself loyal to the Creator."[13] Today, however, the religious nature of most of these early organizations has been replaced by the social and material aspects of success in American society.

While religion may not have been a central focus for early fraternities, several fraternities established after the Civil War "had rituals that were heavily permeated with Christian symbolism." For example, Alpha Tau Omega (1865) had as one of its purposes "to foster a Christian Brotherhood," while Phi Sigma Kappa (1873) was founded upon "the principle of the Golden Rule."[14]

Rise of Religious Fraternities and Sororities

It was between 1885 and 1927 that the majority of religious fraternities and sororities were established, nearly three-quarters of all such organizations. Although several organizations were still writing religious ideas into their constitutions, strictly speaking, they were not classified as a religious fraternity. For example, Alpha Chi Rho (1895) has on its badge the labarum, an ancient symbol of Christianity. In the fraternity's oath, reference is made to several symbols representing Christianity including the cross as a symbol of suffering and the crook as a symbol of shepherding. "The Cross makes us humble, but uplifts us to the high plain of brotherhood."[15] Sigma Pi (1897) tied its theme of brotherhood to one's relationship with God, or a Supreme Being. The spirit of brotherhood took on a deeper meaning since all men were considered a son of God. Having this common parentage brought brothers closer together. The ceremony, ritual, and symbols of the fraternity reflected this ideal.[16]

Though established as a religious fraternity, Sigma Phi Epsilon is no longer classified as such. The beginning of this organization, however, is certainly based on religion. This fraternity was established in 1901 at the University of Richmond (Richmond College at the time) by twelve men, of which seven went on to become Baptist ministers. Desiring to join one of the national fraternities already on campus, the group was turned down. In petitioning the college for a new fraternity, this group of young men had to defend why they chose not to join one of the five national organizations already on campus. Their defense was that these groups did not accept individuals planning on becoming a minister, so a brotherhood of students under Judeo-Christian standards was established based on a scripture from the New Testament: *Thou shalt love the Lord thy God with all thy heart, and with all thy soul, and with all thy mind. This is the first and great commandment. And the second is like unto it, Thou shalt love thy neighbor as thyself.*[17]

The story behind this comes from one of the founders, Carter Jenkins:

> I dreamed that I saw a great black cloud over this University and I saw lightning, and heard the reverberations of the thunder. I saw nations at war, I saw homes destroyed; I saw ten hundred thousand monuments to the newly dead soldiers of the earth. And I asked the Recording Angel, who stood by my side, what such a scene meant in the University of God. And he answered me quietly, saying, "Men have failed to understand the simple teachings of

> the prince of the earth." I woke, and I bowed my head and when I slept the Angel returned and he showed me a world in which the cloud had broken. I saw children, neatly clad, wending their way to school. I saw workmen singing for joy at their work. I saw the churches filled, institutions of learning crowded, and the nations of the earth were at peace, every nation with its brother nation. And I asked the Angel of God what had brought about this change in the old universe. And he pointed me to a passage of Scripture, in Matthew 22: 37–40. (Quotes Scripture). Thus the name of Sigma Phi Epsilon was born in the philosophy of love—the only foundation on which the world can have peace. This is the principle on which our Fraternity was founded.[18]

John Robson, a strong proponent of fraternities and sororities, not only penned *Educating for Brotherhood* but was also editor for several editions of *Baird's Manual of American College Fraternities and Sororities.* A member of Sigma Phi Epsilon, *Educating for Brotherhood* was published by this fraternity in 1965 and served as a manual for its members. The book is steeped in religious references as Robson weaves various aspects of religion into the fabric of the fraternity. For example, several pages are used to discuss the importance of the altar from a religious perspective and its significance to the fraternity.[19]

While religious aspects permeated the origins of social fraternities, there were two groups who found themselves excluded from the traditional fraternity. One group were non-Christian, the Jews, while the other group were Catholic students. Jewish students represented both a religious as well as an ethnic group, while Catholics certainly could not belong to an organization comprised of young men who were primarily Protestants. Or was there ethnic bias as well? Although there were Catholics in this country from Spain and France at this time, the vast majority came from Ireland or had Irish descent.

Rise of Religious Fraternities and Sororities: Denomination-Specific

The period of 1889 to 1927 was a fertile time for establishing fraternities and sororities on college campuses, including at least thirty-eight organizations associated with different religious, Jewish, or nonsectarian groups. This represents about one-third of all the new fraternities and sororities during this period.

Two divisive camps emerged on the role of fraternities and sororities. Since these organizations were private, one group argued, they should be allowed to admit whomever they felt met their requirements of membership. The second group desired to eliminate any religious or racial membership restrictions. In 1955, Dr. Alfred McClung Lee wrote a book for the Committee on Fraternities in Education. Titled *Fraternities Without Brotherhood*, Dr. Lee made the point that a true brotherhood could only exist if everyone was allowed to participate. By the 1960s, this thought process had expanded to include male and female members in a coed fraternity.[20]

While some fraternities and sororities freely removed any restrictive clauses they had for membership requirements, many other organizations had to be forced to make these changes. While in place, these restrictive clauses banned Jewish and Catholic students from joining, resulting in these students creating their own fraternity brotherhood. While the number of Catholic fraternities established was only a handful, the number of Jewish fraternities and sororities numbered eighteen, along with another nine organizations called nonsectarian, which included many Jewish students. When the restrictive clauses were removed, the Jewish organizations suffered the most as Jewish students were now able to join a traditional gentile fraternity at the expense of the predominately Jewish fraternity. Thus, a great deal of consolidation took place as several Jewish fraternities and sororities merged together.[21]

Nonsectarian Organizations

While some fraternities excluded certain religious groups and other fraternities were sectarian, there were still several groups of college students who found themselves left out of the national social fraternity scene. One such group included Jewish students. In 1895, three Jewish students at Yale University had been denied admission because of their religious and racial backgrounds. They envisioned "a fraternity in which all men were brothers, no matter what their religion," and thus religion could not be used to bar someone from joining their organization. Thus, Pi Lambda Phi "was established as a protest and living example against the tendency of fraternities to discriminate against students for religious and racial reasons." The group opposed fraternities that excluded Jews but also opposed fraternities that were exclusively for Jews. Despite this nonsectarian view, the fraternity membership consisted of mainly Jewish students. By 1900, the organization was relatively inactive and remained so for the next twelve years. After being revitalized, the fraternity later absorbed several Jewish fraternities.[22]

This first nonsectarian fraternity gave rise to eight other organizations that fall into the same classification. In 1899, Delta Sigma Phi was founded at the City College of New York (CCNY) by a group of Jewish and Christian young men that had been affiliated during their high school days. Desiring to continue this affiliation through membership in a fraternity, they were disappointed as the fraternities at CCNY barred any mixing of religions. Thus, these young men formed their own fraternity based on the universal brotherhood of man.[23]

In 1904, Phi Epsilon Pi, was also established at CCNY. This fraternity had great success in expanding as it incorporated numerous local Jewish fraternities into its national organization. With a nonsectarian constitution, this fraternity acknowledged its Jewish members but also left any practice of the religion to its individual members. Phi Epsilon Pi grew even larger when it absorbed Sigma Lambda Pi in 1932 and Kappa Nu in 1961. The fraternity, however, ceased to exist in 1970, when it merged with Zeta Beta Tau.[24]

Over the next fourteen years, an additional six nonsectarian organizations were organized. Two of them, Phi Beta Delta (1912) and Sigma Lambda Pi (1915), merged with other fraternities, while the others are still active today: Kappa Delta Rho (1905), Alpha Phi Delta (1914), and Phi Mu Delta (1918). The only sorority established as a nonsectarian organization was Phi Sigma Sigma (1913) at Hunter College. The founders "believed that women of different faiths could come together and work toward common goals." This sorority was open to all and its rituals had no reference to religious scriptures.[25]

In 1948, an intercultural fraternity (nonsectarian) was established at Roosevelt (Illinois). Beta Sigma Tau had many Jewish students as members; however, they did not dominate the fraternity. Since most fraternities had membership restrictions, this organization was established to be totally nonrestrictive in who could become a member. This fraternity had great success in the beginning as it established chapters, but by 1960, the organization had merged with Pi Lambda Phi.[26]

Jewish Fraternities

The most prolific group of fraternities and sororities for a specific religion were Jewish. Of course, one could argue these were also ethnic organizations. Eighteen organizations were established between 1903 and 1920; only eight remain active today. This expansion was enhanced by an increasing Jewish alumni and the establishment of a fraternity network. The first Jewish fraternity had its beginnings in 1898 at the Jewish Theological Seminary in New York City and was the idea of Professor Richard J. H. Gottheil. Seeking to form a Zionist fraternity, symbols representing the Zionist movement were used including the Star of David. The organization also used Hebrew names for its officers. The goal of this organization was "to promote the cause of Zionism and the welfare of Jews in general." The name of the organization, Z.B.T., was an acronym for a Zionist motto. In 1903, this group merged with a local Jewish fraternity at the City College of New York, which became the official date of founding. The focus of the fraternity changed as less emphasis was placed on Zionism and more on providing Jewish students with the same opportunities of belonging to a fraternity that other college students had. The acronym became Zeta Beta Tau, the first fraternity strictly for Jewish students. Its constitution and ritual were deeply Jewish. As part of the initiation one had to say "I am a believer in God and the Brotherhood of Man; I am a Jew." As the oldest Jewish fraternity, it became the fraternity of choice for upper-echelon Jews and those who had been in the United States for some time. This tended to exclude other Jewish groups and led to a proliferation of Jewish fraternities.[27]

Table 13 Nonsectarian (NS) and Jewish Fraternities and Sororities

Organization	F/S	Place of Origin	Date	Type
Pi Lambda Phi	F	Yale	1895	NS
Delta Sigma Phi	F	City University of NY	1899	NS
Zeta Beta Tau	F	City University of NY	1903	Jewish
Iota Alpha Pi*	S	Hunter (NY)	1903	Jewish
Phi Epsilon Pi*	F	City University of NY	1904	NS
Kappa Delta Rho	F	Middlebury (VT)	1905	NS
Phi Sigma Delta*	F	Columbia	1909	Jewish
Sigma Alpha Mu	F	City University of NY	1909	Jewish
Alpha Epsilon Phi	S	Barnard (NY)	1909	Jewish
Beta Sigma Rho*	F	Cornell	1910	Jewish
Tau Epsilon Phi	F	Columbia	1910	Jewish
Tau Delta Phi	F	City University of NY	1910	Jewish
Kappa Nu*	F	Rochester	1911	Jewish
Omicron Alpha Tau*	F	Cornell	1912	Jewish
Phi Beta Delta*	F	Columbia	1912	NS
Alpha Epsilon Pi	F	NYU	1913	Jewish
Phi Sigma Sigma	S	Hunter College (NY)	1913	NS
Phi Alpha*	F	George Washington	1914	Jewish
Sigma Omega Psi*	F	City University of NY	1914	Jewish
Alpha Phi Delta	F	Syracuse	1914	NS
Alpha Mu Sigma*	F	Cooper Union (NY)	1914	Jewish
Sigma Lambda Pi*	F	NYU	1915	NS
Sigma Delta Tau	S	Cornell	1917	Jewish
Delta Phi Epsilon	S	NYU	1917	Jewish
Sigma Tau Phi*	F	Penn	1918	Jewish
Phi Mu Delta	F	Connecticut	1918	NS
Tau Alpha Omega*	F	NYU	1920	Jewish

*No Longer Active

Beginning in 1909, and for the next six years, Jewish-leaning fraternities were organized every year. Sigma Alpha Mu at the CCNY and Phi Sigma Delta at Columbia University were founded in 1909; the latter merged with Zeta Beta Tau in 1969. The establishment of Sigma Alpha Mu signaled a shift in Jewish membership. While membership in earlier organizations were elite Jews of German descent, the membership of this new fraternity were descendants of Eastern European immigrants. In 1910, three organizations were established, including Tau Epsilon Phi at Columbia University, Tau Delta Phi at CCNY, and Beta Sigma Rho at Cornell University. Beta Sigma Rho was the first Jewish fraternity established outside the New York City area, although most of its members were from the New York metropolitan area. In 1972, Beta Sigma Rho merged with Pi Lambda Phi.[28]

Kappa Nu was founded in 1911 at the University of Rochester and merged with Phi Epsilon Pi in 1961. Omicron Alpha Tau was established in 1912 at Cornell University and ceased to exist in 1934. This group was reportedly "the most Jewish" of all the fraternities as supposedly they had "strictly kosher kitchens for its members."[29] In 1913, Alpha Epsilon Pi was established at New York University and in 1914, three organizations—Alpha Mu Sigma at Cooper Union Institute in New York City, Sigma Omega Psi at CCNY, and Phi Alpha at George Washington University—were established. Alpha Mu Sigma declined over the years until it no longer came to exist in 1963, Sigma Omega Psi merged with Alpha Epsilon Pi in 1940, and Phi Alpha also merged in 1959 with Phi Sigma Delta. Sigma Tau Phi was established at the University of Pennsylvania in 1918 and merged with Alpha Epsilon Pi in 1947. In 1920, Tau Alpha Omega was organized at CCNY, but ceased to exist during the 1930s. During the 1920s, a number of nonsectarian and Jewish fraternities were established in New York City and expanded to other campuses in the metropolitan area. With limited expansion and weak central organizations, these fraternities died during World War II. These short-lived organizations are not identified.[30]

The founding of the first Jewish sorority took place in 1903, at Hunter College in New York City. Iota Alpha Pi was a local sorority until 1913, when it became national, eventually disbanding in 1971. Four other sororities were established, all remaining active today. Alpha Epsilon Phi was founded at Barnard College in 1909 and catered to the elite Jewish female collegian. Sigma Delta Tau and Delta Phi Epsilon were both established in 1917 at Cornell University and New York University respectively.[31]

During the rise of Jewish fraternities, an internal cultural debate ensued within the Jewish community. At opposite ends of the spectrum were Pi Lambda Phi and Zeta Beta Tau. As a nonsectarian fraternity,

Pi Lambda Phi did not stress the Jewish religion or heritage. Zeta Beta Tau was limited to Jewish students and incorporated the religion and heritage as part of the organization. All other Jewish fraternities fell somewhere between these two organizations. Most Jews viewed fraternities and sororities as being divisive and a waste of time, for students should be studying Jewish religion and culture.[32] While nonfraternity sentiment opposed exclusion in fraternities and sororities, others argued for their exclusiveness. One such individual, Louis Levinthal, felt Jewish fraternities were needed to help maintain one's Jewish identity. He said:

> How can we Jews hope to continue to be Jews if we mingle freely with the non-Jews? Where shall the line be drawn? If we eat and sleep with non-Jews in fraternity houses and in hotels, why should we not marry their sisters and daughters? Isn't it a fact that those Jews who do mix freely with their non-Jewish neighbors drift away from the faith of their fathers into baptism and intermarriage? It is only by maintaining . . . as many separate factors as possible that we Jews can remain Jews amid non-Jewish surroundings. An exclusively Jewish fraternity, such as the Sigma Alpha Mu, with its ideals essentially Jewish, is a separative factor in the life of the American-Jewish college war. Long life to it![33]

Thus, the above quotation represents the argument for maintaining Jewish fraternities and sororities, an argument that could be applied to any other fraternity and sorority based on religious membership. In fact, arguments similar to this have been used by other Greek-letter organizations to exclude individuals of different race, ethnicity, or religion.

Catholic Fraternities

The exclusion of Catholics from college fraternities only reflected society at the time, for Catholics were not allowed to join the Masonic organization. In response to this, the Knights of Columbus was established in 1882. A college fraternity would follow in 1889. The Catholics were the first to establish a fraternity to serve the needs of a religious group of students. Known as Phi Kappa, this fraternity was established at Brown University. There were nine existing fraternities already on campus and Catholic students attending Brown were not allowed to join them. Over two years, a group of twelve men frequently gathered together before they established a club for individuals who shared this common faith. Their motto was *Loyalty to God and College*. They selected the name Phi Kappa Sigma, meaning a fraternity of Catholic students, but changed the name to Phi Kappa in 1900, since there was already another fraternity by the earlier name. Like other fraternities, the purpose of this organization was to create a bond between students through social and intellectual exchange as they pursued their college education. The only difference was the entire group belonged to one religion.[34]

Theta Kappa Phi was established at Lehigh University in 1919. Prior to this, a club for Catholic students, called the Newman Club, was very active during the school year but ceased to exist by the end of the year. Several of these students desired to have an organization that continued from year to year and focused on the idea of a social fraternity. This group held "the belief that religious and scholarly ideals could be fostered in a homelike environment." The group was also "motivated by the idea that there was virtue in the mystic rites associated with Greek letter fraternities." This fraternity and Phi Kappa later merged their sixty-three chapters in 1959 to form Phi Kappa Theta. The merger was unique as it was more of a union than a merger; one organization did not incorporate the other organization. Both entered the merger on equal footing with a new name for the fraternity.[35]

A third Catholic fraternity was established in 1924 at Loyola University of Chicago. While the other Catholic fraternities existed at colleges around the country, this organization limited its chapters to Catholic schools. Again, the four students who founded this fraternity saw a need for an organization that was different from the existing organizations already on campus. The founders "envisioned a new concept in fraternities based upon the traditions, ideals of true brotherhood, and missionary zeal of Ignatius Loyola, Francis Xavier and Isaac Jogues." From the original national creed, several references are made to the religious nature of the organization. "Alpha Delta Gamma believes in the unity of fraternal brotherhood. The true principle of fraternalism is one of Christian friendship strengthened by the bond of common ideals." Later the creed says, "He may turn with confident steps to face his Creator happy that he has preserved undimmed the jewel of Christian manhood in the struggle with grasping greed, palsied fear, creeping treachery and leprous lust." In 1952, the fraternity adopted its national prayer. The motto of the fraternity is "To the Glory of God," while the first principle states: "Man was created to praise, do reverence to serve God, Our Lord, and thereby to save his soul; and other things on the face of the earth were created for man's sake and to help him in the following out of the end for which he was created."[36]

A fourth Catholic fraternity was established in 1943 at St. Bernard's College in Alabama. The purpose of this fraternity was to instill a strong sense of Christian morality and to create a bond between the students. Although a Catholic organization, it does allow others to join but requires at least half of the membership to be of the Catholic faith. One cannot be refused admission based on religious belief. Each chapter must also adopt a secondary purpose that involves some form of Catholic action involving volunteer work.[37]

The first national Catholic sorority was originally established in 1912 as a local organization for Catholic women. Known as Theta Phi Alpha, it went national in 1919. The founders wanted to create a sorority that would "resemble the Catholic homes from which they had come." Today, the sorority is open to all women regardless of their religion. Another local sorority was established at Marquette University in 1917 but did not go national until 1947. Known as Kappa Beta Gamma, it is the smallest of the national organizations that had a Catholic beginning as it limited expansion to Catholic universities. A third national Catholic sorority was organized in 1921 at Boston University, but it would later merge with Theta Phi Alpha in 1952. A fourth sorority was established in 1987. Known as Mu Epsilon Theta, the sorority was founded at the University of Texas. It was established on Catholic principles "to unite college women by promoting academics, leadership and community service as well as moral and spiritual well-being." Along with spiritual activities during the month and a weekly rosary, a spiritual retreat is held every semester.[38]

The majority of chapters established by these fraternities and sororities are found on universities that have strong Catholic ties. Thus, there membership consists of students who are predominately Catholic. Most of these organizations, however, do accept non-Catholics into their membership. Of the above Catholic fraternities and sororities, Alpha Delta Gamma is a member of the National Interfraternity Conference and Theta Phi Alpha a member of the National Panhellenic Conference. As such, both are recognized as general college fraternities, along with the traditional organizations established in the 1800s.

Religious Diversity among Fraternities and Sororities

The period from 1928 to 1977 saw a precipitous decline in the number of new fraternities and sororities. Only twenty-four organizations emerged during this period with four of them being religious: two Mormon, one Catholic, and one Methodist. From the 1950s through the 1970s, a great deal of conflict occurred between entrenched societal organizations, like the college fraternity and sorority, and changes occurring in American society. As the civil rights movement emerged, the college campus became the arena in which conflicts took place. Greek-letter social organizations became the target for those who felt everyone should have the opportunity to join an organization regardless of their race, color, or religion. It did not matter if that individual was different from other members of the organization, his or her individual right to associate with a group superseded the organization's right to include who it may. A second group joined this attack on fraternities and sororities. These individuals opposed the fraternal and sororal organizations on grounds they were "snobbish, non-intellectual, and self-centered." While the first group desired a more equitable membership enrollment, the second group desired to exterminate the organization.[39]

While Catholic, nondenominational, and Jewish fraternities and sororities were established in response to their exclusion from the traditional organizations, a couple of other denomination specific organizations were also established. These fraternities and sororities were designed for college students of a specific religion and others of like mind so they could associate with individuals who had similar religious values.

The Church of Jesus Christ of Latter-day Saints (Mormons) organized a social fraternity in 1920, at the University of Utah. Initially called the Friars Club, it was established for returned missionaries. This organization provided a group for young men with the same religious ideals, and their charge was to keep "the high and worthy ideals of manhood which become a servant of the Master." The fraternity was actually open to anyone who had served at least six months as a missionary for any Christian denomination or was attending a school of divinity and had done enough religious service to equal six months of missionary work. In 1931, the named changed to Delta Phi, as the club merged with this local fraternity. The name was changed again in 1961 to Delta Phi Kappa to avoid confusion with another fraternity. In 1978, this fraternity merged with and was replaced by Sigma Gamma Chi, another Mormon fraternity.[40]

In 1937, Lambda Delta Sigma was established in Salt Lake City as a coed student association for church members. In 1967, the organization split with the sorority keeping the original name and the fraternity taking the name Sigma Gamma Chi. Both the fraternity and sorority were social and service organizations that focused on brotherhood or sisterhood, service, spirituality, and scholarship. While the fraternity stressed leadership and patriotism, the sorority focused on the supporting role of women. These organizations were not associated with any church schools, for the student congregation (ward) provided the functions of the fraternity system. For small numbers of LDS students attending colleges and universities around the country, these organizations became the social vehicle.[41]

The first Lutheran fraternity established was Beta Sigma Psi at the University of Illinois in 1925. As the Lutheran student population increased at colleges and universities around the country, the Lutheran

Church recognized the need to support these students. With early beginnings in 1919, ten young men and the local minister, who was also in charge of students at the university, organized the Lutheran Illini League. It was later called the Concordia Club. The minister was concerned about Lutheran students maintaining "contact with each other and the church of their childhood and youth." Besides meeting several times a week for religious discussion, the group also planned activities for socialization. Over the next several years the idea of a national organization was discussed and finally realized in 1925. The mission of the fraternity was "to promote an organization of communicant Lutheran men who recognize that life rooted with Christ in God is the only true goal of human existence and who therefore foster, encourage, and inspire activities and relationships which promote this end."[42]

It was not until 1978 that a sorority was established for Lutheran women. Phi Beta Chi was also established at the University of Illinois. Its creed reads, "We, the sisters of Phi Beta Chi, shall strive to be faithful and energetic Christian leaders and shall celebrate the Lutheran heritage," and "in all of our activities, we shall strive to be living symbols of the Rose of Sharon and shall use Love through Life in Christ as the ideal which shall guide our lives." Although not limited to Lutheran students, the members of the sorority were to "share a common bond—the desire to uphold Christian ideals." Along with Beta Sigma Psi, there was now a Lutheran sorority.[43]

For those of the Methodist faith, Sigma Theta Epsilon had its beginnings as Phi Tau Theta in 1924 in Lincoln, Nebraska. Its meaning stood for "Friends of God." Sigma Epsilon Theta was another Christian fraternity established in 1936 at Indiana University. In 1941, these two fraternities merged to create Delta Sigma Theta. In 1949, the name changed to Sigma Theta Epsilon and remained a Methodist fraternity until 1968, when the organization became a National Christian Service Fraternity. Its name means "Fellow Workers with God." One of its purposes is "to attempt with the guidance of God to live Christian lives of faith and service." The organizations brotherhood is "divided into three parts: service, religious, and social."[44]

Christian Fraternities and Sororities

Along with the denomination-specific fraternity or sorority, a [illegible]l number of organizations, not denomination specific, were estab[illegible]d for Christians. Two fraternities and one sorority were establishe[illegible]-ing the early 1900s. The first was Alpha Kappa Lambda at the University of California-Berkeley. Originally called Los Amigos and established in 1907, the organization was a house club on campus until 1914, when the name was changed and the organization became national. The house club was established "out of the need . . . of Christian men for a place to live and study that was within their means." Besides Christian brotherhood, the group also hoped to save costs on housing while attending school. A fraternity without any secret signs, pledges, or passwords, some of the ideals of the organization included the development of religious character and the fostering of Christian principles. This fraternity has the distinction of being the first national fraternity established on the West Coast.[45]

In 1927, a group of young men attending UCLA desired to establish a Christian Club or fraternity that was "founded on Christian ideals and fellowship." Desiring to name their organization Alpha Omega, representing the beginning and the end, they discovered that another organization was already using that name. The founders decided to insert Gamma, becoming Alpha Gamma Omega. Gamma represented Jesus Christ, the focus of the fraternity. One of the founders, in a letter seventeen years later, stated, "The primary purpose of Alpha Gamma Omega was to provide for born again men thrown into an atmosphere of Godlessness and to give forth a testimony to others of the saving and keeping power of the Lord Jesus Christ."

To be eligible for membership in this fraternity one must be a Christian, "born again in Christ knowing they are redeemed by the blood of the Lamb." Calling itself a "Christ-Centered Fraternity," its aim is to "win others to a saving knowledge of Jesus Christ, promote Christian fellowship, present Christian ideals in word and deed, search reverently for truth, and deepen the spiritual lives of its members."[46]

While Alpha Gamma Omega was the first religious fraternity on campus at UCLA, it was not the first social religious organization. Two years earlier, in 1925, ten women organized Alpha Delta Chi as an organization "where Christian women could participate in Greek life without compromising their beliefs." One of the key purposes of the sorority was "to promote spiritual growth" while enjoying social activities and focusing on one's education. The goal of the sorority was to strengthen each member's "personal relationship with Jesus Christ while earning a college degree." Alpha Delta Chi is the sister sorority to Alpha Gamma Omega.[47]

The Evangelical Movement

It would be nearly sixty years before another nonspecific religious fraternity or sorority was established. As more and more college students sought out friendships with those of similar cultural, ethnic, social, racial, or religious backgrounds, the number of ethnic, multicultural,

African American, and religious organizations increased throughout the 1980s and '90s. The religious groups comprised 10 percent of these new organizations.

During the mid-1980s, the rise of the Evangelical Christian movement in the country saw it spread to several college campuses, particularly in Texas, where three sororities and three fraternities were established. In 1985, Beta Upsilon Chi was established at the University of Texas declaring itself as an alternative to the typical social fraternity. With the moniker "Brothers Under Christ," this fraternity sought to wear their religion on their sleeve. This group wanted to "demonstrate that one could remain true to one's faith and yet enjoy life in fellowship with others."[48]

A few years later, Sigma Phi Lambda or Sisters for the Lord, was founded in 1988. Considered by many to be Beta Upsilon Chi's sister sorority, the purpose of the organization is "glorifying our Lord Jesus Christ and making His name great." This comes from Colossians 3:23, *Whatever you do, work at it with all your heart, as working for the Lord.* The group "provides a source of fellowship to Christian women, who sincerely seek to know His person, His will and His ways." This is accomplished through fellowship in the sorority. Becoming a member involves answering questions concerning one's "desire to grow in a personal relationship with Jesus Christ." In the organization's constitution, under statement of beliefs, the sorority has adopted the Apostles' Creed, which states: "I believe in God, the Father almighty, creator of heaven and earth. I believe in Jesus Christ His only son our Lord. He was conceived by the power of the Holy Spirit and born of the Virgin Mary. He suffered under Pontius Pilate, was crucified, dead, and buried. He went down to the dead. On the third day He rose again. He ascended into heaven and is seated at the right of the Father. He will come again to judge the living and the dead. I believe in the holy catholic (universal) church, the communion of saints, the forgiveness of sins, the resurrection of the body, and the life everlasting."[49]

While these first two religious organizations attracted a white clientele, many evangelical African Americans also desired a similar organization. In 1988, an African American fraternity was established at the University of Texas. A group of young men met together for fellowship and Bible study. In their search for an existing fraternity they felt that if they joined a fraternity they would be compromising their morals and beliefs. Desiring to have the fraternity experience while maintaining their principles, they organized Gamma Phi Delta Christian Fraternity. The pillars of the fraternity are fellowship, evangelism, and discipleship. All focus on Christ in which members provide service as Christ did, spread the message about Christ, and help each other to understand Christ.[50]

In 1990, an African American sorority, Alpha Lambda Omega Christian Sorority, was established to correspond with Gamma Phi Delta at the University of Texas. The group was "committed to uplifting the name of the Lord through fellowship with others, community service and discipleship." Its members were to "be exceptional examples of Christian womanhood," and to "exemplify true sisterhood in Christ by sharing the love of God with one another through fellowship." The sorority's statement of faith consists of thirteen items dealing with the Bible, God, Jesus Christ, or the Holy Spirit.[51]

Another Christian organization, known as Kappa Upsilon Chi Christian Fraternity, was established in 1993 at Texas Tech University. The purpose of the fraternity included glorifying Jesus Christ, maintaining biblical Christian standards, service in the community, having a positive attitude and spirit, and helping others in their academics. This is accomplished by "submitting to the Lord, our God, and allowing Him to direct our lives as Psalm 139: 23–34 states, '*Search me, O God, and know my heart, test me and know my thoughts. See if there is any wicked way in me, and lead me in the way everlasting.*'" All the symbology of the fraternity relates in some way to Jesus Christ. For example, the colors include white, green, and royal and represent purity under Christ, growth under Christ, and leadership under Christ, respectively. Even the fraternity's abbreviation KUC means Keeping Under Christ.[52]

The first coed religious organization, Chi Alpha Omega, was founded in 1987 at East Carolina University. The purpose of this group was to worship the Lord in whatever they did and be closer together in a Christ-centered brotherhood. Beyond the social activities associated with fraternities, other activities this group performed included Bible studies and prayer meetings.[53]

The first African American coed fraternity was established in 1988 at Morgan State University in Maryland. This organization was founded by Shirley K. Russell, a mathematics instructor, and called Alpha Nu Omega. Her vision was for an organization that was more than just a club or Christian organization. Everything in the organization was to be based on scripture including the purpose of the organization, its symbols, and code of conduct. If it was not in the Bible then the group would not incorporate that practice. While the organization operates under a single constitution, both the fraternity and sorority are separate entities.[54]

A second African American coed fraternity was established in 1990. Known as Zeta Omicron Epsilon Fraternity, it is also called the ZOE Posse. However, the early beginnings of this African American fraternity were in Chicago. The Reverend Harvey Carey was working with the Salem Baptist Church of Chicago Youth Ministries and asked the youth what they enjoyed doing. The answer was stepping. Stepping emerged in early African American fraternities and sororities and is a performance combining folk traditions and popular culture. It involves the synchronization of body movements and includes singing, speaking, chanting, and theater.[55]

Searching the Bible for a reference that gave a purpose for stepping, Reverend Carey found a reference in Ezekiel which said, "*Thus saith the Lord God Almighty; Smite with thy hand and Stamp with thy foot.*" Out of this came the fraternity. In 1996, many of the ladies in the church felt they had a similar calling to preach the gospel through stepping. These Female Steppers for Christ became known as Zeta Alpha Omicron. These Greek words were chosen for their meaning, "to give the Life of God to others causing them to live." After participating in a Greek step show at Eastern Illinois University, Reverend Willie Comer asked why there was no Christian stepping for Christ on college campuses. He was inspired to take the principles of both organizations and combine them into Zeta Phi Zeta Fraternity and Sorority in 2001. The first chapter was established at Eastern Illinois. There is no pledging or hazing in this organization, and if one desires to become a member they go through a six-week process of grafting. During this time they are taught the "biblical principles that govern every movement, clapping, stamping, stomping, spinning, and turning."[56]

In 1992, Delta Psi Epsilon Christian Sorority was established at Oakwood College in Alabama. This African American sorority has four foundations for its ministry: faith, wisdom, honor, and sisterhood. Each of these foundations is based on a scriptural quote that provides the core for that foundational point.[57]

The last national organization covered is Mu Omicron Gamma Christian Fraternity, an African American organization founded in 2001 at Old Dominion University. Also known as M.O.F.I.A., it means Men of Faith in Action. Their vision is "to develop godly young men of valor who will be living epistles that will correctly represent the Lord Jesus Christ in a world were he is misrepresented." Of the five areas of emphasis, one is spirituality which is accomplished through meetings and lectures focusing on biblical teachings. The group believes in 1) the only true God, the almighty Creator of all things, existing eternally in three persons—Father, Son, and Holy Spirit—full of love and glory, 2) the unique divine inspiration of the Bible in all matters of belief and practice, 3) the value and dignity of all people created in God's image but alienated from God because of our sin and guilt, 4) justification by God's grace to all who repent and put their faith in Jesus Christ alone for salvation, 5) the indwelling presence and transforming power of the Holy Spirit, 6) the unity of all believers in Jesus Christ manifest in worship and witnessing churches.[58]

In August of 2006, three organizations, Alpha Nu Omega, Delta Psi Epsilon, and Men of God Christian Fraternity came together to organize the United Council of Christian Fraternities and Sororities. Following the dream of its founder, Shirley K. Russell, this umbrella organization seeks to bring together other Christian fraternities and sororities to work together in spreading the Christian message. The purpose of this organization has five points: 1) Unity—bringing together the various Christian fraternities and sororities into a unified body that will make it easier to go into communities to spread their message, 2) Navigation—help its member organizations to work with the university and other college fraternities and sororities on campus, 3) Inspection—be an advisor to Christian fraternities and sororities to "provide guidance, oversight, legitimacy, and credibility," 4) Training and Development—provide leadership and development training to the officers of each fraternity or sorority member, and 5) Eminent Domain—by combining the resources of all the umbrella's organizations, the goal it to become more effective and efficient in spreading the message of Christianity.[59]

An Armenian Fraternity

In 2000, three Armenian men attending California State University at Northridge formed Alpha Epsilon Omega. While open to all ethnic backgrounds, the purpose of this organization is to promote Armenian history, language, and culture. Part of that Armenian culture is its heritage as the first Christian kingdom in the world and a country today where 94 percent of the population is Christian. Thus, similar to Jewish fraternities, this fraternity represents an ethnic/religious group of students. In 2006, the fraternity established the Armenian Educational Relief Foundation as part of its philanthropic mission. The fraternity focuses on raising money to resupply the seventeen kindergarten schools in Armavir, Armenia. The fraternity also established the "Never Again Campaign" to help prevent future genocides. Through educating people about the Armenian Genocide, the fraternity hopes to prevent anything like this from happening again.[60]

A Muslim Sorority

With the student population mirroring the population of the United States, a new group of religious students emerged—Muslims. While international students tend to form organizations for students from specific countries or regions, the idea of a Muslim fraternity and sorority is of recent origin. In April 2005, a sorority for Muslim women, Gamma

Gamma Chi, was established by Imani Abdul-Haqq and her mother, Dr. Alithia F. Collins. With national headquarters in Alexandria, Virginia, this neophyte organization is looking for Muslim women on college campuses to establish chapters. This is the first sorority based on Islamic principles with its mission to promote positive examples of Islam. This is to be accomplished by becoming more involved in the community. The motto of the group is "striving for the pleasure of Allah through sisterhood, scholarship, leadership, and community service." Although no chapters have been established to date, the desire of the organization

Table 14 Religious Fraternities and Sororities

Organization	F/S	Place of Origin	Date	Affiliation
Phi Kappa (Sigma)*	F	Brown	1889	Catholic
Theta Phi Alpha	S	Michigan	1912	Catholic
Alpha Kappa Lambda	F	Cal-Berkeley	1914	Christian
Kappa Beta Gamma	S	Marquette	1917	Catholic
Theta Kappa Phi*	F	Lehigh	1919	Catholic
Delta Phi Kappa	F	Utah	1920	Mormon
Pi Lambda Sigma*	S	Boston	1921	Catholic
Alpha Delta Gamma	F	Loyola-Chicago	1924	Catholic
Beta Sigma Psi	F	Illinois	1925	Lutheran
Alpha Delta Chi	S	UCLA	1925	Christian
Alpha Gamma Omega	F	UCLA	1927	Christian
Sigma Theta Epsilon	F	Nebraska/Merger	1925/ 1941	Methodist
Sigma Beta Kappa	F	St. Bernard's (AL)	1943	Catholic
Sigma Gamma Chi	F	Salt Lake City	1967	Mormon
Lambda Delta Sigma	S	Salt Lake City	1967	Mormon
Phi Beta Chi	S	Illinois	1978	Lutheran
Beta Upsilon Chi	F	Texas	1985	Christian
Chi Alpha Omega	Coed	East Carolina	1987	Christian
Mu Epsilon Theta	S	Texas	1987	Catholic
Alpha Nu Omega	Coed	Morgan State (MD)	1988	Christian-Af Am
Gamma Phi Delta	F	Texas	1988	Christian-Af Am
Sigma Phi Lambda	S	Texas	1988	Christian
Alpha Lambda Omega	S	Texas	1990	Christian-Af Am
Delta Psi Epsilon	S	Oakwood (AL)	1992	Christian-Af Am
Kappa Upsilon Chi	F	Texas Tech	1993	Christian
Alpha Epsilon Omega	F	Cal State-Northridge	2000	Armenian
Zeta Phi Zeta	Coed	Eastern Illinois	2001	Christian-Af Am
Mu Omicron Gamma	F	Old Dominion	2001	Christian-Af Am
Gamma Gamma Chi	S	Alexandria, Virginia	2005	Muslim

*No Longer Active

is to become a national sorority. The founding of an organization based on another religion is certainly foreign to the historical development of the fraternity and sorority establishment; however, it certainly is in keeping with the idea of forming a bond between students who share something in common, in this case the Islamic religion.[61]

Exclusion and Discrimination

While religion has been a fundamental characteristic of many social fraternities and sororities since their inception, it has also been used to exclude individuals from joining an organization. In the 1930s, nearly all of the major social fraternities had exclusion clauses written into their constitution limiting membership to whites or Christians. Under pressure from college administrations, most fraternities and sororities dropped their Christian-only requirement over the years and rewrote their rituals and constitution to replace the many references to Jesus Christ. By 1955, not quite a dozen organizations still had these exclusionary clauses in their constitution. By the mid-1960s, many universities had adopted specific policies that condemned this discrimination and ordered any fraternity or sorority on their campus to get rid of any bias clauses.[62] Today, the majority of historic fraternities and sororities as well as cultural interest organizations do not restrict their membership. Many of the religious fraternities and sororities, however, maintain that since their emphasis is on religious principles, the members of their organization need to adhere to these beliefs.

This social institution has now come full circle. While early fraternities and sororities restricted membership, the battle to eliminate these membership restrictions resulted in the vast majority of national fraternities and sororities allowing no restrictions based on race, religion, color, sex, or sexual orientation. Today, however, many religious fraternities and sororities argue for the right to restrict their membership. As a result, universities often deny permission to these groups to be recognized as a student organization on campus. The religious organization, in return, argues they are being discriminated against. At the University of Georgia, a chapter of Beta Upsilon Chi was not recognized by the administration as a student organization in 2006. Without this recognition, the fraternity would not be allowed to use campus facilities or advertise on campus. The school cited the fraternity's requirement that its members and officers share the organization's Christian beliefs. Therefore, the university's nondiscrimination policy cited the fraternity for "religious discrimination" as it required its members and officer to profess faith in Christ. One of the arguments against the policy was if the Young Democrats could require its officer and members to be Democrats, then why could not a Christian group have the same requirements? The final outcome included Beta Upsilon Chi being recognized as a student organization and the university revising its nondiscrimination policy. This fraternity is fighting the same battle at the University of Florida. Since the fraternity only allows men to join and requires it members to be Christians, the school charges that the fraternity is involved in sexual and religious discrimination.

At the Universities of North Carolina, Minnesota, and Oklahoma, Pennsylvania State University, Gonzaga University, and Southwest Missouri State University, actions have been taken to disband Christian fraternities and sororities. These schools argued that because Christian organizations require one to pledge their loyalty to God and to adhere to the principles of Christianity, these organizations are discriminatory to non-Christians and homosexuals. Perhaps to appease this criticism leveled at them, religious fraternities and sororities could rework their charters to include a broader membership. Requirements for membership would now include any individual who supported the "ideals, values and standards of behavior of that group." Thus, individuals could join who desired to learn more about the specific teachings of that fraternity or sorority, with the possibility of becoming a member of the religious denomination sponsoring that fraternity or sorority.[63]

Conclusion

This discussion of religious diversity in college fraternities and sororities examined three areas. Early fraternities established were inherently religious, given the structure and focus of colonial American colleges and universities. Thus, while these organizations may not have been overtly religious in nature, their underlying principles were enveloped in a religious context. The same cannot be said for some fraternities and sororities established in the late 1800s and early 1900s. The traditional fraternities had been filled with white, Protestant young men that excluded Jews and Catholics. New religious organizations were established to be nondenominational, Catholic, or Jewish in its membership. Others followed, including Mormon, Lutheran, Methodist, Christian, and Evangelical Christian.

While many of the fraternities and sororities established during the 1800s incorporated or were founded on Christian principles, there are several differences between these organizations and the organizations that identify themselves as a Christian fraternity or sorority. The fraternities and sororities of this latter group were established based on biblical scripture, tended to be more open, rather than secretive, and had as their central focus Jesus Christ. All the good works performed by the fraternity or sorority were done so to glorify Christ. The rise of the Evangelical Movement in the United States, therefore, and its manifestation on college campuses in the form of fraternities and sororities is an area that requires further research.[64]

While nonreligious fraternities and sororities focus on a variety of character-building traits, religious fraternities and sororities include a spiritual aspect the others tend not include. All fraternity and sorority groups have the same underlying aspirations to better themselves through physical, academic, and social fellowship, as well as service. By coming together with common ideals, a group of young men or women can develop a bond that will last throughout their college days and beyond. Religious fraternities and sororities are no different and desire their voices to be heard like all the other cultural interest fraternities and sororities on college campuses. They aspire to provide the Greek-letter experience for its members within the context of religious values or goals.

Since some of the behavior found in social fraternities and sororities is not viewed favorably by their religious counterparts, an area of further research would be on these various behaviors. In research done by a sociology class at the University of North Carolina, some basic differences between religious and nonreligious fraternities and sororities yielded statistics that were really no surprise. Eight organizations were selected, four fraternities and four sororities. Two of the fraternities and two of the sororities were classified as religious, while the other four were not, although one had been established as a Jewish organization. The main reason for joining a fraternity or sorority was to meet new friends or to join the group with friends. This was the response for 88 percent of the nonreligious interviewees, while 39 percent did the same for religious organizations. Almost 60 percent joined because of the religious affiliation. This is then reflected in church attendance, where 76 percent of those interviewed attended church at least once a week, while that figure was only 25 percent for the nonreligious organizations. Further research examined various activities that members were involved in including drinking, taking drugs, premarital sex, and using profanity. The response of those belonging to the religious organizations for these four areas ranged from 0–10 percent, while that figure was 20–60 percent for the nonreligious groups. A couple of other areas were examined to identify differences between the two groups. While limited in its research to one campus, the findings provide insights into the behavior of individuals who join a religious fraternity or sorority. While the nonreligious groups were viewed as social organizations, members still had opportunities to practice their faith. Conversely, religious organizations provided opportunities for social activities that agreed with the beliefs of the group. Thus, the religious organizations did not focus solely on religion.[65] More research like this in comparing religious and nonreligious organizations on a national scale could be useful, as well identifying differences between the different religious organizations. Coupled with this would be more research on the religious social experience of fraternity and sorority members.

In the 230-year history of this social organization, religion has always had a role, for good or bad, and it remains the same today. While some may view these religious organizations as part of the problem, nevertheless, when viewed as a cultural interest group within the context of the other fraternities and sororities examined, it becomes apparent this type of organization fulfills a need, or a niche, for a portion of the college student body.

Notes

1. http://pages.ago.org/jesus_tribute.html; http://www.unc.edu/~hurt4evr/con clusions.html
2. Frederick Rudolph, *The American College and University* (New York: Vintage Books, 1962), 70–80.
3. Clyde Sanfred Johnson, *Fraternities in Our Colleges* (New York: National Interfraternity Foundation, 1972), 38.
4. Oscar M. Voorhees, *The History of Phi Beta Kappa* (New York: Crown Publishers, 1945), 1.
5. Voorhees, *History of Phi Beta Kappa*, 2; Richard Nelson Current. *Phi Beta Kappa in American Life: The First Two Hundred Years* (New York: Oxford University Press, 1990), 8–9.
6. Rudolph, *American College and University*, 136–41.
7. Ibid., 144–50.
8. http://www.phikaps.org
9. George S. Toll, "Colleges, Fraternities, and Assimilation," *Journal of Reform Judaism* (Summer 1985): 93.
10. Dr. Theodore Burton Appel, *The Chronicles of Chi Phi: 1824–1976* (Atlanta: Chi Phi Educational Trust, 1993), 26.
11. John Robson, *The College Fraternity and Its Modern Role* (Menasha, WI: George Banta, 1966), 16.
12. Ritter Collett, *In the Bond: Phi Delta Theta at 150* (Dayton, OH: Landfall Press, 1998), 24–25.
13. William Baird, 1st edition (William Baird, 1879).
14. Toll, "Colleges, Fraternities, and Assimilation," 93.
15. Toll, "Colleges, Fraternities, and Assimilation," 93–94; Exoteric Manual of Alpha Chi Rho at http://www.alphachirho.org
16. *I Believe: The Sigma Pi Manual* (Sigma Pi Fraternity, International, 2000), 59.
17. Jack L. Anson and Robert F. Marchesani Jr., *Bairds Manual of American College*

Fraternities, 20th ed. (Indianapolis: Baird's Manual Foundation, 1991), III-127; http://www.sigep.org; Robson, "The College Fraternity," 39.

18. John P. Adams, ed., *The Lifetime Responsibility of Brotherhood* (Sigma Phi Epsilon Fraternity, 2000), 70.

19. John Robson, *Educating for Brotherhood: Guidelines to the Meaning of Fraternity* (Richmond, VA.: Sigma Phi Epsilon Fraternity, 1965), 30–34.

20. Toll, "Colleges, Fraternities, and Assimilation, 28–29.

21. Ibid., 28–30; Marianne Rachel Sanua, *Going Greek: Jewish College Fraternities in the US, 1895–1945* (Detroit: Wayne State University Press, 2003), 28.

22. http://www.pilambdaphi.org; Anson and Marchesani, *Baird's Manual*, III-106; Sanua, *Going Greek*, 28.

23. http://www.deltasig.org

24. Anson and Marchesani, *Baird's Manual*, VII-16, 22; Sanua, *Going Greek*, 28.

25. http://phisigmasigma.org

26. George S. Toll, *Alpha Epsilon Pi: The First Sixty-Five Years 1912–1978* (Alpha Epsilon Pi Foundation, 1980), 25.

27. Sanua, *Going Greek*, 30–34, 69.

28. Sanua, *Going Greek*, 69, 74–76; Anson and Marchesani, *Baird's Manual*, III-17, 116, 140, VIII-5, 24.

29. Ibid.

30. Toll. *Alpha Epsilon Pi*, 24–25.

31. Sanua, *Going Greek*, 76; Anson and Marchesani, *Baird's Manual*, VIII-32, IV-8, 61, 35.

32. Sanua, *Going Greek*, 30–34, 69.

33. Louis E. Levianthal, "Jewish Brotherhood," *Octagonian of Sigma Alpha Mu* 4, no. 4 (April 1915) as quoted in Sanau, *Going Greek*, 83.

34. Anson and Marchesani, *Baird's Manual*, VIII-15.

35. "Phi Kappa Theta's Heritage" and "Early Days of Phi Kappa and Theta Kappa Phi," http://www.phikaps.org

36. "History of Alpha Delta Gamma," http://alphadeltagamma.org; *The History of Alpha Delta Gamma, 1924 to 1995*, 2nd ed. (Alpha Delta Gamma Educational Foundation, 1995), 1–2; "A Mark of Honor," *Candidate Education Manual* (Alpha Delta Gamma Educational Foundation, 1997), 9–10.

37. Anson and Marchesani, *Baird's Manual*, III-173.

38. http://www.studentorgs.utexas.edu/metheta/general_infor.php; Anson and Marchesani, *Baird's Manual*, IV-68, 88, VIII-34.

39. Toll, "Colleges, Fraternities, and Assimilation," 27.

40. Laura Smith, "The LDS Greeks: Lambda Delta Sigma and Sigma Gamma Chi," *Ensign* (September 1986): 27–31; Anson and Marchesani, *Baird's Manual*, III-172–74, IV-88.

41. Ibid.

42. http://www.betasigmapsi.org

43. http://www.phibetachi.org

44. http://www.sigmatheta.org

45. "Our Founding," http://www.akl.org; Anson and Marchesani, *Baird's Manual*, III-5.

46. "National History," http://ieee.ee.calpoly.edu/ago; http://www.ago.org

47. http://www.geocities.com/CollegePark/Quad/5545/links.html.

48. http://www.betaupsilonchi.org

49. http://studentorgs.utexas.edu/philamb/

50. http://www.gphid.org

51. http://Studentsorgs.utexas.edu/utalo/History.htm
52. http://www.kyx.org
53. http://www.barnabas.com/; http://www.unc.edu/student/orgs/xaeomega/; http://www.ncsu.stud
54. http://www.alphanuomega.org
55. For more information on stepping, see Elizabeth C. Fine, *Soulstepping: African American Step Shows* (Urbana: University of Illinois Press, 2003).
56. http://www.zetaphizeta2000.org
57. http://www.angelfire.com/ca2/deltapsiepsilon/foundations.html
58. http://www.angelfire.com/va3/mog/Who.html
59. The Official Website of the United Council for Christian Fraternities and Sororities at http://www.uccfs.org
60. Alpha Epsilon Omega at http://alpha.alphaepsilonomega.org
61. http://gammagammachi.org; Jenny Jarvie, "One Sorority's Modest Start," *Los Angeles Times* November 23, 2005.
62. "Fraternities Get the Grip," *Time Magazine* 85, no. 26 (June 25, 1965).
63. "Religious Clubs/Fraternities on State Campuses," Stanislaus Dundon at http://insidehighered.com/news/2006/12/29/qt
64. "Christian Fraternities and Sororities," at http//www.greekchat.com
65. "Sociology 10 Group Project," at http://www.unc.edu/~hurt4evr/sociology.html

Rushing the Wall, Crossing the Sands: Cross-Racial Membership in U.S. College Fraternities and Sororities

Matthew W. Hughey

> The problem of the Twentieth Century is the problem of the color-line . . . Between me and the other world there is ever an unasked question: . . . How does it feel to be a problem? . . . Why did God make me an outcast and a stranger in mine own house? The shades of the prison-house closed round about us all: walls strait and stubborn to the whitest, but relentlessly narrow, tall, and unscalable to sons of night who must plod darkly on in resignation, or beat unavailing plans against the stone, or steadily, half-hopelessly, watch the streak of blue above.
>
> —W. E. B. Du Bois, *The Souls of Black Folk*, 1903

> The idea of "race" represents one of the most dangerous myths of our time, and one of the most tragic. Myths are most effective and dangerous when they remain unrecognized for what they are. . . . In earlier days we believed in magic, possession, and exorcism, in good and evil supernatural powers, and until recently we believed in witchcraft. Today many of us believe in "race." "Race" is the witchcraft of our time. The means by which we exorcise demons. It is the contemporary myth. Man's most dangerous myth. . . . Myths perform the double function of serving both as *models of* and *models for* cultural attitudes and behavior. Built, as they are, into the structure of social relationships, racial myths often have a force which exceeds even that of reality itself.
>
> —Ashley Montague, *Man's Most Dangerous Myth*, 1942

I BEGIN THIS CHAPTER WITH AN EPIGRAPH OF DU BOIS' AND MONTAGUE'S words because the poignancy of their language helps us frame the issues of racial segregation, inequality, and racial identity in a historic continuum of human struggle that reaches as far back in time as it will also reach forward.[1] Whereas the early 1900s bore witness to the sociolegal conditions of rampant inequality that legally protected and propagated racism and white supremacy, today we are often prompted to tell a different story. In our contemporary moment, we have a post–civil rights doctrine that posits racism and segregation are either in serious decline or vanquished altogether, and that as a result, we are steadily moving toward a "color-blind" and equitable society. However, such discourse does not reflect the material realities of our present conditions. The rhetoric of "color-blindness," and even politically correct buzzwords like "diversity" and "multiculturalism," need to be recognized as discursive strategies of obscuration, hoodwinking the modern realities of racial inequities. The U.S. is becoming increasingly racially segregated every year in such diverse registers as education, employment, and housing to medical treatment, incarceration, and religion. Such "resegregation" has increased to the point that, in 2008, we are more racially divided than we were in the 1960s, and of all racial groups, whites are the most segregated.[2]

The rampant increase in racial segregation is fundamentally impacting access to both material and symbolic resources as well as the life chances of many people: From Judeo-Christian traditions that help to keep 11:00 a.m. on Sunday the most segregated hour of the week, to the juggernaut "prison-industrial complex" that relies upon racist policing and sentencing to transform black and Latino/a populations into "human capital" in order to fund the privatization of "for profit" prisons, to the growing health disparities that have made insurance, access to doctors, competent diagnoses, treatment, and education effectively out of the reach for many people of color, to the recent trends of immigration that, according to the U.S. Census of 2000, predict by the year 2050, whites will become less than one-half of the U.S. population.[3] Such demographic changes are uncharted territory and could precipitate one of the largest cultural shifts in U.S. history, as even the meaning of racial categories and boundaries will be altered. These differences are neither arbitrary nor essential. Rather, these dynamics reflect the racial order (a racialized social system) that has developed over human history to, as sociologist Eduardo Bonilla-Silva writes, "award systemic privileges to Europeans (the people who became 'white') over non-Europeans (the people who became 'nonwhite'). . . . Racial structures and racial inequality the world over [exists] because they benefit members of the dominant race."[4] As evidenced, the problem of the twenty-first century remains the color-line, and "racial progress" is our most dangerous myth. Still, racial lines of separation are, and will continue to be, contested and negotiated in a strikingly different United States than the one in which Du Bois and Montague first pronounced their words.

While notions of "progress" via Enlightenment principles of "liberty, equality, and fraternity" are said to be mainstream and commonplace, the aforementioned continuation and growth of nouveau forms of racism come as an uncomfortable and disquieting reality. For some, such cultural contradictions are too much to bear. From laypersons, to political pundits, to academics, many now go to great lengths to explain away racial inequality and instead emphasize the great legal and attitudinal progress of the nation over the past century. Indeed, many great strides have taken place, in large part due to the sacrifices laid down by the children, women, and men of the civil rights movement (that still continues today). However, it is apparent that many of these gains are now under attack.

One of the preeminent places to clearly view such antagonisms over race, policy, and equality is within the realm of higher education: From public ballot initiatives like the 1996 passage of "Proposition 209" in California and the "Michigan Civil Rights Initiative" (MCRI)[5] that effectively banned all "affirmative action" programs resulting in a "Whitening" of colleges and universities in Michigan, to the recent Supreme Court decisions of *Gratz v. Bollinger* (2003) and *Meredith v. Jefferson County Board of Education* (2007)[6] that facilitates the already entrenched racial segregation of educational structures. Together, these debates signal a paradigm shift in our nation's approach to racial inequality, and are already having widespread repercussions in our institutions of higher learning. For instance, while judicial doctrine has made racial exclusion in U.S. college fraternities and sororities an illegal action, the laissez-faire approach to racial separation only facilitates an already entrenched pattern of segregation that prevails through tradition, custom, and preference. The existence of the extreme racially homogenous character of fraternal organizations, which exist amid a campus climate that claims to have moved "beyond race," presents a blatant contradiction and multiple challenges to researchers.

Accordingly, this chapter labors to elucidate how patterns of cross-racial Greek membership have altered and shifted over time. The first part of this chapter examines the politics of Greek-racial border crossing. The second section inspects nonwhite membership in traditionally white fraternities and sororities, and the third section analyzes non-black membership in Black Greek-Lettered Organizations (BGLOs). In so doing, this work provides a glimpse into not only the microlevel campus social and political affairs that underpin how Greek racial boundaries have been both reproduced and challenged, but also the larger macrolevel cultural logic of our racialized society as a whole. Specifically, this study adds nuance to the predominant account of "diversity" within U.S. college fraternities and sororities by identifying, describing, and constructing a picture of the trials and tribulations of Greek cross-racial membership and the tremors of those color boundaries as they have been challenged and defended.

Why Raced Fraternities and Sororities, Why Now?

In an era of educational and race-relations reform, scholars, practitioners, and students have taken pause concerning the still racially segregated system of U.S. higher education. The separate worlds of racial formations on U.S. campuses often result in profoundly different interpretations and perspectives on campus life. In the dominant historical account of Helen Horowitz, Greek members are depicted as the ultimate campus "insiders" who set the tenor of campus life.[7] If indeed Greek organizations act as a dominating influence, the possibility exists that at their best, cross-racial Greek memberships—as individual and organizational instances of racial boundary breaking—promote intimacy, increased racial tolerance, integration, understanding, and social change. While at their worst, cross-racial Greek memberships represent the exploitive tokenism of racialized "others" within the scope of the minstrelesque theme that earns the host organization "multicultural capital,"[8] thus credentialing the organization among the politically correct communities of both "town and gown" in a manner that only reinscribes and maintains the racial order.

Today, many scholars argue that college campus racism is a vestige of the past; colleges are no longer hostile social and cultural environments for students of color.[9] While some aspects of racial tensions have eased due to many of the changes of the 1960s and '70s, many suggest a newfound rekindling of racial animosity in the 1980s, '90s, and in the new century. As Jon C. Dalton states, "racial and ethnic hostility on college campuses was the inevitable culmination of fundamental changes in the values of college students, increased competition and stress in higher education, a lack of sufficient personal experience and knowledge among students about racial and cultural diversity, and a societal shift away from concerns about civil rights and social justice to interest in issues of individual rights and consumerism."[10] Racial attitudes in white Greek organizations appear as an intense reflection of the overall white campus population. Researchers have found that those who live in Greek housing (usually white Greeks) are much less conscious of social injustice and less culturally aware than non-Greek whites[11]—a finding that is similar to earlier work that found white Greeks more

Eurocentric in their worldviews than their non-Greek white peers.[12] Racial exclusion and racism appear to be prevalent among white Greek organizations, creating an understandable apprehension among many black student communities. When white Greek organizations do accept nonwhite members they often are not perceived or treated as full members and face, as Carol Thompson writes, "ostracism and criticism from other black students who view their membership as a 'sellout.'"[13] As Schmitz and Forbes found, "the social structure of Greek segregation in this setting is self-perpetuating. Although racial prejudice is a factor in the systemic exclusion of minorities, the root causes of racial separatism are systemic and endemic to the sorority recruitment process itself. Even those women who want to change the system are powerless in the face of a recruitment structure that subverts integration."[14]

Cross-racial membership does blur previously firm and entrenched boundaries in once racially homogenous Greek organizations. Yet, the mere empirical support of a new destabilization of fraternity and sorority racial boundaries within the context of a still racially stratified globe, country, and campus does not address why some decide to transgress the color-line while others abide by it and effectively use it to shape their identity in college. Accordingly, cultural sociologists Lamont and Molnar underscore the necessity to study "key mechanisms associated with the bridging, crossing, and dissolution of boundaries."[15] When categorical boundaries are strong, as in the case of the raced Greek system in our contemporary moment, boundary transgression is rare. In his insightful account of ethnic and racial identities, Fredrik Barth suggested that the "boundary . . . defines the group, not the cultural stuff that it encloses."[16] Building on Barth, the work of Hannan and Freeman postulated that racial segregating processes establish those boundaries. I suggest that the categories launched within the raced Greek system establish both social and symbolic boundaries and constitute a large portion of the identity of the members involved. Further, strong categorical boundaries are a prerequisite for segregation. This suggests that the raced Greek system involves a cultural code of conduct that imposes sanctions on code violators. However, these categorical boundaries can be undermined, and the "clarity of a set of boundaries is not a permanent property of a set of classifications. Rather, the realism of the distinction . . . depends on the degree of institutionalization that has occurred."[17]

While Greek organizations open to cross-racial membership may be transgressive, progressive, and antiracist, sociologist Bethany Bryson demonstrates that racial and cultural inclusivity can simultanously be used as a tool of political intolerance and exclusion. Even Greek organizations that incorporate members from other racial groups do not destroy racial boundaries, but rather, reestablish them in differing forms. Bryson writes, "Cultural tolerance should not be conceptualized as an indiscriminate tendency to be non-exclusive, but as a reordering of group boundaries."[18] Cross-racial transgression should not be mistaken as dissolution of boundaries, but as Richard Alba maintains, mutability of racial boundaries can be forms of crossing, blurring, and shifting social forces that simply redefine the characteristics of a group.[19] By displaying certain credentials, multicultural capital, authentic familiarity, and cultivated dispositions, Greek cross-racial membership does not destroy but remakes racial boundaries.

While a large amount of scholarship on race and the Greek system exists, there is minimal research on Greek cross-racial membership. Where it has taken place, it has been small and specific to precise contexts. Kimbrough devoted only four pages toward the subject of nonblacks in BGLOs.[20] Bankhead examined White women in Black sororities,[21] Chen analyzes Asian American women in white, Asian, and black sororities,[22] Matthews examines black men in white fraternities,[23] and Thompson investigated the factors that influence a range of minority participation in historically white Greek organizations.[24] My own work encompasses a broad array of settings and political dimensions: from studies of the first white social fraternity to establish a chapter at the flagship HBCU (Historically Black College or University) Howard University,[25] in-depth qualitative studies of nonblack members in BGLOs,[26] theoretical analysis regarding how BGLO racial homogeneity is a key factor in group stigmatization as an "educated gang,"[27] how racial identity and homogeneity is assumed, "performed," and understood by BGLO members in virtual chat rooms,[28] to historical overviews of challenges to Greek racial homogeneity.[29] Other scholars who are concerned with the intersection of race and the Greek system have studied the role of BGLOs on predominately white campuses[30] and the differentials between black fraternities and sororities values and attitudes.[31] Despite the strong persistence of both white and black Greek systems, not to mention the growing number of Asian, Latino/a, and American Indian Greek-letter organizations, more work must speak specifically to the cultural phenomenon of cross-racial membership. This chapter aims to add to this burgeoning literature.

The Politics of Border Crossing: Toward A Theory of Cross-Racial Membership

Research indicates that nonwhite students on predominately white campuses are unlikely to become involved in campus-wide student organizations or engage in social activities with white students.[32] While

Greek racial discrimination is less structurally formal today, it is no less culturally strong due to the power of status quo racial homogeneity. The accounts that follow demonstrate that the small shifts toward racial heterogeneity have been tumultuous.

Phi Beta Kappa was the first Greek-letter organization in the U.S. It was founded in 1776 at the College of William and Mary in Williamsburg, Virginia. From that day to the late 1800s, U.S. colleges and universities had a rather homogenous student population—white, male, and Christian. Greek organizations simply mirrored the student body. But just before the turn of the nineteenth century, racial and religious restriction issues were voiced as nonwhites began to gain access to formerly all-white institutions of higher learning. Therefore, some white Greek organizations incorporated specific racially exclusionary policies into their constitutions in order to retain both tradition and restrictive systems of social relations. Sociologist Alfred M. Lee wrote in *Fraternities Without Brotherhood* that "the chief defect in . . . the social fraternity . . . [can be] summed up as 'Aryanism'—the acceptance and rejection of persons for membership on grounds of race, religion, and national origin. To the extent that Aryanism persists in them, social fraternities represent a basic threat to democracy in the United States."[33]

While Lee's pronouncement might be considered Machiavellian to some, his work is saturated with historical evidence. Racial demographic changes in university and college student bodies resulted in traditionally white Greek organizations adopting official policies of discrimination against African Americans, Jews, and other people of color. The racial and ethnic proscriptions were stringent and inflexible. As late as 1953 it was the national policy of Lambda Chi Alpha to pledge only those people "who are members of the Caucasian race who are of non-Semitic blood and believe in the principles of Christianity, [rejecting those with] one-eighth of proscribed blood." One commentator noted that the Greek system in the U.S. was "even more restrictive than Hitler's definition of the 'Semite' in his infamous Nuremberg laws: his edicts applied only to those who had one-fourth or more of ancestry identifiable as Jewish."[34]

Consequently, Pi Lambda Phi was formed in 1895 as the nation's first nonsectarian fraternity, accepting men of all religions. Jewish students who would not be accepted by other fraternities often founded local chapters of Pi Lambda Phi. "As minority-group members began to attend American colleges in greater numbers, one of their first reactions to the generally exclusionist practices of fraternities was to set up their own minority group."[35] Many BGLOs have been formed over the years, but today nine such organizations (five fraternities and four sororities) are codified as the "Divine Nine," or the National Pan-Hellenic Council (NPHC). The nine member organizations of the NPHC are "among the oldest black campus organizations on most predominately white campuses and are possibly the strongest nationwide social institutions in black America."[36] The NPHC was founded in 1930 as a counterpart to the National Interfraternity Council (NIC) for white fraternities and the National Panhellenic Conference (NPC) for white sororities.

One of the first questions to arise regarding cross-racial membership was the issue of power and autonomy. Who held the ultimate authority over membership decisions: the campus administration or Greek national offices? At a 1952 NIC conference, the State University of New York (SUNY) administrator William S. Carlson suggested that SUNY should implement a nondiscrimination policy that structurally banned racially restrictive barriers among fraternities and sororities. The outraged members shot down his suggestion, and after extensive debate the resolution failed by a three-to-one vote.[37] Despite losing the vote, the next year Carlson ordered all student social organizations in the SUNY system to eliminate "artificial criteria" in the selection of their members and to sever their affiliations with their national offices if they held racially restrictive agencies. Sigma Tau Gamma fraternity immediately filed suit against the SUNY system for denying the rights of free assembly and the lack of due process.[38] However, the SUNY regulation was upheld, even after appeal to the United States Supreme Court that resulted in a dismissal.

On April 1, 1954, Dartmouth imposed a student referendum that ended fraternity discrimination by requiring the twenty-four local fraternities to provide written proof that their constitutions contained no discriminatory language. However, four fraternities (Delta Tau Delta, Phi Gamma Delta, Sigma Chi, and Sigma Nu) failed to submit a compliance form. They would have to disaffiliate from their national offices or close down.[39] Similar actions occurred at the University of Pennsylvania whereby Sigma Chi, Alpha Tau Omega, and Sigma Nu received orders to either change their constitutions or disaffiliate from their national offices.[40] At UCLA, Acacia fraternity and Pi Beta Phi sorority filed a suit against the California Board of Regents in an effort to evade the September 1, 1964, deadline to abolish fraternal racial discrimination. Superior Court Judge Newell Barrett upheld the right of the Regents to enforce the policy. Afterward, all UCLA Greek organizations signed the pledge with the exception of one sorority.[41]

By the end of the 1960s amid social pressures from campus and governing administrations, advice from IFC and NPC lawyers, and partially due to the changing culture of the times, predominately white Greek-letter organizations eliminated official constitutional stipulations that prohibited membership based on race. Many of the black fraternities also originally held racially exclusionary doctrine but changed their positions much earlier then their white counterparts. Alpha Phi Alpha fraternity, a BGLO, revised its constitution to enable the entrance of a white man into Howard University's Theta chapter in 1946. The BGLO Phi Beta Sigma fraternity never had racial restrictions. It was founded both in response to white Greek discrimination and also to the developing skin-tone politics among the young and burgeoning BGLOs that were quickly setting a standard of selecting blacks of lighter skin tones for membership while declining membership to darker-skinned African Americans.

In response to white discrimination against Asians on the U.S. West Coast, several Asian American organizations were begun: Pi Alpha Pi fraternity was founded in 1926 at the University of California, Berkeley; Chi Alpha Delta sorority was founded in 1928 at the University of California, Los Angeles, and Sigma Omicron Phi sorority was founded at San Francisco State Teachers' College in 1930. Shirley Lim's work outlines the many Asians in the early and mid-twentieth century that did not want to seek membership in white Greek organizations because of the discrimination that was both a part of the white Greek process and also representative of the larger social dynamics between whites and Asians.[42] The first Asian American fraternity was Rho Psi, founded at Cornell University in 1916, and later expanded to the Rho Psi Society that today includes women as well as a multiethnic membership. Since the 1980s, amid a budding multicultural logic, many Greek organizations, based on Asian, Latino/a, and American Indian identities, were created. Today, none of the Greek organizations have exclusionary official structure, but the symbolic boundary of the color-line persists.

While all the national fraternities and sororities eliminated racial discriminatory clauses from their constitutions and charters by the end of 1960s, Alfred M. Lee astutely predicted a decade earlier that "the abolition of restrictive clauses is merely a first step; it ignores other means for maintaining restrictive practices. It may remove an obstacle; it does not promote integration."[43] Even in the absence of such conscious efforts to subvert the elimination of official discrimination, other forces work to restrict access to minority students, even in the face of the best of intentions. A charge often leveled against white fraternities on many campuses today, despite the lack of official policies of discrimination, is that they continue to informally discriminate and are in fact, overtly racist organizations. Some of these charges are based on continued de facto segregation, parties with racially insensitive themes or white-supremacist overtones, mock "slave auctions," and numerous accounts of white fraternity members dressing in "blackface" for parties and other social gatherings.

Hazing activities have often included the use of racial stereotypes. For example, in the early 1990s, a Texas A&M white fraternity held a "jungle" theme party in which pledges blackened their faces, donned grass skirts, carried spears, and were "hunted" by fraternity members dressed in military fatigues. A similar event at the Rider College chapter of Phi Kappa Psi in the early 1990s gained national media coverage. Pledges of the all-white fraternity were made to dress "like black people," have X's painted on their foreheads (as a slight against slain human rights leader Malcolm X), and talk in a stereotypical form of black vernacular while cleaning the fraternity house. A message posted on a public electronic mailing list, known as "Nigger Night," by a representative of the fraternity, claimed that the event was the sole work of a deviant brother and that the fraternity "condemn[s] the incident and neither condone[s] nor tolerate[s] insensitive or inappropriate behavior of this nature." A week later however, the Phi Kappa Psi national offices announced in a press release that "the actions were premeditated and conducted with the full knowledge of the chapter officers . . . the chapter officers conspired to lie and obstructed both the Fraternity's and the college's investigations." The press release further stated that "Phi Kappa Psi . . . does not condone or tolerate actions or language which are insensitive to others" and "action is pending to expel from the Fraternity the members who were involved."[44] In 2001 a Whitewater State College white fraternity held a party with members in blackface, and in 2002 two fraternities at the University of Virginia held a similar party with members in blackface. According to University of Virginia professor and race scholar Eric Lott in his work *Love and Theft*, "The black mask offered a way to play with the collective fears of a degraded and threatening—and male—Other while at the same time maintaining some symbolic control over them."[45]

While some members are crossing the color-line, the transgression is not without a simultaneous and significant increase in the maintenance of the tradition of racial homogeneity. In the accounts that follow, I delineate the history of attempts to integrate organizations coupled with an overview of the social and political milieu in which those attempts were situated.

Rushing the Wall: Nonwhites in White Greek Organizations

Recent academic discourse indicates that black students on predominately white campuses are disproportionately likely to deal with social isolation, racism, and alienation.[46] John Smyth writes, "white students have more negative attitudes toward African Americans . . . while African Americans are more likely to appreciate and value their interracial experiences."[47] Further, students of color are often vastly underrepresented in campus student populations. Studies conducted by Balenger and Sedlacek as well as Fleming suggest that many black students do not join mainstream campus organizations because most of these organizations "do not directly help disadvantaged groups or advance the cause of racial equality."[48]

The tensions of cross-racial membership and desegregation by non-whites into historically white Greek organizations usually transpired through one of three situations. First, a chapter could be forced to desegregate by its national offices; second, a chapter could be forced to desegregate by the college or university administration; third, the chapter wanted to voluntarily desegregate but was not allowed by its national offices—making the chapter either abide by the decision until the constitution was changed or disaffiliate from their national offices. These tensions were motivated largely by the rearticulation of the concept of democracy following increased political discourse resulting from the aftermath of WWII. Additionally, there was contentious debate over the question of how to navigate egalitarian principles and notions of individualism pragmatically while simultaneously embracing the social networks that afford upward mobility that are characteristic of exclusive Greek societies.

Greek racial membership statistics are not kept. However, it is estimated at least 750,000 students (about one in seventeen) belong to Greek organizations.[49] The issue of cross-racial membership came to national attention, and a direct confrontation, in the 1940s. National Interfraternity Conference (NIC) President David A. Embury said in 1947 that people should "stop shivering at the word discrimination. . . . I love the discriminating tongue, the discriminating eye, the discriminating ear, and, above all, the discriminating mind and . . . soul. The person for whom I can find no love and no respect is the indiscriminate person. To be indiscriminate is to be common, to be vulgar."[50] President Embury masked the segregation ideology in democratic thought, arguing that organizations should have the right to restrict membership to whomsoever they choose. Eduardo Bonilla-Silva explains this type of racism as the "language of liberalism" which effectively allows whites the ability to argue against all measures to eradicate de facto racial inequality while seeming reasonable and moral.[51] Continuing at the 1947 NIC convention, Embury stated: "I, for one, will fight to the last ounce of my strength to defend the right—the democratic right—of any man or group of men to form a fraternity or other association with any membership restriction or qualification that they, in their absolute discretion, may see fit to impose: a fraternity of blacks for blacks, of whites for whites, of Jews for Jews, of Gentiles for Gentiles, of Catholics for Catholics, of Protestants for Protestants."[52]

Because of the staunch opposition to racial integration, some campuses responded by banning organizations that codified discrimination in their policies. In 1949, the president at the University of Connecticut forced Lambda Chi Alpha, Sigma Nu, Kappa Sigma, and Sigma Chi to disaffiliate from their national offices.[53] In other situations, national offices would suspend their undergraduate chapters if they attempted to bring in nonwhite members. After the initiation of a black pledge, Robert Thomas, into Phi Sigma Kappa at Boston University, its national offices suspended the chapter. At Phi Kappa Sigma's 1952 convention a resolution was passed that "no Negro could be initiated into the fraternity without the consent of all chapters."[54] In 1953 the Phi Delta Theta national offices suspended their chapters at Williams and Amherst colleges for pledging "non-Aryans." Although the national offices changed their official membership intake requirements from "full Aryan blood" to "socially acceptable" the following year in 1954, the suspensions of the Amherst and Williams chapters were still upheld. Resistance to discriminatory policies grew quickly in the 1950s, both from university administrations and undergraduate students. Some local chapters adopted nondiscriminatory policies even though it meant losing the recognition of their national offices. According to a student at Wesleyan at the time; "We view with shame the paradoxical situation presently existent at Wesleyan—of a community explicitly dedicated to the principles of democracy and brotherhood which yet allows discriminatory practices to persist within its own area of jurisdiction."[55]

Ward Connerly, the controversial black opponent of affirmative action, was one of only fifty African American students on a campus of two thousand at Sacramento State in the late 1950s, where he was also the first African American to pledge the all-white Delta Phi Omega (now Sigma Phi Epsilon). In 1961 at the University of Iowa, the Delta Chi fraternity offered membership to an African American student, Andrew J. Hankins. Shortly thereafter, Delta Chi's national offices warned the local chapter not to continue with the pledging of Hankins and the bid was withdrawn.[56] Later on that year in the fall, Yale University's chapter of Delta Psi fraternity initiated Wendell Mottley, a West Indian student from Trinidad. Upon hearing of Mottley's acceptance, a delegation from the University of Virginia chapter of Delta Psi flew to New Haven to protest Mottley's membership, but the Yale chapter ignored the protests and Mottley was successfully inducted.[57] At the same time, Duke University's chapter of Delta Theta Phi disaffiliated with their nationals so they could pledge Walter Johnson, a black student.[58]

One of the most notable cases of early cross-racial membership took place in the Stanford University chapter of Sigma Chi, who in 1965 pledged the black student Kenneth M. Washington, resulting in the chapter being suspended by the national offices. Harry V. Wade, leader of Sigma Chi's national offices cited "contemptuousness for the fraternity and ritual" as the reason for the suspension that hid the racial motivation behind Washington's membership deferment. Stanford University strongly supported the decision of the chapter that was already becoming racially conscious as they previously sent two chapter members on the dangerous Mississippi "Freedom Summer" rides of 1964. Stanford officials attempted to intercede between the chapter and their national offices to no avail. The situation was quickly becoming a debate between the Civil Rights Act of 1964 which stated that "no person in the United States shall, on the ground of race, color, or national origin, be excluded from participation in . . . any program or activity receiving Federal financial assistance," and the Meader Amendment which prevented investigations into the internal affairs of private fraternal organizations.[59] After widespread debate that reached the U.S. Congress, Commissioner of Education Francis Keppel stated that the Civil Rights Act would be applicable to the Sigma Chi case. Keppel made this statement after a 1964 letter surfaced that outlined a chapter member urging the national offices against "pledging a black student."[60] Still Sigma Chi was able to evade changing the racial makeup of their fraternity by retaining a clause in their constitution that stated new members must be "socially acceptable."

It would appear that the Stanford debacle reverberated throughout the Sigma Chi fraternal structure as well as other fraternities. Over the next couple of years, notable "firsts" across the color-line took place. In 1965, Brown University ordered its Sigma Chi chapter to disaffiliate from the national organization, arguing that their "socially acceptable" clause masked discrimination. In that same year, Yale University Phi Gamma Delta chapter accepted its first black member—the first in Phi Gamma Delta's history.[61] In April of 1966 Sigma Chi reinstated the Stanford Chapter following their yearlong suspension, but later that year disaffiliated from the national offices after chapter members stated "there is no white clause in the fraternities [*sic*] constitution, but an individual member may use any criterion he wishes to bar a prospective member."[62] In 1967, Michael Maloy was the first black member of Davidson College's Sigma Chi chapter, and in the same year, University of North Carolina (UNC) freshman basketball player Charlie Scott, also an African American, pledged a white fraternity.[63]

However, not all cases of these "firsts" were without conflict and even violence. In the spring of 1968 two black Colgate University students, Robert L. Boney and Naceo Giles, were walking past the Sigma Nu fraternity house when threats were yelled and several gunshots fired at them. The Sigma Nu student who fired the shots was apprehended but later released citing "lack of evidence." Many of the black Colgate students, who were also members of the Association of Black Collegians (ABC), held a meeting about what should be done. Shortly afterward on April 7, 1968, thirty-five ABC members entered the Sigma Nu house in order to take the guns so they would no longer be a threat to the black student population. They also issued the demand that the fraternity be banished from campus—the campus administration agreed with their demands.[64] Ironically, the Colgate Sigma Nu chapter was, at the time, working toward the removal of the national constitutions restrictive ban on blacks and Jews and had earlier that year pledged their first black member. Still, bridging the Greek color-line did not stop one of its members from trying to shoot Boney and Giles, leaving the attempts at desegregation to appear as either hollow legal gesturing or political maneuvering.

In 1971, a black undergraduate student named Alvin Kellog joined a white fraternity at UNC and quickly found himself ostracized from the larger black campus community and ignored by many of his fraternity brothers. Asking a poignant question, Kellog stated, "I don't understand why the first black athlete and first black cheerleader was praised, but the black in a fraternity is an outcast." The president of the UNC Black Student Union at the time, Warren Carson, stated of the Kellog case, "Fraternities are geared to the white middle-class and really have nothing to offer blacks."[65] Statements like Carson's draw upon a logic that considers the effects of centuries of segregation, leading people on both sides of the color-line to praise exclusivity and the vestiges of segregation even if they feel them to be structurally unfair.

While early integrationist stories in the 1950s, '60s, and '70s began to take shape, a segregationist backlash began to emerge that presented a severe empirical complication and competition with the predominant discourse of multiculturalism that took hold in the 1980s. That is, the few desegregationist "victories" appeared to level off. By the 1990s cross-racial membership was rare. For instance, in 1994 at the University of Florida (the largest Greek system in the Southeastern U.S. at the time), had almost no nonwhite members among the more than two thousand members in seventeen recognized Greek organizations (just among the sororities alone). As Esther Wright explains in *Torn Togas:* "Researchers studied sorority integration at the University [of Florida]. . . . Not one African-American lived in any of the sixteen white sorority houses. . . . Most black women interested in joining the Greek system were encouraged to join one of the three black sororities, only one of which was recognized by the college. None of three black sororities had houses."[66]

Courtney Bishop, the first black student to join the Acacia fraternity in the late 1980s at Cornell University, stated, "There isn't a lot of crossover between black and white fraternities. It's still the unwritten rule."[67] Marcela Hahn, president of the Cornell chapter of Delta Delta Delta stated of black students wishing to involve themselves in the predominantly white Greek system, "I think they're more comfortable in their own system."[68] This tactic of appealing to "comfort" allows for racial segregation to appear as "natural" and "just the way things are." As a consequence, many on both sides of the color-line begin to use this discourse of naturalism to utilize or to explain phenomena such as segregation as a natural, and nonracial, occurrence. White writer-activist Tim Wise recounted during his senior year of college in 1989 at Tulane University that a cross was burned on the lawn of a white fraternity due to its first-ever bid to a black student. Wise writes, "many white students and administrators said they didn't think the incident was racially-motivated, especially since 'it was only a two-foot cross.'" Sarcastically, Wise concluded, "No sir, no racism in these here parts."[69]

In 2000, the chapter of Alpha Gamma Delta at the University of Georgia (UGA) was put under the microscope when a black student was systematically barred from membership—a story that was broken when one of its white female members, Alison Davis, decided to leak the story and leave both the sorority and UGA. Partially because of Davis's actions, Alpha Gamma Delta became the only Greek-letter organization suspended on allegations of racial discrimination in the school's 200-plus-year history. As is the case at many universities, at UGA: "When alumni visit their white-columned chapter house on football Saturdays, almost no dark faces look out from the veranda or from the composite portraits in the hallways. Every school year brings new reports of anachronistic racial pranks. . . . Auburn University suspended two fraternities after photos surfaced on the Internet showing members dressed in Klan robes and blackface staging a mock lynching at a Halloween party. Similar displays led to recent fraternity sanctions at Ole Miss and the University of Louisville."[70]

The black female freshman that showed up to rush at UGA's Alpha Gamma Delta mixer was the only African American out of approximately one-thousand women who signed up for possible Greek recruitment that year. After the mixer, the members retired to evaluate the guests, wherein Davis maintained that one member stated, "She's black. I don't even know why she'd want to come to our rush." Again, this form of rhetoric frames segregation as natural and commonplace, putting the burden of rationalizing membership on the outsider. Another member stated of the black potential member, "If we let a black girl in our sorority, none of the fraternities would want to do anything with us." Amazingly, these comments are attempts to justify white privilege and exclusion by rationalizing racial exclusions as harmful and restrictive to the dominant group. That is, the discussion of which Davis bore witness allowed the white sorority members to adopt white-victimology arguments that explained away racial inequality without using racial epithets. After the sorority decided not to offer the girl membership based on her race, Davis returned to the house two days later, packed her things and left Athens, GA and the sorority.[71]

While the UGA-Davis story created a brief media frenzy, perhaps the most notorious, notable, and newsworthy cases of modern attempts at crossing the white Greek color-line have transpired at the University of Alabama (hereafter UA). In 1986, a chapter of Alpha Kappa Alpha (AKA), the first black sorority founded at Howard University in 1908, became the first black sorority to move to "sorority row," a street lined with all-white sorority houses. Days later, a burning cross was put in the front lawn of the AKA house. Joyce B. Stallworth, president of UA's chapter of AKA at the time stated, "People have to decide to change their attitudes. You can't force that." Yet others, like Kimberly McCord, a black UA junior in 1997 remarked, "They [Traditionally White Greek Organizations] didn't want to open their doors to us until they had to. . . . Why would we want to join them now?"[72]

In the early 1990s, UA fraternity members booed a black homecoming queen while sorority women made headlines in the *New York Times* when they appeared in blackface and Afro wigs to a "Who Rides the Bus?" social.[73] In a 1994 interview with Everett Whiteside (a white member of a UA chapter of the black fraternity Phi Beta Sigma), Lawrence R. Stains recalls the event (with the assistance of Whiteside). Stains wrote: "'There was a blackface incident here that made national news,' Everett says matter-of-factly. In 1991, Sigma Chi and Kappa Delta sorority had a party called a swap; swaps usually have themes. "The theme of this party was Who Rides the Bus?" says Everett. "Some of the members of both organizations dressed up in blackface. One girl put a basketball in her shirt.'"[74]

Dr. Charles Brown, UA's interim vice president of student affairs in 1997, maintains that the segregation at UA is not an aberration—citing that the Universities of Arkansas, Georgia, and Auburn had no black members in white fraternities at the time.[75] However, UA professor Pat Hermann is convinced that a handful of white racists, along with the normalization of status quo segregation, are behind the maintenance of the all-white Greek system at UA. Reportedly, an underground group of white Greek members who call themselves "The Machine" have controlled student government elections and a majority of the informal respect for an all-white Greek tradition at the University of Alabama since at least the 1920s. Herman stated: "One thing about the South, is that rules against integrating are deeply embedded in the consciousness of both blacks and whites. I know white Greek students, they will not break the color-line unless they are forced to do so. The alumni, who are the planter aristocracy of the state of Alabama, will not let them do it."[76] A UA committee exploring the issue found that "invisible barriers" bar blacks from membership, causing many black students to selectively avoid what they feel is an inherently racist system, pushing black students to either avoid the Greek life altogether or join one of the BGLO chapters on campus.

But Hermann says these committees give only "the illusion of progress." As early as 1985, the faculty senate passed a resolution asking for Greek integration. And in 1991 Hermann chaired the Greek Accreditation Committee, which targeted 1996 as the year for integration. In 1999 two black female students rushed for membership in the white sorority system but received no bids. Now the university is "reinventing the wheel," says Hermann.[77]

As of 2001, none of the 37 white fraternities and sororities at UA had ever accepted a black member.[78] In context, that is over 170 years after the founding of UA and almost a century since it desegregated as an institution. Recently, UA passed a Faculty Senate resolution that called for white Greek organizations to accept nonwhite members or risk severe penalties. However, both the president of the White IFC and the NAACP opposed any administrative actions that would force integration on either side of the Greek color-line. In 1999, Jamese Young, president of the black sorority Delta Sigma Theta, stated that forcing integration would "degrade the quality of membership"[79] for both white and black Greek organizations.

Despite the opposition, UA administration backed the 2001 candidacy of African American Melody Twilley for membership in a white sorority. However, Twilley declined an invitation to join any of the white sororities, despite a rush acceptance rate of over 80 percent that year. However, after the official rush process of 2001, a young member of Gamma Phi Beta sorority, named Christina Houston, announced that she had already broken the color-line, divulging that she was a biracial child of a white mother and a black father. Houston, when applying to UA, marked "White" on her application, and sources indicate that members of Gamma Phi Beta did not know that she was biracial when she was accepted.[80]

However, that same year in 2001, Calvin Johnson, a black student, joined Lambda Sigma Phi, a new Christian fraternity that joined the IFC after Johnson was already a member. Technically, this did not represent a break of the color-line as Lambda Sigma Phi was not a part of the IFC when Johnson joined. However, Johnson and Houston do represent the first two African Americans in predominately white Greek organizations in the history of UA. Shortly thereafter in 2003, Carla Ferguson became the first known black woman to join one of the established historically white Greek organizations post-IFC/NPC. Ferguson, along with twenty-eight white women, was offered membership in the Epsilon Lambda chapter of Gamma Phi Beta sorority.[81] At the completion of the academic year, the chapter was named as the Most Outstanding Sorority at UA for 2003–4, and Carla Ferguson was named the "Most Outstanding New Member."[82]

An often-overlooked aspect of cross-racial membership has been that of Asian members who have more successfully crossed the color-line into white Greek organizations. As Chew and Ogi write, "Asian American students experience unique struggles, living in a multicultural existence. Having one foot embedded in American values and the other foot in Asian values provides a richness and depth that monocultural experience lacks." One of the most significant works on this topic is Elizabeth Chen's study that used ethnographic, archival, and interview data to explain why some Asian American women decided to remain or cross the Greek color-line. One respondent in Chen's study, an Asian American woman named "Leslie" remarked of one popular white sorority house: "They all had that 'all American' look. I remember them being almost all White, maybe a couple of Asian people at most. I don't remember there being any African American women in the sorority. They just seemed a little bit cold. They were all, accordingly to whatever beauty myth there is, that [American ideal] look of attractiveness—tall, thin, and blond."[83]

Chen argues that low status white sororities are more likely to have cross-racial membership. This is attributed to both *selectivity;* high-status white sororities are more selective of whom they choose as members, and *recruiting;* low-status white sororities have a harder time recruiting members in order to maintain their numbers and must be less discriminate than the high-status sororities. Therefore, those sorority houses that were depicted as "going down" tended to have more diverse members.

While many might be tempted to paint the low-status sororities as possessing a commitment to change and racial egalitarianism, Elizabeth Chen writes, "the inclusion of more types of women in less popular houses is not because of an alternative ideology to the hierarchical nature of Panhellenic sororities."[84] Further, low-status sororities with greater numbers of nonwhite women still highlight the white women with Eurocentric standards of beauty. Another respondent in Chen's work named "Mary" stated: "One house that I really liked was Beta Chi, because I thought it was the "pretty girl" house. . . . all of the rushees that come in see all the girls standing on the staircase. . . . But then I remember at the first meeting, it was such a let down. . . . I was shocked, kind of disappointed. . . . I realized that there was a whole strategy behind that. Because during rush, what they do is they pick the twelve most beautiful women in the house, and they put them on the stairwell purposefully, so that you get that first impression."[85] This tactic is affirmed in *Torn Togas:* "It is usually the less-popular sororities that accept minority rushees. Because these houses often have a hard time recruiting members—without enough members to pay the bills, they would have to shut down—they usually accept whoever wants to join just to stay afloat. 'Frankly, my sorority is not a very desirable sorority to be in socially. We just aren't,' admitted one sorority member. 'Because we are not all beauty queens, we are probably more flexible [about minorities]. If we were more popular, I am sure that would change. Let's face it—sororities are social and exclusive, and that is that.'"[86]

In a particularly reflexive moment of research, Chen described how the various sorority members of her study received her own Asian American subjectivity. She stated that Asian American sorority members went out of their way to avoid her. However, she stated that white sorority women spoke to her frequently and attempted to recruit her into their sorority. She concluded that Asian American sorority women may have felt uncomfortable being identified as Asian American and hence, "disassociated themselves from other Asian Americans"[87] like herself.

Chen illuminates how Asian Americanness is used as "Social Capital." Sociologist Pierre Bourdieu describes social capital as the actual or potential resources that are linked to a durable network of institutionalized relationships of mutual acquaintance and recognition. Those relationships then serve as a form of "collectively-owned capital, a 'credential' which entitles them to credit."[88] That is, Chen's Asian identity was seen as a possible credential for white sororities wishing to both boost their membership and to be perceived as inclusive organizations. That is, tokenized subjectivities that appear "authentically" nonwhite make the organizations appear more diverse and "politically correct."

Additionally, by taking Bourdieu's theory and "turning it on its head," I specify that there were instances in which Chen's Asianness was not used as social capital, but instead as *social debt.* Chen was ignored by Asian American sorority women because of the salient role that race continues to play in their lives (even as they were "accepted" into predominately white sororities as "sisters"); they saw the display of familiarity with other Asians as a debt that would hinder their continued negotiation of acceptance into a Eurocentric sorority order. Chen writes: "Despite their visible presence within predominately White sororities, Asian American women often embrace Western middle-class notions of femininity and accept assimilationist notions of what it means to be American, thereby reinforcing notions of Anglo American cultural superiority. Being Asian—whether this is positively embracing Asian cultural values or behavior, having Asian Americans as close friends, or exploring issues of race and ethnicity—is not seen as something positive within the context of Panhellenic sororities."[89] As Wright maintains, "Incidents like these . . . provide overwhelming proof that the Greek system discriminates against minorities and perpetuates segregation."[90] Established patterns of stereotyping and prejudicial violence directed specifically at minorities are structurally a part of Greek organizations, which means that Greek organizations cannot become tolerant overnight.

The work of anthropologist Mary Douglas specifies that institutions, especially traditionally formal organizations like white Greek-lettered organizations are social vehicles that create and even control how people perceive reality. Within these frameworks, "objectivity" is formed and diffused to individuals leaving them little space for them to "think" independently. From this standpoint, Douglas attempts to explain social behavior as an aggregate of individuals' actions by departing from a macrolevel explanation and elaborates how institutions act like a person and determine collective actions in four distinct ways: First, institutions confer identity to individuals. Second, institutions remember and forget through so-called "public memory." Third, institutions create classifications. And fourth, institutions influence major social decision-making processes.[91] This picture may be bleak, but it can explain the continued support and growth of BGLO by black members, and possibly the reason why some progressive whites who wish to be a part of the Greek system, seek membership by pledging BGLOs.

Crossing the Sands: Nonblacks in Black Greek-letter Organizations

Before engaging the discourse of nonblacks who seek membership in BGLOs, it is prudent to outline many of the distinguishing characteristics between the NPHC and NIC/NPC organizations. There are many differences between white and black Greek traditions. First,

Whipple et al. and Berkowitz and Padavic argue that there are fundamental value orientations, family backgrounds, educational objectives, and significant differences in the very organizational ontology of black and white Greeks. Whipple et al.'s study of over 620 fraternity and sorority members found that "Black Greeks generally come from a lower socioeconomic background, are more academically motivated, more liberal, more socially conscious, and more peer independent than White Greeks."[92] Berkowitz and Padavic, by means of twenty-six open-ended in-depth interviews, investigated the reasons behind why white and black women joined sororities in regard to academic and social life, career plans, and the role of their respective sororities toward those ends. White sorority members seemed more focused on using the Greek structure to "get a man," whereas black sorority members appear more focused on community service and career advancement.[93]

Secondly, Berkowitz and Padavic found that black sorority members had widely differing worldviews regarding the role of their organizations as a lifelong commitment, opposed to something that one is simply a part of while in college, a belief widely held by white sorority members. As a consequence, BGLOs have a much larger percentage of alumni who remain active in both alumni chapters and as formal and informal advisors to undergraduate chapters.[94]

Third, white Greeks afford less value and importance to achieving high marks academically than their nonwhite Greek counterparts.[95] Simultaneously, black Greeks provide much of the major social structure for the black community on campus,[96] while white Greek counterparts generally do not work to extend programs or activities far beyond Greek social networks. Black Greeks appear to be more service oriented than white Greeks, as some estimates state that BGLOs devote as many as five times the amount of hours to community service than white Greeks.[97]

Fourth, and most notably, the membership intake processes between both white and black systems are very different. Both systems receive a large amount of negative press regarding hazing. Hazing in higher education stretches back to the first European universities founded circa 1000 CE, and affects both organizations today.[98] However, pledging and hazing take on a distinctive characteristic within BGLOs due to the length and intensity of the process. Walter Kimbrough writes in *Black Greek 101:*

> [Pledging] could be defined as a cultural appendage that has taken on a life of its own. It has evolved over time into a complex culture that has birthed numerous customs and traditions associated with Black Greek life. . . . it is an integral part of the Black fraternal experience. . . . The idea of pledging

> actually emerged as early as 1919 at Ohio State University. During that year, Kappa Alpha Psi began the Scrollers Club. . . . Two years later, Alpha Phi Alpha created the Sphinx Club at Howard University. . . . At Wilberforce in 1923, Delta Sigma Theta defined the Pyramid Club. . . . In less than ten years from the beginnings of pledging in Black fraternities and sororities, the signs of hazing emerged.[99]

These differences between the raced systems of Greek life add to a complexity that both enables and constrains or "structurates"[100] the initial appeal, recruitment, and retention of nonblacks who would cross the burning sands, and the color-line, into BGLOs.

The first collegiate fraternity for African American men still existent today, Alpha Phi Alpha, was established in 1906 at Cornell University. However, like their white counterparts, fraternities for nonwhite groups often excluded students who were not members of their particular racial group. Accordingly, when questioned about the need for fraternities for nonwhite students in 1949, Alpha Phi Alpha President Wilbert Whitsett responded, "If we are not permitted to join other fraternities, we must form a fraternity of our own. We have no other choice."[101] E. Franklin Frazier affirms in *Black Bourgeoisie* that BGLOs were founded in direct response to the refusal to allow blacks to join white Greek organizations. So too, Swedish economist Gunnar Myrdal, in his classic study *An American Dilemma*, remarked that "America has an unusual proliferation of social clubs, recreational organizations, lodges, fraternities and sororities. . . . Despite the fact that they are predominately lower class, Negroes are more inclined to join associations than are whites; in this respect. . . . Negroes are "exaggerated" Americans. . . . With rare exception, these associations have only Negroes as members, and their large number is in some measure a product of the prohibitions against having Negro members in white associations."[102]

While Myrdal praised black fraternal organizations for their "exaggerated" Americanness of civic participation, he went on to decry black fraternal organizations as "pathological" and "a poor substitute [for] . . . political activity." Sadly ironic, he missed how BGLOs were vehicles for political and social change. Skocpol, Liazos, and Ganz argue: "To gain critical leverage against U.S. white racism and build as much black solidarity as possible . . . African American fraternalists, had always been internationalists. They became human rights universalists, as it were, long before this stance became fashionable. . . . and thus enhanced the power and dignity of appeals for racial equality inside the United States."[103] Accordingly, while many white Greek organizations were excluding black members, BGLOs were breaking the color-line. Even though BGLOs were either changing their constitutions early on in their organizational history, or never possessed racial restrictive clauses, nonblack membership (especially for whites) was often framed as a taboo topic. Walter Kimbrough writes, "Whites who go against the grain of societal norms and seek membership in groups founded to serve the Black community. This is a definitely a controversial subject."[104]

Instances of nonblack membership in BGLOs started to make headlines in the 1940s. Alpha Phi Alpha fraternity pledged Bernard Levin, a senior at the University of Illinois College of Dentistry on June 21, 1946.[105] "Pledging a white student, the opposition maintained, would violate an ancient Alpha tradition of seeking recruits from the cream of college-bred Negroes. Supporters of the admission of Bernard Levin attacked these arguments as smug bigotry. To oppose creation of an interracial fraternity amounted to justifying Jim Crow, they said. After hours of heated wrangling, the interracialists finally triumphed and Levin was pledged."[106] In 1949 Mrs. Marjorie T. Ware and Miss Olive Young became the first two white women initiated into Alpha Kappa Alpha sorority. Both members attributed their choice of membership in the black sorority to their belief in human rights and racial integration. In 1953 at the University of Kansas, a white man named Roger L. Youmans pledged Alpha Phi Alpha and moved into the fraternity house during the next fall semester. After Youmans gained media attention for his move, a cross was burned on the front lawn of the fraternity house.[107]

Chi Delta Mu (one of the first BGLOs, no longer existent today), along with Omega Psi Phi fraternity at Howard University, admitted white members in 1949.[108] In 1954 at Philander Smith College, Georg Iggers (who fled Nazi Germany when he was twelve years old when the German army began rounding up Jewish citizens to put in concentration camps) became possibly the first white member of Phi Beta Sigma fraternity.[109] Five years later in 1959 at the Omega Psi Phi conference, Herbert E. Tucker, the assistant attorney general of Massachusetts, urged all BGLOs to encourage interracial membership and challenged the members in attendance by stating, "Negro fraternities had only token white membership."[110] These patterns of sporadic nonblack membership continued into more recent years. As a corollary to the University of Alabama (UA) attempts at cross-racial membership that were discussed in the preceding section, several BGLOs have succeeded in obtaining white membership long before the aforementioned Twilley, Johnson, and Houston examples at UA. In 1986 a white student made headlines when she joined the UA chapter of Zeta Phi Beta sorority. In 1987, Mark Brafford became a white member of Zeta Phi Beta's brother organization—Phi Beta Sigma fraternity. Jeff Choron became a white member of Phi Beta Sigma fraternity at the UA in 1990 because he felt "they are more tolerant, because differences are to be expected." The next semester in the spring of 1990, Everett Whiteside also became a white member of Phi Beta Sigma fraternity at the UA. Whiteside stated, "Being part of a trend never crossed my mind. . . . Make your own reasons why I joined."[111]

A December 2000 issue of *Ebony* included the article "Whites in Black Sororities and Fraternities" which examined both the white and black members' perceptions of cross-racial membership in BGLOs. The article concentrates on the heterogeneity of white members: "White members fit no easy stereotypes. Instead, they come from all backgrounds. . . . Some grew up surrounded by Blacks, while others had little contact with African Americans before college." Then president of the NPHC Cassandra Black writes, "Our organizations, every one of them, have had some sort of White infusion probably almost since our founding, so to speak, whether through actual membership, honorary membership or support."[112]

Barbara Bartsch-Allen became a white member of Delta Sigma Theta sorority in 1993 at Southern Methodist University and remarked on her reasons for joining: "I am involved in women's rights and being associated with women who are doing good things is really important to me. . . . The Deltas really stood out for doing community service and sisterhood." Allen Pulsifer became the first white member of the Dartmouth University chapter of Kappa Alpha Psi fraternity in 1986. He remarked that while the positives of his membership are many, that involvement in the fraternity also comes with challenges. "Sometimes I get a look or sometimes I get questioned. It's interesting. But once they talk to me, they know that I belong."[113] Brodey Milburn, a white student who pledged Kappa Alpha Psi fraternity at Indiana University stated, "There are black people who don't appreciate my presence in a black fraternity, just as there are white people who can't understand why I did it in the first place." Accordingly, L. R. Stains wrote, "It's rarely the black fraternity members who resent whites; it's the bystanders who are bothered."[114] Research reports that much of the harshest criticisms of nonblacks joining BGLOs come not from blacks but from within the racial group of the nonblack member.[115] Such intraracial antagonism can be explained by the notion that whites may feel compelled to police racial-ontological boundaries, as well as feel more comfort in confronting "one of their own" now that the predominant logic of "color-blindness" is prevalent "politically correct" restrictions often dictate how one "appropriately" speaks of race.

Some white members receive more than just challenging looks from fellow members that are absolved upon a personal connection, or mere misunderstanding from outsiders. Lisa Terrell became a white member of Alpha Kappa Alpha sorority at Texas Tech University. She stated,

"Most people didn't want me to be a part of the chapter. They didn't want to be known as the ones who allowed a White soror to slip in." Davina Brown, a black member of Zeta Phi Beta sorority remarked, "we service the special needs of our Black communities—it just makes me feel uncomfortable in knowing that, here again, is a tradition that is slowly being taken away from us."[116] Yet, Lawrence C. Ross Jr., author of *The Divine Nine*, argues that the fear of whites taking over BGLOs is unfounded and almost impossible, and that even though white membership in BGLOs has grown, it is far from a "white stampede."[117] Accordingly, a white professor at the University of Central Oklahoma, Jere Roberson, pledged Omega Psi Phi fraternity in 1977 and stated that his fraternity brothers, "make me feel at home, comfortable and happy." Many feel that contemporary racial politics would be an impediment to cross-racial amity due to prejudicial attitudes based on white stereotypes. However, Damien L. Duchamp, who became a white member of Phi Beta Sigma fraternity at Clemson University in 1997 stated, "Some of my brothers would say I'm the Whitest guy they know. . . . I grew up in a very Caucasian environment."[118] Despite these differences, most white BGLO members report substantial accord and unity. Writing in a *Cornell Sun* online discussion forum in conjunction with the coverage of the one-hundredth anniversary of Alpha Phi Alpha, White Alpha member Karl Rainhold stated: "While it would be understandable if I were not well received amongst the ranks of the organization, given the still persistent divisions and inequities in our society today, my experience for the last 15 years has been quite to the contrary. Does it raise eyebrows? Yes, but not with feelings of animosity or exclusion, only curiosity at the visual singularity of my presence. I am welcomed and embraced as a Brother in the organization, an inspiring testament to working by example, fellowship and brotherhood, without preoccupation or undue regard to my racial or cultural background."[119]

While many white members express elation and recall positive social and service experiences as members of BGLOs, a different take on cross-racial Greek membership began to surface recently at one of the premier HBCUs, Howard University. In February of 2006 the historically white fraternity Pi Kappa Alpha started a colony to work toward establishing a formal chapter at Howard University. Pi Kappa Alpha did not lift its "Whites only" racial clause until 1964. Despite the high ideals of the organization, many questioned why Pi Kappa Alpha was trying to charter a chapter at Howard University given the fraternity's blatant racism of the past, as well as the recent activities in the late 1990s that includes Auburn University chapter members dressing as Ku Klux Klan members for a Halloween party, or the "Straight Outta Compton" party at a Georgia State chapter in which members came in blackface. As reported in *The Hilltop*, Howard University's campus newspaper, student reaction was mixed, but largely negative.

> "Howard has enough Greek organizations on campus that students have no need to establish new ones, especially ones that weren't designed with us in mind," said Dalontee Edgarton, a senior physical therapy major. He added, "as a member of Kappa Alpha Psi Fraternity, Inc. I feel that it is an embarrassment to add a historically white and racist fraternity to Howard" historically rich Greek legacy." . . . Some students [are] questioning the intent and purpose of this organization on Howard's campus. "As a member of the Divine Nine I am disappointed to see the fabric of the Howard Greek legacy and traditions be torn by this new addition," said senior marketing major A.C. Onyia, member of Alpha Phi Alpha Fraternity, Inc.[120]

The move has made shockwaves throughout the BGLO community, and Howard alumni have heard of the move and have written to the school paper:

> There is not the same standard or set of virtues and values connected to their [Pi Kappa Alpha] Greek life. To put it bluntly, their affiliation with their sororities and fraternities appear to be primarily about drinking, drugging and hooking up sexually. Of course we are not immune to this mentality, but there is definitely a cultural divide that separates what it means for us to be affiliated with our historical sororities and fraternities versus theirs. . . . I do hate to see the lines begin to get blurred and our black fraternity/sorority life and lifestyle begin to become diluted with the lack of values and the different emphasis that white fraternity/sorority life displays.[121]

Sean Eric Mickens, a Howard University student wrote:

> I also don't see anything wrong with an organization that is working to erase color-lines. After reading this article, I saw more of a racial threat coming from Howard students than from members of Pi Kappa Alpha. It is a step forward for the organization to want to include African Americans by founding a chapter at an HBCU [Historically Black College or University]. . . . Too often, we as African Americans are quick to check white people's racism without taking in the fact that we possess our own degrees of racism and discrimination. Although blacks are subject to racism, we are not above being advocates of it, whether willingly or unwillingly.[122]

The issue of the Greek color-line on the flagship Historically Black College or University (HBCU) campus is complex. Many are polarizing themselves around whether Pi Kappa Alpha should be welcomed or shunned–centering the debate around the fraternity's racist past, and possibly, present. However, Alicia M. Johnson wrote in *The Hilltop*, "perhaps the arrival of Pike [Pi Kappa Alpha] reflects the current state of historically black fraternities and sororities. While Pike had the blackface incidents and exclusionary clause [*sic*], didn't (don't) we have the paper-bag test[123]and classism?"[124]

This event garnered a great deal of attention because of the contentious history of white and black Greek organizations, coupled with the status of Howard as one of the premier black institutions of higher learning.[125] However, white organizations on black campuses or white members in BGLOs are neither the only cases of Greek cross-racial membership, as some Latino/a and Asian students seek membership across the color-line and present their own distinct challenges to the questions of integration, acceptance, and identity. In the mid 1990s at the University of Florida (UF), Rhonda Chung-DeCambre was invited to an academic forum by Sigma Gamma Rho sorority. She knew that she wanted to be involved in the Greek system, but she was not interested in the traditional white groups. She later joined Sigma Gamma Rho and also shared her sisterhood with two Latina women that were also members in the traditionally black sorority.[126] In 1995 Kenneth A. Lynch, Jr., a white student at Brown University pledged Lambda Upsilon Lambda fraternity as a freshman. As to why he joined, he answered, "I was really familiar with the Latino culture from going to public schools and growing up in Providence. . . . I thought the Latino culture could better meet my needs as opposed to the other organizations I looked at."[127]

As Elizabeth Chen writes of her study at the institution of higher learning "PCU," a moniker for a large Pacific Coast University: "At least ten Asian American women participated in African American sororities at some point between 1992 and 1997 at PCU. Their participation illustrates another form of incorporation that departs from the classical model of assimilation. The participation of Asian American women . . . reveals social processes that underly [*sic*] one form of incorporation, in which minority members become integrated into another minority community that is not socially defined as their own."[128] Chen goes on to identify the process of Asian American women in joining BGLOs as a strategy for both further developing their identities as women of color and directly challenging racial hierarchies in which Asianness is juxtaposed against black and white. Specifically, the subjects of her study were found to use their membership in a BGLO to first, construct a nonwhite identity; second, identify with other racial minorities; third, articulate an Asian American identity. These all work together to foster oppositional racial identities. Accordingly, racial scholar Mari J. Matsuda wrote: "If white, as it has been historically, is the top of the racial hierarchy in American, and black, historically, is the bottom, will yellow assume the place of the racial middle? . . . if it refuses to be the middle, if it refuses to buy into racial hierarchy, and if it refuses to abandon communities of black and brown people, choosing instead to forge alliance with them."[129] Perhaps many Asian Americans who join BGLOs are expressing a form of subtle resistance with racial categories. The women in Chen's study had already developed a sense of racial consciousness prior to joining and did not view black and Asian struggles as completely separate.

Different schools of thought exist to explain the continued significance of race and racism. These can be organized into roughly four different debates. First, an *optimistic standpoint* campaigns for the view that antiblack prejudice is in hasty retreat.[130] Second, some scholars show that racial perspectives are filled with a *mixture of approval and bigotry*. This is exemplified by idealistic approval of racial liberalism in the abstract with a staunch disapproval of racial policies (like affirmative action) in the specific.[131] Third, other scholars argue that a *latent White supremacy* governs racial relations.[132] Fourth, work like Sears and Kinder and Kinder and Sanders[133] shows how antiblack attitudes and traditional Western value systems such as meritocracy and individualism merge together to form a "*symbolic racism*" that rationalizes and/or hides racist intent in mainstream ideology. Advances in multicultural-spawned "political correct" attitudes that reflect an increasingly racial egalitarianism in higher education exist simultaneously with the empirical evidence of a harsh segregation that is one of the hallmarks of the U.S. Greek-letter system. Accordingly to follow, some of the causes, mechanisms, and effects of cross-racial Greek membership are further examined.

The Structured Culture of Cross-Racial Greek Membership

There are many factors that influence the decision, ability, and benefits of people who decide to cross the Greek racial line. Many inquiries into Greek racial homogeneity have been interpretations that are strong on action, but weak on structure. That is, they portray human beings as purposive agents, who are aware of themselves as independent thinkers and doers, who challenge the status quo of Greek racial homogeneity. Yet, other theorists have given little explanation to how human beings cope with the problems of structural and symbolic constraint, power and the large-scale social organizations that are Greek fraternities and sororities. This approach is strong on structure, but is weak on action as it treats human beings as if they are "cultural dopes"—inert and inept beings. This presents a dualism of theoretical perspectives and reifies the separation between the "individual" and the "institution."

To illustrate the mechanisms of Greek racial transgression, I draw upon scholar Anthony Giddens theory of "structuration."[134] At its center, his theory is a cyclical relationship between social structure and human action, or the "duality of structure." As applied to cross-racial Greek boarder transgression, I emphasize that the social structure of historically racially homogenous Greek fraternities and sororities both enable and constrain the ability of people actively seeking to cross the color-line, while simultaneously, human behavior produces and reproduces the social structures that are Greek organizations in a relatively consistent manner. Accordingly, I delineate how the Greek structural system both constrains and enables human agency (for example, economic factors), while also emphasizing cultural factors that constrain and enable the institution from bringing in different racial groups (for example, stereotypes and informal practices). First, I address why people might be motivated to join Greek organizations that are racially different than themselves; second, I discuss the cultural factors that influence the ability to join; and third, I illuminate the effects of cross-racial membership.

Cross-Racial Motivations

Many nonwhites who joined the traditionally white Greek system (NPC and IFC) report doing so in order to make friends, to get involved in campus life, and because they succumbed to substantial "peer pressure" from their friends who were already members or who planned to join. Conversely, many nonblacks who joined the historically black Greek system (NPHC) report doing so because of certain members, to seek out a feeling of unity, and to have a support system that serves as a haven away from home.

Two divergent themes are manifest. First, many nonwhites who join NPC and IFC organizations report doing so mainly because of anticipated payoffs to their social capital networks (both socially while in college, and afterward via economic and employment opportunities). Second, nonblack members of NPHC organizations report joining because they wanted a fraternal bond that would reach past their collegiate years. NPHC organizations have a significantly higher rate of postgraduate involvement due to a heavy focus on alumni chapter activity. Additionally, nonblacks in NPHC organizations report that because of the original racial segregation that motivated the founding of BGLOs, they feel that the black fraternity and sorority structure is a more inclusive, tight-knit, and socially cohesive organization than their white counterparts. Many attribute the BGLO legacy of resistance as to having created a culture of progressive thinking and more open-minded individuals that accrue nicely with the mission of many liberal-arts college and university agendas.

Cultural Factors

In all cases of black, white, Asian and Latino students, the ability to join organizations of vastly different racial composition seems dependent on having support from friends and family. Additionally, having close friends who were already members that both encouraged the person to join, and who served as an advocate during the pledging/rushing procedures, increased the chances of successful membership intake processes. Many other cultural factors serve as constraints toward the membership of nonwhites in NPC and IFC organizations. Mostly notably, the amount of money that it costs to rush and remain a member of a NPC or IFC organization is significantly larger on average than NPHC organizations. Also, because of the public acknowledgment of the heavy recreational side of white Greek organizations, many people report a worry over whether joining an NPC or IFC organization would serve as a detriment to their academic performance.

Many black students report that joining a NPC or IFC organization is something that is simply just not done in the status quo of the majority of black students in college and universities today. As a rationale, many cite that NPC and IFC interests and goals do not relate to the issues and problems affecting black populations and that many minority students also have a lack of interest in what they believe are the white community's goals. Many nonwhite students also report that the white Greek system has the stereotype of being either excessive partygoers or of being overly pretentious and bourgeois—both affiliations that many students of color try to shun due to already increased, and often racist, focus on minority student behavior.

Traditionally white Greek organizations are not perceived as a racially "diverse" structure, and both the empirical nature of that homogenous population, coupled with the discourse about its racial homogeneity, greatly diminishes the opportunities to communicate possible benefits for minority members, or even that white attitudes might be changing toward the desire of racial inclusivity. This means that many people of color may not feel comfortable participating in the white Greek system because they see so few racial minorities. In Carol Thompson's study of factors that influence minority participation in white Greek organizations, one participant stated, "Kappa Alpha was founded in the deep South in the late 1800s and their founding was during slavery and on slavery."[135] Acknowledgment of the racist history of many white Greek organizations works like a discursive framework that is a significant barrier to nonwhite membership in NPC and IFC organizations—both the empirical evidence and symbolic belief that these organizations are deeply committed to racial exclusivity and maintaining white homogeneity.

On the other side of this racial divide, many nonblack students report different circumstances regarding why they would or would not pledge a BGLO. First, many white students are not aware of the tradition or even existence of BGLOs due to the fact that it is rare for a BGLO to have a physical house on campus. BGLOs are many times simply outside of the social network of much of the white community, and the lack of white knowledge about their processes, traditions, or even existence, makes cross-racial Greek membership a nonissue for many white students. This divide between the black and white social circles led scholar Andrew Hacker to write in the preface to his work *Two Nations* that blacks and whites are "two nations, between whom there is no intercourse and no sympathy; who are as ignorant of each others habits, thoughts, and feelings, as if they were dwellers in different zones, or inhabitants of different planets."[136] When BGLOs are recognized by white audiences, they are often viewed through a lens that results in stereotypical and reductive conclusions as a repercussion. Often BGLOs are talked about as if they are little more than gangs of deviant students, even under the empirical evidence that shows black Greeks academically achieve at a much higher rate then their white Greek counterparts and that they often contribute more than five times the amount of community service.

However, some constraints toward cross-racial membership are common to all Greek organizations. Most common is a fear of hazing—that membership intake procedures will be intensified in their case, as they are not racial members of the established tradition. Many students on both sides of the color-line also report that they feel they would not be welcome and that the racial separation of the Greek system is a good thing that allows for people to choose places of institutional comfort. Additionally, many black students worry over the notion of being perceived as a "sell-out," while many white students worry over being ostracized by the white community.

Effects of Cross-Racial Membership

Of a positive scope, increased leadership opportunities, networks, and the structural inclusion and validation of students of color in previously closed and powerful institutions have been noted. However, cross-racial membership also leads to many organizations fetishizing and tokenizing the few members who do cross the color-line. Particularly on college campuses that already lack a diverse population of students, underrepresented racial groups have an increased chance of being viewed as tokens. Tokenism contributes to the enhanced visibility of underrepresented groups, the exaggeration of group differences, and the alteration of images to fit existing stereotypes.[137] On predominantly white campuses, the fact that students of color are underrepresented produces both negative social stigma and "minority status" stressors that adversely affect student achievement.[138]

Further Questions and Issues

This study focuses on cross-racial Greek membership, in both the scope of its history and the contemporary mechanisms that guide its behavior. However, more research must be undertaken in order to develop more of the latter aspect. Here I outline six areas in which future research would gain the most purchase. The first four are more or less straightforward, while the last two are more significant in their reach and scope.

First, scholars must explore the conditions in which Greek racial lines are more or less fluid. That is, under what conditions are students of color accepted into the social circles of the dominant group, and conversely, what conditions have allowed many nonblack students entry into BGLOs? Second, what types of students, particularly students of color, participate in these organizations and what do these findings suggest about racial identity? Third, how might findings regarding the fluidity of racial identity in our (post)modern moment affect the relatively solid and fixed agenda of racial identity politics that is characteristic of many of these Greek institutions? Fourth, and of a democratic and ethical posture, if our goal is to eradicate racial strife, assumptions emphasizing differences between races and our willingness to uphold these differences should be reexamined.

Fifth, while this chapter presents a solid first step in gathering the histories of cross-racial membership, future research should build on this historical foundation to wrestle more closely with issues of power, representation, and voice. That is, illuminating the interplay of power, representation, and voice also encourages us to imagine the ways in which we are all constituted as raced subjects: whether in the specific context of a particular fraternal organization or in society *writ large*. Accordingly, members of raced organizations are cast in positions that carry with them explicit and implicit expectations. These social requirements, however, require members' consent for them to remain formative. Consent, however, is a sticky issue: as sometimes it is implicit, assumed, unconsciously given or an essential part of hegemonic social relations. Thus, understanding the role of power in the organizational and individual formative process is of utmost importance. Sixth, we must rearticulate the methodology by which we make truth claims regarding the past and the telling of the history of cross-racial membership, as well as the future, by which we make predictions regarding the Greek cross-racial memberships to come. That is, for a robust and multifaceted approach to this issue, it is imperative to start with the idea that every act of racial boundary transgression is composed of certain rudiments. These rudiments draw upon subjective experiences but also transcend them. The moments of cross-racial membership must be first understood as a personal experience, but then also as a representative experience that reflects an increasing pattern that takes place between divergent people and different places, all at the same conjuncture, in the same time.

Regardless of these anticipated courses of research, at the center of these inquires should remain an attention to the crisis of a monocultural Greek system and identity that is increasingly being framed as out of place in the world. This is indicative of a certain historical moment in the geopolitics of decolonization, the moment in which Frantz Fanon's "politics of the skin" and Greek racial homogeneity is coming to a crisis while simultaneously entrenching itself in mystified and normalized behaviors. Therefore, this Greek out-of-placeness, is both lived from the inside as a subjective fact, and yet at the same moment, it is a matter of objective historical conjuncture. This experience of racial dislocation is a particular moment that is a new configuration that must be continually rearticulated and simultaneously connected to the genealogy of cross-racial contact in the Western tradition. Failure to do so will only result in myopic scholastic narratives about race and fraternal culture that will tell us little about why this area of study matters for the illumination of the dynamics of organizations, race and ethnicity, racism, power, and democratic theory and practice.

Notes

1. Gratitude for assistance in data collection is extended to Phi Beta Sigma Fraternity, Inc. International Executive Director Mr. Donald J. Jemison; Kappa Alpha Psi Fraternity, Inc. Executive Director Mr. Richard L. Snow; Kappa Alpha Psi Fraternity, Inc. Director of Undergraduate and University Affairs Mr. Andre G. Early; Alpha Phi Alpha Fraternity, Inc. General President Mr. Darryl R. Matthews; Alpha Phi Alpha

Fraternity, Inc. Executive Director Mr. Willard C. Hall, Jr; and the coeditors Craig Torbenson and Gregory S. Parks.

2. For more information on the growing trends of "resegregation," see the numerous reports published by "The Civil Rights Project" at http://www.civilrightsproject.ucla.edu/. Such data shows that nearly a half-century after the anniversary of *Brown v. Board of Education* (1954) racial segregation continued to intensify. On top of the intensification of segregation, many of the "gains" for black and Latino students was eliminated throughout the 1990s and 2000s due to the Supreme Court limiting desegregation remedies. Latinos, now the nation's largest minority, have become increasingly isolated since the 1970s, with Latino segregation surpassing that of blacks. For instance, in specific regard to education, the growing gap in segregation is affecting the quality between the schools that are being attended by white students and those serving a large proportion of nonwhite students. In specific, in spite of the rapid increase in minority enrollment in schools, white students remain the most segregated racial group in U.S. education. The average white student attends a school where more than 80% of the students are white, compared to the average black and Latino student that attends a school with 53% to 55% students of their own group, respectively. Even in the District of Columbia, where fewer than one student in twenty was white, the typical white student was in a class with a slight majority of whites. Racial segregation persists even among the faculty at the nation's elite institutions of higher learning. For instance, a recent report from Evelynn M. Hammonds, senior vice provost for faculty development and diversity at Harvard University, identifies only 46 blacks among the nonmedical tenure or tenure-track faculty at Harvard. This is equal to 3.5 percent of the total nonmedical faculty with tenure or on the tenure track. Additionally, there are only 27 blacks who hold tenure at Harvard, which is only 3.2 percent of all tenured nonmedical faculty. "Black Faculty at Harvard: A Mixed Record," *Journal of Blacks in Higher Education*, Weekly Bulletin (October 18, 2007).

3. The 2000 U.S. Census report detailed that the U.S. population was 281,421,906 people. Of that, 194,552,774 (69.1%) were white; 33,947,837 (12.1%) were black; and 35,305,818 (12.5%) were of Latino/a origin. Additionally, 2,068,883 (0.7%) were Native American, and 10,123,169 (3.8 %) were Asian.

4. E. Bonilla-Silva, *Racism Without Racists: Color Blind Racism and the Persistence of Racial Inequality in the United States* (New York: Rowman and Littlefield, 2003), 9; M. T. Hannan and J. Freeman, *Organizational Ecology* (Cambridge, MA: Harvard University Press, 1989): 57.

5. "Proposition 209" was a 1996 California ballot proposition which amended the state constitution to prohibit public institutions from "discriminating" on the basis of race, sex, or ethnicity. Proposition 209 was voted into law on November 5, 1996, with just 54 percent of the vote and the similar proposition "MCRI" was voted into law with just 58 percent of the vote on November 7, 2006.

6. *Gratz v. Bollinger* (2003) was a United States Supreme Court case regarding the University of Michigan undergraduate affirmative action admissions policy. In a 6-3 decision announced on June 3, 2003, the Supreme Court ruled the university's point system was too mechanistic and therefore unconstitutional. *Meredith v. Jefferson County Board of Education* (2007) was a United States Supreme Court case regarding "racial quotas" and explicit racial desegregation in public education. The U.S. Supreme Court handed down its opinion on June 28, 2007 that rejected the use of a student's race in student assignment plans. This latter decision will effectively overturn the historic decision of *Brown v. Board of Education of Topeka* (1954) that overturned the earlier rulings of *Plessy v. Ferguson* (1896), by declaring that state laws that established separate public schools for black and white students denied black children equal educational

opportunities. Handed down on May 17, 1954, the Warren Court's unanimous (9–0) decision stated, "separate educational facilities are inherently unequal." As a result, de jure racial segregation was ruled a violation of the Equal Protection Clause of the Fourteenth Amendment. However, while the decision of *Brown* was widely viewed as a progressive victory for human and civil rights, it was not instituted or enforced on a structured or regular basis and de facto racial segregation in many of the nation's schools remained largely unaltered or worsened.

7. See: H. L. Horowitz, *Campus Life: Undergraduate Cultures from the End of the Eighteenth Century to the Present* (New York: Alfred A. Knopf, 1987).

8. For discussions on the use of "multiculturalism" for the antithetical creation of social and cultural boundaries of distinction and exclusion, see B. Bryson. "Anything but Heavy Metal: Symbolic Exclusion and Musical Dislikes." *American Sociological Review* 61, no. 5 (1996): 881–96.

9. For accounts of racism in higher education, see J. C. Dalton, ed., *Racism on Campus: Confronting Racial Bias Through Peer Interventions* New Directions for Student Services 56. (San Francisco: Jossey-Bass, 1991); J. Helms, *Black and White Racial Identity: Theory, Research and Practice* (Westport, CT: Greenwood Press, 1990); R. A. Siggelkow, "Racism in Higher Education: A Permanent Condition?" *NASPA Journal* 28, no. 2 (1991): 98–104.

10. Dalton, "Racism on Campus," 3.

11. J. R. Morris, "Racial Attitudes of Undergraduates in Greek Housing," *College Student Journal* 25 (1991): 501–5.

12. A. W. Astin, *Four Critical Years: Effects of College on Beliefs, Attitudes and Knowledge* (San Francisco: Jossey-Bass, 1977), and D. Wilder, A. Hoyt, B. Surbeck, J. Wilder, and P. Carney, "Greek Affiliation and Attitude Change in College Students," *Journal of College Student Personnel* 27 (1986): 510–19.

13. C. D. Thompson, "Factors that Influence Minority Student Participation in Predominately White Fraternities and Sororities" (Ph.D. diss., Northern Arizona University, 2000), 23.

14. S. Schmitz and S. A. Forbes, "Choices in a No-Choice System: Motives and Biases in Sorority Segregation," *Journal of College Student Development* 35 (March 1994): 107.

15. M. Lamont and V. Molnar, "The Study of Boundaries Across the Social Sciences," *Annual Review of Sociology* 28 (2002): 187.

16. F. Barth, *Ethnic Groups and Boundaries: The Social Organization of Culture Difference* (Boston: Little, Brown, 1969), 15.

17. M. T. Hannan and J. Freeman, *Organizational Ecology* (Cambridge, MA: Harvard University Press, 1989), 57.

18. Bryson, "Anything but Heavy Metal," 892.

19. R. Alba, "Bright vs. Blurred Boundaries: Second-Generation Assimilation and Exclusion in France, Germany, and the United States," *Ethnic and Racial Studies* 28, no. 1 (2005): 20–49.

20. W. M. Kimbrough, *Black Greek 101: The Culture, Customs, and Challenges of Black Fraternities and Sororities*, (Madison, NJ: Fairleigh Dickinson University Press, 2003).

21. M. L. Bankhead, "A Qualitative Exploration of White Women in Historically Black Sororities at Predominately White Institutions in the Midwest" (master's thesis, Eastern Illinois University, 2003).

22. E. Wen-Chu Chen, "The Continuing Significance of Race: A Case Study of Asian American Women in White, Asian American, and African American Sororities" (Ph.D. diss., University of California, Los Angeles, 1998).

23. E. Matthews, "'I'm Still an African American but with a Similar but Different

Story to Tell.' The Racial Identity Development of African American Males Who Join Historically Caucasian Fraternities" (master's thesis, Smith College School of Social Work, 2005).

24. Thompson, "Factors that Influence Minority Student."

25. M. W. Hughey, "Black, White, Greek . . . Like Who? Howard University Student Perceptions of a White Fraternity on Campus," *Educational Foundations* 20, no. 1–2 (Winter–Spring 2006): 9–35.

26. M. W. Hughey, "'I Did It For The Brotherhood': Non-Blacks Members of Historically Black Greek-Lettered Organizations," in *Black Greek Letter Organizations in the Twenty-First Century: Our Fight Has Just Begun*, ed. G. S. Parks (Lexington: University Press of Kentucky, 2008), 313–43.

27. M. W. Hughey, "''Cuz I'm Young and I'm Black and My Hat's Real Low?': A Critique of Black Greeks as 'Educated Gangs,'" in *Black Greek Letter Organizations in the Twenty-First Century: Our Fight Has Just Begun*, ed. G. S. Parks (Lexington: University Press of Kentucky, 2008), 385–417.

28. M. W. Hughey, "Virtual (Br)others and (Re)sisters: Authentic Black Fraternity and Sorority Identity on the Internet," *Journal of Contemporary Ethnography* 37, no. 4 (forthcoming 2008).

29. M. W. Hughey, "Crossing the Sands, Crossing the Color-Line: Non-Black members of Historically Black Greek Organizations," *Journal of African American Studies* 11 no. 2 (2007): 55–75.

30. J. H. Daniel, "A Study of Black Sororities at a University with Marginal Integration," *Journal of Non-White Concerns in Personal Guidance* 4 (1976): 191–201; A. R. O'Reilly, "The Impact of Membership in Black Greek-letter Organizations on the Identity Development of Black Students on Predominantly White Residential Campuses." (PhD diss., Ohio University, 1990); J. Rice-Mason, "An Assessment of Black Fraternities' and Sororities' goals On Predominantly White Campuses" (PhD diss., Southern Illinois University at Carbondale, 1989); M. Tyler, "Role Expectations for Black and White Greeks at a Predominantly White Institution," (PhD diss., University of Missouri–Columbia, 1990).

31. W. E. Sedlacek, "Black Students on White Campuses: 20 Years of Research," *Journal of College Student Personnel* 28 (1987): 519–23; E. G. Whipple, J. L. Baier, and D. Grady, "A Comparison of Black and White Greeks at a Predominately White University," *NASPA Journal* 28, no. 2 (1991): 140–148; R. B. Winstong Jr., W. R. Nettles III, and J. H. Opper, Jr., *Fraternities and Sororities on the Contemporary College Campus*, New Directions for Student Services 40 (San Francisco: Jossey-Bass, 1987).

32. B. Barol, C. Camper, C. Pigott, R. Nodalsky, and M. Sarris, "Why White and Black Students Choose to Segregate," *Newsweek on Campus* (March 1985); D. M. Bourassa, "How White Students and Students of Color Organize and Interact on Campus," in *Racism on Campus*, ed. J. C. Dalton 13–24, New Directions for Student Services 56 (San Francisco: Jossey-Bass, 1991).

33. Alfred Lee McClung, *Fraternities Without Brotherhood* (Boston: Beacon Press, 1955), ix.

34. R. Plotkin, "A Brief History of Racial and Ethnic Discrimination in Greek-Letter Organizations," *Alternative Orange* 2, no. 6 (1993): 9.

35. Lee, *Fraternities Without Brotherhood*, 21–22.

36. C. W. McKee, "Understanding the Diversity of the Greek World," in *Fraternities and Sororities on the Contemporary College Campus*, ed. R. B. Winston, Jr., W.B. Nettles, III, and J. H. Opper, Jr., (San Francisco: Jossey-Bass, 1987), 27.

37. "Autonomy Urged for Fraternities," *New York Times*, November 29, 1952.

38. "State University Bars Student Bias," *New York Times*, October 9, 1953.

39. "Dartmouth Tells 4 Fraternities to End Discrimination by Fall," *New York Times*, April 17, 1960.
40. "3 Penn Fraternities Must End Race Bars," *New York Times*, May 27, 1960.
41. C. Kerr, "A Statement of University Policy," *California Monthly* 19 (1964): 19.
42. S. Lim, *A Feeling of Belonging: Asian American Women's Popular Culture, 1930–1960* (New York: New York University Press, 2005).
43. Lee, *Fraternities Without Brotherhood*, 19.
44. Plotkin, "A Brief History . . . of Discrimination," 11.
45. E. Lott, *Love and Thef: Blackface Minstrelsy and the American Working Class* (New York: Oxford University Press, 1993): 25.
46. E. V. Guloyan, "An Examination of White and Non-White Attitudes of University Freshman as They Relate to Attrition," *College Student Journal* 20 (1986): 396–402 and C. M. Loo and G. Rolinson, "Alienation of Ethnic Minority Students at a Predominately White University," *Journal of Higher Education* 57 (1986): 58–77.
47. J. Smyth, "Developing and Sustaining Critical Reflection in Teacher Education," *Journal of Teacher Education* 40, no. 2 (1989): 2–9.
48. J. Fleming, *Blacks in College: A Comparative Study of Students' Success in Black and White Institutions* (San Francisco: Jossey-Bass, 1984), 204.
49. "The Sister Who Spoke Up," *Atlanta Journal-Constitution*, February 10, 2002.
50. Plotkin, "A Brief History . . . of Discrimination," 7.
51. Bonilla-Silva, *Racism Without Racists.*
52. Plotkin, "A Brief History . . . of Discrimination," 7.
53. "Michigan to Bar Bias on Campus," *New York Times*, March 9, 1951.
54. "B.U. Fraternity Chapter is Suspended by National for Initiating Negro," *Boston Daily Globe*, May 6, 1953, 1.
55. Plotkin, "A Brief History . . . of Discrimination," 11.
56. "Fraternity Refuses A Negro," *New York Times*, May 4, 1961.
57. "Fraternity at Yale Shuns Racial Plea," *New York Times*, October 27, 1961.
58. "Fraternity at Duke Acts to Accept Negro Members," *New York Times*, October 7, 1962.
59. See Meader Amendment (1964) Congressional Record, Vol. 110, part 2, Washington, DC: 2291–96.
60. T.C. Huston, "Congress, Federal Aid to Education, and Fraternity Discrimination," *Shield of Phi Kappa Psi*, 89 (Summer 1969): 253–62.
61. "Fraternity Chapter at Yale Accepts Its First Negro," *New York Times*, March 5, 1965.
62. "Stanford Sigma Chi Quits National Unit On Race Bias Issue," *New York Times*, November 11, 1966.
63. "Carolina College Fraternity Pledges Its First Negro," *New York Times*, February 17, 1967.
64. "Negro Students Seize Colgate Fraternity House," *New York Times*, April 8, 1968.
65. "A Back Man and a White Fraternity," *Washington Post*, March 11, 1973.
66. E. Wright, *Torn Togas* (Minneapolis, MN: Fairview Press, 1996), 162.
67. "Black Fraternities Thrive, Often on Adversity," *New York Times*, October 2, 1989.
68. Ibid.
69. T. Wise, "I Can Explain . . .: Racism and the Culture of Denial," *Louisiana Weekly*, November 26, 1994.
70. "The Sister Who Spoke Up," *Atlanta Journal-Constitution*, February 10, 2002.
71. Ibid.

72. B. Gose, "U of Alabama Studies Why Its Fraternities and Sororities Remain Segregated by Race," *Chronicle of Higher Education*, December 5, 1997. Accessed at http://chronicle.com/che-data/articles.dir/art-44.dir/issue-15.dir/15a00101.htm.

73. J. Dash, "Raging Against 'The Machine,'" *Salon*, March 19, 1999.

74. L R. Stains, "Black Like Me," *Rolling Stone*, March 24, 1994, 70.

75. Gose, "U of Alabama Studies."

76. "The University of Alabama: Where Racial Segregation Remains a Way of Life," *Journal of Blacks in Higher Education* 32 (Summer 2001): 23.

77. Dash, "Raging Against 'The Machine.'"

78. "Alabama University Attacks Fraternity Bias," *New York Times*, September 2, 2001.

79. Dash, "Raging Against 'The Machine.'"

80. "The Continuing Segregation of Fraternities and Sororities at the University of Alabama," *Journal of Blacks in Higher Education* 33 (Autumn 2001): 69–70.

81. "Black Student Gets Bid to White Sorority at University of Alabama," *Black Issues in Higher Education* 20, no. 15 (September 11, 2003): 17.

82. "In Celebration," *Crescent*, April 15, 2004.

83. Chen, "The Continuing Significance of Race," 53.

84. Ibid, 54.

85. Ibid.

86. Wright, *Torn Togas*, 163.

87. Chen, "The Continuing Significance of Race," 54.

88. P. Bourdieu, "The Forms of Capital" in *Handbook of Theory and Research for the Sociology of Education*, ed. John G. Richardson (New York: Greenwood Press, 1986), 254.

89. Chen, "The Continuing Significance of Race," 56.

90. Wright, *Torn Togas*, 156.

91. M. Douglas, *How Institutions Think* (Syracuse, NY: Syracuse University Press, 1986).

92. Whipple, Baier, and Grady, "A Comparison of Black and White Greeks," 146.

93. A. Berkowitz and I. Padavic, "Getting a Man of Getting Ahead: A Comparison of White and Black Sororities," *Journal of Contemporary Ethnography* 27, no. 4 (1999): 530–57.

94. Whipple, Baier, and Grady, "A Comparison of Black and White Greeks."

95. See R. Binder, M. B. Schaub, W. Seiler, and T. Lake. "Greek Academic Achievement Update: Gamma Sigma Alpha and Bowling Green State University Partnership." Paper presented at the 2002 annual meeting of the Association of Fraternity Advisors (Columbus, OH, December 2002), and J. Kunjufu, *Black College Student Survival Guide* (Chicago: African American Images, 1997).

96. McKee, "Understanding the Diversity of the Greek World."

97. Stains, "Black Like Me."

98. Kimbrough, *Black Greek 101*.

99. Ibid., 38, 41–43.

100. Sociologist Anthony Giddens's "Structuration Theory" is one of his best-known ideas. At its center is a cyclical relationship between social structure and human action. For more, see A. Giddens, *The Constitution of Society* (Berkeley: University of California Press, 1984).

101. Plotkin, "A Brief History . . . of Discrimination," 12.

102. G. Myrdal, *An American Dilemma: The Negro Problem and Modern Democracy, Vol 2.* (New York: Harper Brothers Publishers, 1944), 952

103. T. Skocpol, A. Liazos, and M. Ganz, *What A Mighty Power We Can Be: African American Fraternal Groups and the Struggle for Racial Equality* (Princeton, NJ: Princeton University Press, 2006), 94.

104. Kimbrough, *Black Greek 101*, 169.

105. J. H. Mims, "Another Chapter in Theta's History," *Sphinx* 32, no. 3 (1946): 348–49.

106. "Negro Frat Admits 'White Brother,'" *Ebony* 1, no. 11 (1946): 24, 26.

107. "White Student Belongs to Negro Frat at K.U.," *Lawrence Daily Journal-World*, October 24, 1953

108. "Negro Joins Fraternity," and "Admits White Student," *New York Times*, March 25, 1949 and April 12, 1949.

109. Phi Beta Sigma Fraternity, Inc. "Brother Dr. Georg Iggers, the Man Who Helped Bring Down the Berlin wall." Accessed October 25, 2007 at: http://www.pbs1914.org/archivedspotlights/georgiggers1220041.asp

110. "Negro Clubs Told to Enroll Whites," *New York Times*, December 28, 1959.

111. Stains, "Black Like Me," 70–71.

112. "Whites in Black Sororities and Fraternities," *Ebony* (December 2000): 173.

113. Ibid., 174.

114. Stains, "Black Like Me," 72.

115. As a nonblack, specifically white, member of the BGLO Phi Beta Sigma Fraternity, Inc., my experiences also support most of the research on this topic. For the twelve years of which I have been a member of my BGLO, the harshest challenges have come from other whites. Whether this means that whites possess more negative attitudes about my racial boundary crossing, or that they feel simply more or a right to overtly confront me about my BGLO membership, calls for more qualitative inquiries on the subject.

116. Ebony, "Whites in Black Sororities and Fraternities," 174.

117. L. C. Ross, Jr., *The Divine Nine: The History of African American Fraternities and Sororities* (New York: Dafina Books, 2002).

118. Ebony, "Whites in Black Sororities and Fraternities," 176.

119. K. Rainhold, "First African-American Fraternity Celebrates 100," *Cornell Daily Sun*, November 21, 2005. Available at http://www.cornellsun.com/vnews/display.v/ART/2005/11/21/438172c976e2c.

120. L. Goodwin, "Fraternity with Racist Past Comes to Howard," *Hilltop*, February 17, 2006.

121. J. B. Winston, "Greek Responds to Pi Kappa Alpha's Arrival at Howard," *Hilltop*, February 21, 2006.

122. S. E. Mickens, "In Defense of Howard Pikes," *Hilltop*, February 23, 2006.

123. The "brown paper bag test" was (and some argue still is) a ritual practiced by certain African American sororities and fraternities who discriminate[d] against people who were "too Black." Organizations would deny membership to anyone whose skin tone was darker than a brown paper bag. Spike Lee's film *School Daze* (1988) satirizes this practice. This is also recognized as a form of "colorism," or black-on-black racism, based on skin tone, exemplified in terms such as "high yellow" or "blue vein." There is an implicit racist ideology behind this belief that makes the goodness of the individual inversely related to the darkness of his/her skin. "Classism" can be defined by a form of prejudice or oppression against people who are in, or who are perceived as being like those who are in, a lower social class (especially in the form of lower or higher socioeconomic status) within a class-stratified society. It is similar to social elitism.

124. A. M. Johnson, "The Problem with Pike," *Hilltop*, February 22, 2006.

125. See Hughey, "Black, White, Greek . . . Like Who?" In particular, this work notes the heterogeneity of black student responses to a white fraternity at Howard University.

126. A. Burkdoll, "Greek Differences: Black, White," *Alligator On-Line*, University of Florida, October 7, 1996.

127. S. Martinez, "The Pulse," *Providence Journal*, November 19, 1998.

128. Chen, "The Continuing Significance of Race," 106.

129. M. Matsuda, *Where is Your Body? And Other Essays on Race, Gender and the Law* (Boston, MA: Beacon Press, 1996), 150.

130. See G. Firebaugh and K. Davis, "Trends in Antiblack Prejudice, 1972–1984: Region and Cohort Effects," *American Journal of Sociology* 94 (1988): 251–72; S. Lipset, *American Exceptionalism* (New York: Norton, 1996); and P. Sniderman and E. Carmines, *Reaching Beyond Race* (Cambridge, MA: Harvard University Press, 1993).

131. See H. Schuman, C. Steeh, L. Bobo, and M. Krysan, *Racial Attitudes in America: Trends and Interpretations* (Cambridge, MA: Harvard University Press, 1997).

132. See D. Roediger, *Towards the Abolition of Whiteness* (London: Verso, 1994); L. Bobo and J. Kluegel, "Opposition to Race-targeting: Self-interest, Stratification Ideology, or Prejudice?" *American Sociological Review* 58 (1993): 443–64; G. Lipsitz, "The Possessive Investment in Whiteness," *American Quarterly* 47, no. 3 (1995): 369–86; R. Dyer, *White* (New York: Routledge, 1997); and J. Sidanius, P. Singh, J. Hetts, and C. Federico, "It's Not Affirmative Action: It's the Blacks," in *Racialized Politics: The Debate about Racism in America*, ed. D. Sears, J. Sidanius, and L. Bobo (Chicago: University of Chicago Press, 2000).

133. See D. Sears and D. Kinder, "Racial Tensions and Voting in Los Angeles," in *Los Angeles: Viability and Prospects for Metropolitan Leadership*, ed. W. Hirsch (New York: Praeger, 1996); D. Kinder and L. Sanders, *Divided by Color: Racial Politics and Democratic Ideals* (Chicago: University of Chicago Press, 1971).

134. Giddens, *The Constitution of Society*.

135. Thompson, "Factors that Influence Minority Student Participation," 77.

136. A. Hacker, *Two Nations: Black and White, Separate, Hostile, Unequal* (New York: Macmillan Publishing, 1992), 19.

137. R. M. Kanter, *Men and Women of the Corporation* (New York: Basic Books, 1977).

138. See S. Prillerman, H. Myers, and B. Smedley, "Stress, Well-being, and Academic Achievement in College," in *Black Students*, ed. G. L. Berry & J. K. Asamen (Newbury Park, CA: Sage, 1989), 198–215; B. D. Smedley, H. F. Myers, and S. P. Harrell, "Minority-status Stresses and the College Adjustment of Ethnic Minority Freshmen," *Journal of Higher Education* 64, no. 4 (1993): 434–52.

Appendix
National College Fraternities and Sororities

Organization	F/S	Place of Origin	Date	Affiliation
Phi Kappa Beta	F	William and Mary	1776	Traditional
Kappa Alpha	F*	North Carolina	1812	T
*No Longer Active				
FIRST WAVE (1824–74)				
Chi Phi Society	F*	Princeton	1824	Traditional
Kappa Alpha Society	F	Union (NY)	1825	T
Delta Phi	F	Union	1827	T
Sigma Phi Society	F	Union	1827	T
Alpha Delta Phi	F	Hamilton (NY)	1832	T
Psi Upsilon	F	Union	1833	T
Delta Upsilon	F	Williams (MA)	1834	Nonsecret
Mystic Seven	F*	Wesleyan (GA)	1837	Traditional
Beta Theta Pi	F	Miami (OH)	1839	T
Chi Psi	F	Union	1841	T
Delta Kappa Epsilon	F	Yale	1844	T
Alpha Sigma Phi	F	Yale	1845	T
Delta Kappa	F*	Yale	1845	T
Delta Psi	F	Columbia	1847	T
Zeta Psi	F	New York University	1847	T
Theta Delta Chi	F	Union	1847	T
Phi Delta Theta	F	Miami (OH)	1848	T
Phi Gamma Delta	F	Wash & Jefferson (PA)	1848	T
Rainbow (W.W.W.)	F*	Mississippi	1848	T
Phi Kappa Sigma	F	Pennsylvania	1850	T
Alpha Delta Pi	S	Wesleyan (GA)	1851	T
Phi Kappa Psi	F	Wash & Jefferson (PA)	1852	T
Phi Mu	S	Wesleyan (GA)	1852	T
Pi Rho Phi	F*	Westminister (PA)	1854	T
Epsilon Alpha	F*	Virginia	1855	T
Sigma Chi	F	Miami (OH)	1855	T
Theta Chi	F	Norwich (VT)	1856	T
Sigma Alpha Epsilon	F	Alabama	1856	T

Organization	F/S	Place of Origin	Date	Affiliation
Phi Sigma	F*	Lombard (IL)	1857	Traditional
Chi Phi	F	North Carolina	1858	T
Delta Tau Delta	F	Bethany (WV)	1858	T
Alpha Kappa Phi	F*	Centre (KY)	1858	T
Phi Mu Omicron	F*	South Carolina	1858	T
Sigma Delta Pi	F*	Dartmouth	1858	T
Sigma Alpha	F*	Roanoke (VA)	1859	T
Order Chi Phi	F	Hobart (NY)	1860	T
Delta Epsilon	F*	Roanoke (VA)	1862	T
Kappa Phi Lambda	F*	Wash & Jefferson (PA)	1862	T
Upsilon Beta	F*	Gettysburg (PA)	1863	T
Theta Xi (Engineer)	F	Rensselaer Poly (NY)	1864	T
Alpha Tau Omega	F	Virginia Military Inst.	1865	T
Kappa Alpha Order	F	Wash & Jefferson (PA)	1865	T
Pi Beta Phi	S	Monmouth (IL)	1867	T
Alpha Gamma	F*	Cumberland (TN)	1867	T
Kappa Sigma Kappa	F*	Virginia Military Inst.	1867	T
Pi Kappa Alpha	F	Virginia	1868	T
Sigma Nu	F	Virginia Military Inst.	1869	T
Kappa Sigma	F	Virginia	1869	T
Zeta Phi	F*	Missouri	1870	T
Kappa Kappa Gamma	S	Monmouth (IL)	1870	T
Phi Kappa Alpha	F*	Brown (RI)	1870	T
Theta Nu Epsilon	F*	Wesleyan (CT)	1870	T
Kappa Alpha Theta	S	DePauw (IN)	1870	T
Alpha Sigma Chi	F*	Rutgers	1871	T
Alpha Phi	S	Syracuse	1872	T
Delta Gamma	S	Lewis School (MS)	1873	T
Phi Sigma Kappa	F	Massachusetts	1873	T
Gamma Phi Beta	S	Syracuse	1874	T
Phi Delta Kappa	F*	Wash & Jefferson (PA)	1874	T
Sigma Kappa	S	Colby (ME)	1874	T
SECOND WAVE (1885–1928)				
Psi Theta Psi	F*	Washington & Lee (VA)	1885	Traditional
Alpha Chi Omega	S	DePauw (IN)	1885	T
Delta Delta Delta	S	Boston University	1888	T
Beta Sigma Omicron	S*	Missouri	1888	T
Phi Kappa (Sigma)	F*	Brown (RI)	1889	Religious
Delta Chi	F	Cornell	1890	Traditional
Alpha Xi Delta	S	Lombard (IL)	1893	T
Phi Phi Phi	F*	Austin (TX)	1894	T
Pi Kappa Sigma	S*	Eastern Michigan	1894	T
Alpha Chi Rho	F	Trinity (CT)	1895	Religious

Organization	F/S	Place of Origin	Date	Affiliation
Pi Lambda Phi	F	Yale	1895	Nonsectarian
Mu Pi Lambda	F*	Washington & Lee (VA)	1895	Traditional
Chi Omega	S	Arkansas	1895	T
Delta Sigma	S*	Brown (RI)	1896	T
Kappa Delta (Educational)	S	Longwood (VA)	1897	T
Sigma Pi	F	Vincennes (IN)	1897	T
Alpha Omicron Pi	S	Barnard (NY)	1897	T
Sigma Sigma Sigma (Educational)	S	Longwood (VA)	1898	T
Zeta Tau Alpha	S	Longwood (VA)	1898	T
Delta Sigma Phi	F	City U. of New York	1899	Nonsectarian
Alpha Sigma Tau (Educational)	S	Eastern Michigan	1899	Traditional
Tau Kappa Epsilon	F	Illinois Wesleyan	1899	T
Kappa Delta Phi	F	Bridgewater State (VA)	1900	T
Sigma Phi Epsilon	F	Richmond	1901	T
Alpha Sigma Alpha (Educational)	S	Longwood (VA)	1901	T
Omega Pi Alpha	F*	City U. of New York	1901	Interracial
Beta Kappa	F*	Hamline (MN)	1901	Traditional
Delta Zeta	S	Miami (OH)	1902	T
Zeta Beta Tau	F	City U. of New York	1903	Jewish
Nat. Federation Common Clubs	F*	Wesleyan (CT)	1903	Traditional
Iota Alpha Pi	S*	Hunter (NY)	1903	Jewish
Pi Kappa Phi	S	Coll. of Charleston (SC)	1904	Traditional
Sigma Iota	F*	Louisiana State	1904	Hispanic
Phi Eta	F*	Pennsylvania	1904	Traditional
Phi Epsilon Pi	F*	City U. of New York	1904	Nonsectarian
Acacia (Masons)	F	Michigan	1904	Fraternal Order
Alpha Kappa Psi	S*	St. Mary's (NC)	1904	Traditional
Alpha Gamma Delta	S	Syracuse	1904	T
Farmhouse (Agriculture)	F	Missouri	1905	T
Kappa Delta Rho	F	Middlebury (VT)	1905	Nonsectarian
Phi Kappa Tau	F	Miami (OH)	1906	Traditional
Alpha Phi Alpha	F	Cornell	1906	Black
Triangle (Engineer)	F	Illinois	1907	Traditional
Alpha Kappa Alpha	S	Howard (DC)	1908	Black
Sigma Phi Sigma	F*	Pennsylvania	1908	Traditional
Alpha Gamma Rho (Agriculture)	F	Ohio State	1908	T
Theta Alpha	F*	Syracuse	1909	T
Phi Sigma Delta	F*	Columbia	1909	Jewish
Lambda Chi Alpha	F	Boston University	1909	Traditional

Organization	F/S	Place of Origin	Date	Affiliation
Beta Phi Alpha	S*	Cal-Berkeley	1909	Traditional
Sigma Alpha Mu	F	City U. of New York	1909	Jewish
Alpha Epsilon Phi	S	Barnard (NY)	1909	J
Beta Sigma Rho	F*	Cornell	1910	J
Phi Omega Pi	S*	Nebraska	1910	Traditional
Tau Epsilon Phi	F	Columbia	1910	Jewish
Phi Sigma Epsilon (Educational)	F*	Emporia State (KS)	1910	Traditional
Tau Delta Phi	F	City U. of New York	1910	Jewish
Beta Phi	F*	University of Chicago	1911	Traditional
Kappa Alpha Psi	F	Indiana	1911	Black
Kappa Nu	F*	Rochester	1911	Jewish
Omega Psi Phi	F	Howard (DC)	1911	Black
Theta Phi Alpha	S	Michigan	1912	Religious
Omicron Alpha Tau	F*	Cornell	1912	Jewish
Phi Beta Delta	F*	Columbia	1912	Nonsectarian
Delta Sigma Theta	S	Howard (DC)	1913	Black
Alpha Epsilon Pi	F	New York University	1913	Jewish
Phi Sigma Sigma	S	Hunter (NY)	1913	Nonsectarian
Theta Gamma	F	SUNY-Canton	1913	Traditional
Phi Alpha	F*	George Washington (DC)	1914	Jewish
Phi Beta Sigma	F	Howard (DC)	1914	Black
Sigma Omega Psi	F*	City U. of New York	1914	Jewish
Alpha Phi Delta	F	Syracuse	1914	Nonsectarian
Alpha Mu Sigma	F*	Cooper Union (NY)	1914	Jewish
Theta Upsilon	S*	Cal-Berkeley	1914	Traditional
Delta Sigma Epsilon	S*	Miami (OH)	1914	T
Alpha Kappa Lambda	F	Cal-Berkeley	1914	Religious
Pi Nu Epsilon	S	SUNY-Canton	1914	Traditional
Sigma Lambda Pi	F*	New York University	1915	Nonsectarian
Phi Phi Phi	F*	Northwestern	1915	Traditional
Rho Psi	F*	Cornell	1916	Asian American
Beta Phi Theta	F*	Wisconsin-Milwaukee	1917	Traditional
Sigma Delta Tau	S	Cornell	1917	Jewish
Square/Compass	F*	Washington & Lee (VA)	1917	Fraternal Order
Delta Phi Epsilon	S	New York University	1917	Jewish
Commons Club	F*	Denison (OH)	1917	Traditional
Kappa Beta Gamma	S	Marquette	1917	Religious
Sigma Tau Phi	F*	Pennsylvania	1918	Jewish
Phi Mu Delta	F	Connecticut	1918	Nonsectarian
Theta Kappa Phi	F*	Lehigh (PA)	1919	Religious
Alpha Delta Theta	S*	Transylvania (KY)	1919	Traditional
Delta Alpha Pi	F*	Ohio Wesleyan	1919	T
Alpha Lambda Tau	F*	Oglethorpe (OH)	1920	T

Organization	F/S	Place of Origin	Date	Affiliation
Delta Kappa	F*	SUNY-Buffalo	1920	Traditional
Tau Alpha Omega	F*	New York University	1920	Jewish
Sigma Sigma Omicron	S	New York University	1920	Traditional
Sigma Tau Gamma	F	Central Missouri	1920	T
Phi Lambda Theta	F*	Penn State	1920	Fraternal Order
Alpha Delta Alpha	F*	Coe (IA)	1920	Traditional
Zeta Phi Beta	S	Howard (DC)	1920	Black
Chi Tau	F*	Duke	1920	Traditional
Delta Phi Kappa	F	Utah	1920	Religious
Delta Sigma Lambda	F*	Cal-Berkeley	1921	Fraternal Order
Alpha Kappa Pi	F*	New Jersey Tech	1921	Traditional
Theta Sigma Upsilon	S*	Emporia State (KS)	1921	T
Pi Lambda Sigma	S*	Boston University	1921	Religious
Sigma Delta Rho	F*	Miami (OH)	1921	Traditional
Sigma Mu Sigma	F*	Tri-State (IN)	1921	Fraternal Order
Phi Lambda Alpha	F*	New York City	1921	Hispanic
Alpha Gamma Upsilon	F*	Anthony Wayne Inst.	1922	Traditional
Sigma Gamma Rho	S	Butler (IN)	1922	Black
Lambda Omega	S*	Cal-Berkeley	1923	Traditional
Alpha Gamma Sigma	F	Missouri	1923	T
Theta Upsilon Omega	F*	Bucknell (PA)	1923	T
Theta Kappa Nu	F*	Drury (MO)	1924	Traditional
Alpha Delta Gamma	F	Loyola-Chicago	1924	Religious
Beta Psi	F*	Illinois	1924	Traditional
Phi Lambda Chi (Educational)	F	Central Arkansas	1925	T
Beta Sigma Psi	F	Illinois	1925	Religious
Alpha Delta Chi	S	UCLA	1925	R
Pi Delta Theta	S*	Miami (OH)	1926	Traditional
Pi Alpha Phi	F	Cal-Berkeley	1926	Asian American
Alpha Gamma Omega	F	UCLA	1927	Religious
Sigma Phi Beta	S*	New York University	1928	Traditional
Trianon	S	U. of Cincinnati	1928	T
Interim				
Sigma Omicron Pi	S	San Francisco State	1930	Inactive-1946
		Cal-Berkeley (re-est)	1988	Asian American
Phi Iota Alpha	F (merger)	Rensselaer Poly (NY)	1931	Hispanic
Gamma Tau	F*	Howard (DC)	1934	Black
Zeta Sigma	F*	Fairmont State (WV)	1935	Traditional
Sigma Theta Epsilon	F	Merger	1941	Religious
Sigma Beta Kappa	F	St. Bernard's (AL)	1943	R
Beta Sigma Tau	F*	Roosevelt (IL)	1948	Intercultural

Organization	F/S	Place of Origin	Date	Affiliation
Sigma Phi Omega	S	USC	1949	Asian American
Phi Sigma Beta	S	NY-Pace	1951	Traditional
Phi Kappa Theta	F	Ohio State (merger)	1958	T
Groove Phi Groove	F	Morgan State (MD)	1962	Black
Iota Phi Theta	F	Morgan State (MD)	1963	B
Phi Eta Psi	F	Mott CC (MI)	1965	B
Sigma Beta Chi	F	Northern Michigan	1965	Traditional
Beta Omega Phi	F	USC	1965	Asian American
Sigma Gamma Chi	F	Salt Lake City	1967	Religious
Lambda Delta Sigma	S	Salt Lake City	1967	R
Delta Psi	Coed	Fraternity went Coed	60s	Traditional
Swing Phi Swing	S	Winston-Salem (NC)	1969	Black
THIRD WAVE (1975–99)				
Lambda Theta Phi	F	Kean (NJ)	1975	Latino
Lambda Theta Alpha	S	Kean (NJ)	1975	Latina
Phi Delta Psi	F	Western Michigan	1977	Af American
Malik Sigma Psi	F	C.W. Post (NY)	1977	Af Am
Phi Beta Chi	S	Illinois	1978	Religious
Lambda Sigma Upsilon	F	Rutgers	1979	Latino
Sigma Phi Rho	F	Wagner (NY)	1979	Af American
Chi Upsilon Sigma	S	Rutgers-N Brunswick	1980	Latina
Lambda Phi Epsilon	F	UCLA	1981	Asian American
Mu Sigma Upsilon	S	Rutgers	1981	Multicultural
Lambda Upsilon Lambda	F	Cornell	1982	Latino
Phi Sigma Rho	S	Purdue	1984	Technology
Delta Phi Upsilon	F	Tallahassee, FL	1985	Alternative
Lambda Alpha Upsilon	F	SUNY-Buffalo	1985	Latino
Alpha Psi Lambda	Coed	Ohio State	1985	L
Delta Omega Epsilon	F	Staten Island	1985	Traditional/Mult
Beta Upsilon Chi	F	Texas	1985	Religious
Beta Phi Pi	F	Western Illinois	1986	Af American
Epsilon Sigma Rho	F	Cal State-Sacramento	1986	Multicultural
Phi Omicron Psi	F	Virginia Commonwealth	1986	Af American
Sigma Lambda Beta	F	Iowa	1986	Latino
Lambda Sigma Gamma	S	Cal State-Sacramento	1986	Multicultural
Lambda Theta Nu	S	Cal State-Chico	1986	Latina
Delphic of Gamma Sigma Tau	F	SUNY-New Paltz	1986	Multicultural
Delta Lambda Phi	F	Washington DC	1987	Alternative
Gamma Zeta Alpha	F	Cal State-Chico	1987	Latino
Omega Delta Phi	F	Texas Tech	1987	L
Chi Alpha Omega	Coed	East Carolina	1987	Religious
Kappa Delta Chi	S	Texas Tech	1987	Latina

Organization	F/S	Place of Origin	Date	Affiliation
Sigma Lambda Upsilon	S	SUNY-Binghamton	1987	Latina
Mu Epsilon Theta	S	Texas	1987	Religious
Phi Sigma Phi	F	Indiana (broke away)	1988	Traditional
Alpha Nu Omega	S	Morgan State (MD)	1988	Af Am:Religious
Gamma Phi Delta	F	Texas	1988	Af Am:Rel
Nu Alpha Kappa	F	Cal-Poly SLO	1988	Latino
Lambda Delta Omega	S	UCLA	1988	Alternative
Lambda Delta Lambda	S	Cal-Berkely	1988	A
Lambda Tau Omega	S	Montclair State (NJ)	1988	Multicultural
Lambda Phi Delta	S	SUNY-Buffalo	1988	Latina
Lambda Pi Chi	S	Cornell	1988	L
Omega Phi Chi	S	Rutgers	1988	Multicultural
Sigma Phi Lambda	S	Texas	1988	Religious
Gamma Omega Delta	F	Brooklyn College	1989	Multicultural
Alpha Kappa Delta Phi	S	Cal-Berkeley	1989	Asian American
Chi Delta Theta	S	Cal-Santa Barbara	1989	Asian American
Omega Phi Beta	S	SUNY-Albany	1989	Latina
Kappa Zeta Phi	S	Cal State-LA	1989	Asian American
Phi Gamma Theta	S	Cal State-Chico	1990	Multicultural
Sigma Iota Alpha	S	SUNY-Albany	1990	Latina
Zeta Sigma Chi	S	Northern Illinois	1990	Multicultural
Alpha Lambda Omega	S	Texas	1990	Af Am:Religious
Psi Sigma Phi	F	Montclair State (NJ)	1990	Multicultural
Sigma Lambda Gamma	S	Iowa	1990	Latina
Alpha Pi Sigma	S	San Diego State	1990	L
Sigma Omega Phi	S	Cal State-Chico	1990	Multicultural
Eta Omega Tau	S	NYC-Pace	1990	Multicultural
Zeta Phi Zeta	F	Eastern Illinois	1990	Af Am:Religious
Theta Delta Beta	F	Cal-Irvine	1990	Asian American
Zeta Chi Epsilon	F	San Francisco State	1991	AA
Rho Delta Chi	S	Cal-Riverside	1991	AA
Gamma Phi Omega	S	Indiana	1991	Latina
Phi Alpha Psi	S	Virginia Commonwealth	1991	Af American
Sigma Theta Psi	S	San Jose State	1991	Multicultural
Delta Phi Mu	S	Purdue	1991	Latina
Lambda Pi Upsilon	S	SUNY-Geneseo	1992	L
Sigma Delta Alpha	F	San Jose State	1992	Latino
Sigma Alpha Zeta	S	Cal State-Fresno	1992	Multicultural
Alpha Delta Phi Society	Coed	Chapters broke away	1992	
Gamma Phi Sigma	F	Temple	1992	Latino
Psi Chi Omega	F	Cal-San Diego	1992	Asian American
Delta Phi Beta	F	Cal-Berkeley	1992	AA
Tau Phi Sigma	F	Illinois	1992	Multicultural
Delta Psi Epsilon	S	Oakwood (AL)	1992	Af Am:Religious

Organization	F/S	Place of Origin	Date	Affiliation
Alpha Gamma Psi	S	Michigan	1993	Af American
Phi Lambda Rho	S	Cal State-Stanislaus	1993	Latina
Kappa Upsilon Chi	F	Texas Tech	1993	Religious
Pi Psi	F	Michigan State	1993	Af American
Alpha Rho Lambda	S	Yale	1993	Latina
Gamma Alpha Omega	S	Arizona State	1993	L
Chi Sigma Upsilon	S	New Jersey City Univ.	1993	Multicultural
Upsilon Kappa Delta	S	Cal State-Chico	1993	M
Sigma Psi Zeta	S	SUNY-Albany	1994	Asian American
Chi Delta Beta	F	Cal State-Stanislasus	1994	Multicultural
Iota Nu Delta	F	SUNY-Binghamton	1994	Asian American
Phi Rho Eta	F	Southern Illinois	1994	Af American
Nu Alpha Phi	F	SUNY-Albany	1994	Asian American
Pi Delta Psi	F	SUNY-Binghamton	1994	AA
Alpha Phi Gamma	S	Cal Poly-Pomona	1994	AA
Pi Lambda Chi	S	Colorado	1994	Latina
Delta Xi Phi	S	Illinois	1994	Multicultural
Alpha Pi Omega	S	North Carolina	1994	Native American
Gamma Eta	S	Florida	1995	Latina
Chi Rho Omicron	F	Cal State-Fresno	1995	Asian American
Zeta Phi Rho	F	Cal State-Long Beach	1995	AA
Iota Psi Phi	S	Cal State-Fresno	1995	Multicultural
Kappa Phi Lambda	S	SUNY-Binghamton	1995	Asian American
Omega Phi Gamma	F	Texas	1995	AA
Sigma Delta Lambda	S	Southwest Texas State	1996	Latina
Gamma Phi Eta	F	Georgia Southern	1996	Af American
Sigma Iota Sigma	S	SUNY-Buffalo	1996	Multicultural
Sigma Omega Nu	S	Cal Poly-SLO	1996	Latina
Phi Sigma Chi	F	NYC Tech	1996	Multicultural
Sigma Beta Rho	F	Pennsylvania	1996	Asian American
Zeta Phi Zeta	S	Eastern Illinois	1996	Af Am:Religious
Delta Sigma Chi	S	City U. New York	1996	Multicultural
Lambda Fe Uson	S	SUNY-Stony Brook	1996	Multicultural
Epsilon Chi Nu	F	NC State/E. Carolina	1996	Native American
Alpha Kappa Omega	F	Cal State-Hayward	1996	Asian American
Kappa Psi Epsilon	S	Cal State-Long Beach	1996	Asian American
Phi Sigma Nu	F	North Carolina	1996	Native American
Beta Gamma Nu	F	USC	1997	Multicultural
Omega Delta	F	Illinois	1997	M
Alpha Sigma Omega	S	Syracuse	1997	Latina
Lambda Psi Delta	S	Yale	1997	Multicultural
Theta Nu Xi	S	North Carolina	1997	M
Sigma Delta Phi Epsilon	F	SUNY-Buffalo	1997	Multicultural
Sigma Omicron Epsilon	S	East Carolina	1997	Asian American

Organization	F/S	Place of Origin	Date	Affiliation
Xi Kappa	F	Georgia	1997	Asian American
Alpha Sigma Rho	S	Georgia	1997	AA
Delta Phi Lambda	S	Georgia	1998	AA
Sigma Alpha Phi	S	San Jose State	1998	Native American
Delta Psi Alpha	Coed	Northern Illinois	1998	Latino
Kappa Phi Gamma	S	Texas	1998	Asian American
Delta Epsilon Psi	F	Texas	1998	AA
Delta Gamma Pi	S	Towson State (MD)	1998	Multicultural
Delta Phi Omega	S	Houston	1998	Asian American
Sigma Sigma Rho	S	St. John's (NY)	1998	AA
Alpha Beta Sigma	S	SUNY-Buffalo	1998	Latina
Alpha Lambda Tau	F	Indianapolis	1999	Alternative
Beta Chi Theta	F	UCLA	1999	Asian American
Beta Kappa Gamma	F	Texas	1999	AA
Sigma Lambda Kappa	S	Parsons (NY)	1999	AA
Gamma Mu Phi	F	Richmond, VA	1999	Alternative
INTERIM				
Alpha Psi Rho	F	San Diego State	2000	Asian American
Delta Sigma Iota	F	Penn State	2000	AA
Beta Phi Omega	S	Tallahassee, Florida	2000	Alternative
Alpha Epsilon Omega	F	Cal State-Northridge	2000	Armenian
Mu Omicron Gamma	F	Old Dominion	2001	Af Am:Religious
Zeta Phi Zeta	Coed	Merger	2001	Af Am: Rel
Kappa Psi Kappa	S	Tallahassee, Florida	2001	Alternative
Phi Nu Kappa	F	Tallahassee, Florida	2001	A
Zeta Chi Phi	S	Texas-San Antonio	2003	Multicultural
Kappa Xi Omega	S	Tampa, Florida	2004	Alternative
Sigma Nu Omega	S	Detroit, Michigan	2004	A

Bibliography

Books and Book Chapters

Adam, Barry D. *The Rise of a Gay and Lesbian Movement.* Boston: Twayne, 1987.

Adams, John P., ed. *The Lifetime Responsibility of Brotherhood.* Sigma Phi Epsilon Fraternity, 2000.

Anson, Jack L., and Robert F. Marchesani Jr., eds. *Baird's Manual of College Fraternities.* 20th ed. Indianapolis, IN: Baird's Manual Foundation, 1991.

Appel, Dr. Theodore Burton. *The Chronicles of Chi Phi: 1824–1976.* Atlanta, GA: Chi Phi Educational Trust, 1993.

Astin, Alexander W. *Four Critical Years: Effects of College on Beliefs, Attitudes and Knowledge.* San Francisco: Jossey-Bass, 1977.

Baily, Howard J., ed. *Baird's Manual of American College Fraternities.* Menasha, WI: George Banta Publishing, 1949.

Baird, William. *Baird's Manual of College Fraternities.* William Baird, 1879.

Bank, Barbara J. *Contradictions in Women's Education: Traditionalism, Careerism and Community at a Single-Sex College.* With Harriet M. Yelon. New York: Teachers College Press, 2003.

Banks, James A. "The Canon Debate, Knowledge Construction and Multicultural Education." In *Revisioning Curriculum in Higher Education,* edited by Clifton F. Conrad and Jennifer Grant Haworth, 271–87. Needham Heights, MA: Simon & Schuster Custom Publishing, 1995. Originally published as James A. Banks, "The Canon Debate, Knowledge Construction and Multicultural Education," *Educational Researcher* 22, no. 5 (1993).

———. *Cultural Diversity and Education: Foundations, Curriculum, and Teaching.* 4th ed. Boston: Allyn and Bacon, 2001.

Barrett, F., et al. "Social Construction and Appreciative Inquiry: A Journey in Organization Theory." In *Management and Organization: Relational Alternatives to Individualism,* edited by D. Hosking et al. Aldershot, UK: Avebury Press 1995.

Barth, Frederik. *Ethnic Groups and Boundaries: The Social Organization of Culture Difference.* Boston: Little, Brown, 1969.

Belton, Don, ed. *Speak My Name: Black Men on Masculinity and the American Dream.* Boston: Beacon Press, 1995.

Benitez, Margarita. "Hispanic-serving Institutions: Challenges and Opportunities." In *Minority-serving institutions: Distinct purposes, Common Goals,* edited by J. P. Merisotis and C. T. O'Brien, 57–68. New Directions for Higher Education 102. San Francisco: Jossey-Bass, 1998.

Bennett, William J. "To Reclaim a Legacy: A Report on the Humanities in Higher Education." In *Revisioning Curriculum in Higher Education,* edited by Clifton F. Conrad and Jennifer Grant Haworth, 205–19. Needham Heights, MA: Simon & Schuster Custom Publishing, 1995. Originally published in William J. Bennett, *To Reclaim a Legacy: A Report on the Humanities in Higher Education.* Washington, DC: National Endowment of the Humanities, 1984.

Blachford, Gregg Blachford. "Male Dominance and the Gay World." In *The Making of the Modern Homosexual,* edited by Kenneth Plummer, 184–210. Totowa, NJ: Barnes & Noble, 1981.

Bonilla-Silva, Eduardo. *Racism Without Racists: Color-Blind Racism and the Persistence of Racial Inequality in the United States.* New York: Rowman & Littlefield.

Bourassa, Donna M. "How White Students and Students of Color Organize and Interact on Campus." In *Racism on Campus: Confronting Racial Bias Though Peer Interventions,* edited by J. C. Dalton, 13–24. New Directions for Student Services 56. San Francisco: Jossey-Bass, 1991.

Bourdieu, Pierre. "The Forms of Capital." In *Handbook of Theory and Research for the Sociology of Education,* edited by John G. Richardson. New York: Greenwood Press, 1986.

Brown, Tamara, et al. *African American Fraternities and Sororities: The Legacy and the Vision.* Lexington: University of Kentucky Press, 2005.

Brubacher, John S., and Willis Rudy. *Higher Education in Transition: An American History, 1636–1976.* 4th ed. New Brunswick, NJ: Transaction Publishers, 1997.

Candidate Education Manual. Alpha Delta Gamma Educational Foundation, 1997.

Carby, Hazel. *Race Men.* Cambridge, MA: Harvard University Press, 1999.

Carey, James W. *Communication as Culture: Essays on Media and Society.* New York: Routledge, 1992.

Chan, Jachinson. "Asian American Interest Fraternities: Competing Masculinities at Play." In *Asian Pacific American Genders and Sexualities,* edited by Thomas K. Nakayama, 65–73. Tempe, AZ: Arizona State University, 1999.

Chan, Sucheng. *Asian Americans: An Interpretive History.* Boston: Twayne Publishers, 1991.

Chilman, C. S. "Hispanic families in the United States." In *Family Ethnicity: Strength in Diversity,* edited by H. P. McAdoo, 141–63. Newbury Park, CA: Sage, 1993.

Clawson, Mary Ann. *Constructing Brotherhood: Class, Gender, and Fraternalism.* Princeton, NJ: Princeton University Press, 1989.

Clemens, Elisabeth S. *The People's Lobby: Organizational Innovation and the Rise of Interest Group Politics in the United States, 1890–1925.* Chicago: University of Chicago Press, 1997.

Collett, Ritter. *In the Bond: Phi Delta Theta at 150.* Dayton, OH: Landfall Press, 1998.

Collins, Patricia Hill. *Black Feminist Thought: Knowledge, Consciousness, and the Politics of Empowerment.* New York: Routledge Press, 1991.

Connell, R. W. *Gender and Power: Society, the Person and Sexual Politics.* Stanford, CA: Stanford University Press, 1987.

Cruz, Melany Dela, and Pauline Agbayani-Siewert, "Filipinos: Swimming with and against the Tide." In *The New Face of Asian Pacific America: Numbers, Diversity & Change in the 21st Century,* edited by Eric Lai and Dennis Arguelles, 45–50. San Francisco: Asian Week and UCLA's Asian American Studies Center Press, 2003.

Current, Richard Nelson. *Phi Beta Kappa in American Life: The First Two Hundred Years.* New York: Oxford University Press, 1990.

Dalton, Jon C. "Racism on Campus: Confronting Racial Bias Through Peer Interventions." In *Racism on Campus: Confronting Racial Bias Though Peer Interventions*, edited by J. C. Dalton, 39–52. New Directions for Student Services, 56. San Francisco: Jossey-Bass, 1991.

DeJong, David H. *Promises of the Past.* Golden, CO: North American Press, 1993.

Delta Lambda Phi. Chapter Handbook. No Date.

Douglas, Mary. *How Institutions Think.* Syracuse, NY: Syracuse University Press, 1986.

D'Souza, Dinesh. "The Victim's Revolution of Campus." In *Revisioning Curriculum in Higher Education*, edited by Clifton F. Conrad and Jennifer Grant Haworth, 231–44. Needham Heights, MA: Simon & Schuster Custom Publishing, 1995. Originally published in Dinesh D'Souza, *Illiberal Education: The Politics of Race and Sex on Campus.* New York: Free Press, 1991.

Du Bois, W. E. B. *Souls of Black Folk.* New York: Mass Market Publishers, 1995.

DuCille, Ann. "The Occult of True Black Womanhood." In *Skin Trade.* Cambridge, MA: Harvard University Press, 1996.

Dyer, Richard. *White.* New York: Routledge, 1997.

Escoffier, Jeffrey. *American Homo: Community and Perversity.* Berkeley: University of California Press, 1998.

Espino, M. *Joining a Council or Creating Your Own: A Guide to Working with Other Chapters on Campus.* La Mensajera, 2003.

Espiritu, Yen Le. *Asian American Panethnicity: Bridging Institutions and Identities.* Philadelphia: Temple University Press, 1992.

Fahey, David. *Black Lodge in White America.* Lanham, MD: University Press of America, 1994.

Fleming, Jacqueline. *Blacks in College: A Comparative Study of Students' Success in Black and White Institutions.* San Francisco: Jossey-Bass, 1984.

Frazier, Edward Franklin. *Black Bourgeoisie: The Rise of a New Middle Class.* New York: Free Press, 1965.

Giddens, Anthony. *The Constitution of Society.* Berkeley: University of California Press, 1984.

Giddings, Paula. *In Search for Sisterhood: Delta Sigma Theta and the Challenge of the Black Sorority Movement.* New York: William and Morrow, 1988.

———. *When and Where I Enter: The Impact of Black Women on Race and Sex in America.* New York: William and Morrow, 1984.

Giroux, Henry. "Decentering the Canon: Refiguring Disciplinary and Pedagogical Boundaries." In *Revisioning Curriculum in Higher Education*, edited by Clifton F. Conrad and Jennifer Grant Haworth, 255–70. Needham Heights, MA: Simon & Schuster Custom Publishing, 1995. Originally published in Henry Giroux, *Border Crossings: Cultural Workers and the Politics of Education.* New York: Routledge, 1992.

Golden, Thelma, ed., *Black Male: Representations of Black Masculinity in Contemporary American Art.* Whitney Museum of Art, 1994.

Graham, Otis. *Our Kind of People: Inside America's Upper Middle Class.* New York: Harper Collins, 1999.

Gregory, Dennis E., and Associates. *The Administration of Fraternal Organizations on North American Campuses: A Pattern for the New Millennium.* Asheville, NC: College Administration Publications, 2003.

Guerrero, Andres G. "A Brief History of Chicanos." In *A Chicano Theology*. New York: Orbis, 1993.

Hacker, Andrew. *Two Nations. Black and White, Separate, Hostile, Unequal.* New York: Macmillan Publishing Company, 1992.

Hall, Stuart. "New Ethnicities." In *Critical Dialogues in Cultural Studies: The Stuart Hall Reader*, edited by Kuan Hsing Chen and David Morley. London: Routledge 1996.

Hamamoto, Darrell Y. "The Joy Fuck Club: Prolegomenon to an Asian American Porno Practice." In *Countervisions: Asian American Film Criticism*, edited by Darrell Y. Hamamoto and Sandra Liu. Philadelphia: Temple University Press, 2000.

Handlin, Oscar, and Mary. *The American College and American Culture.* New York: McGraw-Hill, 1970.

Hannan, Michael T., and John Freeman. *Organizational Ecology.* Cambridge, MA: Harvard University Press, 1989.

Harding, Vincent. "Religion and Resistance Among Antebellum Negroes, 1800–1860." In *The Making of Black America*, edited by August Meier and Elliott M. Rudwick. New York: Scribner, 1969.

Hastings, William. *Phi Beta Kappa as A Secret Society.* Washington, DC: United Chapters of Phi Beta Kappa, 1965.

Hatch, James V. "Theatre in Historically Black Colleges: A Survey of 100 Years." In *A Source Book of African American Performance: Plays, People, Movements*, edited by Marie Bean. New York: Routledge Press, 1999.

Helms, Janet E. *Black and White Racial Identity: Theory, Research and Practice.* Westport, CT: Greenwood Press, 1990.

Herdt, Gilbert. "Coming Out as a Rite of Passage: A Chicago Study." In *Gay Culture in America*, edited by Gilbert Herdt, 29–67. Boston: Beacon Press, 1992.

Higginbotham, Evelyn Brooks. *Righteous Discontent: The Women's Movement in the Black Baptist Church, 1880–1920.* Cambridge, MA: Harvard University Press, 1993.

Hine, Darlene Clark, and Kathleen Thompson. *A Shining Thread of Hope: The History of Black Women in America.* New York: Broadway Books, 1998.

Hing, Bill Ong. *Making and Remaking Asian America through Immigration Policy, 1850–1990.* Stanford, CA: Stanford University Press, 1993.

The History of Alpha Delta Gamma, 1924 to 1995. 2nd ed. Alpha Delta Gamma Educational Foundation, 1995.

Hochschild, Arlie Russell. *Managed Heart: Commercialization of Human Feeling.* Berkeley: University of California Press, 1984.

Hofstadter, Richard, and Wilson Smith, eds. *American Higher Education: A Documentary History.* Vol. 2. Chicago: University of Chicago Press, 1961.

Holland, Dorothy C., and Margaret A. Eisenhart. *Educated for Romance: Women, Achievement, and College Culture.* Chicago: University of Chicago Press, 1990.

hooks, bell. *Feminist Theory: From Margin to Center.* Boston: South End Press, 1991.

———. *Where We Stand, Class Matters.* New York: Routledge 2000.

———. *Ain't I a Woman: Black Women and Feminism.* Boston: South End Press, 1981.

Horowitz, Helen Lefkowitz. *Campus Life: Undergraduate Cultures from the End of the Eighteenth Century to the Present.* Chicago: University of Chicago Press, 1988.

Hughey, Matthew W. "'Cuz I'm Young and I'm Black and My Hat's Real Low?': A Critique of Black Greeks as 'Educated Gangs.'" In *Black Greek Letter Organizations in the Twenty- First Century: Our Fight Has Just Begun*, edited by Gregory S. Parks. Lexington: University Press of Kentucky, 2008.

———. "'I Did It For The Brotherhood': Non-Blacks Members of Historically Black Greek-Lettered Organizations." In *Black Greek Letter Organizations in the Twenty-First Century: Our Fight Has Just Begun*, edited by Gregory S. Parks. Lexington: University Press of Kentucky, 2008.

Hull, Gloria, et al. *All the Women Are White, All the Blacks Are Men, But Some of Us Are Brave*. Old Westbury, NY: Feminist Press, 1982.

Hune, Shirley, and Kenyon S. Chan. "Special Focus: Asian Pacific American Demographic and Educational Trends." In *Minorities in Higher Education, 15th Annual Status Report*, edited by Deborah Carter and Reginald Wilson, 39–67 and 103–7. Washington, DC: American Council on Education, 1997.

Jackson, Leon. "The Rights of Man and the Rites of Youth: Fraternity and Riot at Eighteenth-Century Harvard." In *The American College in the Nineteenth Century*, edited by Roger Geiger, 46–79. Nashville, TN: Vanderbilt University Press, 2000.

Johnson, Clyde. *Fraternities in Our Colleges*. New York: National Interfraternity Foundation, 1972.

Jones, Ricky L. *Black Haze: Violence, Sacrifice, and Manhood in Black Greek-Letter Fraternities*. Albany: State University of New York Press, 2004.

Kanter, Rosabeth M. *Men and Women of the Corporation*. New York: Basic Books, 1977.

Kappa Alpha Psi Fraternity Incorporated, San Jose Alumni Chapter Handbook. San Jose, CA: Kappa Alpha Psi Fraternity Alumni Chapter.

Kelly, Robin. *Race Rebels: Culture, Politics, and the Black Working Class*. New York: Free Press, 1996.

Kibria, Nazli. *Becoming Asian American: Second-Generation Chinese and Korean American Identities*. Baltimore: John Hopkins University Press, 2002.

Kimbrough, Walter M. *Black Greek 101: The Culture, Customs, and Challenges of Black Fraternities and Sororities*. Madison, NJ: Farleigh Dickinson University Press, 2003.

Kimmel, Michael S. "Masculinity as Homophobia: Fear, Shame and Silence in the Construction of Gender Identity." In *Theorizing Masculinities*, edited by Harry Brod and Michael Kaufman, 119–41. Thousand Oaks, CA: Sage, 1994.

Kinder Donald R., and Lynn M. Sanders. *Divided by Color: Racial Politics and Democratic Ideals*. Chicago: University of Chicago Press, 1996.

Kunjufu, Jawanza. *Black College Student Survival Guide*. Chicago: African American Annual Images, 1977.

Lerner, Gerda, ed. *Black Women in White America: A Documented History*. New York: Vintage Books, 1972.

Levine, David O. *The American College and the Culture of Aspiration, 1915–1940*. Ithaca, NY: Cornell University Press, 1986.

Levine, Martin P. *Gay Macho*. New York: New York University Press, 1998.

Lim, Shirley. *A Feeling of Belonging: Asian American Women's Popular Culture, 1930–1960*. New York: New York University Press, 2005.

Lipset, Seymour M. *American Exceptionalism*. New York: Norton, 1996.

Lott, Eric. *Love and Theft: Blackface Minstrelsy and the American Working Class*. New York: Oxford University Press, 1993.

MacDonald, Victoria M., and Teresa García, "Historical Perspectives on Latino Access to Higher Education: 1848–1990." In *The Majority in the Minority: Expanding the Rep-*

resentation of Latina/o Faculty, Administrators, and Students in Higher Education, edited by Jeanette Castellanos and Lee Jones, 15–43. Sterling, VA: Stylus. 2003.

Majors, Richard, and Jacob Gordon, eds. *The American Black Male*. Chicago: Nelson Hall Publishers, 1994.

Malone, Jacqui. *Steppin' on the Blues: The Visible Rhythms of African Dance*. Chicago: University of Illinois Press, 1994.

Matsuda, Mari J. *Where is Your Body? And Other Essays on Race, Gender and the Law*. Boston: Beacon Press, 1996.

McClung, Alfred Lee. *Fraternities Without Brotherhood: A Campus Report on Racial and Religious Prejudice*. Boston: Beacon Press, 1955.

McKee, C. William. "Understanding the Diversity of the Greek World." In *Fraternities and Sororities on the Contemporary College Campus*, edited by R. B. Winston, Jr., W. B. Nettles III, and J. H. Opper, Jr., 21–35. San Francisco: Jossey-Bass, 1987.

McWilliams, Wilson C. *The Idea of Fraternity in America*. Berkeley: University of California Press, 1973.

Meirer, August, and Elliott Rudwick, eds. *The Making of Black America*. New York: Athenaeum, 1969.

Mercer, Kobena. *Welcome to the Jungle: New Positions in Black Cultural Studies*. New York: Routledge, 1994.

Montague, Ashley. *Man's Most Dangerous Myth: The Fallacy of Race*. New York: Columbia University Press, 1942.

Munoz, Carlos, Jr. *Youth, Identity, Power: The Chicano Movement*. London: Verso, 1989.

Musgrave, Wayne. *College Fraternities*. New York: Interfraternity Conference, 1923.

Myrdal, Gunnar. *An American Dilemma: The Negro Problem and Modern Democracy, Vol 2*. New York: Harper Brothers Publishers, 1944.

Nardi, Peter M. "Sex, Friendship, and Gender Roles among Gay Men." In *Men's Friendships*, edited by Peter M. Nardi, 173–85. Newbury Park, CA: Sage, 1992.

Newitz, Annalee, and Matt Wray. *White Trash: Race and Class in America*. New York: Routledge, 1997.

Nuwer, Hank. *Broken Pledges: The Deadly Rite of Hazing*. Atlanta: Longstreet Press, 1990.

———. *Wrongs of Passage: Fraternities, Sororities, Hazing, and Binge Drinking*. Bloomington: Indiana University Press 1999.

Osumi, Dick. "Asians and California's Anti-Miscegenation Laws." In *Asian and Pacific American Experiences*, edited by Nobuya Tsuchida, 1–37. Minneapolis: Asian/Pacific American Learning Resources Center, University of Minnesota, 1982.

Parker, Marjorie. *Alpha Kappa Alpha through the Years*. Chicago: Mobium, 1988.

Pascarella, Ernest T., and Patrick T. Terenzini. *How College Affects Students*. Vol. 2. San Francisco: Jossey-Bass, 2005.

Pena, Jesus. *The History of Lambda Theta Phi Latin Fraternity, Incorporated*. New York: Vantage Press, 1994.

Peterson, Richard A. *Creating Country Music: Fabricating Authenticity*. Chicago: University of Chicago Press, 1997.

Polletta, Francesca. *Freedom Is an Endless Meeting: Democracy in American Social Movements*. Chicago: University of Chicago Press, 2002.

Prillerman, Shelly L., Hector F. Myers, and Brian D. Smedley. "Stress, Well-being, and Academic Achievement in College." In *Black Students*, edited by G. L. Berry and J. K. Asamen, 198–215. Newbury Park, CA: Sage, 1989.

Ramirez, R. R., and P. de la Cruz. *The Hispanic Population in the United States: March 2002.* Current Population Reports, P20–545. Washington, DC: U.S. Census Bureau, 2002.

Rao, K. V. "Instant Identity: The Emergence of Asian Indian America." In *The New Face of Asian Pacific America: Numbers, Diversity & Change in the 21st Century*, edited by Eric Lai and Dennis Arguelles, 51–56. San Francisco: Asian Week and UCLA's Asian American Studies Center Press, 2003.

Reel, Jerome Jr. *The Oak: A History of Pi Kappa Alpha.* Memphis, TN: Pi Kappa Alpha Fraternity, 1980.

Renn, Kristen A. *Mixed Race Students in College: The Ecology of Race, Identity, and Community on Campus.* Albany: State University of New York Press, 2004.

Rhoads, Robert A. *Freedom's Web: Student Activism in an Age of Cultural Diversity.* Baltimore: Johns Hopkins University Press, 1998.

Riorden, B. G., and R. Q. Dana. "Greek Letter Organizations and Alcohol: Problems, Policies and Programs." In *New Challenges for Greek Letter Organizations: Transforming Fraternities & Sororities into Learning Communities*, edited by W. G. Whipple, 49–59. San Francisco: Jossey-Bass, 1998.

Robson, John. *Baird's Manual of American College Fraternities.* 19th ed. Menash, WI: Baird's Manual Foundation, Inc., 1977.

———. *The College Fraternity and Its Modern Role.* Menasha, WI., George Banta Company, 1966.

———, ed. *Educating for Brotherhood: Guidelines to the Meaning of Fraternity.* Richmond, VA: Sigma Phi Epsilon Fraternity, 1965.

Roebuck, Julian, and Komunduri Morty. *Historically Black Colleges and Universities: Their Place in American Higher Education.* New York: Greenwood, 1993.

Roediger, David. *Towards the Abolition of Whiteness.* London: Verso, 1994.

Rooks, Noliwe M. *Hair-Raising: Beauty, Culture, and African American Women.* New Brunswick, NJ: Rutgers University Press, 1996.

Ross, Lawrence C., Jr. *The Divine Nine: The History of African American Fraternities and Sororities.* New York: Dafina Books, 2002.

Rudolph, Frederick. *The American College and University.* New York: Alfred Knopf, 1962.

Russell, Kathy, et al. *The Color Complex: The Politics of Skin Color among African Americans.* New York: Harcourt, Brace, Jovanovich, 1992.

Said, Edward. *Orientalism.* New York: Vintage Books, 1979.

Sandy, Peggy Reeves. *Fraternity Gang Rape: Sex Brotherhood, and Privilege on Campus.* New York: New York University Press, 1990.

Santiago, Rorber. *Boricuas: Influential Puerto Rican Writings—An anthology.* New York: Ballantine, 1995.

Sanua, Marianne Rachel. *Going Greek: Jewish College Fraternities in the US, 1895–1945.* Detroit: Wayne State University Press, 2003.

Schuman, H., C. Steeh, L. Bobo, and M. Krysan. *Racial Attitudes in America: Trends and Interpretations.* Cambridge, MA: Harvard University Press, 1997.

Scott, William S. *Values and Organizations.* With the Collaboration of Ruth Scott. Chicago: Rand McNally, 1965.

Sears, David, and Donald Kinder. "Racial Tensions and Voting in Los Angeles." In *Los Angeles: Viability and Prospects for Metropolitan Leadership*, edited by W. Hirsch. New York: Praeger, 1971.

Sheldon, Henry. *Student Life and Customs.* New York: D. Appleton, 1901.

Shepardson, Francis, ed., *Baird's Manual of American College Fraternities.* 12th ed. Menasha, WI: George Banta, 1930.

Shonrock, M. D. "Standards and Expectations for Greek Letter Organizations." In *New Challenges for Greek Letter Organizations: Transforming Fraternities & Sororities into Learning Communities*, edited by W. G. Whipple, 79–85. San Francisco: Jossey-Bass, 1998.

Sidanius, Jim, Pamela Singh, John J. Hetts, and Christopher M. Federico. "It's Not Affirmative Action: It's the Blacks." In *Racialized Politics: The Debate about Racism in America*, edited by D. Sears, J. Sidanius, and L. Bobo. Chicago: University of Chicago Press, 2000.

Sigma Pi Manual. Sigma Pi Fraternity, International, 2000.

Singh, Jane. "South Asians: New Communities and New Challenges." In *The New Face of Asian Pacific America: Numbers, Diversity & Change in the 21st Century*, edited by Eric Lai and Dennis Arguelles, 105–12. San Francisco: Asian Week and UCLA's Asian American Studies Center Press, 2003.

Skocpol, Theda, Ariane Liazos, and Marshall Ganz. *What A Mighty Power We Can Be: African American Fraternal Groups and the Struggle for Racial Equality.* Princeton, NJ: Princeton University Press, 2006.

Sleeter, Christine E. *Multicultural Education as Social Activism.* Albany: State University of New York Press, 1996.

Sniderman, Philip, and Edward Carmines. *Reaching Beyond Race.* Cambridge, MA: Harvard University Press, 1993.

Stecopoulos, Harry, and Michael Uebel, eds. *Race and the Subject of Masculinities.* London: Duke University Press, 1997.

Swain, Scott. "Covert Intimacy: Closeness in Men's Friendships." In *The Gendered Society Reader*, edited by Michael S. Kimmel, 364–82. New York: Oxford University Press, 2000.

Szasz, Margaret Connell. *Education and the American Indian; The Road to Self-determination since 1928.* 3rd ed. Albuquerque: University of New Mexico Press, 1999.

Takagi, Dana. *The Retreat from Race: Asian-American Admissions and Racial Politics.* New Brunswick, NJ: Rutgers University Press, 1992.

Takaki, Ronald. *Strangers from a Different Shore: A History of Asian Americans.* New York: Penguin Books, 1989.

Thelin, John R. *A History of American Higher Education.* Baltimore: Johns Hopkins University Press, 2004.

Toll, George S. *Alpha Epsilon Pi: The First Sixty-Five Years 1912–1978.* Alpha Epsilon Pi Foundation, 1980.

Torbenson, Craig L. "The Origin and Evolution of College Fraternities and Sororities." In *African American Fraternities and Sororities: The Legacy and the Vision*, edited by Tamara L. Brown, Gregory S. Parks, and Clarenda M. Phillips. Lexington: University of Kentucky Press, 2005.

Vaid, Urvashi. *Virtual Equality: The Mainstreaming of Gay and Lesbian Liberation.* New York: Doubleday, 1995.

Vellela, Tony. *New Voices: Student Activism in the '80s and '90s.* Boston: South End Press, 1988.

Voorhees, Oscar M. *The History of Phi Beta Kappa.* New York: Crown Publishers, 1945.

Walker, Alice. *In Search of Our Mothers' Gardens.* New York: Harcourt, Brace, Jovanovich, 1983.

Wallace, Michelle. *Black Macho and the Myth of the Superwoman.* London: Verso 1978; reprint 1991.

Washington, Booker T. *Up From Slavery.* New York: Dover Publications, 1995.

Waters, Mary C. *Ethnic Options: Choosing Identities in America.* Berkeley, CA: University of California Press, 1990.

Wesley, Charles. *The History of Alpha Phi Alpha: A Development in Negro College Life.* Washington, DC: Foundation Publishers, 1948.

West, Cornel. "The New Politics of Difference." In *Social Theory: Multicultural and Classic Readings,* edited by Charles Lemert. Boulder, CO: Westview Press, 1999.

White, Debra Gray. *Too Heavy a Load: Black Women in Defense of Themselves.* New York: W.W. Norton, 1999.

Windmeyer, Shane L., and Pamela W. Freeman, eds. *Out on Fraternity Row: Personal Accounts of Being Gay in a College Fraternity.* New York: Alyson Books, 1998.

———. *Secret Sisters: Stories of Being Lesbian and Bisexual in a College Sorority.* Los Angeles: Alyson Books, 2001.

Winston, Roger B., Jr., William R. Nettles III, and John H. Opper, Jr., eds. *Fraternities and Sororities on the Contemporary College Campus.* New Directions for Student Services, 40. San Francisco: Jossey-Bass, 1987.

Woodson, Carter G. *The African Background Outlined.* Washington, DC: Association of the Study of Negro Life and History, 1936.

Work, Monore N. "Secret Societies as Factors in the Social and Economical Life of the Negro." In *Democracy in Earnest: Southern Sociological Congress, 1916–1918.* New York: Negro Universities Press, 1969.

Wright, Esther. *Torn Togas.* Minneapolis, MN: Fairview Press, 1996.

Yoo, David K. *Growing Up Nisei: Race, Generation, and Culture among Japanese Americans of California, 1924–1949.* Urbana: University of Illinois Press, 2000.

Yung, Judy. *Unbound Feet: A Social History of Chinese Women in San Francisco.* Berkeley: University of California Press, 1995.

Zablocki, Benjamin D. *Alienation and Charisma: A Study of Contemporary American Communes.* New York: Free Press, 1980.

Periodicals

"A Black Man and A White Fraternity." *Washington Post,* March 11, 1973.

Adams, Josh and Vincent J. Roscigno. "White Supremacists, Oppositional Culture and the World Wide Web." *Social Forces* 84, no. 2 (2005): 760–78.

"Admits White Student." *New York Times,* April 12, 1949.

"Alabama University Attacks Fraternity Bias." *New York Times,* September 2, 2001.

Alba, Richard. "Bright vs. Blurred Boundaries: Second-generation Assimilation and Exclusion in France, Germany, and the United States." *Ethnic and Racial Studies* 28, no. 1 (January 2005): 20–49.

Alexander, Kari. "U. Illinois Greek System Expands With New Council." *Daily Illini,* January 26, 2004.

Altamirano, Natasha. "U. Virginia Holds First 'State of the Greek System' Address." *Cavalier Daily*, October 22, 2003.

Amsler, Jennifer. "Sorority Holds Sexual Abuse Forum at U. Arizona." *Arizona Daily Wildcat*, November 18, 2004.

Baldwin, James. "Liberalism and the Negro: A Roundtable Discussion." *Commentary* 37 (March 1964).

Balenger, Victoria J., and William E. Sedlacek. "Black and White Student Differences in Volunteer Differences at a Predominately White University." *NASPA Journal* 30, no. 3 (1993): 203–8.

Barol, B., C. Camper, C. Pigott, R. Nodalsky, and M. Sarris. "Why White and Black Students Choose to Segregate." *Newsweek on Campus*, March 1985.

Barrett, F., et al. "The Central Role of Discourse in Large-Scale Change: A Social Constructionist Perspective." *Journal of Applied Behavioral Science* 31 (1995): 352–72.

Beito, David. "Black Fraternal Hospitals in the Mississippi Delta, 1942–1967." *Journal of Southern History* 56 (February 1999): 109–40.

Berkowitz, Alexandra, and Irene Padavic. "Getting a Man of Getting Ahead: A Comparison of White and Black Sororities." *Journal of Contemporary Ethnography* 27, no. 4 (1999): 530–57.

Bird, Sharon R. "Welcome to the Men's Club: Homosociality and the Maintenance of Hegemonic Masculinity." *Gender & Society* 10 (1996): 120–32.

"Black Faculty at Harvard: A Mixed Record." *Journal of Blacks in Higher Education, Weekly Bulletin*, October 18, 2007.

"Black Fraternities Thrive, Often on Adversity." *New York Times*, October 2, 1989.

"Black Student Gets Bid to White Sorority at University of Alabama." *Black Issues in Higher Education* 20, no. 15 (September 11, 2003): 17.

Blue, Alexis. "U. Arizona Students Find That 'Words Hurt.'" *Arizona Daily Wildcat*, November 14, 2003.

Bobo, Laurence, and James R. Kluegel. "Opposition to Race-targeting: Self-interest, Stratification Ideology, or Prejudice?" *American Sociological Review* 58 (1993): 443–64.

Bonifacio, Lauren. "Minority Greeks Lack Row Home." *Daily Trojan Online*, June 29, 2005, at http://www.dailytrojan.com/media/paper679/previousarchive/V150/N66/01-minor.66c.shtml.

Boswell, A. Ayres Boswell, and Joan Z. Spade. "Fraternities and Collegiate Rape Culture: Why Are Some Fraternities More Dangerous Places for Women?" *Gender & Society* 10 (1996): 133–47.

Bowen, Ezra. "New Look for Thriving Greeks." *Time*, March 10, 1986, 77.

Bryson, Bethany. "Anything but Heavy Metal: Symbolic Exclusion and Musical Dislikes." *American Sociological Review* 61, no. 5 (1996): 881–96.

"B.U. Fraternity Chapter Suspended by National for Initiating Negro." *Boston Daily Globe*, May 6, 1953.

Burgin, Aaron. "USC Struggles With Diversity." *Daily Trojan*, September 1, 2004.

Burkdoll, Amy. "Greek Differences: Black, White." *Alligator On-Line*. University of Florida, October 7, 1996.

"Carolina College Fraternity Pledges Its First Negro." *New York Times*, February 17, 1967.

Case, Douglas N. "A Glimpse of the Invisible Membership: A National Survey of Lesbigay Greek Members." *Perspectives* 22, no. 3 (April/May 1996).

"Changing World New Sororities Lead Way For UA Greek System." *Birmingham News*, May 21, 2003.

Chavez, A., F. Guido-DiBrito, and S. Mallory. "Learning to Value the 'Other': A Framework of Individual Diversity Development." *Journal of College Student Development* 44 (2003): 453–69.

Chernow, Elizabeth. "Greek Life Expands at George Washington U." *GW Hatchet*, July 8, 2003.

Chow, May. "San Jose State Frat Brawl Ends in Death of 23-Year-Old APA." *AsianWeek*, January 31–February 6, 2002, Bay and California News Story, http://asianweek.com/2003_01_31/bay_frat.html.

Cohn, Elizabeth. "A House with No Closets." *Rolling Stone* 30 (September 1993): 87–95.

"The Continuing Segregation of Fraternities and Sororities at the University of Alabama." *Journal of Blacks in Higher Education* 33 (Autumn 2001): 69–70.

Crotty, William J. "Democratic Consensual Norms and the College Student." *Sociology of Education* 40, no. 3 (Summer 1967): 200–219.

Daniel, Jessica H. "A Study of Black Sororities at a University with Marginal Integration." *Journal of Non-White Concerns in Personal Guidance* 4 (1976): 191–201.

"Dartmouth Tells 4 Fraternities to End Discrimination by Fall." *New York Times*, April 17, 1960.

Dash, Julekha. "Raging Against 'The Machine.'" *Salon*, March 19, 1999.

Denizet-Lewis, Benoit. "View Fraternity Life from the Three B-Perspective." *Contra Costa Times*, February 24, 1998.

Eichstedt, Jennifer L. "Problematic White Identities and a Search for Racial Justice." *Sociological Forum* 16, no. 3 (2001): 445–70.

Espino, Michelle. "Joining a Council or Creating Your Own." *La Mensajera* (Summer 2003): 3.

Farrell, Elizabeth. "Four Rules for Saving a Fraternity." *Chronicle of Higher Education*, December 3, 2004, A35.

Fausset, Richard. "A Frat for Misfits at Ole Miss; Cheers! A Motley Band of Foreign Students and Domestic Square Pegs Has Created Its Own Fraternity: The Awesome Dudes of Alpha Delta." *Los Angeles Times*, September 16, 2006, A1.

Firebaugh, Glenn, and Kenneth Davis. "Trends in Antiblack Prejudice, 1972–1984: Region and Cohort Effects." *American Journal of Sociology* 94 (1988): 251–72.

"Fraternities Get the Grip," *Time Magazine* 85, no. 26 (June 25, 1965).

"Fraternity at Duke Acts to Accept Negro Members." *New York Times*, October 7, 1962.

"Fraternity at Yale Shuns Racial Plea." *New York Times*, October 27, 1961.

"Fraternity Chapter Accepts Its First Negro." *New York Times*, March 5, 1965.

"Fraternity Refuses a Negro." *New York Times*, May 4, 1961.

Freeman, Marilyn, and Tina Witcher. "Stepping Into Black Power: Black Fraternities and Sororities Give Their Members Access to a Network of Influence and Power—and Good Times Too. So What's Wrong With That?" *Rolling Stone* (September 1987).

Gadson, Denita. "Greek Power! African American Greek Letter Organizations Wield Massive Influence After School Days." *Black Collegian*, 20, no. 1 (September/October 1989).

Gatlin, Eboni. "Forum Discusses Race, Civil Rights at Indiana U." *Indiana Daily Student*, January 25, 2005.

Giddings, Paula. "Sorority Sisters." *Essence* (July 1988).

Goodwin, Lawrence. "Fraternity With Racist Past Comes To Howard." *Hilltop*, February 17, 2006.

Gose, Ben. "U of Alabama Studies Why Its Fraternities and Sororities Remain Segregated by Race." *Chronicle of Higher Education*, December 5, 1997.

"Greek Life Still Segregated at the University of Alabama." *Journal of Blacks in Higher Education* 19 (October 2002): 17.

Guardia, Juan R. "Latino/a Fraternity-Sorority Ethnic Identity Development." *Hispanic Outlook in Higher Education*, September 10, 2007.

Guloyan, E. V. "An Examination of White and Non-White Attitudes of University Freshman as They Relate to Attrition." *College Student Journal* 20 (1986): 396–402.

Gumz, Jondi. "UCSD Suspends Fraternity Involved in Fight." *Sentinel*, January 25, 2003.

Harris, David R., and Jeremiah Joseph Sim. "Who Is Multiracial? Assessing the Complexity of Lived Race." *American Sociological Review* 67, no. 4 (2002): 614–27.

Harris Robert L, Jr. "Early Black Benevolent Societies, 1780–1830." *Massachusetts Review* 20 (Autumn 1979), 603–25.

Harris, Rosemary Banks. "College Love Affair for Keeps: Sorority, Fraternity Memberships Often Last a Lifetime." *St. Petersburg Times*, April 14, 1998.

HeavyRunner, Iris, and Kathy Marshall, "Miracle Survivors." *Tribal College* 14, no. 4 (2003): 14–19.

Herel, Suzanne, Matthew B. Stannard, Wyatt Buchanan, and Ryan Kim. "Fraternity Feud's Unlikely Victim: Friends Say Man Tried to End Rivalry." *San Francisco Chronicle*, January 26, 2003, http://www.sfgate.com/cgi-bin/article.cgi?file=/c/a/2003/01/26/MN231151.DTL.

Hom, Alice. "In the Mind of An/Other." *Amerasia Journal* (1991): 51–42.

hooks, bell. "Straightening Our Hair." *Z Magazine* (Summer 1988): 14.

Hughey, Matthew W. "Black, White, Greek . . . Like Who? Howard University Student Perceptions of a White Fraternity on Campus." *Educational Foundations* 20, nos. 1–2 (Winter–Spring 2006): 9–35.

———. "Brotherhood or Brothers in the 'Hood? Debunking the 'Educated Gang' Thesis as Black Fraternity and Sorority Slander." *Race, Ethnicity, and Education*, 11, no. 2 (forthcoming 2008).

———. "Crossing the Sands, Crossing the Color-Line: Non-Black Members of Historically Black Greek Organizations." *Journal of African American Studies* 11, no. 2 (2007): 55–75.

———."Virtual (Br)others and (Re)sisters: Authentic Black Fraternity and Sorority Identity on the Internet." *Journal of Contemporary Ethnography*, 37, no. 4 (forthcoming 2008).

Hune, Shirley. "Demographic and Diversity of Asian American College Students." *New Directions for Student Services: Working with Asian American College Students* 97 (2002): 13.

Hurtado, Sylvia. "The Campus Racial Climate: Contexts for Conflict." *Journal of Higher Education* 63, no. 5 (1992): 539–69.

———. "The Institutional Climate for Talented Latino students." *Research in Higher Education* 35, no. 1 (1994): 21–41.

Hurtado, Sylvia, Jeffrey F. Milem, Alma R. Clayton-Pederson, and Walter R. Allen. "Enhancing Campus Climates for Racial/Ethnic Diversity Through Educational Policy and Practice." *Review of Higher Education* 21, no. 3 (1998): 279–302.

Huston, T. C. "Congress, Federal Aid to Education, and Fraternity Discrimination." *Shield of Phi Kappa Psi* 89 (Summer 1969): 253–62.

"In Celebration." *Crescent.* Official Publication of Phi Beta Sigma Fraternity, Inc. April 15, 2004.

Iwata, Edward. "Race without a Face." *San Francisco Focus,* May 1991.

Johnson, Aliciamarie M. "The Problem with Pike." *Hilltop,* February 22, 2006.

Jonsson, Patrik. "South Wrestles with Segregated Sororities." *Christian Science Monitor,* September 18, 2001, 4.

Kalof, Linda, and Timothy Cargill, "Fraternity and Sorority Membership and Gender Dominance Attitudes." *Sex Roles* 25 (1991): 417–23.

"Kappa Alpha Psi: Fraternity Founded at Indiana University Stresses Individual and Group Achievement." *Ebony* 45, no. 7 (1991).

Kenji, Jasper. "A Proud Heritage for Black Greek Groups." *San Diego Union Tribune,* February 24, 1998.

Kerr, C. "A Statement of University Policy." *California Monthly* 19 (January 1964).

Kimbrough, Walter. "The Membership Intake Movement of Historically Black Greek-letter Organization." *NASPA Journal* 34, no. 3 (1997): 229–39.

Kwon, Andres. "U. Michigan Greek Organizations Homophobic, LGBT Students Say." *Michigan Daily,* April 12, 2005.

Lamont, Michelé, and Virág Molnar. "The Study of Boundaries across the Social Sciences." *Review of Sociology* 28 (2002): 167–95.

Levine, Zach. "Sororities 'Step and Stroll' for Charities at Rutgers." *Daily Targum,* November 22, 2004.

Lipsitz, George. "The Possessive Investment in Whiteness." *American Quarterly* 47, no. 3 (September 1995): 369–86.

Loo, Chalsa M., and G. Rolinson. "Alienation of Ethnic Minority Students at a Pedominately White University." *Journal of Higher Education* 57 (1986): 58–77.

Lord, M. G. "The Greek Rites of Exclusion." *Nation,* July 4 and 11, 1987, 10–13.

Martinez, Soljane. "The Pulse." *Providence Journal,* November 19, 1998.

McWilliams, Carey. "Toward Real Fraternity." *Nation,* August 12, 1950, 144.

Mendenhall, Brittany. "Rutgers Sororities, Fraternities Show Pride to Hopefuls." *Daily Targum,* February 15, 2005.

"Michigan to Bar Bias on Campus." *New York Times,* March 9, 1951.

Mickens, S. E. "In Defense of Howard Pikes." *Hilltop,* February 23, 2006.

Mims, J. H. "Another Chapter in Theta's History." *Sphinx* 32, no. 3 (October 1946): 348–49.

Miranda, Monica L., and Martin de Figueroa. "¡Adelante Hacia El Futuro! (Forward to the future) Latino/Latina Students: Past, Present and Future." *Perspectives* (Summer 2000): 6–8.

Morris, J. R. "Racial Attitudes of Undergraduates in Greek Housing." *College Student Journal* 25 (1991): 501–5.

Mourra, Sara. "Fraternity Life Conflicts with the Image of Homosexuality at UC-Berkeley." *Daily Californian*, May 11, 2001.

"Multicultural Classes Should be Required." *Lariat* (Baylor University), November 6, 2003.

Narans, Julie. "Greeks Can Exclude: They Have That Right." *Daily Nebraskan*, October 24, 2000.

"Negro Clubs Told to Enroll Whites." *New York Times*, December 28, 1959.

"Negro Frat Admits 'White Brother.'" *Ebony* 1, no. 11 (October 1946): 24–27.

"Negro Joins Fraternity." *New York Times*, March 25, 1949.

"Negro Students Seize Colgate Fraternity House." *New York Times*, April 8, 1968.

"New Rules for Fraternities, Sororities." *USA Weekend*, January 12–14, 1990.

Nichols, Megan. "U. Alabama Multicultural Sorority Vying to Join Panhellenic." *Crimson White*, September 12, 2003.

Painter, Nell. "Black Studies, Black Professors, and the Problems of Perception." *Chronicle of Higher Education*, December 15, 2000.

"Phi Beta Sigma." *Ebony* 47, no. 5 (March 1992).

Plotkin, Robert. "A Brief History of Racial and Ethnic Discrimination in Greek-Letter Organizations." *Alternative Orange* 2, no. 6 (April 1993).

Potter, Tim. "At KU, Painful Lessons In Sensitivity." *Wichita Eagle*, October 3, 1997.

Puente, Teresa. "Special Report: Hispanics on Campus—Getting Organized." *Hispanic* (March 1992): 31–33.

"The Racially Segregated Fraternity Row at the University of Alabama." *Journal of Blacks in Higher Education* 19 (Spring 1998): 44–45.

Rainhold, Karl. "First African-American Fraternity Celebrates 100." *Cornell Daily Sun Online*, November 21, 2005, http://www.cornellsun.com/vnews/display.v/ART/2005/11/21/438172c976e2c.

Reisberg, Leo. "Ethnic and Multicultural Fraternities Are Booming on Many Campuses." *Chronicle of Higher Education*, January 7, 2000, A60.

———. "Fraternities in Decline." *Chronicle of Higher Education*, January 7, 2000, A59.

Reyes, David, and H. G. Reza. "Fraternity Held Edge at Fatal Ballgame." *Los Angeles Times*, September 1, 2005.

Rich, Adrienne. "Compulsory Heterosexuality and Lesbian Existence." *Signs* 5 (1980): 647–50.

Right, Evan. "Sister Act: Deep Inside the Secret Life of Sorority Girls at Ohio State University." *Rolling Stone*, October 14, 1999.

Rivenburg, Roy. "Asian Frat in Spotllight After Death." *Los Angeles Times*, September 7, 2005.

Roche, Timothy, and Leslie Everton Brice. "Blacks Need Not Apply." *Time*, June 11, 2000, 104.

Rodriguez, Robert. "Hermandades on Campus: Elite Latino Secret Societies and Fraternities of the Past Give Way to Toady's Brotherhoods and Sisterhoods." *Black Issues in Higher Education* 12 (1995): 26–29.

Schmidt, Alvin J., and Nicholas Babchuk. "The Unbrotherly Brotherhood: Discrimination in Fraternal Orders." *Phylon* 34, no. 3 (3rd Quarter 1973): 275–82.

Schmitz, Stephen, and Sean A. Forbes. "Choices in a No-Choice System: Motives and Biases in Sorority Segregation." *Journal of College Student Development* 35 (March 1994): 103–8.

Scott, John Finley. "The American College Sorority: Its Role in Class and Ethnic Endogamy." *American Sociological Review* 30, no. 4 (August 1965): 514–27.

Shea, Christopher. "Racist Acts Roil Nation's Campuses, Igniting Protests." *Chronicle of Higher Education*, November 25, 1992.

Sheng, Yuan. "Minority Greek Council Created at Baylor U." *Lariat*, February 24, 2004.

Sedlacek, William E. "Black Students on White Campuses: 20 Years of Research." *Journal of College Student Personnel* 28 (1987): 519–23.

Sidanius, Jim, Colette Van Laar, Shana Levin, and Stacey Sinclair. "Ethnic Enclaves and the Dynamics of Social Identity on the College Campus: The Good, the Bad, and the Ugly." *Journal of Personality and Social Psychology* 87, no. 1 (2004): 96–110.

Siggelkow, Richard A. "Racism in Higher Education: A Permanent Condition?" *NASPA Journal* 28, no. 2 (1991): 98–104.

"Sigma Gamma Rho: Motto of the Youngest Black Greek Letter Organization is Greater Service, Greater Progress." *Ebony*, 46 no. 4 (February 1991).

"The Sister Who Spoke Up." *Atlanta Journal-Constitution*, February 10, 2002.

Smedley, Brian D., Hector F. Myers, and Shelly P. Harrell. "Minority-status Stresses and the College Adjustment of Ethnic Minority Freshmen." *Journal of Higher Education* 64, no. 4 (1993): 434–52.

Smith, Jim H. "Breaking the Fraternity Color Bar: UConn Led the Way." *Journal of Blacks in Higher Education* 28 (Summer 2000): 114–15.

Smith, Laura. "The LDS Greeks: Lambda Delta Sigma and Sigma Gamma Chi." *Ensign* (September 1986): 27–31.

Smyth, John. "Developing and Sustaining Critical Reflection in Teacher Education." *Journal of Teacher Education* 40, no. 2 (1989): 2–9.

"Stanford Sigma Chi Quits National Unit On Race Bias Issue." *New York Times*, November 11, 1966.

Stains, Laurence A. "Black Like Me: What's Up With White Guys Who Join Black Frats? Are They Trying Too Hard, Or Is It Just a Class Thing?" *Rolling Stone*, March 24, 1994.

"State University Sifts Bias Issue." *New York Times*, November 29, 1962.

"Statue University Bars Student Bias." *New York Times*, October 9, 1953.

Stombler, Mindy. "'Buddies' or 'Slutties': The Collective Sexual Reputation of Fraternity Little Sisters." *Gender and Society* 8, no. 3 (September 1994): 297–323.

Stombler, Mindy, and Irene Padavic. "Sister Acts: Resisting Men's Domination in Black and White Fraternity Little Sister Programs." *Social Problems* 44 (1997): 257–75.

Stombler, Mindy, and Patricia Yancey Martin. "Bring Women In, Keeping Women Down: Fraternity 'Little Sister' Organizations." *Journal of Contemporary Ethnography* 23 (1994): 150–84.

"Studies Show Dividends of Diversity." *Academe*, November–December 1999, 13.

Thompson, Vernon. "Fraternities, Sororities from Howard: Students Draw Renewed Interest; Clubs Offer On Campus Social Life to Off Campus Commuters." *Washington Post*, November 16, 1978.

"3 Penn Fraternities Must End Race Bars." *New York Times*, May 27, 1960.

Tierney, William G., and Kidwell, Clara Sue. "The Quiet Crisis." *Change* 23, no. 2 (1991): 4–5.

Toll, George. "Colleges, Fraternities, and Assimilation." *Journal of Reform Judaism* (Summer 1985): 94–97.

"U. Florida Greeks Apologize for Mekong Delta Theme Party." *Alligator*, April 11, 2001.

"The University of Alabama: Where Racial Segregation Remains a Way of Life." *Journal of Blacks in Higher Education* 32 (Summer 2001): 22–24.

"Waging War on the Greeks." *Time*, April 16, 1990.

Wakayama, Christina. "'Sorority Life' Garners Mixed Reactions on USC Campus." *Daily Trojan*, September 30, 2003.

Weiner, Jon. "Racial Hatred on Campus." *Nation*, February 27, 1989.

Whipple, Edward G., John L. Baier and David L. Grady. "A Comparison of Black and White Greeks at a Predominately White University." *NASPA Journal* 28, no. 2 (1991): 140–48.

"White Student Belongs to Negro Frat at K.U." *Lawrence Daily Journal-World*, October 24, 1953.

"Whites in Black Sororities and Fraternities." *Ebony* (December 2000): 172–76.

Whitlock, Stephen. "The Rise of Greek Civilization." *Equal Times* (Fall 1995).

Wilder, David H., Arlyne E. Hoyt, Beth S. Surbeck, Janet C. Wilder, and Patricia I. Carney. "Greek Affiliation and Attitude Change in College Students." *Journal of College Student Personnel* 27 (1986): 510–19.

Wingett, Yvonne. "Minorities Find Connection in Ethnic Greek Organizations." *Arizona Republic*, October 31, 2004.

Winston, Jerralyn B. "Greek Responds to Pi Kappa Alpha's Arrival at Howard." *Hilltop*, February 21, 2006.

Wise, Tim. "I Can Explain . . .: Racism and the Culture of Denial." *Louisiana Weekly*, November 26, 1994.

Wood, Alex K. "First African-American Fraternity Celebrate 100." *Cornell Daily Sun Online*, November 23, 2005. http://www.cornellsun.com/vnews/display.v/ART/2005/11/21/438172c976e2c.

Woodson, Jacqueline. "Common Ground." *Essence*, 30 no. 1 (May 1999).

Wright, Bobby, and William G. Tierney. "American Indians in Higher Education." *Change*, 23, no. 2 (1991): 11–19.

Yeung, King-To, and Mindy Stombler. "Gay and Greek: The Identity Paradox of Gay Fraternities." *Social Problems* 47 (2000): 134–52.

Yeung, King-To, Mindy Stombler, and Renée Wharton. "Making Men in Gay Fraternities: Resisting and Reproducing Multiple Dimensions of Hegemonic Masculinity." *Gender & Society* 20 (2006): 5–31.

"Zeta Phi Beta: Founded at Howard University, Group Celebrates 71st Anniversary with Innovative Programs." *Ebony* 46, no. 7 (May 1991).

Zott, Stacey. "Out, Proud, Greek?" *Indiana Daily Student Supplement*, February 2, 1998.

Dissertations and Theses

Bankhead, Mary L. "A Qualitative Exploration of White Women in Historically Black Sororities at Predominately White Institutions in the Midwest." Master's thesis, Eastern Illinois University, 2003.

Bowan, Mary. "Educational Work of a National Professional Sorority of Negro College Women." Master's thesis, University of California Berkeley, 1935.

Chen, Elizabeth Wen-Chu. "The Continuing Significance of Race: A Case Study of Asian American Women in White, Asian American, and African American Sororities." PhD diss., University of California, Los Angeles, 1998.

Dickerson Charles Edward, III. "The Benevolent and Protective Order of Elks and the Improved Benevolent and Protective Order of Elks of the World." PhD diss., University of Rochester 1981.

Garcoa, Gina Ann. "The Relationship and Perceptions of Campus Climate and Social Support to Adjustment to College for Latina Sorority and Non-Sorority Members." Master's thesis, University of Maryland, College Park, 2005.

Guardia, Juan R. "Nuestra identidad y experiencias (Our identity and Experiences): Ethnic Identity Development of Latino Fraternity Members at a Hispanic-Serving Institution." PhD diss., Iowa State University, 2006.

Hernandez, J. C. "En sus voces (in their voices): Understanding the Retention of Latino/a College Students." PhD diss., University of Maryland—College Park, 1999. Abstract in *Dissertation Abstracts International*, 60A (2000): AAT 9957158.

James, Anthony Wayne. "The Defenders of Tradition: College Social Fraternities. Race, and Gender, 1945–1980." PhD diss., University of Mississippi, 1998.

Kessler, Thomas R. "The Logistic Model: A Study of the Growth of Fraternities," Master's thesis, Kent State University, 1963.

Lim, Shirley Jennifer. "Girls Just Wanna Have Fun: The Politics of Asian American Women's Public Culture, 1930–1960." PhD diss., University of California, Los Angeles, 1998.

Lou, Deborah. "We're All Sisters Here: Asian American Women's Experiences from Leftist Politics to Sorority Membership." Master's thesis, University of California, Santa Barbara, 1998.

Lourie, Stephen J. "The Historical Development of the Relationship Between the Fraternity and the University in the United States." Master's thesis, University of Missouri-Columbia, 1971.

Malone, Susan Carole. "Gender Role Attitudes and Homogamy Preferences of College Greeks." PhD diss., University of Florida, 1996.

Matthews, Erin. "'I'm Still an African American but with a Similar but Different Story to Tell.' The Racial Identity Development of African American Males Who Join Historically Caucasian Fraternities." Master's thesis, Smith College School of Social Work, 2005.

McKenzie, Andre. "Fraters: Black Greek-Letter Fraternities at Four Historically Black Colleges, 1920–1960." PhD diss., Teachers College, Columbia University, 1986.

Montrose, Marjorie A. "Sororities: Present and Potential." PhD diss., Columbia University, 1956.

Nuñez, Jennifer G. "The Empowerment of Latina University Students: A Phenomenological Study of Ethnic Identity Development through Involvement in a Latina-Based Sorority." Master's thesis, Iowa State University, 2004.

O'Conor, Andi. "The Cultural Logic of Gender in College: Heterosexism, Homophobia and Sexism in Campus Peer Groups." PhD diss., University of Colorado-Boulder, 1998.

O'Reilly, A. R. "The Impact of Membership in Black Greek-letter Organizations on the Identity Development of Black Students on Predominantly White Residential Campuses." PhD diss., Ohio University, 1990.

Park, Julie. "Melting Pot or Greek Salad: A Study of Asian American Women and Sororities at a Predominantly White Institution." Undergraduate Thesis, Vanderbilt University, 2004.

Patterson, Marcella M. "Latina Sisterhood: Does It Promote or Inhibit Campus Integration?" PhD diss., University of Southern California, 1998. Abstract in *Dissertation Abstracts International* 60 (1998): 1477.

Reyes, Gabriel Allan. "Does Participation in an Ethnic Fraternity Enable Persistence in College?" PhD diss., University of Southern California, 1997.

Rice-Mason, Jennifer. "An Assessment of Black Fraternities' and Sororities' Goals on Predominantly White Campuses." PhD diss., Southern Illinois University at Carbondale, 1989.

Robinson, Linda Kay. "The Influence of Curricular and Co-Curricular experiences on Students' Openness to Diversity at a Predominantly White, State Supported University in the South." PhD diss., Union Institute, 2000.

Tanaka, Gregory Kazou. "The Impact of Multiculturalism on White Students." PhD diss., University of California, Los Angeles, 1996.

Thompson, Carol D. "Factors that Influence Minority Student Participation in Predominately White Fraternities and Sororities." PhD diss., Northern Arizona University, 2000.

Trevino, Jesus G. "Participation in Ethnic/Racial Student Organizations." PhD diss., University of California, Los Angeles, 1992.

Tyler, Matthew. "Role Expectations for Black and White Greeks at a Predominantly White Institution." PhD diss., University of Missouri—Columbia, 1990.

Torbenson, Craig L. "College Fraternities and Sororites: A Historical Geography, 1776– 1989." PhD diss., University of Oklahoma, 1992.

Web sites

Alpha Chi Rho, http://www.alphachirho.org.

Alpha Delta Chi: The Christian Sorority, http://www.geocities.com/CollegePark/Quad/5545/links.html.

Alpha Delta Gamma, http://alphadeltagamma.org.

Alpha Delta Sigma Sorority, Inc., http://www.alphadeltasigma.org/?pg=history.

Alpha Epsilon Omega: The Armenian Fraternity, http://alpha.alphaepsilonomega.org.

Alpha Kappa Alpha, http://www.mit.edu: 8001/ activities/ akas /home2.html.

Alpha Kappa Lambda, http://www.akl.org.

Alpha Gamma Omega: Christ Centered Fraternity, http://www.ago.org.

Alpha Nu Omega Fraternity and Sorority, Inc., http://www.alphanuomega.org.

Alpha Pi Omega Sorority, Inc., http://geocities.com/alphapiomegasorority.

Alpha Psi Lambda National Inc., http://www.alpha-psi-lambda,org/.

ASPIRA Association, http://www.aspira.org/about.html.

Association of Fraternity Advisors, "Special Interest Fraternities & Sororities." http://www.fraternityadvisors.org/Links/Fraternal_Organizations/Special_Interest.asp.

Bacone College, http://www.bacone.edu/information/mission.html.

Beta Gamma Nu, Inc., http://www.betagammanu.com/.

Beta Sigma Psi: National Lutheran Fraternity, http://www.betasigmapsi.org.

Beta Sigma Epsilon, Alpha Chapter, http://clubs.asus.arizona.edu/~bse/.

Beta Upsilon Chi: Brothers Under Christ, http://www.betaupsilonchi.org.

Chi Delta Beta Fraternity, http://www.chideltabeta.com/.

Chi Sigma Upsilon Sorority, Inc., http://www.angelfire.com/nj/csu93/.

Chi Upsilon Sigma Sorority, Inc., http://www.justbecus.org.

Christian Fraternities and Sororities, http://www.greekchat.com.

"Cultural interest fraternities and sororities." *Wikipedia, The Free Encyclopedia.* http://en.wikipedia.org/wiki/Cultural_interest_fraternities_and_sororities.

Decision and Planning Support (DAPS). University of Arizona, http://daps.arizona.edu.

Delphic of Gamma Sigma Tau, http://www.delphic-gst.org/.

Delta Lambda Phi National Social Fraternity, http://www.dlp.org/national.

Delta Phi Epsilon Christian Sorority, Inc., http://www.angelfire.com/ca2/deltapsiepsilon/foundations.html.

Delta Sigma Chi Sorority, Inc., http://dsc1996.org/history.html.

Delta Sigma Phi, http://www.deltasig.org.

Delta Xi Phi Multicultural Sorority, Inc., http://www.geocities.com/%7Edeltaxiphi/.

Dundon, Stanislaus, "Religious Clubs/Fraternities on State Campuses," http://insidehighered.com/news/2006/12/29/qt.

Epsilon Chi Nu, Inc., http://www.epsilonchinu.org/.

Epsilon Sigma Rho Fraternity, Inc., http://www.epsilonsigmarho.org/.

Gamma Delta Pi, Native American Indian Sorority, http://students.ou.edu/W/Robin.S.Williams-1/homepage.html.

Fraternities, Sororities and Christian Beliefs, http://www.unc.edu/~hurt4evr/conclusions.html.

Gamma Gamma Chi Sorority: The First Islamic-based Sorority, http://gammagammachi.org.

Gamma Omega Delta Fraternity, Inc., http://www.gamma-omega-delta.org/.

Good Voice, C. Native Sisterhood, http://www.reznetnews.org/student/041203_sisterhood.

Iota Lambda Phi Fraternity, Inc., http://www.truegentlewomen.org/herstory.htm.

Iota Psi Phi, http://www.csufresno.edu/StudentOrgs/IOTAPSIPHI/.

Charles Johnson and Patricia Smith. "Beneficial and Charitable Societies." Teaching Guide for PBS documentary *Africans in America*, http://www.pbs.org/wgbh/aia/part3/3h480.html.

Kappa Upsilon Chi: Keeping Under Christ, http://www.kyx.org.

Lambda Fe Uson Sorority, Inc., http://www.sinc.sunysb.edu/Clubs/divas/.

Lambda Phi Epsilon, www.lambdaphiepsilon.com.

Lambda Pi Chi Sorority, Inc., http://www.lambdapichi.org.

Lambda Psi Delta Sorority, Inc., http://lambdapsidelta.org/.

Lambda Sigma Gamma Sorority, Inc., http://www.lambdasigmagamma.org/.

Lambda Sigma Upsilon, Inc., http://www.lsu79.org.

Lambda Tau Omega Sorority, Inc., http://www.geocities.com/CollegePark/Lab/8874/.

Lambda Theta Alpha Latin Sorority, Inc., http://www.lambdalady.org/prn-history.htm.

Lambda Theta Nu Sorority, Inc., http://lambdathetanu.org.

Latino Greek-lettered Organization—Fraternal Societies, http://www.lglo.com/modules.php?name=News&file=pring&sid=1.

La Unidad Latina. "A Movement Starts at Cornell University: The Story of "la unidad Latina," http://www.launidadlatina.org/story.htm.

Mu Sigma Upsilon Sorority, Inc., http://www.musigmaupsilon.org/.

NALFO—National Association of Latino Fraternal Organizations, Inc., http://www/halfo.org.

National Center for Educational Statistics, http://nces.ed.gov/help/sitemap.asp.

National Asian Pacific American Legal Consortium, "2001 Audit of Violence Against Asian Pacific Americans, Ninth Annual Report." February 2003. http://www.advancingequality.org.

The offical site of the Lumbee Tribe of North Carolina, http://www.lumbee tribe.com/lumbee/index.htm.

Office of Workforce Diversity, Equity and Life, Quality, "The Cornell University Story: A Holistic Approach to Diversity and Inclusiveness." Cornell University, Sept 8th, 2005. http://www.ohr.cornell.edu/commitment/ publications/Cornell_Story_2005.pdf.

Omega Delta, http://www.omegadelta.org/index.php.

Omega Phi Chi, Inc., http://www.omegaphichi.org/.

Phi Beta Chi National Sorority, http://www.phibetachi.org.

Phi Iota Alpha Fraternity, Inc., http://www.phiota.org/history.html.

Phi Kappa Theta National Fraternity, http://www.phikaps.org.

Phi Sigma Chi, http://www.phisigmachi.com/home.html.

Phi Sigma Nu, Native American fraternity, http://phisgmanu.com/.

Phi Sigma Sigma, http://phisigmasigma.org.

Pi Alpha Phi fraternity, http://www.pialphaphi.com/?page_id=4.

Pi Lambda Phi, http://www.pilambdaphi.org.

Psi Sigma Phi Multicultural Fraternity, Inc.: http://www.psisigmaphi.org/php/begin.php.

Rho Psi Society, http://www.rhopsi.org/history.html.

Sigma Alpha Zeta Sorority, Inc., http://orgs.sa.ucsb.edu/saz/.

Sigma Chi Omega Fraternity, Inc., http://www.chideltabeta.com/.

Sigma Lambda Beta Fraternity, http://www.sigmalambdabeta.com.

Sigma Omicron Epsilon Beta Chapter, http://soebetachapter.tripod.com/id17.html.

Sigma Phi Epsilon, http://www.sigep.org.

Sigma Phi Lambda: Sisters for the Lord, http://studentorgs.utexas.edu/philamb/.

Sigma Theta Epsilon National Christian Fraternity, http://www.sigmatheta.org/.

Sigma Theta Psi Multicultural Sorority, http://www.sigmathetapsi.com/page/page/2375754.htm.

Theta Kappa Phi, http://www.thetakappaphi.com/history.html.

Theta Nu Xi Multicultural Sorority, Inc., http://thetanuxi.org/.

United Council for Christian Fraternities and Sororities. http://www.uccfs.org.

University of Albany—Greek Life. "Latino Greek Council at SUNY Albany." http://www.albany.edu/~lgc/history.html

University of Arizona. 2005. Students by Ethnicity and Gender, Headcount Enrollment, Fall 2004. Office of Institutional Research & Evaluation.

University of North Carolina at Pembroke, http://www.uncp.edu.

Upsilon Kappa Delta, http://www.upsilonkappadelta.org/.

White Dove's Native American Indian site eastern universities and Indians, http://users.multipro.com/whitedove/encyclopedia/eastern-universities-and-indians.html.

Zeta Phi Zeta, Inc, http://www.zetaphizeta2000.org.

Zeta Sigma Phi Multicultural Sorority, Inc., http://www.zetasigmachi.com/.

Presentations

Binder, R. M. B. Schaub, W. Seiler, and T. Lake. "Greek Academic Achievement Update: Gamma Sigma Alpha and Bowling Green State University Partnership." Paper presented at the 2002 annual meeting of the Association of Fraternity Advisors, Columbus, OH, December 2002.

Chang, Mitchell. "Race Identity and Race Relations in Higher Education: Fraternity and Sorority Membership Among Students of Color." Paper presented at the Association for the Study of Higher Education National Conference, Orlando, Florida, November 2–5, 1995.

Layzer, Carolyn. "Strategic Sisterhood in a Latina Sorority: Affiliation, Recognition, and Solidarity." Paper presented at the annual meeting of the American Educational Research Association, New Orleans, LA, April 27, 2000. ERIC Document #: ED 441887.

Olivas, Margarita. R. "Latina Sororities and Higher Education: The Ties that Bind." Paper presented at the AESA convention, Montreal, Canada, November 9, 1996. ERIC Document #: ED 407194.

Ortiz, David, Susana Muñoz, and Dennos Camacho. "Latino Greeks: A Training Module for Advisors and Allies." Paper presented at the pre-convention of the American College Personnel Administrators, Minneapolis, MN, March 2003.

Stombler, Mindy, Renee Wharton, and King-To Yeung, "A House with No Closets: Exploring the Structure of and Dynamics within Gay Fraternities." Paper presented at the annual meeting of the Society for the Study of Social Problems, Toronto, Canada, August 10, 1997.

Other

Barrera, C., N. Nevarez, C. Vernia, A. Thorne-Thompson, J. Vargas, V. Hernandez II, *Concilio Nacional de Hermandades Latinas & National Association of Latino Fraternal Organizations Joint Exploratory Committee Report and Proposal.* Davis, CA: Exploratory Committee. September 1999.

Black Women's Oral History Project, Arthur and Elizabeth Schlesinger Library at Radcliffe College.

Slaying the Dragon, Film. Directed by Deborah Gee. Executive producer, Asian Women United; 60 minutes, National Asian American Telecommunications Association, 1988.

Taylor, Janis Swenson. 1999. "America's First People: Factors Which Affect Their Persistence in Higher Education." (ERIC Document Reproduction Service No. ED437874).

Contributers

Edith Wen-Chu Chen is an Associate Professor of Asian American Studies at California State University, Northridge. She received her PhD in Sociology from UCLA. Her research and teaching interests include Asian American women, race and ethnicity, Chinese in the Americas, and visual sociology. She is the editor (co-edited with Glenn Omatsu) for the pioneering teaching anthology and resource guide, *Teaching about Asian Pacific Americans: Effective Activities, Strategies, and Assignments for Classrooms and Workshops* (Rowman & Littlefield Publishers INC, 2006). She has also previously published, "Constructing a Non-Asian Identity: Asian American Sisters in 'White' Sororities," in *Changing Cultures from Within: Communication and Asian American Women*, (ed.) Elizabeth Kunimoto (Kailua, HI: Patina Productions, LLC, 2006). She is currently co-editing, *The Greenwood Encyclopedia of Asian American Issues Today*, with Grace Yoo. (Westport, CT: Greenwood Publishing Group).

Mark K. Dolan is an Assistant Professor at the University of Mississippi. He earned his PhD in Journalism and Mass Communications from the University of South Carolina. His research interests include black press history and cultural approaches to multimedia. Dolan's work recently appeared in the fall 2007 Second Annual Music Issue of *Southern Cultures*, published by the University of North Carolina at Chapel-Hill. He has written for several daily newspapers, including the *Savannah Morning News*, the *Naples Daily News*, and *The (SC) State*. Highlights from his newspaper work include interviews with novelists Toni Morrison, Reynolds Price, and Salmon Rushdie. As a journalism educator, he has generated student-written feature packages for the Pulitzer Prize winning *Sun-Herald* (2006). He has presented research on the black press at annual conventions of the Association for Education in Journalism and Mass Communication (AEJMC) and the American Journalism Historians Association (AJHA).

Juan R. Guardia is Director of the Office of Multicultural Affairs and Visiting Instructor in the Higher Education graduate program at

Florida State University in Tallahassee. He received his AA from Miami-Dade Community College, BS in Communication and MS in Higher Education from Florida State University, and PhD in Educational Leadership—Higher Education Administration from Iowa State University. His dissertation explored the factors influencing the ethnic identity development of Latino fraternity members at a Hispanic Serving Institution and has been published in the May/June 2008 issue of the *Journal of College Student Development.* In 2007, he received the inaugural Richard McKaig Outstanding Doctoral Research Award from the Center for the Study of the College Fraternity and the Fraternity Executives Association at Indiana University-Bloomington. He is a member of Phi Iota Alpha Fraternity, Inc.

Matthew W. Hughey is an adjunct instructor in African American studies, media studies, and sociology at the University of Virginia. He earned his BA in Sociology from the University of North Carolina–Greensboro, his MEd from Ohio University, and is a PhD candidate in sociology at the University of Virginia. His research focuses on processes of racial identity formation, racial organizations and racial media representations. He has several peer-reviewed journal articles, book chapters, and presentations to his credit. He is a member of Phi Beta Sigma Fraternity, Inc.

Linda Kelly is a professor at Delgado Community College as the Occupational Therapy Assistant Program Director. She received an endowed professorship while working at Delgado. She received a bachelor's degree in occupational therapy from the University of Illinois at the medical center. Her master's degree was from the University of New Mexico in special education. In 2008, she completed her dissertation, "Higher Education in Louisiana through a Native American Lens" in Educational Administration at the University of New Orleans. Her love of travel has allowed the experiences of working as an occupational therapist in Brazil, Germany and Zimbabwe. When in the United States, one of her favorite jobs was working with Indian Health Services and providing consultation to various tribes in Arizona and New Mexico. She is an active member of her American Occupational Therapy Association and has been most recently the second alternate delegate to the World Federation of Occupational Therapy. Her professional career has provided the venue for presentations at conferences around the world including Portugal, Germany, Belgium, Sweden, Canada, and Australia. She has published some of these papers in foreign journals.

Susana M. Muñoz is a doctoral candidate in Educational Leadership and Policy Studies at Iowa State University. She has 10 years of experience working in higher education in areas of Multicultural Affairs, Residence Life, Leadership Development, and First-Generation student issues. She received her bachelor's degree in political science and international studies from Iowa State University and her master's degree in student affairs in higher education from Colorado State University. She has been a member of Sigma Lambda Gamma National Sorority, Inc. since 1992 and is a past national board member. She is also a Association for the Study of Higher Education-Lumina Dissertation Fellow.

Gregory S. Parks earned his BA from Howard University, his MS from the City University of New York, and an MA and PhD from the University of Kentucky. He will earn his JD from Cornell University in 2008. He is also the editor of two other books on "Greek"-life: *African American Fraternities and Sororities: The Legacy and the Vision* (with Tamara Brown and Clarenda Phillips), and *Black Greek-Letter Organizations in the Twenty-First Century: Our Fight Has just Begun.* He is also the author of several articles on Black Greek-Letter Organizations in publications such as *Black College Wire, Diverse Issues in Higher Education, Ebony, Essentials* (Association of Fraternity Advisors publication). Dr. Parks has given invited lectures on BGLOs at California State University-Long Beach, Hampton University, Kentucky State University, Syracuse University, and University of South Carolina. He is a Life Member of Alpha Phi Alpha Fraternity, Inc.

Craig. L. Torbenson is an Associate Professor of Geography at Wichita State University. He graduated with a BS in Cartography and an MS in Geography from Brigham Young University and a PhD in Geography from the University of Oklahoma. His dissertation was a historical geography of college fraternities and sororities that examined the origins and diffusion of this social institution.

Amy E. Wells is an Associate Professor of Higher Education at the University of Mississippi. She is in the department of Leadership and Counselor Education and was a 2006 Faculty Research Fellow. Her research interests include the history of higher education, Rockefeller philanthropy to southern universities, and co-curricular student organizations in campus life. Her historical research has been supported by the Rockefeller Archive Center in Tarrytown, New York and has appeared in the *History of Higher Education Annual*, *The Community College Journal of Research and Practice*, and *Urban Education*.

Deborah E. Whaley is an Assistant Professor of American Studies and African American Studies at the University of Iowa. Her teaching and research fields include American Cultural History, Comparative Ethnic Studies, Black Cultural Studies, Popular and Visual Arts, and Feminist Theory. Whaley has published widely in peer-reviewed journals and anthologies on BGLOs, popular culture, and film. Her recently completed first book project, *Disciplining Women: Alpha Kappa Alpha, Black Counter-publics, and the Cultural Politics of Black Sororities*, is an interdisciplinary examination of a historically Black sorority. She is currently working on her second book project, which concerns women comic book and graphic novel characters of African descent.

King-To Yeung is Assistant Professor of Sociology at Princeton University. He attained his doctoral degree in Sociology at Rutgers University. His other works on gay fraternities have been published in *Social Problems* and *Gender & Society*.

Index